Fingal, 1603–60

Maynooth Historical Studies

GENERAL EDITOR, RAYMOND GILLESPIE

Over the last three generations the study of Irish history has been transformed almost out of recognition. The work of scholars such as J.C. Beckett, R. Dudley Edwards, R.B. McDowell, T.W. Moody and D.B. Quinn established scholarly standards within which the study of Irish history could proceed and, with their students, demonstrated in their writing how those standards could be applied. In the main these writings concentrated on the traditional historical themes, dealing with the political and constitutional problems which Ireland encountered in the past. More recently a new generation of scholars have built on these insights but have also looked again at the traditional canon of Irish history. Some have re-examined older problems in the light of fresh evidence or new conceptual models. Others have broadened the range of the debate on the Irish past by insisting on the importance of economic, social, local or cultural factors in shaping the Irish historical experience.

The result of this expansion in historical research has been a dramatic growth in publications dealing with the whole range of Irish history and hence a series of lively debates on the nature of the study of the Irish past. Maynooth Historical Studies is part of that new phenomenon. The series contributes to the debate on the interpretation of the Irish past by presenting the results of new research which either looks again at old problems or casts light into hitherto dark corners of the historical landscape. Both the individual volumes, and the series as a whole, reflect the complexity of understanding the evolution of Irish society and in so doing presents the study of Irish history as the vibrant and challenging discipline that it is.

IN THIS SERIES

Alison Forrestal, *Catholic synods in Ireland, 1600–1690*

Patrick Carroll-Burke, *Colonial discipline: the making of the Irish convict system*

Mary Ann Lyons, *Church and society in county Kildare,* c.*1470–1547*

Bridget McCormack, *Perceptions of St Patrick in eighteenth-century Ireland*

Vincent P. Carey, *Surviving the Tudors: the 'wizard' earl of Kildare and English rule in Ireland, 1537–1586*

Colmán N. Ó Clabaigh, OSB, *The Franciscans in Ireland, 1400–1534: from reform to Reformation*

Séamus Ó Maithiú, *Dublin's suburban towns, 1834–1930*

Simon Kingston, *Ulster and the Isles in the fifteenth century: the lordship of the Clann Domhnaill of Antrim*

John Crawford, *The Church of Ireland in Victorian Dublin*

Fingal, 1603–60

Contending neighbours in North Dublin

Maighréad Ní Mhurchadha

FOUR COURTS PRESS

This book was set in 10 on 12 point Ehrhardt by
Mark Heslington Ltd, Scarborough, North Yorkshire for
FOUR COURTS PRESS LTD
7 Malpas Street, Dublin 8, Ireland
Email: info@four-courts-press.ie
and in North America for
FOUR COURTS PRESS
c/o ISBS, 920 NE 58th Avenue, Suite 300, Portland, OR 97213.

A catalogue record for this title
is available from the British Library.

SPECIAL ACKNOWLEDGMENT

The publisher would like to thank Fingal County Council
for its generous financial support of this publication.

ISBN 1-85182-804-4

Printed in England
by Antony Rowe Ltd, Chippenham, Wilts.

For my sisters, Mary Brown, Jeanne Leaney and Betty Hodgins, their families and the people of Fingal, in celebration of their heritage and mine

Contents

LIST OF ABBREVIATIONS 8

LIST OF ILLUSTRATIONS 9

TECHNICAL NOTES 11

ACKNOWLEDGMENTS 13

PREFACE 15

PART I: LIVING IN FINGAL
1 'An odd corner of the country' 19
2 People, houses and homes 41
3 The Hoar Stone and the Lady Bush 69
4 'Neptune's neighbour' 92

PART II: EXPRESSING COMMUNITY VALUES
5 'The race of the English' 115
6 'Drinking, piping and dancing' 140
7 Every house and hamlet a sanctuary 170
8 'The holy company of heaven' 204

PART III: NEIGHBOURS AT WAR
9 'Universal desolation' 229

CONCLUSION: THE BROKEN PITCHER 285

BIBLIOGRAPHY 287

INDEX 305

Abbreviations

Anc. Rec. Dublin	*Calendar of ancient records of Dublin in the possession of the municipal corporation of that city*, ed. John T. Gilbert and Rosa Mulholland Gilbert (19 vols, Dublin, 1889–1944)
BL	British Library
Cal. S. P. Ire.	*Calendar of the state papers relating to Ireland*
Civil Survey	*The Civil Survey, A.D. 1654–56*, ed. R.C. Simington (Irish Manuscripts Commission, 10 vols, Dublin, 1931–61)
DNB	*Dictionary of national biography*
'Fingal 1603–60'	Maighréad M.B. Ní Mhurchadha, 'Contending neighbours: society in Fingal 1603–60' (NUI Maynooth, unpublished PhD thesis, 2 vols, 2002)
Griffith, *Inquisitions*	*Calendar of inquisitions formerly in the office of the chief remembrancer of the exchequer prepared from the mss of the Irish Record Commission*, ed. Margaret C. Griffith (Dublin, 1991)
IHS	*Irish Historical Studies*
NAI	National Archives of Ireland
NLI	National Library of Ireland
NUI	National University of Ireland
OED	*Oxford English Dictionary*
PRO	Public Record Office, Kew
RCBL	Representative Church Body Library
RSAI	Royal Society of Antiquaries of Ireland
Stat. Ire.	*The statutes at large passed in the parliaments held in Ireland*
TCD	Trinity College Dublin

Illustrations

1.1 Map of Ireland, *c.*1609, by Baptista Boazio (detail) 21
1.2 Down Survey barony map of Newcastle and Uppercross, 1657 (detail) 22
1.3 Map of Co. Dublin in the seventeenth century (Sir William Petty) 30
1.4 Approximate boundaries of Fingal parishes in the mid-seventeenth century 32
1.5 Contemporary representations of roads in seventeenth-century Fingal 39
2.1 Percentage of Fingal residents assessed for poll tax, classified as Irish, by parish, 1660 42
2.2 Percentage of Fingal houses assessed on more than one hearth by parish, *c.*1664 44
3.1 Map of Glasnevin parish, 1640, by Richard Francis 78–9
3.2 Extract from map of Glasnevin parish, 1640, by Richard Francis showing Glasnevin village 81
4.1 The barony of Nethercross in the county of Dublin, Down Survey, 1657 (detail) 94
4.2 Detail of map of part of the archbishop's lands in and near the town of Swords by John Tormer, 1656 95
4.3 Map of the archbishop of Dublin's lands at Lusk, abstracted by El. Arnoldi in 1668 from an original map of 1656 by John Turmor 110
5.1 Percentage of Fingal occupants with Gaelic-Irish surnames by parish, *c.*1664 117
5.2 Areas of Fingal situated within three miles of a known Catholic school, *c.*1630 121
6.1 Seventeenth-century manor courts in Fingal 144
6.2 Some inns, taverns and alehouses in seventeenth-century Fingal 151
6.3 Holy wells and other pattern sites in Fingal 156
6.4 Plot of Killshane, parish of Finglas, abstracted by El. Arnoldi in 1668 from an original map of 1656 by John Turmor 157
7.1 Churches of the established church in Fingal still available for use in 1615, 1630 and 1654–6 173
7.2 Fingal Mass-centres in 1630 178
7.3 Responsibility for parishes of the established church in Fingal, 1615, by status of clergyman 182
7.4 Responsibility for parishes of the established church in Fingal, 1630 184
7.5 Location of Commonwealth ministers in and near Fingal in the 1650s 187
8.1 Dedications of holy wells in Fingal 209

9.1 Robberies and seizures in Fingal November 1641 to January 1642 (incl.) 240
9.2 Places in Fingal at which burnings were recorded 1641–7 (incl.) 242
9.3 Down Survey barony map, 1657 – barony of Balrothery (detail) 250
9.4 Targets and their known attackers in north-east Fingal during the 1641 rising 259
9.5 Residences of gentlemen who attended the meeting of rebels at Swords, December 1641 263

Technical notes

Except where otherwise indicated dates are old style, but with the year starting on 1 January.

Spelling and punctuation have been modernized in quotations. The spelling of place-names has, where possible, been standardized in line with that used in the *General alphabetical index to the townlands and towns, parishes and baronies of Ireland* (1851). For surnames, especially those of proprietors, the spelling adopted by L.J. Arnold in *The Restoration land settlement in County Dublin, 1660–1688* has been used as a guide.

The parish maps in this study are based generally on a map of the parishes of Co. Dublin in Brian Mitchell, *A new genealogical atlas of Ireland* (Baltimore, 1986). The parish boundaries have been amended to approximate the situation in the mid-seventeenth century.

The publishers have allowed me to keep my style of reference and notation, even though it differs from the Four Courts Press house style.

Acknowledgments

I should like to express my sincere thanks to all those who assisted me in preparing this study. In particular I am grateful to the directors, librarians and staff of the following organizations, libraries and repositories: Armagh Public Library, Capuchin Archives, Dublin, Cheshire Record Office, Dublin City Library and Archive, Fingal County Council Archives, National Archives of Ireland, National Library of Ireland, National Monuments Service of the Department of the Environment, Heritage and Local Government (formerly Dúchas–the Heritage Service), John Paul II Library, National University of Ireland, Maynooth, Public Record Office of Northern Ireland, Representative Church Body Library, Royal Irish Academy, Royal Society of Antiquaries of Ireland, Skerries Historical Society and Trinity College Dublin.

Special thanks are due to the Representative Church Body Library for permission to make use of maps from their collections and to reproduce maps in figures 3.1, 3.2, 4.2, 4.3 and 6.4, to the Manuscripts Department of the National Library of Ireland for access to copies of the Down Survey parish maps, to the librarian of Trinity College Dublin for permission to consult two unpublished theses by Dr Bríd McGrath, to Revd Benedict Cullen, OFM, Cap., for giving so much of his time to facilitating access to the Capuchin Archives in Church Street, Dublin, and to Dean Cassidy and the staff of Armagh Public Library for their kindness and hospitality to me during my brief visit to that city. I wish to thank Dr Joe Brady and Stephen Hannon of the Department of Geography, UCD, for arranging to have the maps in Figures 2.1, 2.2, 5.1, 7.3 and 7.4 produced electronically.

I am grateful to many friends, particularly those in the local history societies in Fingal, for information on local history, advice on computing, encouragement and prayers. Special thanks are due to Maree and Jack Baker, Betty and Fred Balcombe, Peadar Bates, Rory McKenna, Denis Murphy, Dave O'Connor, Kit Sheridan, Jim Walsh and Paddy Weston. I deeply appreciate the help with graphics given by John Harte.

I am grateful to Dr Jane Ohlmeyer, Trinity College, Dublin, for taking the trouble to send me copies of her work and to Revd Ignatius Fennessy, OFM, Killiney, for valuable information and advice. I should also like to acknowledge the support of Professor R.V. Comerford and the staff and students of the Department of Modern History of the National University of Ireland, Maynooth and, in particular, the help and encouragement given me by Dr Jacqueline Hill and Dr Colm Lennon.

Finally, I owe an enormous debt of gratitude to my doctoral supervisor, Dr

Raymond Gillespie, who encouraged me to undertake this work, helped me to develop the germ of an idea into a full-blown thesis, shared with me his extensive knowledge about seventeenth-century Ireland and assisted with comments which were perceptive, constructive and always challenging.

Preface

This study aims to tell the story of a community during a relatively short period of its history. The community lived and worked in Fingal, an area of approximately 50,000 hectares, comprising the baronies of Balrothery, Castleknock, Coolock and Nethercross, north of the river Liffey in Co. Dublin, during the reigns of James I, Charles I and the Commonwealth. The study, based on a PhD thesis submitted to the National University of Ireland, Maynooth, takes a comprehensive view of society and, insofar as the source documents allow, pays particular attention to non-élite groups.[1] Omitted from this publication are a chapter on leadership in the Fingal community as well as all statistical tables and appendices. These can be found in the original thesis.

The present work is concerned with a traditional multi-cultural community within the Pale. Apart from the contributions of Francis Elrington Ball and Joseph Byrne there is little, if anything, available in print specifically devoted to the history of Fingal or, indeed, any part of it for the period 1603–60.[2] This study aims to look at this ancient territory as an entity and to examine what lifestyles, values and norms were shared by its people and what tensions divided them. The population of Fingal at the period has been estimated at not much more than 15,000. The area was relatively small and compact and contained no natural barriers. In normal times people moved around freely within the territory, facilitated by the good road network, the fragmented manorial system of landholding and the easy access to markets, particularly in Dublin, the capital. They assembled at churches, chapels and holy wells. They had no difficulty in getting to know each other as neighbours. Despite differences of language, culture, class and religion they managed to co-exist peacefully for the period 1603–41, as they had already done for many centuries. It will be one of the tasks of this study to analyze the factors which caused the breakdown of this peaceful, prosperous, and, on the whole, tolerant society.

A community study is concerned with people. In seeking to learn how people lived and felt we seek first the personal documents which tell us about their daily lives. Unfortunately, collections of personal letters, diaries and estate papers are virtually non-existent for Fingal for the period. As is well known, most of the wills have been destroyed. There are relatively few portraits or other pictures. Even more surpris-

1 Maighréad Ní Mhurchadha, 'Contending neighbours: society in Fingal 1603–60' (NUI Maynooth, unpublished PhD thesis, 2 vols, 2002). Copies of this thesis have been deposited in the library of NUI, Maynooth and in the Dublin City Library (Gilbert Library), Pearse St, Dublin 2. 2 Francis Elrington Ball, *A history of the County Dublin* (6 vols, Dublin, 1902–20, reprinted 1995); Joseph Byrne, *War and peace: the survival of the Talbots of Malahide 1641–1671* (Dublin, 1997).

ingly there are few physical remains. It is doubtful if there is a single residence in the area of which one could say with certainty that it dates from the period 1603–60 although a few probably do. Most of the churches which then existed and which still remain, mostly in ruins, were built in an earlier period. Almost all the early seventeenth-century gravestones have disappeared. If there are other local artefacts dating from that period they have either not been recognized as such or have not found their way into the public domain. Even the landscape has changed. Much of what was rural Fingal even as late as the early twentieth century, is now part of Dublin city, while villages such as Blanchardstown, Swords and Malahide have become, by Irish standards, large towns.

Despite the limitations already mentioned a wealth of documentary material concerning the area still remains. This is partly due to the assiduous compilation, collection and preservation of documents by church and state institutions. But it is also due to the fact that Fingal in the early seventeenth century had more than its fair share of writers and, in particular, historians. Fingallians were keen travellers and much exciting material, which has been found in libraries in Britain and on the continent, is now available as transcripts or on microfilm in Irish repositories. It is likely that additional documentation will come to light in future.[3]

The study is divided into three parts. Part I examines the physical environment in which people lived and worked. It is subdivided into four chapters. Chapter 1 portrays the landscape, chapter 2, broad issues relating to, among other topics, population, housing, food, clothing, occupations, transport, illness and poverty, chapter 3, the rural economy and chapter 4, the urban and maritime economies. Part II, which is subdivided into five chapters, focuses on the beliefs, values and norms of the community. Chapter 5 looks at the Fingallian identity, taking into account such factors as marriage and the family, education, literature, the legal profession and crime. Chapter 6 concentrates on social interaction in the secular sphere, looking at venues such as the workplace, manor courts and patterns and at activities such as drinking, music, dancing and sport. The structures and membership of the churches are examined in chapter 7 while the beliefs and religious practices of the people are considered in chapter 8. Finally, part III, consisting of a single chapter (chapter 9), traces the progress of the war which broke out in 1641 and its effect on the community.

3 For a discussion of the sources and methodology used in this study see 'Fingal 1603–60', i, pp 5–9.

Part I
Living in Fingal

1

'An odd corner of the country'

> ... the first of December one thousand six hundred forty and one, one Captain Cusack, Lieutenant Fleming, Richard Murphy and divers of the neighbours of Fingal namely Mr Russell of Seatown, Mr Bellings of Ardla, a servant of Robert Arthur of Dublin, alderman, a servant of Mr Thomas Fitzwilliams of Baldongan (since executed) and many others to the number of forty persons came about dinner time to Holmpatrick aforesaid ...[1]

This extract is taken from the opening of Margaret Huiberts Verveer's dramatic account of an attack by rebels on her home at Holmpatrick, near Skerries, in Co. Dublin, on 1 December 1641. On 14 March 1644 she made a formal deposition about the attack and the subsequent murder of her husband, Dirrick, to two of the commissioners, Henry Brereton and Henry Jones, who had been appointed to hear evidence concerning the rebellion which began in the autumn of 1641.

Neither Margaret Huiberts Verveer nor the secretary to the commission needed to explain the term 'Fingal'. This region, which had neither an administrative nor an ecclesiastical basis, was evidently familiar to all concerned. The four 'neighbours of Fingal', mentioned specifically were two local proprietors, Bartholomew Russell of Seatown near Swords and Laurence Bellings of Ardla, which was situated in the parish of Lusk, not far from Holmpatrick, and the servants of two other local gentlemen, Robert Arthur, whose home was at Hacketstown in the parish of Lusk, also close to Holmpatrick, and Thomas Fitzwilliam, who lived in the neighbouring parish of Baldongan.[2] Richard Murphy was also a Fingallian who leased property at Blackhall in the parish of Balrothery.[3] Captain James Cusack of Rathaldron in Co. Meath was the son of a proprietor of land in Balrothery which had been leased to Murphy.[4] Lieutenant Fleming has not been identified with certainty but he may have been Thomas Fleming of Santry.[5] All the places mentioned (apart from Rathaldron in Co. Meath) lay well within the boundaries of the territory known as 'Fingal'. The precise boundaries are difficult to pinpoint accurately. In fact there is some evidence that people's perceptions of where the borders of Fingal lay changed over time and may even have altered even during the relatively short period covered by this study.

Traditional Fingal (*Fine Gall* – the territory of the foreigners) is often defined as that part of north Co. Dublin which lies between the rivers Delvin and Tolka.[6] The

1 Deposition of Margaret Huiberts, 14 March 1644 (TCD, MS 810, f. 239). 2 *Civil Survey, vii, county of Dublin,* pp 102, 58, 59 and 67. 3 *Civil Survey, vii, county of Dublin,* p. 12. 4 *Civil Survey, vii, county of Dublin,* pp 11–12. 5 *Civil Survey, vii, county of Dublin,* pp 196–7. 6 Robert Walsh, *Fingal and its*

name of the territory is of great antiquity. The Annals of Inisfallen made three mentions of the territory for the years 1013, 1084 and 1100.[7] The Annals of Ulster referred to the men of 'Brega and Fine Gall' in its entry for the year 1100 suggesting that the Fingallians were already seen as a distinctive group of people.[8] By the sixteenth century the area was not only recognized but had, in the eyes of observers, taken on a unique character, being described in *Holinshed's Irish chronicle* as an 'odd corner of the country'.[9]

Map-makers in the sixteenth and seventeenth centuries acknowledged the existence of the territory. Fingal (spelt in a variety of ways) was marked on several maps dating from the Elizabethan to the later Stuart periods though in no case were its precise boundaries delineated. These maps ranged from Ortelius's map of 1574 to that of Blome published in 1673.[10] In all the cases examined the name of the territory was printed north of the river Tolka and in most cases it was shown north of the river Broadmeadow (see fig. 1.1). This may, of course, have had more to do with cartographic design than with accurate representation. Only one reference to Fingal has been found in the Down Survey maps.[11] The map for the baronies of Newcastle and Uppercross, which also included Dublin city, showed a road, outside the northern boundaries of the city, leading to Fingal (fig. 1.2). This was clearly the road to Santry and Swords. Two other roads on the same map were shown as 'leading to the Cabragh' and 'the high way to Clontarf'. Both Clontarf and Cabragh would be regarded as part of Fingal under a broader definition of the term. However it is not possible to fix the boundaries of Fingal with cartographic precision. Even the county boundaries do not seem to have been fixed with certainty in the minds of contemporaries. As well as occasionally confusing the river Nanny with the Delvin, John Speed and other early cartographers placed the boundaries of Co. Dublin further to the west than did those who drew the Down Survey maps and those who compiled the Civil Survey. Some early maps show the Co. Meath towns of Ardcath, Greenogue, Piercetown, Ratoath and Stamullen, for example, as part of Co. Dublin.[12] There is further confirmation of this practice in an examination dated 2 June 1642 of a priest named Conor Donnogh, probably a local man, which referred to 'Greenogue in Fingal'.[13]

The documentary evidence presents an even more confusing picture. With Irish-speaking writers it is necessary to know the context in which the name, *Fine Gall*, was

churches ... (Dublin, 1888), pp 2–3. 7 *The Annals of Inisfallen (MS Rawlinson B 503)*, ed. and trans. Seán Mac Airt (Dublin, 1944, reprinted 1988), pp 182, 238 and 256. 8 *The Annals of Ulster (to A.D. 1131)*, ed. and trans. Seán Mac Airt and Gearóid Mac Niocaill, part 1 (Dublin, 1983), p. 536. 9 Richarde Stanyhurst, *A treatise contayning a playne and perfect description of Irelande* ... in Raphaell Holinshed and Richarde Stanyhurst, *Holinshed's Irish chronicle* ..., ed. Liam Miller and Eileen Power (London, 1577, republished Dublin, 1979), p. 13. 10 Ortelius, 'Eyrn-Hiberniae Britannicae Insulae Nova Descriptio' in Ortelius, *Theatrum orbis terrarum* (Antwerp, 1574); Blome, *Ireland* (1673). Other examples include Mercator (Dusseldorf, 1595); Baptista Boazio, *Map of Ireland, c.1609* (facsimile Dublin, 1990, from original printed in Antwerp in 1609); John Speed, *The theatre of the empire of Great Britain, the fourth book containing the kingdom of Ireland* ... (London, 1631) and Jan Jansson, *Hibernia Regnum* (1647). 11 Down Survey baronial maps, 1657 (reproduced Ordnance Survey Office, 1908, from the originals in the Bibliothèque Nationale, Paris); Down Survey parish maps ... (NLI, MS 714). 12 John Speed, 'The county of Leinster with the city Dublin described' (Map) in *The theatre of the empire of Great Britain, the fourth book containing the kingdom of Ireland* ... (London, 1631). 13 Examination of Conor Donnogh, 2 June 1642 (TCD, MS 816, f. 192).

Fig. 1.1 Map of Ireland, *c.*1609, by Baptista Boazio (detail)

Fig. 1.2 Down Survey barony map of Newcastle and Uppercross (detail)

being used. John O'Donovan, when editing *Annála Ríoghachta Éireann* (The Annals of the Kingdom of Ireland), noted that the Four Masters, as well as Geoffrey Keating, used the Irish form of the name to express both the English Pale and a smaller district within the Pale lying north of Dublin city.[14] Another contemporary

14 *Annála ríoghachta Éireann: Annals of the kingdom of Ireland by the Four Masters from the earliest period to the year 1616*, ed. and trans. John O'Donovan (7 vols, Dublin, 1851; facsimile edition, Dublin, 1990), v, p. 1691 (footnote).

Irish-speaking writer, Philip O'Sullivan Bear, who left Ireland as a young boy, also regarded Fingal as encompassing the entire Pale.[15] Edmund Hogan, in his *Onomasticon Goedelicum*, listed a number of definitions of Fine Gall from manuscripts and printed works almost all of which placed the southern boundary of the territory at the Liffey or at Dublin city.[16] Richard Stanihurst, whose views, because of his close family connections with the area, must be given weight, placed Fingal 'directly to the north of Dublin'.[17] An anonymous writer, in a book published in 1642, but which, according to the internal evidence, seems to have been written much earlier in the century, having referred to the coastal towns of Howth and Malahide, went on to say that 'more within the country is Fingal, a little place, but very well husbanded'.[18] This suggests that in the eyes of some, at least, Fingal meant a restricted inland area, probably in the neighbourhood of Swords. This accords with the evidence of the Down Survey map of Newcastle and Uppercross mentioned earlier. The contemporary Latin records of the Irish Capuchins, who worked in the area in the late 1620s and 1630s, referred to the conversion of a Welshman in the Naul in Fingal and also mentioned that Father Barnabas who was working at Garristown, made a pilgrimage '*in Connatiam*' (presumably into Connaught) to St Brigid's holy well and returned to Fingal after six days.[19] The views of another seventeenth-century writer, Sir James Ware, would have been valuable since he owned a great deal of land in the area. However, the section on Fingal in *The whole works of Sir James Ware concerning Ireland*, published in 1764, seems to have been added by the editor, Walter Harris.[20] Harris (or Ware) took the view that Fingal was on the north side of the river Liffey and comprehended a good part of the Co. Dublin.

Patrick Weston Joyce, relying on Irish-language authorities, defined Fingal as the district lying north of Dublin, between it and the Delvin river.[21] Francis Elrington Ball agreed with this wider definition and, in his foreword to *Southern Fingal*, published in 1920, having examined the evidence, concluded as follows: 'During more recent times the extent of Fingal has been defined by some writers as stretching from the river Tolka to the river Delvin; but for this limitation of its extent no authority has been found.'[22] Another early twentieth-century local historian, Patrick Archer, while accepting the Tolka as the southern boundary, argued that Fingal's western boundary should be drawn somewhat to the east of the county boundary.[23] Archer considered that a line of natural and man-made elevations marked the western boundary of Fingal and claimed that this alignment was in exact agreement with

15 Philip O'Sullivan Bear, *Ireland under Elizabeth: chapters towards a history of Ireland in the reign of Elizabeth being a portion of the history of Catholic Ireland by Don Philip O'Sullivan Bear*, translated from the Latin by Matthew J. Byrne (Dublin, 1903, originally published Lisbon, 1621), pp 50 and 56. 16 Edmund Hogan, *Onomasticon Goedelicum locorum et tribuum Hiberniae et Scotiae. An index, with identifications, to the Gaelic names of places and tribes* (Dublin, 1910), p. 419. 17 Richard Stanihurst, *De rebus in Hibernia gestis* (originally published Antwerp, 1584), translated from the Latin by Colm Lennon in *Richard Stanihurst the Dubliner* (Dublin, 1981), p. 143. 18 G.N., *A geographicall description of the kingdom of Ireland* ... (London, 1642), p. 17. 19 Nicholas Archbold, The historie of the Irish Capucins, 1643 (Bibliothèque Municipale, Troyes, ff 171 and 176). 20 James Ware, *The whole works of Sir James Ware concerning Ireland, revised and improved*, ed. Walter Harris (2 vols, Dublin, 1764), ii, p. 49. 21 P.W. Joyce, *The origin and history of Irish names of places* (3 vols, Dublin, 1869–1913), i, p. 97. 22 Francis Elrington Ball, *Southern Fingal* ... (originally published 1920, reprinted Dublin, 1995), pp vii–viii. 23 Patrick Archer, *Fair Fingall*, ed. Bob Browne and Jarlath Duffy (2nd ed., Dublin, 1975), p. 1.

local tradition.[24] While this may well have been the case, Archer did not adduce any further evidence for this conclusion.

It is tentatively suggested here that the older southern boundary was, in fact, the river Liffey but that, as Dublin city expanded towards the north, the southern boundary of Fingal, in the popular perception, was also moved towards the north. Like the Liffey, the Tolka was a convenient natural boundary which stretched across the entire width of the area. For the purposes of this study, however, it is proposed to use the wider definition which appears to have been accepted at least up to the start of the seventeenth century and which, in general, coincides to the north and west with the county boundaries and to the south with the city of Dublin and the river Liffey. Excluded are that part of St Michan's parish within the city boundaries, that part of the parish of Kilmainham (or St James) in the barony of Newcastle and Uppercross, known as 'Newtown and the Phoenix', and the townlands of St Catherine's and Westmanstown (then in the parish of Lucan) in the same barony, also lying north of the Liffey.[25] Fingal, therefore, is taken to mean the four baronies of Balrothery, Castleknock, Coolock and Nethercross as described in the Civil Survey.

The distance from the Liffey to the Delvin is approximately 32km while Fingal's widest extent, from Howth Head to its western boundary, is 28km. It is a low-lying region although there is a range of hills to the north and north-west of the area. The highest point of this range is Knockbrack (176m). Apart from these hills the only significant heights are Knockbane (126m) on Lambay Island and Howth Head (163m), described by Gerard Boate in 1652 as 'a great high mountain'.[26] Boate, relying for his information on accounts sent to him by his brother, Arnold, was impressed by the fact that Howth could be seen from a great distance both on its eastern (seaward) and western sides.

The anonymous seventeenth-century writer already referred to described Co. Dublin as 'Neptune's neighbour'.[27] This description was even more appropriate to Fingal. Despite the fact that it covered a relatively small area it had a long coastline due to the fact that there were two major estuaries, at the Broadmeadow and Rogerstown, and a number of peninsulas, notably the Howth peninsula. There were also several small islands, Rockabill, Colt Island (shown on early seventeenth-century maps as 'St Clare' or 'St Clere'), *Inis Phádraig* ('Island Patrick') or St Patrick's Island and Shenick Island ('Skerries'), all of which lay close to the fishing-port of Skerries. The larger island of Lambay was conveniently situated to guard the entrances to the estuaries and the island known as Ireland's Eye lay off Howth. Lambay was probably the only one of the islands inhabited at this period. Gerard Boate described it as follows:

> Three or four miles beyond Irelands Eye lieth the Isle of Lambay, belonging to Sir William Ussher of Dublin, who hath there a fine little castle of free-

24 Patrick Archer, *Fair Fingall*, ed. Bob Browne and Jarlath Duffy (2nd ed., Dublin, 1975) pp 1–2. Archer's suggested boundary line is marked from south to north by the rath of Cappagh (Knock Maeldoid), Knockbrush, the hill of the Broughan, the moat of Kilshane, the hill of the Ward, the moat of Coolatrath, the rath of Kilsallaghan, the moat of Palmerstown, the moat of Knockineek and the moat of Knocklyon. Acceptance of Archer's definition would mean excluding places such as Mulhuddart and a small area north of Garristown. 25 *Civil Survey, vii, county of Dublin*, p. 292. 26 Gerard Boate, *Ireland's naturall history* ... (London, 1652), pp 37–8. 27 G.N., *A geographicall description of the kingdom of Ireland* ... (London, 1642), p. 14.

> stone, and close by it a village, wherein dwell divers families, of fishers and husbandmen, who plough part of this island, and upon the rest feed cattle and sheep. The whole island being about three miles in compass, is high land wherefore it may be seen a great way off. On the north-side of this island ships may anchor in twelve or thirteen fathoms for a southerly wind. For a sea-wind the ships must ride on the west-side, over against the castle but that road is not very good, because always in that sound, being about three miles broad, goeth a great sea-sect.[28]

Two other areas, then described as islands – Haven Island, on which the harbour of Skerries was situated, and Clontarf Island, which was of particular importance to Dublin city – may have been accessible on foot at certain times only. Small islands, whatever about their other attractions, presented a hazard to shipping, Because of their proximity to the busy port of Dublin these small islands were a particular danger to navigators and, consequently, together with the coastal towns of Fingal, attracted the attention of map-makers in the late sixteenth and early seventeenth centuries.

The long mainly east-facing coastline and proximity to Dublin city together with some good natural harbours ensured that many of the people of Fingal would obtain their livelihood from the sea. However, in the early seventeenth-century access to the sea facilitated not only trade and the fishing industry but also the movement of people and ideas not just to and from England and Wales, Scotland and the Isle of Man but also to and from the continent of Europe. Control of even a small harbour was important. Writing in *Holinshed's Irish Chronicle* (published in 1577) Richard Stanihurst listed eighty-seven haven towns in Ireland, of which nine were in Fingal. The Fingal havens were Balbriggan and Bremore (parish of Balrothery), Baldoyle, Holmpatrick and Skerries (parish of Holmpatrick), Howth, Malahide and Rogerstown and Rush (parish of Lusk).

Another late sixteenth-century list of seventy Irish havens, found among the papers of Meredith Hanmer, mentioned seven Fingal havens, Skerries and its islands (as part of Holmpatrick), Rush, Malahide, Rogerstown, Baldoyle, Howth and Bremore.[29] A further list of thirty-six havens, prepared in 1598, contained just four Fingal references.[30] While this decrease in the number of havens might have been due to the particular criteria applied by the various writers the evidence from Skerries, in particular, seems to indicate a temporary decline in maritime activity in the region during the late sixteenth and early seventeenth centuries followed by a period of recovery.

Examining the individual havens more closely we find that the Newhaven of Bremore (also known as Orde or Horde) was an important local harbour throughout the period covered by this study. The proprietors were the Barnewalls of Bremore, a staunchly Catholic family.[31] Newhaven was described in the Civil Survey as 'a fishing town' while the Down Survey, in its comments on the barony, stated

28 Gerard Boate, *Ireland's naturall history ...* (London, 1652), p. 33. 29 *Cal. S. P. Ire., 1601–3*, p. 677. 30 *The description of Ireland and the state thereof as it is at this present in anno 1598*, ed. Edmund Hogan (Dublin, 1878), pp 238–9. 31 Griffith, *Inquisitions*, p. 352 and pp 440–443; Stephen B. Barnwell, 'The

> On the north of this barony stands a point or north [*sic*] of land (extending itself into the sea) called New Haven it being by the industry of the inhabitants of the town which stands near this point made a secure harbour for boats and is a considerable place of fishing.[32]

In the Down Survey terriers on the parish it was also described as 'a town of fishing'. There was no mention of fishing in relation to Balbriggan in either the Civil Survey or the Down Survey. It would appear that the haven declined in importance some time between 1577 and 1641. Its decline may have paralleled the rise of the port of Newhaven which was only about 2km away and perhaps reflected the growing importance of the Barnewall family of Bremore.

Stanihurst's listing of two havens in the parish of Holmpatrick is also puzzling. Holmpatrick may refer to the harbour of Mellock or Meloke, built on one of the islands, which has not been identified but which evidently ceased to be important before the manor of Holmpatrick was granted to the earl of Thomond in 1605.[33] The history of the second haven in the parish, the harbour at Skerries, is reasonably well documented. In 1545 the harbour had been able to able to cope with the logistics of transporting 2,000 men in twenty-eight ships under the earls of Lennox and Ormond via Olderfleet to Scotland to assist Henry VIII but in *c.*1596, when writing to Sir Robert Cecil seeking a lease of Holmpatrick, Nicholas Fitzwilliam reported that the creek and haven there had fallen into decay.[34] In 1605 the grant of the manor of Holmpatrick to the earl of Thomond described the decline of the port pointing out that the haven of Skerries was

> very ruinous; by reason whereof there are now only in Skerries two boats, out of which the lord or tenant of Holmpatrick had the best fish, whenever they took fish, for a custom; but when said port was built, many ships and boats from England, France, Spain and Scotland came thereto annually, as well as for security as to fish, and there paid customs ...[35]

A revised grant to the earl of Thomond in 1610 made no mention of the problems which had existed only five years previously but went on to detail the customs suggesting that they were again in operation.[36] Confirmation that Skerries was once again engaged in trade with the continent can be found in the Irish wine trade lists

Barnewall family during the sixteenth and seventeenth centuries (part 6)' in *The Irish Genealogist*, iii, no. 11 (October 1966), pp 445–54. 32 Down Survey parish maps ... (NLI, MS 714). 33 *Letters and papers foreign and domestic of the reign of Henry VIII* (21 vols, London, 1862–1932), xvi, p. 374; *A repertory of the inrolments on the patent rolls in chancery in Ireland; commencing with the reign of King James I*, ed. John Caillard Erck (2 pts, Dublin, 1846–52), part i, pp 220–1; John D'Alton, *The history of the county of Dublin* (Dublin, 1838), pp 435–6. 34 Dean Guntner White, 'Henry VIII's Irish kerne in France and Scotland, 1544–1545' in *The Irish Sword*, iii, no. 13 (Winter, 1958), p. 224; Historical Manuscripts Commission, *Calendar of the manuscripts of the most hon. the marquis of Salisbury preserved at Hatfield House, Hertfordshire* (24 vols, London, 1883–1976), xiii, p. 598. 35 *A repertory of the inrolments on the patent rolls in chancery in Ireland; commencing with the reign of King James I*, ed. John Caillard Erck (2 pts, Dublin, 1846–52), part i, pp 220–1. 36 *A repertory of the inrolments on the patent rolls in chancery in Ireland; commencing with the reign of King James I*, ed. John Caillard Erck (2 pts, Dublin, 1846–52), part ii, pp 732–3.

of 1614–15 when an unidentified ship's master from Skerries brought two tons of French wine worth £3 into a Co. Louth port in his ship, the *Bryde* of Skerries.[37] The owner of the ship, Jasper Hurlston, was probably an uncle of the Jasper Hurlston who played a prominent role in the 1641 rising in Fingal (see chapter 9). The name of one of the victims of the rising, Dirrick Huiberts Verveer (also known as Dirrick Hubbartes), who later lived at Holmpatrick, also appeared in the list as the owner of two ships.[38] From about this time Skerries was one of the two Fingal ports (the other being Malahide) which were regularly listed along with Dublin and Wicklow in the appointments to the offices of collector and receiver or searcher and gauger in the Dublin region.[39] In 1621 Skerries was granted a charter of the staple.[40] While there is little further information about the harbour in the years that followed it is clear that, by 1641, there was a great deal of activity in the harbour.[41] The Civil Survey reported only on the tithe and custom fish and the charge for anchorage at Skerries while the parish of Holmpatrick, which was not forfeited, was omitted from the Down Survey.[42]

Although there is evidence that Rush had been used for trade in the mid-sixteenth century it seems to have concentrated mainly on fishing during the seventeenth.[43] Edward Leech recorded the involvement of eight or nine boats from the vicinity of Rush in the 1641 rising.[44] The Civil Survey noted that several copyholds in the town of Rush belonged to poor fishermen who also grazed their cattle on the commons. As the proprietor was the Protestant earl of Ormond there is little qualitative information in the Down Survey. The evidence suggests that Rush was a lively fishing port in the mid-seventeenth century.

Rogerstown (on Stanihurst's list) and Portraine, both in the barony of Nethercross and both in Protestant ownership, were not noted as fishing ports in either the Civil Survey or the Down Survey, though there is evidence that Portraine had been a small fishing port in 1529 when it was owned by the convent of Gracedieu.[45] There is a comment in the baronial summary of the Down Survey for Nethercross that 'it would be no inconsiderable benefit would arise to this barony by reason the sea lies so near it were the inhabitants as ingenious and laborious in making up fencing and preserving certain havens and brooks there for fishing, riding safe of large vessels and coming in of lesser as nature has been bountiful in affording them so great a means of nighreaching themselves.'[46] This suggests that there was little maritime activity in the area although the natural surroundings offered considerable possibilities.

Moving towards the south the next haven in the series, Malahide, was probably a

37 H.F. Kearney, 'The Irish wine trade, 1614–15' in *IHS*, ix, no. 36 (September 1955), p. 411. 38 H.F. Kearney, 'The Irish wine trade, 1614–15' in *IHS*, ix, no. 36 (September 1955) pp 408 and 410. 39 *Irish patent rolls of James I*, ed. M.C. Griffith (Dublin, 1966), pp 227, 256, 302–3, 495–6, 505 and 591; *Calendar of the patent and close rolls of chancery in Ireland of the reign of Charles the first, first to eighth year, inclusive*, ed. James Morrin (London, 1863), pp 109, 266 and 430. 40 *Irish patent rolls of James I*, ed. M.C. Griffith (Dublin, 1966), p. 498. 41 Examination of Christopher Hampton, 11 December 1641 (TCD, MS 809, f. 212); deposition of Anthony Huiberts, 29 January 1642 (TCD, MS 809, f. 311); 'County Louth depositions, 1641' ed. Thomas Gogarty in *Journal of the County Louth Archaeological Society*, iii, no. 1 (December, 1912), pp 71–2. 42 *Civil Survey, vii, county of Dublin,* p. 54. 43 Griffith, *Inquisitions*, p. 152; *Civil Survey, vii, county of Dublin,* pp 61–2. 44 Deposition of Edward Leech, 18 March 1644 (TCD, MS 810, f. 244). 45 Griffith, *Inquisitions*, p. 77. 46 Down Survey parish maps ... (NLI, MS 714).

busy fishing port in the earlier part of the seventeenth century. Like Skerries it was specifically named in the appointments to offices in the customs service.[47] Joseph Byrne noted that the port appeared to have contained a formal quayside.[48] The Civil Survey also mentioned a fishing harbour, and the Down Survey noted that 'there are also several thatched houses and cabins by the seaside or bay where fishermen dwelleth …'[49] Like the Barnewalls of Bremore, the Talbots of Malahide were Catholic proprietors. Baldoyle, also in the barony of Coolock, was somewhat unusual in that it was in the possession of the city of Dublin, the lessee at the time of the Civil Survey being Alderman Preston.[50] It was clearly prospering in the mid-1650s as the survey noted the presence of several fishing boats as well as the proprietor's right to the choice fish. This small parish did not appear in the Down Survey. Howth, in the same barony, was also in Protestant ownership. The Civil Survey recorded that there were several fishing boats 'that take such fish as is usual on that coast'.[51] The Down Survey did not comment on the unforfeited lands in Howth.

Of the nine havens mentioned by Stanihurst in 1577 three, Balbriggan, Holmpatrick and Rogerstown appear to have ceased activity, at least in any serious way, by 1641. The other six were still functioning. The building or revival of the harbours of Loughshinny and Portraine seems to have been a later development. A surprising omission from Stanihurst's list is the ancient port of Clontarf. The seventeenth-century history of this haven illustrated, perhaps better than any other district, the tension between, as well as the interdependence of, Dublin city and Fingal.[52] Gerard Boate described the difficulties which affected the port of Dublin in the mid-seventeenth century and which resulted in its dependence on other ports such as Clontarf:

> Dublin haven hath a bar in the mouth, upon which at high-flood and spring-tide there is fifteen and eighteen feet of water, but at the ebb and neap-tide but six. With an ordinary tide you cannot go to the quay of Dublin with a ship that draws five feet of water, but with a spring-tide you may go up with ships that draw seven and eight feet. Those that go deeper cannot go nearer Dublin than the Ringsend, a place three miles distant from the bar, and one from Dublin. This haven almost all over falleth dry with the ebb, as well below Ringsend as above it, so as you may go dry-foot round about the ships which lye at an anchor there, except in two places, one at the north-side half way betwixt Dublin and the bar, and the other at the south-side not far from it. In these two little creeks (whereof one is called the Pool of Clontarf, and the other Poolbeg) it never falleth dry, but the ships which ride at an anchor remain ever afloat; because at low water you have nine or ten feet of water there. This haven, besides its shallowness, hath yet another great incom-

47 *Irish patent rolls of James I*, ed. M.C. Griffith (Dublin, 1966), pp 227, 256, 302–3, 495–6, 505 and 591; *Calendar of the patent and close rolls of chancery in Ireland of the reign of Charles the first, first to eighth year, inclusive*, ed. James Morrin (London, 1863), pp 109, 266 and 430. 48 Joseph Byrne, *War and peace: the survival of the Talbots of Malahide 1641–1671* (Dublin, 1997), p. 19. 49 *Civil Survey, vii, county of Dublin*, p. 195; Down Survey parish maps … (NLI, MS 714). 50 *Civil Survey, vii, county of Dublin*, pp 173–4. 51 *Civil Survey, vii, county of Dublin*, p. 169. 52 *Anc. rec. Dublin*, iii, pp 132, 146 and 239.

modity, that the ships have hardly any shelter there for any winds, not only such as come out of the sea, but also those which come off from the land, especially out of the south-west; so as with a great south-west storm the ships run great hazard to be carried away from their anchors, and driven into the sea; which more than once hath come to pass, and particularly in the beginning of November, *Anno.* 1637, when in one night ten or twelve barks had that misfortune befallen them, of the most part whereof never no news hath been heard since.[53]

Clontarf possessed 'a fishing' *c.*1655 and, like Newhaven and Malahide, had a Catholic owner in 1641.[54] The proprietor of Clontarf was George King.

A number of rivers flowed through Fingal into the Irish Sea. Those shown in figure 1.3 from south to north were the rivers Liffey, Tolka, Broadmeadow, Clogher (or Pill), and Delvin. Boate wrote of the Irish brooks that, besides watering the land and drenching the cattle and other beasts, they 'do also serve the inhabitants for another good use, to wit the grinding of their corn, whereunto the windmills are very little used in Ireland, because they have the conveniency, through the great number of brooks, to erect water-mills in every quarter where it is necessary: which bring a great profit to the owners, being kept and maintained with less cost and labour'.[55] This was not quite true of Fingal, where there were at least four windmills situated in Lusk, Raheny, Clontarf and Feltrim.[56] A further windmill is known to have existed in Holmpatrick earlier in the century. This was required because the local watermill ground only in winter due to lack of water.[57] Boate also commented on the dangerous nature of some rivers, in particular the Tolka and the Dodder, and mentioned that there had been a stone bridge over the Tolka near Drumcondra since ancient times.[58]

While it was possible to treat the islands and ports of Fingal's coastal region as discrete units examination of the inland district presented certain difficulties. In order to find a convenient unit for comparative analysis it was necessary to chose between the baronies, of which there were four, the parishes (forty-one according to the Civil Survey or thirty-eight according to the Books of Survey and Distribution) and the townlands (500–600). The parish was selected as the most convenient unit of analysis although, in practice, Fingal parishes were far from being neat and tidy units.[59] The parishes of Finglas, Lusk and Swords crossed barony boundaries. In some accounts the parishes of Ballymadun, Clonmethan and Hollywood were split into more than one entity. We find detached townlands or holdings, such as Ardla (in the parish of Lusk but surrounded by the parish of Holmpatrick) or Dellabrown (in the parish of Holmpatrick but surrounded by the parish of Lusk).[60] Nevertheless, on balance, the parish seemed to be the most useful unit on which to base analyses. For the purpose

53 Gerard Boate, *Ireland's naturall history* ... (London, 1652), pp 25–6. 54 *Civil Survey, vii, county of Dublin*, p. 176. 55 Gerard Boate, *Ireland's naturall history* ... (London, 1652), p. 57. 56 *Civil Survey, vii, county of Dublin*, pp 120, 172, 176 and 184. 57 *A repertory of the inrolments on the patent rolls in chancery in Ireland; commencing with the reign of King James I*, ed. John Caillard Erck (2 pts, Dublin, 1846–52), part i, p. 220. 58 Gerard Boate, *Ireland's naturall history* ... (London, 1652), pp 59–60. 59 The reasons for the choice of parish are given in 'Fingal 1603–60', i, p. 25. 60 Jocelyn Otway-Ruthven, 'The medieval church lands of County Dublin' in *Medieval studies presented to Aubrey Gwynn, S.J.* ed. J.A. Watt, J.B. Morrall and F.X. Martin (Dublin, 1961), p. 68.

Fig. 1.3 Map of County Dublin (Sir William Petty, *A geographical description of the kingdom of Ireland*, 1728 edition). Barony boundaries are indicated by dotted lines.

of analysing parish data the Civil Survey, despite its deficiencies, was selected as the most comprehensive of the three main seventeenth-century surveys.[61] The size of parishes varied enormously.[62] There were less than 200 acres in the smallest parish, Killester, while the largest, Lusk, contained over 6,600. The average (mean) parish size was 1,394 acres and the median parish was St Margaret's (1,094 acres). On the whole, the larger parishes were in the more northerly baronies of Balrothery and Nethercross while the smaller were in the baronies of Castleknock and Coolock. There were, however, exceptions. Balrothery contained one small parish, that of Baldongan (435 acres) while the large parish of Castleknock (3,112 acres) was situated in the barony of the same name. Figure 1.4 shows the approximate boundaries of the parishes in the mid-seventeenth century.

A detailed analysis of land quality and land use for Co. Dublin as a whole has been carried out by William Smyth.[63] Writing about the county as a whole, he estimated that close on 70 per cent of Co. Dublin was 'arable', that is, land capable of producing good tillage crops, in the time of the Civil Survey. Smyth noted the fact that the Civil Survey did not make a distinction between arable and pastoral lands for the barony of Nethercross. The compilers of the Down Survey, however, described the quality of the soil in Nethercross as 'very good and profitable', compared with 'good' in Balrothery, 'generally good' in Castleknock and 'indifferent good' in Coolock.[64]

Land quality in Fingal was analyzed on a parish by parish basis.[65] As well as showing a high proportion of arable land this analysis indicated that the amount of unprofitable land was negligible except in the barony of Balrothery and in the parish of the Ward. A breakdown of profitable and unprofitable land in the barony of Balrothery by type of proprietor in 1641 indicated that 9 per cent of the land held by Catholic proprietors was classified as unprofitable compared with 35 per cent of that held by Protestants and 19 per cent of church land.[66] The figures for the parish of Holmpatrick, which showed the highest percentage of unprofitable land (39 per cent), could not be cross-checked, as the parish was wholly owned by the Protestant earl of Thomond and consequently did not appear in the Down Survey. It must be questioned if the juries for the barony of Balrothery adopted the same standards as those in other baronies. In the Ward parish (barony of Castleknock) where over 17 per cent of the land was classified as unprofitable the same pattern occurred. Just under 9 per cent of Catholic-owned land was classified as unprofitable while almost 25 per cent of Protestant-owned land was so classified.

The statistical evidence on quality of land in Fingal is complemented by the observations of contemporary and near-contemporary writers who extolled its virtues. Over the centuries invaders had been attracted to Fingal not just by its ease of access but also by the fertility of its soil. In his description of Ireland in *Holinshed's Irish chronicle* Richard Stanihurst commented that Fingal, Meath, Kildare and Louth

61 The reasons for this choice are given in 'Fingal 1603–60', i, pp 27–8. 62 'Fingal 1603–60', ii, appendix A, tables A.1 to A.3, pp 6–8. 63 William J. Smyth, 'Exploring the social and cultural topographies of sixteenth and seventeenth-century County Dublin' in F.H.A. Aalen and Kevin Whelan (eds), *Dublin City and County: from prehistory to present* (Dublin, 1992), pp 125–9. 64 Down Survey parish maps ... (NLI, MS 714). 65 'Fingal 1603–60', ii, appendix B, tables B.1 to B.8, pp 9–14. 66 'Fingal 1603–60', i, p. 30.

Fig. 1.4 Approximate boundaries of Fingal parishes in the mid-seventeenth century

were noted for their good husbandry and rich soil while in a later work he described Fingal and Meath as 'the barn of Ireland' and commented that they produced spectacular crop yields.[67] At the end of the sixteenth century an anonymous author

67 Richarde Stanyhurst, *A treatise contayning a playne and perfect description of Irelande* ... in Raphaell Holinshed and Richarde Stanyhurst, *Holinshed's Irish chronicle* ..., ed. Liam Miller and Eileen Power (London, 1577, republished Dublin, 1979), p. 13; Richard Stanihurst, *De rebus in Hibernia gestis* (originally published Antwerp, 1584), translated from the Latin by Colm Lennon in *Richard Stanihurst the Dubliner* (Dublin, 1981), p. 143.

indicated how the very abundance of corn caused problems for the people, problems which were to recur in the mid-seventeenth century.[68]

> This county of Dublin is very fruitful and yieldeth great plenty of all kind of corns; but if the rebels fear prosecution, they burn the corn that the subject may not have means to relieve the soldiers in the time either of prosecution or cessation, whereupon ensueth extreme misery either to the country man, soldier or both; for the soldiers being for the most part disordered and very licentious, will violently draw from the poor husbandman that which should sustain himself and his family, and so doth daily drive him to beg, or if the soldier be restrained which seldom falleth out, he perisheth for want of food, of both which these last years hath given infinite examples, and it is to be feared that if the corns be burnt up this winter that there will be little sowing of summer corn this year, and consequently a dearth and plague, which commonly followeth dearth, the next year.

The anonymous author of the *Geographicall description* (published in 1642) noted that Dublin was 'a plentiful county both in corn and cattle, abounding also with game for pleasure' and that Fingal was 'even the garner and store-house of this kingdom, so great store of corn it yieldeth every year'.[69] Occasionally one finds details about individual baronies and parishes. According to the Civil Survey the soil of the barony of Balrothery was 'for the most part rye and meslin land and the rest wheat land; and part bog, mountain and furze'.[70] The Down Survey comments were also pertinent.[71] The soil of Coolock barony was deemed to be 'indifferent good but the west is much better than the east, it is for the most part arable and furzy pasture. There is but little meadow therein.' Of Howth it was stated that 'the eastern part of the parish is a high and barren mountain, namely the lands of Howth and Sutton except above the manor house of Howth. There it is more fertile and also above the house of Sutton'. Portmarnock was 'arable, pasture and meadow excepting the coneyburrow of Portmarnock. The eastern part thereof is a sandy bank formerly driven up from the sea by the easterly winds. Only fit for coneys.' The surveyor of Nethercross was particularly enthusiastic, summarizing the barony's benefits as follows:

> The quality of the soil is very good and profitable, consisting of arable, pasture and meadow; there is some little woodland and bog, the former being advantageous for fuel, building, shelter of cattle, repair, fencing and the like and the latter in respect of the smallness of its quantity not considerable.

The soil of the individual parishes in Nethercross was rated as follows:

Clonmethan	no information;
Finglas, Lusk and Portraine	good and profitable;
Swords	generally good.

68 *The description of Ireland and the state thereof as it is at this present in anno 1598*, ed. Edmund Hogan (Dublin, 1878), pp 43–4. 69 G.N., *A geographicall description of the kingdom of Ireland* ... (London, 1642), p. 14. 70 *Civil Survey, vii, county of Dublin*, p. 3. 71 Down Survey parish maps ... (NLI, MS 714).

While the general Down Survey rating of the barony of Balrothery was good arable, pasture and meadow, 'mountain' land was an additional feature in the parishes of the Naul and Hollywood and in the detached townland of Ardla in the parish of Lusk, which was less than 50 m above sea level.

There is one rather interesting pattern to be found in the north-west of the barony. The Civil Survey listed twenty-eight denominations for the parish of Garristown.[72] The Down Survey terriers recorded ninety-two while the Books of Survey and Distribution enumerated 188.[73] A glance at the Down Survey maps shows a pattern of landholding in the parish which differed from that found elsewhere. Many of the tiny holdings were in the form of long narrow strips which may have indicated a type of landholding and/or cultivation dating from an earlier era.

Travellers observed and commented on the country they passed through though their perspective was necessarily more restricted than that of surveyors and residents. Sir William Brereton travelled from Drogheda to Dublin via Swords on 9 July 1635.[74] He described his trip from Drogheda to Swords as follows:

> The way from Drogheda hither as dainty fine way as I ever rid, and a most pleasant country, greatest part corn upon the very sea-coast, almost Wirral-like, and very good and well-eared corn; the barley now beginning to turn, and will be ripe before the rye ... About two or three miles from Swords my lord chief baron hath a dainty, pleasant, high-built house, and much rich and brave land about it ...

Another traveller, going from Dublin to Drogheda in the opposite direction in 1666, noted some differences.[75] He saw a number of ruined castles as well as 'some meadows, and many herds of oxen, cows and calves ...' Corn was not mentioned.

The chief deficiency noted by contemporary writers was the lack of fuel. Fynes Moryson noted that Co. Dublin, despite having a fertile soil and rich pastures was 'wanting in wood, so as they burn turf or sea-coal brought out of England'.[76] The anonymous author of the *Geographicall description* stated that Co. Dublin's greatest want was fuel, which was 'a heavy turf or English sea-coal'.[77] The compilers of the Down Survey, commenting on the barony of Coolock, noted that the 'inhabitants of this barony have no other firing but only furze'.[78] Gerard Boate gave the following graphic description of the results of the general deforestation:

> Ireland hath been made so bare of woods in many parts, that the inhabitants do not only want wood for firing (being therefore constrained to make shift with turf, or sea-coal, where they are not too far from the sea) but even timber

72 *Civil Survey, vii, county of Dublin,* pp 16–25. 73 Books of Survey and Distribution for County Dublin (NAI, Quit Rent Office papers, pp 58–72). 74 William Brereton, *Travels in Holland, the United Provinces, England, Scotland and Ireland, M.DC.XXXIV–M.DC.XXXV*, ed. Edward Hopkins (Manchester, 1844), pp 136–7. 75 Jorevin de Rocheford, 'Description of England and Ireland after the Restoration' in C. Litton Falkiner (ed.), *Illustrations of Irish history and topography* (London, 1904), p. 417. 76 Fynes Moryson, *An itinerary* ... (London, 1617), part iii, chap. v, p. 158. 77 G.N., *A geographicall description of the kingdom of Ireland* ... (London, 1642), p. 14. 78 Down Survey parish maps ... (NLI, MS 714).

> for building, so as they are necessitated to fetch it a good way off, to their great charges, especially in places where it must be brought by land. And in some parts you may travel whole days long without seeing any woods or trees except a few about gentlemen's houses; as namely from Dublin, and from places that are some miles further to the south of it, to Drogheda, Dundalk, the Newry, and as far as Dromore, threescore miles, one doth not come near any woods worth the speaking of, and in some parts thereof you shall not see so much as one tree in many miles ...[79]

On the subject of fuel, Boate stated that sea-coals were the ordinary firing in Dublin and in places near the sea, where they were brought from England, Wales and Scotland cheaply and in abundance.[80] The availability of fuel was very important. During the early seventeenth century Ireland, like the northern hemisphere in general, was in the middle of the so-called Little Ice Age, which was marked by short summers and long cold winters.[81] Since contemporary writers recorded that the climate in Ireland was milder and more temperate than that in other northern European countries, there was just an occasional clue as to exactly how severe the weather could be. Following a eulogy of the temperate Irish climate Boate provided just such a clue when he wrote:

> There hath been some winters, wherein it hath frozen ten or twelve days together, so as the Liffey and other the like rivers were quite frozen, and might be gone upon by men and beasts. But these are altogether extraordinary, and do come very seldom, hardly once in the space of ten or twelve years.[82]

Additional evidence for the harshness of the winters can be found in Dean Bernard's description of the weather in December 1641.[83] He wrote that 'about the end of December there was a great ice, so that our river of the Boyne was in a night or two so hard frozen, that it could scarce be broken with mallets; horses and men might safely pass over'.

Moving from the physical landscape to the influence of man on that landscape we note that estates were superimposed on the landscape in an extraordinarily complex way. In addition, the landowners themselves had varied backgrounds. There were Catholic and Protestant landowners. Some land was held by the city of Dublin and by a variety of church bodies. There were a small number of women proprietors. Some denominations were in joint ownership. Apart from the church the most influential landlords in Fingal in 1641, in terms of acreage of land held, were Nicholas Barnewall of Turvey and the lord of Howth.[84] However, other proprietors such as

79 Gerard Boate, *Ireland's naturall history* ... (London 1652), pp 121–2. 80 Gerard Boate, *Ireland's naturall history* ... (London 1652), p. 152. 81 P.K. Rohan, *The climate of Ireland* (Dublin, 1986), p. 7; Brendan McWilliams, 'The kingdom of the air: the progress of meteorology' in John Wilson Foster (ed.) in *Nature in Ireland: a scientific and cultural history* (Dublin, 1997), pp 116–7. 82 Gerard Boate, *Ireland's naturall history* ... (London 1652), p. 163. 83 Nicholas Bernard, *The whole proceedings of the siege of Drogheda* ... (London, 1642), p. 34 (NLI, Lough Fea pamphlet no. 74). 84 The complex question of landownership is explored in 'Fingal 1603–60', i, pp 34–5 and ii, appendix C, pp 15–24.

John Bysse, Christopher Fagan and Philip Hore, with fairly modest estates by the standards of the major players, had interests and, no doubt, influence spread over a wide area.

Another possible indicator of influence is the court system. The Civil Survey mentioned twelve manor courts in the area, in most of which court leet and court baron were held. These were Ballymadun (proprietor, Robert Preston), Balscaddan (court leet only, dean of Christ Church), Balscaddan, Whitestown (lord of Ormond) Castleknock (Christopher Barnewall), Garristown (Elizabeth Talbot), Holmpatrick (earl of Thomond), Howth (lord of Howth), Lusk, Jordanstown (lord of Howth), Naul (Christopher Cruise), Naul, Reynoldstown (Martin Dillon), Rush (lord of Ormond) and Swords (archbishop of Dublin, later Trinity College Dublin). In these courts the proprietors could exercise real and important powers. These will be discussed later.

Another set of indicators of influence were features such as mills, brew-houses, malt-houses, kilns and quarries which indicated a degree of economic power. Quarries became increasingly important after the introduction of the Highways Act which placed the onus for repair of roads on individual parishes.[85] Also listed were pigeon houses, rabbit warrens and fishing weirs, which could be used to provide emergency supplies of food as well as luxuries in normal times. Included also were castles, which by the 1650s had probably lost much of the strategic importance they still held at the time of the rising of 1641 though, no doubt, they still had a symbolic significance. The use of Fingal castles during the early years of the wars of the 1640s is discussed later. Stables and the single coach-house specifically mentioned are included since horses were important, not just for farm work and transport, but also for military purposes. Finally, a decision was made to list houses of office, a catch-all category which may have indicated farm buildings but in many cases, judging by the building valuations, must have represented substantial economic concerns such as inns and perhaps even manufacturing concerns.

These additional indicators were analyzed by parish.[86] Parishes for which none of these features were listed were Palmerstown in the barony of Balrothery and Cloghran (Swords), Coolock and Glasnevin in the barony of Coolock, though, there was a mill in Glasnevin in 1640. All these parishes were below average size but they were not among the smallest parishes in the area. Not surprisingly, the largest parishes of Lusk and Swords had twenty-eight and twenty-four entries respectively, but the third largest parish, Balrothery, had only eight (of which four were castles) as compared with sixteen entries for Howth, which was less than half its size. A distribution of the selected indicators by type made it clear that Fingal, despite the effects of the recent wars, was still richly endowed in the 1650s.[87] It is noticeable, however, that only twenty-six of the forty-one parishes had one or more corn mills but the mill at Glasnevin and perhaps others were omitted. A listing of the additional indicators by proprietor showed that once again, the major proprietors tended to have most entries on the list but there were some owners of smaller estates, for example, Henry

85 An act for repayring and amending of high-ways and cashes, and cutting or clearing of paces, 11, 12 and 13 J.I, c.7, *Stat. Ire.* (1786), i, pp 444–8. 86 'Fingal 1603–60', i, pp 35–6 and ii, appendix D, pp 25–38. 87 'Fingal 1603–60', ii, appendix D, table D.2, pp 29–33.

Segrave of Cabragh and Sir Henry Power of Chapelizod, who appeared several times.[88] It was also possible to identify family groups, for example, the Barnewalls, the Plunkets and the Talbots, who between them had several entries.

With the possible exception of Swords Fingal had no large towns. An examination of the populations of selected towns based on figures in the so-called 'Census of Ireland' or poll tax returns of 1659 gave rise to the question as to whether these figures were inflated by large rural populations in their immediate hinterlands.[89] This seems unlikely except in the case of Garristown which had a very great number of tiny holdings. Joseph Byrne has drawn attention to the particular circumstances of Malahide, where there was a small colony of officials, retainers and soldiers.[90] Of the towns listed Malahide had the highest proportion of 'English'.

In 'A survey of Ireland' written about 1574 the author listed Swords, Lusk and Balrothery as 'throughfare towns between Drogheda and Dublin'.[91] In a further description of Co. Dublin prepared in 1598 Swords and Lusk were listed as market towns 'unwalled and without privileges'.[92] (In this *Description* the Co. Meath towns, Dunboyne and Ratoath were included as part of Dublin.) Balrothery, Howth, Fieldstown, Kilsallaghan and Finglas were listed among the best villages in the county. Sir William Brereton preserved in his diary a little cameo of Swords in 1635 as follows:

> Jul.9 – From Drogheda we came to the Swords, which is fourteen miles thence, and six from thence to Dublin. Here we lodged at the sign of the Boot, a tavern, and were well used, and found far better accommodation in so mean a village than could be expected.[93]

Perhaps the most significant development relating to the towns was the decline of Balrothery, which was described in the Down Survey (description of the barony) as 'the chiefest town in the barony' of the same name although by 1659, according to the poll tax returns, it had less than half the population of Rush.[94] The Down Survey went on to say that Balrothery 'hath been in former times a town of repute, but now remains only the ruins of it ...' The terriers relating to the parish noted that 'in Balrothery there hath been a fair town; the castle is standing still and some old walls.' The town had clearly suffered greatly during the Confederate and Cromwellian wars.

While the coastal towns had access by sea inland towns required roads to enable them to communicate with each other and with the population in the countryside as well as with the ports. Writing about Ireland as a whole R.A. Butlin stated that inland communication was notoriously bad, necessitating the use of sea and river routes.[95]

88 'Fingal 1603–60', ii, appendix D, table D.3, pp 34–8. 89 'Fingal 1603–60', i, table 1.3, p. 37. 90 Joseph Byrne, *War and peace: the survival of the Talbots of Malahide 1641–1671* (Dublin, 1997), pp 20–1. 91 *Calendar of the Carew manuscripts preserved in the archiepiscopal library at Lambeth* (6 vols, London, 1867–73), iv, pp 446–7. 92 *The description of Ireland and the state thereof as it is at this present in anno 1598*, ed. Edmund Hogan (Dublin, 1878), pp 36–7. 93 William Brereton, *Travels in Holland, the United Provinces, England, Scotland and Ireland, M.DC.XXXIV–M.DC.XXXV*, ed. Edward Hopkins (Manchester, 1844), p. 136. 94 Down Survey parish maps ... (NLI, MS 714); *A census of Ireland c.1659* ... ed. Séamus Pender (Dublin, 1939), p. 385. 95 R.A. Butlin, 'Land and people, *c.*1600' in T.W.

Donald Woodward, on the other hand, has pointed out that 'internal communications were not sufficiently bad to preclude a massive and rapid commercialization of the economy'.[96] What was the situation in Fingal? The early cartographers tended to omit roads from their maps. The Down Survey maps occasionally included roads but, in this respect, those for the Fingal parishes and baronies are disappointing. In the Civil Survey the usual method of describing boundaries was to list the townlands, or natural features such as the sea, a river or even a bog, to the north, south, east and west of the denomination being recorded. There was no reason to mention roads or bridges, unless they provided information about boundaries, yet a surprising number of land routes appeared in the records, particularly in the vicinity of the towns of Swords and, to a lesser extent, Finglas, where other townlands/natural features could not easily be used to delineate boundaries. Figure 1.3 shows the map of Co. Dublin, with the main roads through Fingal, contained in Sir William Petty's *Hiberniae delineatio*, published in 1685 though possibly prepared as early as the 1660s.[97] An attempt has been made in figure 1.5 to reconstruct as much as possible of the road network from the available information in the surveys and to superimpose it on an outline of Petty's map. It is clear that the picture is incomplete. While there is a mention of the road leading from Balrothery to the then tiny hamlet of Balbriggan, the roads in virtually the whole of the eastern part of the area, containing all the important havens and the homes of the two major proprietors, Turvey (Nicholas Barnewall) and Howth (lord of Howth), are not represented in these contemporary records.[98] Despite these omissions enough remains to suggest that Fingal had a good network of roads, Swords and Finglas being particularly well favoured. A number of bridges, some with descriptive names, are also listed, for example, the wooden bridge of Balheary, the white bridge of Kilbarrack and (on the Down Survey barony map) the stone bridge at Portmarnock.[99] The bridges at Kilbarrack and Portmarnock provide evidence of other unrecorded roads in the coastal area. As for the quality of the roads Fynes Moryson made some interesting comments as early as 1617.[100] He wrote that 'in Ireland, since the end of the civil war, some lords and knights have brought in coaches to Dublin, but they are not generally used, neither are there any to be hired, though the ways be most plain and generally good for coaches'. This tribute to the state of the roads by a seasoned traveller must be taken into account when assessing their condition. The use of the road name 'Stony booter', which still survives as Stoneybatter, and the frequent occurrence of the word 'batter' (*bóthar*) in the vicinity of Swords, as well as references to the Irish Street in Swords, raise questions about the survival of the Irish language in parts of Fingal

Moody, F.X. Martin and F.J. Byrne (eds), *A new history of Ireland*, iii, *early modern Ireland 1534–1691* (originally published Oxford, 1976, reprinted 1999), p. 162. **96** Donald Woodward, 'Irish Sea trades and shipping from the later middle ages to *c.*1660' in Michael McCaughan and John Appleby (eds), *The Irish Sea: aspects of maritime history* (Belfast and Cultra, 1989) pp 38–9. **97** William Petty, *Hiberniae delineatio* (London, 1685); J.H. Andrews, *Shapes of Ireland: maps and their makers 1564–1839* (Dublin, 1997), pp 128–38. **98** *Civil Survey, vii, county of Dublin*, p. 12. **99** *Civil Survey, vii, county of Dublin*, pp 108, 169 and 170; Map of the barony of Nethercross (Down Survey baronial maps, 1657, reproduced Ordnance Survey Office, 1908, from the originals in the Bibliothèque Nationale, Paris). **100** Fynes Moryson, *An itinerary* … (London, 1617), part iii, chap. 2, p. 62.

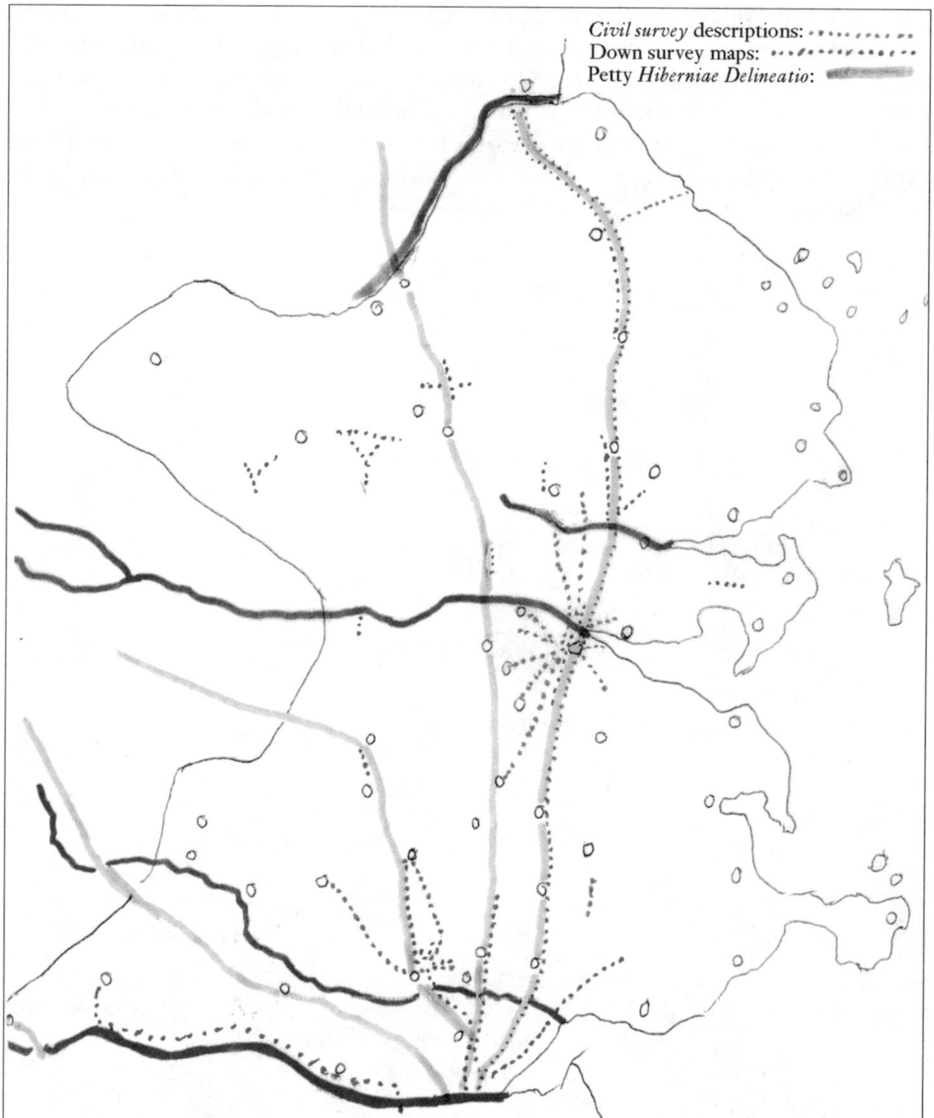

Fig. 1.5 Contemporary representations of roads in seventeenth-century Fingal

and the possible existence of two cultural traditions in Swords, questions that will be addressed later.

In summary, seventeenth-century Fingal was a prosperous area endowed with fertile land and easy access to rich fishing grounds. The only obvious deficiency was lack of fuel. The territory had a number of small towns and was close to the important market of Dublin city. There appears to have been a good road network though the evidence for this is fragmentary. A great deal of power was concentrated in the hands of a small number of major proprietors but the complex pattern of land-holding was such that a number of smaller landholders and principal tenants had interests, and most probably, influence over a wide area. The material welfare of the people of Fingal in the early and mid-seventeenth century will be discussed in the next chapter.

2

People, houses and homes

> Rachaidh mise, rachaidh tusa síos go Fine Gall;
> íosaidh mise, íosaidh tusa, gach ni dhá bhfuighe mé ann.[1]

These lines from a sixteenth-century quatrain encapsulate one of the most vivid images of early modern Fingal, that of the constant movement of people. Travellers, many of them Irish-speaking, journeyed along the Fingal roads described in the previous chapter between the Gaelic world of the north and west and the English-speaking capital. During the seventeenth century these travellers included armies and refugees, scholars and soldiers, chapmen and clergymen, drovers and debt-collectors. But they also included local people such as landlords visiting their properties, servants going to market to sell their masters' corn and men, women and children walking a mile or two to the nearest mass-house, school or holy well. In this chapter some surviving evidence of the way of life and material well-being of the people who lived in seventeenth-century Fingal will be examined. The topics to be dealt with include population, housing, the hearth, furniture and furnishings, food and drink, the use of tobacco and snuff, dress, jewellery and ornaments, weapons, occupations, transport and travel, illness and poverty.

An analysis of housing and population led me to the conclusion that the number of dwellings in the area was of the order of 2,500 and the population in the region of 15,000 or perhaps somewhat higher.[2] An interesting feature which emerged from the analysis was the high proportion (80 per cent) of the population of Fingal classified as 'Irish' at the end of the Commonwealth period (figure 2.1).

Descriptions of the construction and appearance of dwelling houses in Fingal at this period are also difficult to find. Allowing for underreporting the number of houses built of stone was probably not much greater than the total number of castles, mills, malt-houses and stone houses identified in the Civil Survey and probably amounted to well under 10 per cent of the total housing stock. The information on roof types is patchy but it suggests that the number of tiled or slated roofs was small. There is no information in the Civil Survey on doors or windows. Many houses had gardens or orchards attached to them.

1 Gerard Murphy, 'A folksong traceable to Elizabethan times' in *Éigse*, vii, part 2, pp 117–20. The full quatrain reads as follows in normalized spelling: 'Rachaidh mise, rachaidh tusa síos go Fine Gall; / íosaidh mise, íosaidh tusa, gach ni dhá bhfuighe mé ann. / Crochfaidhear mise agus crochfaidhear tusa, agus cad 'a-ghean[f]aid ar gclann? / Nuair ásfaid fiacla acu féin, éirghid féin fén ghleann.' The translation in Gerard Murphy's modernized spelling reads: 'You and I will go to Fingall; / You and I will eat such meat as we find there. / I shall be hanged and you shall be hanged, [and] what shall our children do? When teeth do grow unto themselves, let them go to the glens!' 2 For a detailed discussion of this analysis see 'Fingal 1603–60', i, pp 42–3 and ii, appendix E, pp 39–58.

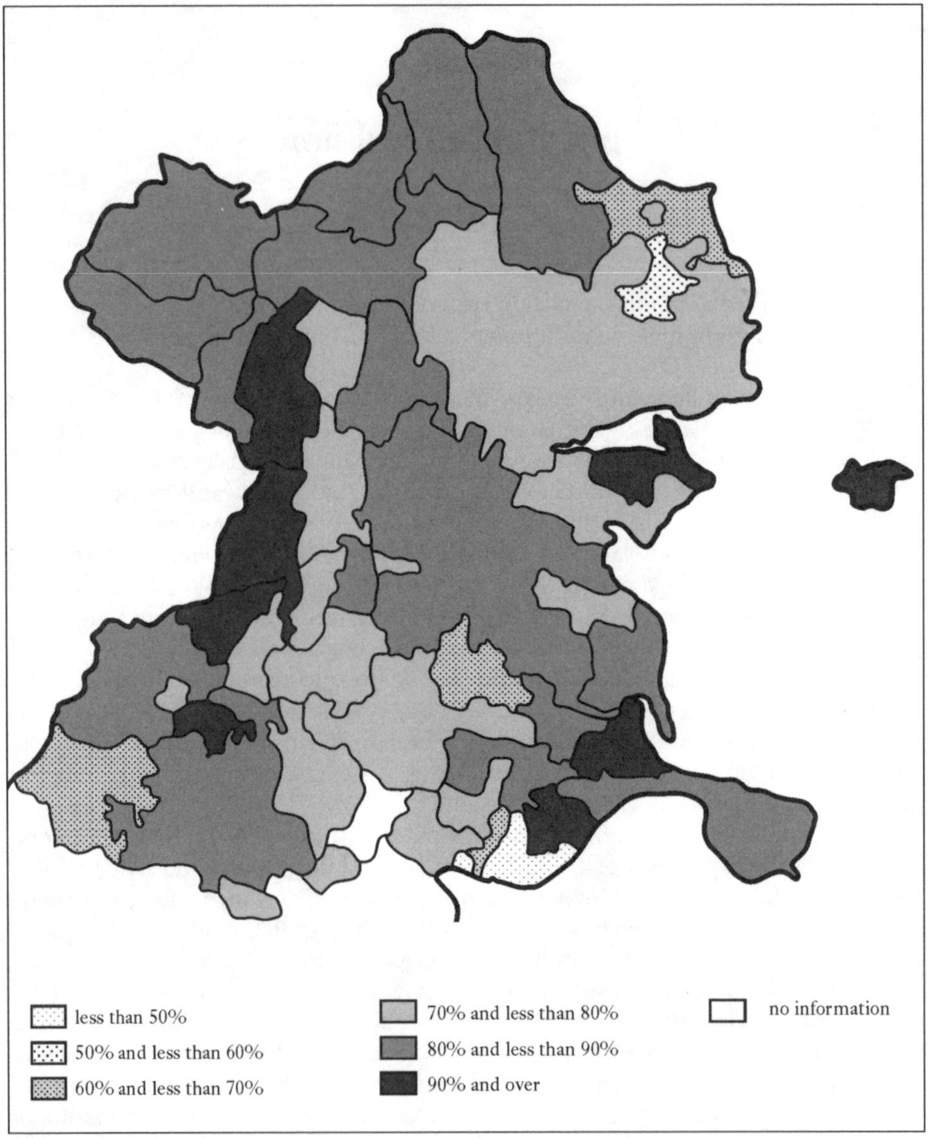

Fig. 2.1 Percentage of Fingal residents assessed for poll tax, classified as Irish, by parish, 1660

Information on the number of hearths, and by extension on the general quality of housing, can be obtained from the hearth money roll for Co. Dublin for 1664.[3] Single-hearth houses amounted to 92 per cent of the total. This preponderance of single-hearth houses (generally the poorest or the lowest class of house within the

3 'Hearth money roll for County Dublin, 1664' (second part), *Journal of the County Kildare Archaeological Society*, xi (1930–33), pp 386–466.

taxation net) listed in the hearth money roll may have been exaggerated somewhat because of attempts at tax evasion by occupiers who reported houses with two or more hearths as houses with a single hearth.[4] On the other hand the houses of the very poor were exempt from tax and were excluded from the roll.[5] If they could have been quantified they would have boosted the number of 'poorer' houses. In proportional terms this would have compensated, in part at least, for the reporting of multiple-hearth households as single-hearth households. All in all, therefore, this survey is likely to have reflected the general *pattern* of housing quality, if not the actual number of houses. Geographically, the parishes of Clontarf, Chapelizod, Finglas and St Michan's, all close to Dublin city, had the highest percentages of multiple-hearth houses (figure 2.2). This was probably a reflection of the number of wealthy officials, merchants and professional men who worked in the city and lived or had a second home in the adjoining countryside.

For further information about the type of housing in the area it is necessary to look at contemporary accounts as well as modern descriptions of surviving buildings or those recently demolished. Travellers occasionally made passing references to the buildings. In July 1635 Sir William Brereton wrote that at the sign of the Boot in Swords he and his party 'found far better accommodation in so mean a village than could be expected'.[6] He also noted that about 'two or three mile from Swords my lord chief baron [Sir Richard Bolton] hath a dainty, pleasant, high-built wood house, and much rich and brave land about it, this placed on the right hand ...'. Perhaps this was one of the lesser Bolton homes as it was about this time that the main residence, a stone and brick house at Brazil, was being built.[7] It seems unlikely that Brereton saw Brazil on his route from Drogheda to Dublin since it was situated some distance to the west of Swords. If, on the other hand, Brereton did travel by Brazil and saw a wooden house there it is possible that, following the burning of the house by Eoghan Rua O'Neill in 1647, the house was rebuilt in the more solid form in which it survived into the twentieth century.[8] About half a mile further along the road Brereton noted another 'gallant pleasant seat' but did not record the owner's name. In the early 1650s Gerard Boate, basing his account on information supplied by his brother and others noted that Sir William Ussher had 'a fine little castle of freestone' on Lambay Island.[9] In 1666 Jorevin de Rocheford travelling from Dublin to Drogheda in the

4 *Heads and hearths: The hearth money rolls and poll tax returns for Co. Antrim 1660–69*, ed. S.T. Carleton (Belfast, 1991), pp 178 and 180. 5 *Heads and hearths: The hearth money rolls and poll tax returns for Co. Antrim 1660–69*, ed. S.T. Carleton (Belfast, 1991), p. xii. 6 William Brereton, *Travels in Holland, the United Provinces, England, Scotland and Ireland, M.DC.XXXIV-M.DC.XXXV*, ed. Edward Hopkins (Manchester, 1844), p. 136. 7 Maurice Craig, *Classic Irish houses of the middle size* (London and New York, 1976), pp 5–8, 19 and 55; the Knight of Glin, David J. Griffin and Nicholas K. Robinson, *Vanishing country houses of Ireland* (2nd ed., Dublin, Antrim, 1989), p. 59. 8 H.C., *News from Dublin in Ireland relating how Colonell Jones ... fell upon the rebells ...* (London, 1647), p. 3 (NLI, Lough Fea pamphlet no. 221). 9 Gerard Boate, *Ireland's naturall history, being a true and ample description of its situation, greatness, shape and nature; of its hills, woods, heaths, bogs; of its fruitful parts and profitable grounds, with the several ways of manuring and improving the same: with its heads or promontories, harbours, roads and bays; of its springs and fountains, brooks, rivers, loughs; of its metals, minerals, freestone, marble, sea-coal, turf, and other things that are taken out of the ground, and lastly, of the nature and temperature of its air and season, and what diseases it is free from, or subject unto, conducing to the advancement of navigation, husbandry and other profitable arts and possessions* (London, 1652), p. 33.

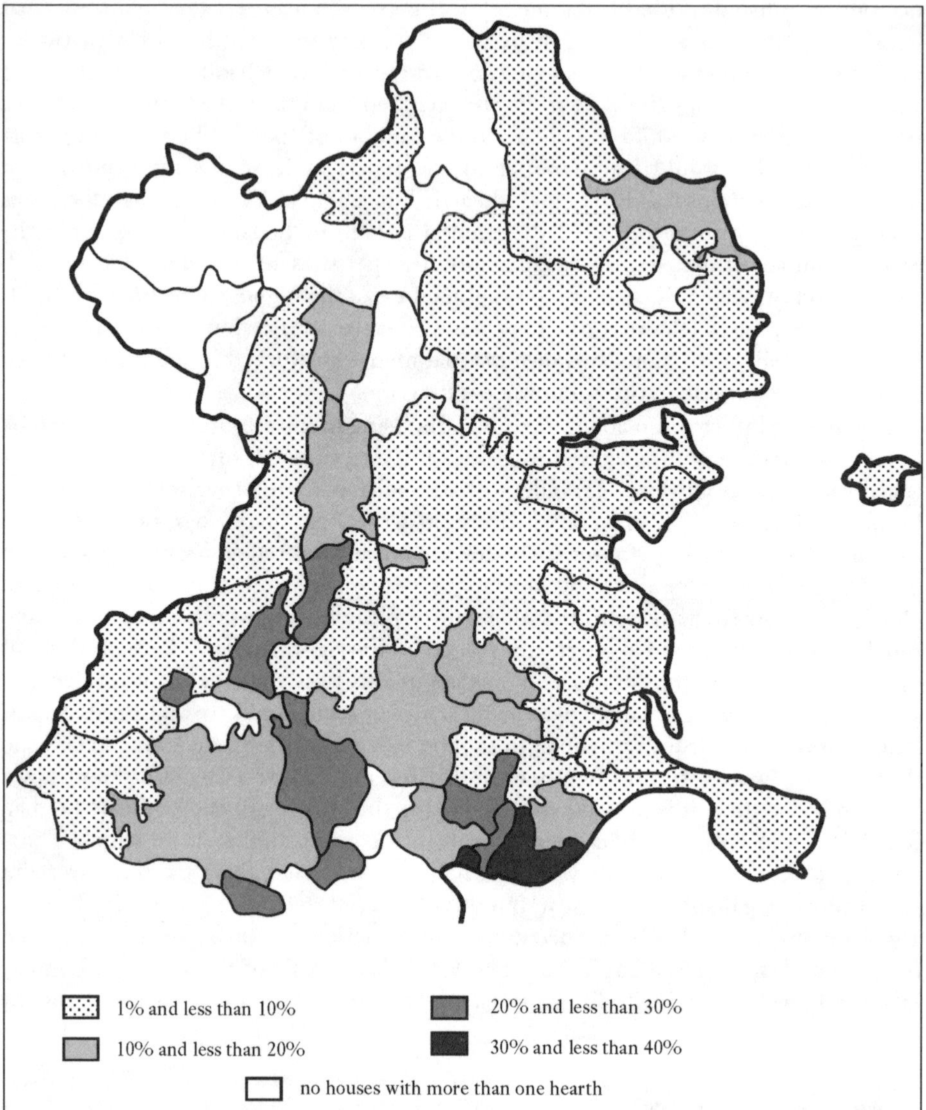

Fig. 2.2 Percentage of Fingal houses assessed on more than one hearth by parish, *c.*1664

opposite direction to that taken by Brereton noted the ruined castle at Swords as well as 'several of these small castles, all ruined in the last wars'.[10]

Among the few detailed contemporary accounts there are two contained in grants to the earl of Thomond which described the manor house of Holmpatrick in the

10 Jorevin de Rocheford, 'Description of England and Ireland after the Restoration' in C. Litton Falkiner (ed.), *Illustrations of Irish history and topography* (London, 1904), p. 417.

early years of the seventeenth century.[11] The house, on the site of the former priory, was built of stone and had three turrets. It had one hall with six chambers and four cellars and one kitchen. There was a bake-house near the house, as well as a stone granary and a haggard or bawn. Other out-buildings included two stone stables and two stone granaries, both covered with tiles, three houses for heifers, sheep and swine, a kiln and a pigeon house. The precinct also included six cottages as well as a garden and orchard. Not far away stood the water-mill. Some of the buildings were described as ruinous in the earlier grant, though not in the later. On the outbreak of the rising of 1641 the occupants and chief tenants of the earl of Thomond, the Verveer family, were warned to leave the house as a priest was coming to say Mass there, 'it being an old abbey', which suggests that the house, whether it was original or had been rebuilt, was, like the adjoining church, part of the priory complex which dated from pre-reformation times.[12] By the time of the Civil Survey only the walls of the church remained, the house was in ruins and some of the out-buildings had disappeared.[13] It is not clear if the house at Holmpatrick, which was assessed on six hearths in 1664, was the same house or a completely new building.[14]

Few dwellings built in the early seventeenth century survive in Fingal. There are, of course, some castles and many tower houses which date from an earlier period as, for example, Malahide and Howth Castles, and tower houses at Balrothery and Dunsoghly. One building which almost certainly contains an early seventeenth-century wing is the late eighteenth-century vernacular house, Tankard Ville, in the townland of Tankardstown, now within the town of Balbriggan.[15] According to a survey carried out by the Dublin Heritage Group in 1992–3 the house was probably that shown on the Down Survey maps and described in the Civil Survey as a farmhouse.[16] In 1641 the owner was Thomas Delahide of Loughshinny. Another interesting complex which may date from the seventeenth century is the mill complex at Killossery.[17] Yet another possible candidate for inclusion in the short list of surviving vernacular buildings is the White Hart Inn, a two-storey building with seven bays, at Stephenstown, on the old main road north of Balrothery.[18] It is impossible to say with certainty that these buildings survive from the seventeenth century since vernacular buildings are notoriously difficult to date.

It is, perhaps, worthy of note that the Bolton residence described by Sir William Brereton was a wooden structure and the surviving farmhouse at Tankardstown is a mud-walled building. The use of perishable materials for construction partly explains why so few seventeenth-century buildings survive while so many stone-built

11 *A repertory of the inrolments on the patent rolls in chancery in Ireland; commencing with the reign of King James I*, ed. John Caillard Erck (2 pts, Dublin, 1846–52), i, part i, pp 220–1 and i, part ii, pp 732–3. 12 Deposition of Margaret Huiberts, 14 March 1644 (TCD, MS 810, ff 238–9). 13 *Civil Survey, vii, county of Dublin*, p. 54. 14 'Hearth money roll for County Dublin, 1664' (second part), *Journal of the County Kildare Archaeological Society*, xi (1930–33), p. 404. 15 A note on Dúchas – the Heritage Service, County Dublin, file no. DU002–011 reads: 'At Tankardville in this townland the west end of L-shaped building incorporates a mud-walled structure. The building itself dates from 1785 so it is likely that the earlier structure is the dwelling marked on the Down Survey 1650 and described in the *Civil Survey*, 1654, p. 4, as one 'farme house' in Tankerstown. Ext. dms. 11.10m. N-S, 5m. E-W, thickness of wall 0.60m. It is steeply gabled.'. 16 Dublin Heritage Group, *Vernacular buildings of east Fingal* (Dublin, 1993), pp 19–20. 17 Dúchas – the Heritage Service, County Dublin, file no. DU011–05702. 18 Dúchas – the Heritage Service, County Dublin, file no. DU005–005.

structures of earlier centuries can still be seen in the area. Further evidence for the use of wood and other perishable materials can be found in the verse of the period, which, of course, must be treated with some caution. The description of the 'high and mighty edifice' in 'Purgatorium Hibernicum' refers to a gate with wooden hinges, bars of oak and bolts of wood, the sides of the building of mud and the house itself built of 'hay and straw confirmed with usual lime and mortar'.[19] The author no doubt used his imagination but the materials he mentioned are likely to have been familiar to his readers or listeners.

The hearth was an important feature of Fingal homes and inns since fires were essential in the cold seventeenth-century climate. Margaret Cooper described how she discussed the Dublin city defences while chatting with one of the Darcys of Platten sitting by the fire in the lower room of her husband's inn at Oxmantown.[20] Some months later a visitor to Carrickmines in south Co. Dublin found the Fingallian, 'old Mr Fagan of Feltrim' sitting by the fire.[21] 'Purgatorium Hibernicum' contained a description of an open fireplace in a mortuary building which gives some idea of what might have been found in the poorer households. It reads as follows (spelling modernized):

On either side there was a door
Extent from roof unto the floor
Which they like hedgehogs stopped with straw
Or open as the wind does blow.
Betwixt which two there was a spot
I' the middle to hang o'er the pot
Pendent in wattle free from roof
And pothooks of the self same stuff
And hath an engine in the nick
For pair of legs a broken stick
A pair of bellows on each side
I mean the door to open wide.[22]

At the other end of the social scale, Walter Segrave had four iron grates and two sets of handirons (probably andirons) as well as a pair of iron-racks in his home at Little Cabragh in 1619 while fifty years later Sir James Ware mentioned the iron grates for the chimneys of his house at Meakstown near Santry in his will.[23]

There are several references in the 1641 depositions to fuel which, as has been explained in the previous chapter, was one of the few essential commodities permanently in short supply in the area. The local people were prepared to go to great lengths to get coal. A Liverpool barque ran aground at Clontarf on 11 December 1641.[24] One of the inhabitants of the village, David Powell, accused the local fish-

19 Purgatorium Hibernicum ..., *c.*1670 (NLI, MS 470, pp 106–8). **20** Examination of Margaret Cooper, 8 November 1641 (TCD, MS 809, f. 138). **21** Examination of John Brackenbury, 27 May 1642 (TCD, MS 810, f. 198). **22** Purgatorium Hibernicum ..., *c.*1670 (NLI, MS 470, p. 47). **23** Abstract of will of Walter Segrave, 9 March 1619 (RSAI, Elrington Ball MSS, vol xii, f. 27); will of Sir James Ware, 10 August 1669 (NAI, Prerogative will book, 1664–84, f. 178). **24** Examination of David Powell,

ermen of taking away coals from it on 14 December and promptly reported the robbery. This was almost certainly the same incident as that seen by Edward Leech as he passed through Clontarf on his way to Dublin after his expulsion from Lambay Island.[25] He described it as follows:

> He also saith that at the same time as he passed by Clontarf, he saw some coals carried away by some of the inhabitants there adjoining from aboard a ship that came into the harbour with coals which they pillaged, but whither they carried the coals he knoweth not. All this was performed before the burning of Clontarf, and (as he conceiveth) was one of the causes thereof, he having upon the said fourteenth of December showed the said pass to some near friends of the Lords Justices and related the said proceedings ...

The theft of timber, fuel or firing was mentioned in some of the 1641 depositions.[26] Turf was listed once, significantly by William Tedder, vicar of Garristown.[27] This suggests that there was some turf still available in the 'turf moor or bog, commonly called the Moor of Garristown'.[28] Furze was also used as fuel.[29] Though it is not possible to be certain of this, it seems probably that furze was used to make the fire which signalled to the fishermen of Rush that Lambay was about to be invaded on 12 December 1641.[30] The presence of furze ricks in the suburbs of Dublin city was a serious cause of concern to the inhabitants of the area.[31] Writing to his brother in February 1642 Robert Bysse, junior, mentioned that, in the opinion of some people, the wood at Artaine, which could have provided a refuge for wood-kernes, must come down 'to prevent mischief and serve for fuel'.[32]

Detailed records of house furnishings in the early seventeenth century are difficult to find. Fortunately, one inventory, an abstract from the will of Walter Segrave of Little Cabragh, has been preserved in the Elrington Ball manuscripts in the library of the Royal Society of Antiquaries of Ireland.[33] This represents a listing of only those items of furniture which Walter Segrave wished to ensure would not be dispersed after his death. Bearing in mind that some thirty-five years after he made his will Little Cabragh was valued in the Civil Survey at £1,400, that is, far and away the most valuable building complex in the whole Fingal area, the furnishings cannot be regarded as in any way typical of the ordinary household but they do indicate what was considered desirable when it could be afforded.

Straw and rushes were commonly used for bedding in the seventeenth century and at much later periods.[34] Yet there is evidence for the widespread use of bedsteads in

14 December 1641 (TCD, MS 809, f. 214). **25** Deposition of Edward Leech, 18 March 1644 (TCD, MS 810, f. 245). **26** Deposition of John Smith, 19 January 1642 (TCD, MS 809, f. 222); deposition of John Husband, 11 March 1642 (TCD, MS 809, f. 281); deposition of Anthony Huiberts, 29 January 1642 (TCD, MS 809, f. 310); deposition of Thomas Waller, 29 March 1642 (TCD, MS 810, f. 187). **27** Deposition of William Tedder, 25 January 1642 (TCD, MS 809, f. 332). **28** *Civil Survey, vii, county of Dublin*, p. 16. **29** Deposition of Darby Lea, 25 January 1642 (TCD, MS 809, f. 288); deposition of William Fleming, 7 November 1643 (TCD, MS 810, f. 233). **30** Deposition of Edward Leech, 18 March 1644 (TCD, MS 810, f. 244). **31** Examination of Margaret Cooper, 8 November 1641 (TCD, MS 809, f. 138); examination of Anthony Pile, 29 June 1643 (TCD, MS 810, f. 282). **32** Robert Bysse, junior, to John Bysse, 16 February 1642 (TCD, MS 840, f. 9). **33** 'Fingal 1603–60', ii, appendix F, table F.1. **34** Edward MacLysaght, *Irish life in the seventeenth century* (paperback ed., Dublin, 1979) pp 66–7

Fingal, at least among the more affluent members of society. As early as 1615 Ambrose Browne of Grangegorman left a bedstead to his sister Ellen, in 1619 Little Cabragh had at least twelve bedsteads while on 27 August 1621 Anthony Delahide of Loughshinny cited in his will a bedstead left him by the dowager lady of Howth.[35] Another dowager lady of Howth, Cecily Finglas, left a feather bed to her cousin in 1635, specifying at the same time that her other beds were to be sold.[36] Thomas Luttrell of Luttrellstown bequeathed four feather beds to his wife and bedsteads to his son, Simon, in 1633.[37] In 1641 the rebels stole bedding from the elderly Grallagh couple, James Smith and his wife.[38] Henry Partington of Killelane in the parish of Balrothery reported that Thomas Daly of the nearby townland of Darcystown had 'carried away his bedsteads' about the same time.[39] In 1665 Sir James Ware left his 'purple bed' and the furniture in his bedchamber to his daughter-in-law while in the following year Christian Purfield of the Ward bequeathed 'a feather bed' to her son, Thomas.[40] Bequests such as these probably created a demand for such items of furniture. A description of a mortuary building in which 'the floors and rooms with rushes laid 'stead of tapestry, no bed or bedstead' in 'Purgatorium Hibernicum' also suggests that, while rushes as bedding were still known and probably used in Fingal, beds and bedsteads were by no means uncommon by the middle of the seventeenth century.[41]

Items of wooden furniture, such as tables, were mentioned in the depositions and in wills.[42] Early in 1642 Robert Benyon described how he saw 'about the quantities of six car-loads of tables, chests and other wooden ware' belonging to himself, his mother and Sir Samuel Mayart (who also lived at Santry) taken away by a John Joyner.[43] The limited evidence which remains to us suggests that seating was in the form of stools rather than chairs even in great houses.[44] Locked chests and trunks were the normal means of storing valuables. Eleven chests and trunks were listed in the will of Walter Segrave as compared with eight cupboards which probably reflects the balance in mansions at the period.[45] Walter Segrave used one of the chests for 'his evidence', that is documents belonging to himself and his son and was careful to specify in his will who should hold the keys to this chest. Security in Luttrellstown may have been even tighter for, as well as storing his 'evidences' in a 'cupboard counter or press', Thomas Luttrell kept evidence concerning his son, John, together with ready money in silver and gold, intended for legacies, in an iron-plated trunk or

and 104–6. 35 Abstracts of wills of Ambrose Browne, 3 March 1615 and Anthony Delahide, 27 August 1621 (NLI, Fisher will abstracts, GO MS 290, pp 21and 133); abstract of will of Walter Segrave, 9 March 1619 (RSAI, Elrington Ball MSS, vol xii, f. 27); Francis Elrington Ball, *Southern Fingal* … (originally published 1920, reprinted Dublin, 1995), p. 92. 36 Abstract of will of Cecilia, dowager lady of Howth, 1 August 1635 (RSAI, Elrington Ball MSS, vol ix, f. 94). 37 Abstract of will of Thomas Luttrell, 20 March 1633 (RSAI, Elrington Ball MSS, vol vii, f. 17). 38 Deposition of James Smith, 26 April 1642 (TCD, MS 810, f. 104). 39 Deposition of Henry Partington, 9 June 1642 (TCD, MS 810, f. 171). 40 Wills of Sir James Ware, 10 August 1665 and Christian Purfield, 23 April 1666 (NAI, Prerogative will book, 1664–84, ff 178 and 117). 41 Purgatorium Hibernicum …, *c.*1670 (NLI, MS 470, p. 47). 42 Abstract of will of Anthony Delahide (NLI, Fisher will abstracts, GO MS 290, p. 133); will of Sir James Ware, 10 August 1665 (NAI, Prerogative will book, 1664–84, f. 178); abstract of will of Cecilia, dowager lady of Howth, 1 August 1635 (RSAI, Elrington Ball MSS, vol ix, f. 94). 43 Examination of Robert Benyon, 21 January 1642 (TCD, MS 809, f. 230). 44 'Fingal 1603–60', ii, appendix F. 45 Abstract of will of Walter Segrave, 9 March 1619 (RSAI, Elrington Ball MSS, vol xii, f. 27).

chest and evidence concerning his wife in a little black trunk.[46] Patrick Gough of Sutton also kept his money in a chest.[47] When the rebels arrived at the home of Margaret Huiberts Verveer and her husband in Holmpatrick in 1641 Captain Cusack called for the keys of the house and the trunks 'and broke open several trunks and took what pleased them'.[48] In 1669 Thomas Bourke of the city of Dublin, who asked to be buried in Raheny, listed in his will a number of items to be found in his 'brown chest'.[49] Furniture mentioned in the verse of the period included stools, tables, kishes and creels.[50]

Metal goods were also used. Brass and pewter were among the items taken from the homes of Darby Lea of Balrothery and Anthony Huiberts of Ballimad during the 1641 rising while the same items, as well as gold, silver and rings, were listed in Anthony Huiberts's account of the attack on the home of his late father at Holmpatrick.[51] Pots and pans, in particular, brewing pans and brass pans, were often left as legacies.[52] 'A copper to brew, with all the necessary vessels' appeared in the Segrave inventory.[53] Items of silver mentioned included bowls, cups, a tankard inscribed with a coat of arms, an *aqua vitae* cup, salts (salt-cellars), spoons, a knife, a fruit dish and basins and ewers.[54] Michael Caddell left his eldest son a candlestick in 1635.[55] Books, pictures and musical instruments were mentioned in a few cases.[56]

Household linen and woollen goods were occasionally referred to in the depositions and bequests of these goods were frequently made. Among the items specified were carpets, curtains, tapestry, hangings, rugs, including caddows (rough woollen mantles or coverings), bolsters, coverlets, a counterpane, sheets, pillow-covers, blankets, table cloths, napkins and, in one instance, a towel.[57]

46 Abstract of will of Thomas Luttrell, 20 March 1633 (RSAI, Elrington Ball MSS, vol vii, f. 17); Francis Elrington Ball, *A history of the County Dublin ... part fourth* (originally published 1906, reprinted Dublin, 1995), pp 10–11. 47 Abstract of will of Patrick Gough, 24 July 1624 (RSAI, Elrington Ball MSS, vol x, f. 29); Francis Elrington Ball, *Howth and its owners ...* (originally published 1917, reprinted Dublin, 1995), p. 116. 48 Deposition of Margaret Huiberts, 14 March 1644 (TCD, MS 810, f. 238). 49 Will of Thomas Bourke, 6 April 1669 (NAI, Prerogative will book, 1664–84, f. 166). 50 Purgatorium Hibernicum ..., *c.*1670 (NLI, MS 470, pp 4, 9 and 48). 51 Deposition of Darby Lea, 25 January 1642 (TCD, MS 809, f. 288); depositions of Anthony Huiberts, 29 January 1642 (TCD, MS 809, ff 310 and 311). 52 Will of Christian Purfield, 23 April 1666 (NAI, Prerogative will book, 1664–84, f. 117); abstracts of wills of Edward Adale (or O'Dale), 16 May 1623, William Corbally, 19 September 1636 and Anthony Delahide (NLI, Fisher will abstracts, GO MS 290, pp 4, 91 and 133); abstract of will of Thomas Luttrell, 20 March 1633 (RSAI, Elrington Ball MSS, vol vii, f. 17); Francis Elrington Ball, *A history of the County Dublin ... part fourth* (originally published 1906, reprinted Dublin, 1995), p. 10; abstract of will of Bartholomew Talbot, 13 November 1616 (RSAI, Elrington Ball MSS, vol xi, f. 73. 53 Abstract of will of Walter Segrave, 9 March 1619 (RSAI, Elrington Ball MSS, vol xii, f. 27). 54 Wills of Christian Purfield, 23 April 1666, Thomas Bourke, 6 April 1669 and Sir James Ware, 10 August 1665 (NAI, Prerogative will book, 1664–84, ff 117, 166 and 178); abstract of will of Thomas Luttrell, 20 March 1633 (RSAI, Elrington Ball MSS, vol vii, f. 17); Francis Elrington Ball, *A history of the County Dublin ... part fourth* (originally published 1906, reprinted Dublin, 1995), p. 10; will of Richard Nettervill, 11 April 1607 (NAI, Deeds and wills extracted from inquisitions, exchequer series, vol 1, Carlow and County Dublin, RC 10/1, p. 354). 55 Abstract of will of Michael Caddell, 15 May 1635 (NLI, Fisher will abstracts, GO MS 290, p. 73). 56 Wills of Thomas Bourke, 6 April 1669 and Sir James Ware, 10 August 1665 (NAI, Prerogative will book, 1664–84, ff 166, 178); abstracts of wills of Richard Berford, proved 21 November 1662, and Bennett Arthur, dated 18 July 1673 (RSAI, Elrington Ball MSS, vol xi, ff 41 and 43); abstract of will of Walter Segrave, 9 March 1619 (RSAI, Elrington Ball MSS, vol xii, f. 26); Francis Elrington Ball, *Southern Fingal ...* (originally published 1920, reprinted Dublin, 1995), pp 25, 27 and 92. 57 Deposition of Darby Lea, 25 January 1642 (TCD, MS 809, f. 288); deposition of Anthony Huiberts, 29 January 1642 (TCD, MS 809, f. 310); deposition of Edward Leech,

No detailed description of the Fingallian diet has been found. However it has been possible to reconstruct the diet of those who were reasonably prosperous by occasional references to meals and by looking at what was readily available on the farm. For many Fingallians their nearest market was in Dublin city. This meant that a wide variety of foodstuffs was available to them. The main meals were dinner, in the middle of the day, and supper, which was an evening meal. Margaret Huiberts (Verveer) described how the rebels came to her home at Holmpatrick in December 1641 at dinner time and stayed till evening.[58] A supper, attended by Nicholas Darcy of Platten, which subsequently attracted the attention of the authorities, took place at Cooper's tavern at Oxmantown, on the boundaries of Fingal, on the 7 November 1641.[59] It began sometime after six o'clock and finished before ten o'clock in the evening. Some references to the food consumed at meals are to be found in a manuscript poems 'The Fingallian hunting of the hare' and 'Purgatorium Hibernicum'. Further information about the availability of food comes from the 1641 depositions and has been generally derived from the lists of items taken from individual deponents. Meat and fowl appear to have been plentiful. In 1607 Richard Nettervill asked in his will that beef, mutton and pork, as well as bread and drink, be provided on the occasions of his month's mind and year's mind.[60] In 'The Fingallian hunting of the hare' the three gentlemen who went hunting were given 'hot waters, good meat and strong ale' at Howth before they set out on their expedition and, at the end of the day, consumed a meal of salt pork and yellow bacon, 'which they then just cut down from the smoke', together with good bread and liquor at Baldoyle.[61] 'Purgatorium Hibernicum' contained references to beef, bacon, pork, ham, mutton, black pudding, puttoges, hens, ducks and geese.[62] Cattle, veals (calves), sheep, hogs, sows and poultry were mentioned in the 1641 depositions.[63]

There were some references to seafood in the depositions. Thomas Benet of Johnstown and Irishtown (near Lusk) lost some barrels of herrings during the rising of 1641.[64] Edward Leech referred to the lands of Clontarf as 'the usual place of salting herrings'.[65] Another deposition recorded the adventures of a Sligo man, Bryan O'Hara, who travelled through Fingal from Navan to Dublin 'with purpose to get his living by catching and making up of herrings and that upon Thursday was fortnight he went to the place where herrings were taken and there made up two barrels of herrings and got a pennyworth of tobacco for his labour and came back to his lodging on Friday at night and on Saturday morning was apprehended'.[66] While it is

18 March 1644 (TCD, MS 810, f. 244); wills of Christian Purfield, 23 April 1666, Thomas Bourke, 6 April 1669 (NAI, Prerogative will book, 1664–84, ff 117, 166); abstract of will of Alice Segrave, 13 October 1660 (RSAI, Elrington Ball MSS, vol xii, f. 40). **58** Deposition of Margaret Huiberts, 14 March 1644 (TCD, MS 810, f. 238). **59** Examination of Margaret Cooper, 8 November 1641 (TCD, MS 809, f. 138); examination of Nicholas Darcy, 8 November 1641 (TCD, MS 809, f. 140). **60** Will of Richard Nettervill, 11 April 1607 (NAI, Deeds and wills extracted from inquisitions, Exchequer series, vol 1, Carlow and County Dublin, RC 10/1, p. 354). **61** The Fingallian hunting of the hare (BL, Sloane MS 900, ff 54–5). **62** Purgatorium Hibernicum …, *c.*1670 (NLI, MS 470, pp 4, 26, 42, 54–6, 84 and 118). **63** For example, deposition of Mary Bucklie, 17 February 1642 (TCD, MS 809, f. 234); deposition of Nicholas Barry, 5 March 1642 (TCD, MS 809, f. 241); deposition of Henry Mawdesley, 22 April 1642 (TCD, MS 810, f. 167); deposition of Henry Partington, 9 June 1642 (TCD, MS 810, f. 171). **64** Deposition of Thomas Benet, 26 February 1642 (TCD, MS 809, f. 243). **65** Deposition of Edward Leech, 18 March 1644 (TCD, MS 810, f. 244). **66** Examination of Bryan O'Hara, 6 November 1641 (TCD, MS 809, f. 122).

not possible to be certain that Bryan O'Hara worked north of the Liffey his experiences were probably similar to those of many who did. Scaddan ore (*scaddán ór*), presumably a form of herring, was mentioned in the verse.[67] Another type of fish available locally was ling. In 1638 the tenant, then Thomas Fitzsimons, of the Grange of Baldoyle, which was Dublin corporation property, was obliged to pay 'one dozen of good large ling at Christmas to the mayor'.[68] Fish were also available from the inland salmon weirs at Chapelizod and Luttrellstown and probably also from some of the smaller rivers.[69] The deposition of Edward Leech suggests that cockle-gathering was an important industry on the coast between Howth and Dublin.[70]

The vegetable crops recorded in the depositions were peas and beans.[71] The same foodstuffs were mentioned in 'Purgatorium Hibernicum' as well as nuts, leek and onions 'preserved on hurdles and in kesh to serve our friends instead of flesh'.[72] The poem also contained a reference to 'nettles tall, beans and cabash' (probably from the Irish *cabáiste* meaning cabbage).[73] The wild fruits, 'froghans' (probably *fraocháin* or bilberries) and 'bogberries' were also mentioned.[74] No doubt these were used to supplement the fruit and vegetables grown in the many orchards and gardens mentioned in the Civil Survey. Allowing for the fact that the 1641 depositions were generally, though not exclusively, made by the more prosperous members of society it is, nevertheless, rather surprising that no specific claims for the loss of potatoes have been found, particularly as potatoes were mentioned several times in the burlesque, 'Purgatorium Hibernicum'.[75] References to 'potato plots five acres long', to a valley 'planted with galleries of pleasure and orchards rich with Irish treasure' (with a marginal note explaining that this meant potatoes) and to the fact that potatoes served instead of 'peas and bacon, beef and bread' appear to confirm a change of diet towards potatoes in the middle of the seventeenth century.[76]

Cereals were usually returned in the depositions under 'corn' or 'grain' but there were also reports specifying wheat, oats, barley and bear.[77] Needless to say bread was a major item in the diet in this rich grain-growing area. The large number of windmills and water-mills in the area has been noted in the previous chapter. Evidence that the quern was still used is contained in 'Purgatorium Hibernicum'.[78] It appears that those living just outside Dublin tried to sell not just corn but also bread within the city limits. In October 1622 Dublin corporation imposed a ban on unfree bakers living within a mile of the franchises of the city selling bread within the city.[79] Strict controls were placed on the sale of bread in the city by these so-called 'foreign' bakers.[80]

67 Purgatorium Hibernicum . . ., *c.*1670 (NLI, MS 470, p. 118). 68 *Anc. rec. Dublin*, iii, p. 350. 69 *Civil Survey, vii, county of Dublin*, pp 223 and 231. 70 Deposition of Edward Leech, 18 March 1644 (TCD, MS 810, f. 245). 71 Deposition of Nicholas Barry, 5 March 1642 (TCD, MS 809, f. 241); deposition of John Husband, 11 March 1642 (TCD, MS 809, f. 281). 72 Purgatorium Hibernicum . . ., *c.*1670 (NLI, MS 470, p. 56). 73 Purgatorium Hibernicum . . ., *c.*1670 (NLI, MS 470, p. 4). 74 Purgatorium Hibernicum . . ., *c.*1670 (NLI, MS 470, p. 55). 75 Purgatorium Hibernicum . . ., *c.*1670 (NLI, MS 470, pp 4, 8, 9, 46, 102 and 150). 76 Purgatorium Hibernicum . . ., *c.*1670 (NLI, MS 470, pp 4, 9 and 150); Austin Bourke, *'The visitation of God?': the potato and the great Irish famine*, ed. Jacqueline Hill and Cormac Ó Gráda (Dublin, 1993), p. 12. 77 Deposition of Henry Baker, 19 February 1642 (TCD, MS 809, f. 240); deposition of Nicholas Barry, 5 March 1642 (TCD, MS 809, f. 241), deposition of Ann Foreside, 5 January 1642 (TCD, MS 809, f. 279); deposition of John Husband, 11 March 1642 (TCD, MS 809, f. 281); deposition of Darby Lea, 25 January 1642 (TCD, MS 809, f. 288). 78 Purgatorium Hibernicum . . ., *c.*1670 (NLI, MS 470, p. 57). 79 *Anc. rec. Dublin*, iii, pp 150–1. 80 *Anc. rec. Dublin*, iii, p. 177.

Alan Bliss provided an interesting commentary on the social, as well as the linguistic, information obtainable from seventeenth and early eighteenth-century Irish texts in English.[81] He noted the frequency with which dairy products, particularly a form of souring milk known as *bainne clabair*, were mentioned in the English-language texts of the period.[82] As well as mentioning bannyclap (*bainne clabair*) 'Purgatorium Hibernicum' contains references to banyrower (*bainne reamhair*), boiled milk, buttermilk, clotted cream and butter.[83] An interesting reference to butter that was 'years buried in the bog' raises questions as to whether dairy produce had to be brought in from outside the area or whether the practice of burying butter was still known in the few remaining bogs in Fingal in the seventeenth century.[84] The importance of dairy produce is confirmed by the many reports of the taking of cows in the depositions.[85] In several of these cases the number of cows in the herd appears to have been quite small. Perhaps farmers kept just enough cows to supply the household's needs. Another possibility is that the rebels did not carry off the whole stock but left some with their owners.

Exotic imported foodstuffs were also known in the area. William Hollis, a soldier captured near Swords and taken as a prisoner to Co. Kildare, described how an Englishman, whose wife was 'one of the rebellious Walshs' brought a number of goods, including fruit, spice and cheese from Dublin to his captors.[86] Spice and sugar were also mentioned in 'Purgatorium Hibernicum'.[87] Fingallians enjoyed special treats at festive times.[88] Eggs and preserved Fingal beef were eaten at Easter and pies were consumed at Christmas.

As well as milk, in its various forms, the people of Fingal drank beer, wine and *aqua vitae*.[89] Brandy was also popular.[90] References in the depositions to the carrying off of malt may indicate the presence of inns or small ale-houses owned by Protestants at Lusk, Johnstown, Coolock, Killelane and Stormanstown.[91] The subject of social drinking, which was clearly important in the area, will be considered in part II, chapter 6.

While there was undoubtedly hardship at certain times during the wars, no reference to actual starvation in Fingal during the period 1603–60 has been found. Elizabeth Parr, whose husband had been killed on the way to Swords while fighting against the rebels 'in the beginning of the present rebellion', claimed that she and her three children 'were like to perish for want of means', while a labourer, Thomas

81 Alan Bliss, *Spoken English in Ireland 1600–1740* (Dublin, 1979), pp 265–76. 82 Alan Bliss, *Spoken English in Ireland 1600–1740* (Dublin, 1979), pp 271–2. 83 Purgatorium Hibernicum ..., *c.*1670 (NLI, MS 470, pp 55–7, 118 and 144). 84 Purgatorium Hibernicum ..., *c.*1670 (NLI, MS 470, p. 118). 85 For example, deposition of John Smith, 19 January 1642 (TCD, MS 809, f. 222); deposition of Mary Bucklie, 17 February 1642 (TCD, MS 809, f. 234); deposition of Huibart Cromphouts, 2 March 1642 (TCD, MS 809, f. 268). 86 Deposition of William Hollis, 27 April 1643 (TCD, MS 810, f. 236). 87 Purgatorium Hibernicum ..., *c.*1670 (NLI, MS 470, p. 56). 88 Purgatorium Hibernicum ..., *c.*1670 (NLI, MS 470, p. 26). 89 Examination of William Stowell, 8 November 1641 (TCD, MS 809, f. 145); examination of Richard Delahide, 19 November 1641 (TCD, MS 809, f. 198); deposition of Darby Lea, 25 January 1642 (TCD, MS 809, f. 288). 90 Purgatorium Hibernicum ..., *c.*1670 (NLI, MS 470, pp 58,103 and 109). 91 Deposition of Mary Bucklie, 17 February 1642 (TCD, MS 809, f. 234); deposition of Thomas Benet, 26 February 1642 (TCD, MS 809, f. 243); deposition of Ann Foreside, 5 January 1642 (TCD, MS 809, f. 279); deposition of Henry Partington, 9 June 1642 (TCD, MS 810, f. 171); deposition of William Fleming, 7 November 1643 (TCD, MS 810, f. 233).

Williams of Santry, although claiming that he had been robbed of certain goods and his house destroyed by the rebels at the beginning of December 1641, reserved his main criticisms for the authorities saying that he 'hath for two years been a soldier against the rebels under Captain Smith, but, having been since sick and weak, got none of his pay or entertainment for near half a year last past: and now with his wife and children is like to starve as they had done if the charity of good people had not relieved them'.[92] Those held in custody in Fingal also had problems but, while there were some threats of starvation, no evidence has been found to suggest that these were carried out.[93]

Tobacco and snuff were popular. As already mentioned, the Sligo man, Bryan O'Hara, who travelled to Dublin to earn his living 'by catching and the making up of herrings', was paid a pennyworth of tobacco for making up two barrels.[94] 'Sneezing' (snuff) was mentioned in two depositions, though in neither case was a Fingallian directly involved.[95] However the popularity of both snuff and tobacco is attested by several references in 'Purgatorium Hibernicum'.[96]

Dress in Ireland by Mairead Dunlevy is the standard work on the history of clothes in Ireland.[97] In this study I attempt to discover if it is possible to throw any additional light on attitudes to dress and the type of clothing worn in Fingal during the period 1603–60 using contemporary documents. The 1641 depositions provided little information. Many deponents reported the theft of apparel, without giving any further details. Others described how they or their friends were stripped naked during attacks. Andrew Mainwaring, a former ensign, described how he had been stripped of his clothes and property and left for dead at Smithstown, Co. Meath, after the battle of Julianstown on the 29 November 1641.[98] A few days later Margaret Huiberts and her sister-in-law were stripped naked on a particularly cold and frosty night at Hacketstown, near Skerries.[99] James Smith of the Grallagh and his wife, who were both very old, were stripped of their clothes about the same time.[100] The deaths of both Margaret Huiberts's sister-in-law and James Smith's wife were attributed in part to these events. In November 1642 Robert Arundell and several companions were ambushed near Castleknock and stripped.[101] The soldier, William Hollis, also reported that he had been stripped of his clothes, money and weapons after an ambush near Swords in March 1643.[102] Following the killing of six people, including Captain Charles Blundell, by a band of tories at the Forrest near Swords in July 1650, five of the corpses were stripped. One of the witnesses, Patrick Maguire of the Ward, recounted how he met one of the tories, Robert Boylan, 'who rid upon

92 Deposition of Elizabeth Parr, 7 January 1644 (TCD, MS 810, f. 237); deposition of Thomas Williams, 10 January 1644 (TCD, MS 810, f. 269). 93 Deposition of Daniel Barwick, 23 May 1642 (TCD, MS 810, f. 114). 94 Examination of Bryan O'Hara, 6 November 1641 (TCD, MS 809, f. 122). 95 Examination of Edmund O Murrohye, 8 November 1641 (TCD, MS 809, f. 146); deposition of William Hollis, 27 April 1643 (TCD, MS 810, f. 236). 96 Purgatorium Hibernicum ..., *c.*1670 (NLI, MS 470, pp 4, 58, 59, 97 and 172). 97 Mairead Dunlevy, *Dress in Ireland* (2nd ed., Cork, 1999). 98 Deposition of Andrew Mainwaring, 15 February 1642 (TCD, MS 809, f. 297). 99 Deposition of Huibart Cromphouts, 2 March 1642 (TCD, MS 809, f. 268); deposition of Anthony Huiberts, 29 January 1642 (TCD, MS 809, f. 311); deposition of Margaret Huiberts, 14 March 1644 (TCD, MS 810, f. 239). 100 Deposition of James Smith, 26 April 1642 (TCD, MS 810, f. 104). 101 Examination of Robert Arundell, 22 November 1642 (TCD, MS 810, f. 203). 102 Deposition of William Hollis, 27 April 1643 (TCD, MS 810, f. 235).

a roan horse, which was the horse of William Donnellan's that was killed, and the said Boylan asked this deponent whether Justice Donnellan [William Donnellan's uncle] had no better horse than this, and when he met the said Boylan he was beating the horse about the head with a pair of boots he had in his hand, which were the boots of them that was killed in the ambush ...'.[103] Another who described this event, Thomas Waltryn of the Forrest, reported that 'the several persons so killed were all stripped by the said tories (except Richard Cooke) who had but ordinary clothes on him'.[104] Such evidence as can be found in the local depositions seems to suggest that stripping, whether of the living or the dead, was carried out for gain and perhaps by a desire to obtain new or fashionable clothes rather than in order to cause humiliation. Soldiers, who often had new clothes, were frequently stripped. One witness, John Heard, claimed that he had recognized 'Captain Blundell's clothes' being worn by one of the tories.[105] The stripping of the two wealthy women near Skerries is likely to have been prompted by the quality of their garments as well as by the fact that they were found to be carrying large sums of money. The partial stripping of Edward St Lawrence, prior to his murder by a group of tories 'near the bridge of Turvey commonly called the Nine streams' in 1651 was described by Arland Ussher of Termonfeckin, Co. Louth, and his servant, Richard Randall.[106] Both recounted how the tories stripped St Lawrence to his shirt and drawers before killing him with his own sword. One of the tories Thomas O Rannahie, otherwise known as Thomas Ne-Muck (or O Muck), while admitting his part in the attack, made no mention of the stripping in his own deposition.[107]

In order to get some idea of the type of clothing favoured in Fingal it may be useful to examine first the articles of clothing worn by both sexes. Mairead Dunlevy described the importance of the mantle in medieval and early modern Ireland, pointing out that woollen weather-proof mantles were worn by everyone in Ireland, 'Irish, English-Irish and English; adult and child; male and female, rich and poor ...'[108] One incident, which suggests that very long cloaks were still being worn in Fingal in the mid-seventeenth century, was described by John Lukey, minister of Ballyboghil.[109] During the rising a man called Horish of Ballyboghil set some mastiff dogs on him and chased him from the church 'which dogs fastened their feet on this deponent's cloak'. Lukey had to rescue himself by using a knife and a small cudgel. William Hollis, the soldier captured near Swords and brought as a prisoner to Co. Kildare, described how, on his return to Dublin, he saw a Captain Fottrell wearing the cloak which had been taken from him (Hollis) in the initial attack.[110] Cloaks were occasionally mentioned in bequests.[111] Thomas White, a fisherman of

103 Examination of Patrick Maguire, not dated (TCD, MS 810, f. 379). **104** Examination of Thomas Waltryn, 1 February 1653 (TCD, MS 810, f. 375). **105** Examination of John Heard, 24 November 1652 (TCD, MS 810, f. 380). **106** Examination of Arland Ussher, not dated (TCD, MS 810, f. 355); examination of Richard Randall, not dated (TCD, MS 810, f. 399). **107** Examination of Thomas O Rannahie, 23 April 1653 (TCD, MS 810, f. 397). **108** Mairead Dunlevy, *Dress in Ireland* (2nd ed., Cork, 1999), pp 39–42 and 78–81. **109** Deposition of John Lukey, 2 March 1643 (TCD, MS 810, f. 168). **110** Deposition of William Hollis, 27 April 1643 (TCD, MS 810, f. 236). **111** Abstract of will of Leonard St Lawrence, 6 November 1608 (RSAI, Elrington Ball MSS, vol ix, f. 94); abstract of will of Henry Burnell, 17 July 1614 (RSAI, Elrington Ball MSS, vol xi, f. 34); Francis Elrington Ball, *Southern Fingal*... (originally published 1920, reprinted Dublin, 1995), p. 21; will of Thomas Bourke, 6 April 1669 (NAI, Prerogative will book, 1664–84, f. 166). **112** Abstract of will of Thomas White, 12 August 1629

Howth, left his daughter Alson his best mantle in 1629.[112] In 'Purgatorium Hibernicum', Nees (*Aeneas*) was described as wearing 'blue bracan' (*breacán* or woollen cloth which was speckled, striped, plaid or checkered) about his shoulders.[113] McChary (*Charon* – the ferryman), the Irish kerne, also wore a blue mantle, in his case fringed, and Shela (*Sibylla*) described in a marginal note as 'an Irish woman' also wore a cloak.[114]

Footwear was worn in Fingal by both sexes. Boots, stolen from the corpses of those killed in the tories' ambush at the Forrest in 1650 were mentioned in the deposition of Patrick Maguire.[115] Brogues were referred to several times in 'Purgatorium Hibernicum'.[116] According to Mairead Dunlevy stockings were worn, even by the poor, in the seventeenth century. A reference in the verse to a pair of stockings 'made of straw' worn by the ferryman McChary, described in a marginal note as 'an Irish kerne', may represent a poetic flight of fancy but a mention of 'suggaun (*súgán*) garters' worn by a woman suggests a poorer version of the garters made of strips of felt in the Tawnamore (Co. Sligo) find described by Dunlevy.[117]

As far as men's attire is concerned there is some pictorial evidence of the dress worn by Fingal men in the early modern period. Unfortunately from the point of view of this study a contemporary (1637) memorial of James Bermingham of Ballough and his wife, Ellinor, daughter of Nicholas Fitzwilliam of Holmpatrick and Baldongan, shows only an image of James, clad in armour of a period almost two centuries earlier than the reign of Charles I.[118] The following caption given to an illustration in *Dress in Ireland* is perhaps more relevant:

> Dancing figures on a whalebone book cover from Donabate, Co. Dublin, late sixteenth century. The figures wear sleeveless jerkins with long skirts over doublets with padded sleeves and chest, decorative detail visible at neck, trunk-hose with canions and codpieces, and halo-brim hats.[119]

As the author made clear, the illustration showed that the soldier-dancers wore introduced styles which had been fashionable in England at an earlier date. In the early seventeenth century a mixture of English and Irish dress appears to have been worn in Fingal. What is rather surprising is that the medieval gown, worn by men, persisted in the district until at least 1621, when Nicholas Begg of Borranstown bequeathed a gown to his brother.[120] The other references to men's gowns found in wills predated 1621. Leonard St Lawrence left a gown to his wife in 1608.[121] Henry Burnell of Castleknock left a broadcloth gown to a woman, Margaret Feakins, who

(RSAI, Elrington Ball MSS, vol x, f. 2). **113** Purgatorium Hibernicum . . ., *c.*1670 (NLI, MS 470, p. 6); Mairead Dunlevy, *Dress in Ireland* (2nd ed., Cork, 1999), p. 187. **114** Purgatorium Hibernicum . . ., *c.*1670 (NLI, MS 470, pp 70 and 83). **115** Examination of Patrick Maguire, not dated (TCD, MS 810, f. 379). **116** Purgatorium Hibernicum . . ., *c.*1670 (NLI, MS 470, pp 34, 54, 70, 83, 95, 137, 138 and 141). **117** Purgatorium Hibernicum . . ., *c.*1670 (NLI, MS 470, p. 70; Mairead Dunlevy, *Dress in Ireland* (2nd ed., Cork, 1999), pp 81–2. **118** Edward Fitzgerald, 'Lusk' in *Journal for the preservation of memorials of the dead in Ireland*, viii, no. 1 (1910), p. 52; Mary McMahon, *Medieval church sites of north Dublin: a heritage trail* (Dublin, 1991), p. 10. **119** Mairead Dunlevy, *Dress in Ireland* (2nd ed., Cork, 1999), p. 63. **120** Abstract of will of Nicholas Begg, proved 24 September 1621 (NLI, Fisher will abstracts, GO MS 290, p. 23). **121** Abstract of will of Leonard St Lawrence, 6 November 1608 (RSAI, Elrington Ball MSS, vol ix, f. 94). **122** Abstract of will of Henry Burnell, 17 July 1614 (RSAI, Elrington Ball MSS,

may have been a relative or servant.[122] It is not clear whether these gifts were intended to be worn as they were or remodelled to suit the new female owners. A short time later in 1619 Walter Segrave, as well as leaving mourning gowns to the poor of St John's Hospital, left 'his three best gowns' and wrought velvet coat to be sold to provide money for 'pious uses'.[123] Perhaps Walter's choice of his gowns, from among his many possessions, as the items which were intended for sale, was an indication that this item of male attire was at last going out of fashion, except as legal or mourning dress. There are several references to the wearing of trouses (trews) and breeches in the 'Purgatorium Hibernicum'.[124] Nees was described as wearing 'trouses of blue frieze'.[125] The ferryman (or Irish kerne), McChary, was 'like Satan dressed in yellow stuff and trouses made of blanket proof' and on his head he wore 'a red barrade'.[126] Men's hats were occasionally mentioned in the depositions. William Hollis described how the Englishman, George Laibourne, brought a hat and feather from Dublin to a Friar Walsh in Co. Kildare.[127] In his account of the incident near Turvey in 1651 Arland Ussher told how one of the tory attackers, Thomas O Rannahie, removed St Lawrence's new castor (beaver) hat and 'clapped on him an old coloured hat in lieu thereof'.[128]

There was, of course, a great difference in the number and variety of garments owned by men at different social levels. Despite the paucity of documentary evidence some idea of the gulf between life-styles can be gauged from just two wills. In 1650 Joseph Woolley of Grangegorman, who described himself as a yeoman, bequeathed his shirt and coat and a pair of new boots to his brother-in-law.[129] The will of Thomas Bourke, on the other hand, made shortly after the end of the period covered by this study, gives a good idea of the range of clothing which a gentleman possessed.[130] His wardrobe included a velvet cap and riding staff, several cloaks, including one of broadcloth, a broadcloth suit, a 'clerk suit', several shirts and half-shirts, a pair of pearl coloured silk stockings, a camlet coat, a cassock and breeches of a whitish-coloured broadcloth and a hat.

Men, in particular, frequently travelled abroad to study, on business or to serve in foreign armies. In the course of these journeys they managed to buy clothes and this was one of the ways in which new fashions were introduced into Ireland. One such traveller was the young William Dongan, who later became recorder of Dublin, and who inherited some property in Ballyboghil as well as a considerable amount of land in counties Kildare and Laois (then Queen's County).[131] In April 1609 while a student at Lincoln's Inn Dongan was detained at Chester on suspicion of attempting to bring 'papistical' books, other books, manuscripts, letters and superstitious relics

vol xi, f. 34); Francis Elrington Ball, *Southern Fingal* ... (originally published 1920, reprinted Dublin, 1995), p. 21. **123** Abstract of will of Walter Segrave, 9 March 1619 (RSAI, Elrington Ball MSS, vol xii, f. 27); Francis Elrington Ball, *Southern Fingal* ... (originally published 1920, reprinted Dublin, 1995), p. 92. **124** Purgatorium Hibernicum ..., *c.*1670 (NLI, MS 470, pp 6, 51, 69 and 171). **125** Purgatorium Hibernicum ..., *c.*1670 (NLI, MS 470, p. 6). **126** Purgatorium Hibernicum ..., *c.*1670 (NLI, MS 470, p. 69). **127** Deposition of William Hollis, 27 April 1643 (TCD, MS 810, f. 236). **128** Examination of Arland Ussher, not dated (TCD, MS 810, f. 355). **129** Will of Joseph Woolley, 10 July 1650 (NAI, Prerogative will book, 1664–84, f. 118). **130** Will of Thomas Bourke, 6 April 1669 (NAI, Prerogative will book, 1664–84, f. 166). **131** Abstract of will of William Dongan, 8 December 1622 (NLI, Fisher will abstracts, GO MS 290, p. 146). **132** Quarter sessions examinations, 1609 (Cheshire Record Office, QSE/8/11–12).

to Ireland.[132] Since both Dongan himself and another witness were required to account for the contents of his two trunks it is possible to gain some impression of the wardrobe of a reasonably prosperous young man. Among the items in the luggage were a black satin doublet, a black serge doublet, a doublet of black fustian cut upon a green sarcenet, a pair of hose of Flanders serge, a pair of hose of black cloth, a cloak of broad cloth in a sad (possibly a dark green) colour with a cape of velvet and lined with russet baize and two laces broad about it, together with boots, shoes, pantoffles, stockings and a hat. The young Dongan clearly favoured the English form of dress.

Details of women's dress are lacking in the depositions relating to Fingal. The surviving wills contain but few references to women's dress. Nevertheless these are of great interest, although they all record bequests made by society women. Elizabeth Ussher (formerly Gough and Berford) of Sutton left her silk gown and petticoat to her sister, Gernon, a curled hood and small scarf to her sister, Cecilia, and a lawn handkerchief to her sister, Bridget.[133] She left her gorget, her old cap, gown and petticoat, and her holland smock to certain named friends or servants but, most significantly, she bequeathed her red waistcoat to her maid, thus indicating one way in which fashion consciousness spread through the community. In the same year Alice Segrave (Alice Noble) mentioned her new gown and petticoat as well as silk gown and silk petticoat with gold lace in her will.[134] Perhaps the most interesting of the three wills is that of Lady Bath (Barbara Gough), who left a golden hatband, a pearl hatband and a hatband with smaller golden buttons.[135] These hatbands were probably used to brighten up the distinctive turban-like linen rolls worn by women in Fingal from the sixteenth to the eighteenth century.[136] Her bequest to provide mourning clothes for forty poor children and thirty poor women will be discussed later but it is worth noting at this point that she made provision for gowns, stockings, bands and hats for these poor mourners. There is a description of 'an Irish woman', Shela, wading through the bogs, in 'Purgatorium Hibernicum'.[137] Her apparel consisted of coats, a voluminous smock, a gown of 'richest scarlet frieze', a cloak, stockings and brogues

The soldier, William Hollis, noticed that an English man named George Laibourne or Laibrum, 'who is now in the city of Dublin ... his wife being one of the rebellious Walshs, doth ordinarily go and pass from hence to and amongst the rebels and had the rebels' pass' and that he supplied the rebels with woollen cloth.[138] The rebels had other ways of obtaining cloth. Giles Dewhurst, a Dublin clothworker, described how, when his barque, which had been driven ashore by tempest at

133 Abstract of will of Elizabeth Ussher, 1 May 1660 (RSAI, Elrington Ball MSS, vol x, f. 29); Francis Elrington Ball, *Howth and its owners ...* (originally published 1917, reprinted Dublin, 1995), p. 116. 134 Abstract of will of Alice Segrave, 13 October 1660 (RSAI, Elrington Ball MSS, vol xii, f. 40). 135 Abstract of will of Barbara Gough (Lady Bath), 23 February 1642 (RSAI, Elrington Ball MSS, vol xii, f. 188); Francis Elrington Ball, *Southern Fingal ...* (originally published 1920, reprinted Dublin, 1995), p. 164. 136 Mairead Dunlevy, *Dress in Ireland* (2nd ed., Cork, 1999), pp 62–3. 137 Purgatorium Hibernicum ..., *c.*1670 (NLI, MS 470, pp 82–3). 138 Deposition of William Hollis, 27 April 1643 (TCD, MS 810, f. 236). 139 Deposition of Giles Dewhurst, 7 February 1642 (TCD, MS 809, f. 273).

Clontarf at the beginning of December 1641 and pillaged by unknown rebels, he lost woollen cloth which had cost him £208 sterling in Yorkshire.[139]

The limited evidence which survives suggests that the Irish love of bright colours persisted in Fingal despite the change to a more sombre form of dress among certain of the upper classes in Ireland which was inspired by changes in England and the continent prior to 1660.[140] Vivid colours, such as red, blue and yellow, were mentioned in the documents. An exception was made in the case of funerals where black predominated. No early seventeenth-century description has been found which details the exact form which mourning clothes took in Fingal. However, it is possible to get some idea of this type of dress from certain of the wills and will abstracts which survive. Early in 1643 Robert Bysse, senior, of Pelletstown, a Protestant, made a will specifying that mourning should be limited to a black velvet cloth on his coffin and pennants with his arms, and mourning for his son and daughter and two of his servants.[141] In 1662 James White of the city of Dublin (formerly of the Ward), who was probably, although not certainly, a Catholic, expressed a wish that there should be no great solemnity at his funeral except that mourning suits and cloaks should be given to three of his friends and ribbons should be bestowed on his dearest and next friends.[142] Walter Segrave, an ardent Catholic, left everyone of the poor of St John's Hospital (in Dublin city) a frieze gown to be worn on the day of his funeral.[143] In 1635 Cecily, dowager lady of Howth, who died a Catholic, specified that gowns were to be given to the poor at her burial and Barbara Gough, Lady Bath, of Drumcondra, also a Catholic, in her will made in 1642, stipulated that thirty poor children and forty poor women were to have mourning gowns, stockings, bands and hats.[144] Her grandson, John Arthur, of the city of Dublin and Hacketstown, near Skerries, left 'so much of black broadcloth ... as will make him a mourning cloak and suit' to his estranged father-in-law, Dr Thomas Arthur of Limerick.[145] He also left money for mourning clothes for his wife and children.[146] Both Catholics and Protestants wore mourning but the scanty evidence that remains to us suggests that, in Fingal at least, Catholics tended to participate in a more elaborate and, perhaps, ostentatious ceremonial.

Priests and students often travelled in disguise. When Luke (later Father Edward) Bath of Drumcondra travelled through England to France to enter the Capuchin order in 1606, he wore 'rich apparel', while his companion, 'another Irish gentleman' attended on him as a serving man and 'two young lads', his half-brother, Humphrey (later Father Paul) Warren and Christopher (later Father Nicholas) Archbold, whom he was escorting to school in Douai, were disguised as pages.[147] When Fathers

140 Mairead Dunlevy, *Dress in Ireland* (2nd ed., Cork, 1999), pp 67–8. 141 Abstract of will of Robert Bysse, senior, 27 January 1643 (RSAI, Elrington Ball MSS, vol xi, f. 44). 142 Abstract of will of James White, 5 September 1662 (RSAI, Elrington Ball MSS, vol xi, f. 87). 143 Abstract of will of Walter Segrave, 9 March 1619 (RSAI, Elrington Ball MSS, vol xii, f. 27); Francis Elrington Ball, *Southern Fingal* ... (originally published 1920, reprinted Dublin, 1995), p. 92. 144 Abstract of will of Cecilia, dowager lady of Howth, 1 August 1635 (RSAI, Elrington Ball MSS, vol ix, f. 94); abstract of will of Barbara Gough (Lady Bath), 23 February 1642 (RSAI, Elrington Ball MSS, vol xii, f. 188). 145 Will of John Arthur, 4 October 1666 (NAI, Prerogative will book, 1664–84, f. 74). 146 Will of John Arthur, 4 October 1666 (NAI, Prerogative will book, 1664–84, f. 74). 147 Nicholas Archbold, The historie of the Irish Capucins, 1643 (Bibliothèque Municipale de Troyes, MS 1103, pp 93 and 133). 148 Nicholas Archbold, Brief records of the beginning, progress and institution of the Capucins in Ireland (Bibliothèque Municipale de Troyes, MS 1103, f. 7).

Nicholas Archbold and Paul Warren returned to Ireland as missionaries in 1626, Nicholas travelled as serving man to Paul.[148]

Early modern Fingallians were fond of jewellery, especially rings. A gold ring worth twenty shillings was taken from Darby Lea of Balrothery in 1641.[149] There were rings among the goods appropriated from Holmpatrick about the same time.[150] Bequests of rings or of money to buy rings occurred frequently in the wills of the period, particularly among the rich.[151] Sometimes a particular ring was specified, for example, a diamond ring, an enamelled ring, a great seal ring, a signet ring.[152] Thomas Luttrell of Luttrellstown left his son Simon the gold ring on his signet finger, whereon his coat of arms was engraved.[153] The wealthy Walter Segrave left his wife a half ring with a heart and death's head as a token of a joyful meeting in eternity.[154] He also left money to buy death's-head rings for his male relatives. Other types of jewellery were also mentioned in bequests: Robert Arthur of Hacketstown left to his wife 'her gold chains and jewels';[155] Thomas Luttrell left his son a gold chain;[156] Alice Segrave left a chain and jewels.[157] Walter Segrave's unusual bequests included the brass flower which he had worn as sheriff of Dublin.[158] Catholics in Dublin city appear to have worn rosary beads as an adornment and, as Fingal was part of the same archdiocese, the practice probably existed there also.[159] George Bursan, a Dublin glover, told how a certain butcher, Patrick Bee, advised him to tell his master, Peter Fletcher, 'that it would be a safe way for him to carry beads either in his pocket or about his arm' in view of the common danger the Protestants were in.

149 Deposition of Darby Lea, 25 January 1642 (TCD, MS 809, f. 288). **150** Deposition of Anthony Huiberts, 29 January 1642 (TCD, MS 809, f. 311). **151** Will of Thomas Bourke, 6 April 1669 (NAI, Prerogative will book, 1664–84, f. 166); abstract of will of Alexander Aylmer, July 1650 (NLI, Fisher will abstracts, GO MS 290, p. 7); abstract of will of Thomas St Lawrence, 27 March 1638 (RSAI, Elrington Ball MSS, vol x, f. 22); Francis Elrington Ball, *Howth and its owners* ... (originally published 1917, reprinted Dublin, 1995), p. 108; abstract of will of Alice Segrave, 13 October 1660 (RSAI, Elrington Ball MSS, vol xii, f. 40); Francis Elrington Ball, *Southern Fingal* ... (originally published 1920, reprinted Dublin, 1995), p. 99. **152** Will of Sir James Ware, 10 August 1665 (NAI, Prerogative will book, 1664–84, f. 178); abstract of will of Elizabeth Ussher, 1 May 1660 (RSAI, Elrington Ball MSS, vol x, f. 29); Francis Elrington Ball, *Howth and its owners* ... (originally published 1917, reprinted Dublin, 1995), p. 116; abstract of will of William St Lawrence, baron of Howth, 14 May 1671 (RSAI, Elrington Ball MSS, vol x, f. 37); Francis Elrington Ball, *Howth and its owners* ... (originally published 1917, reprinted Dublin, 1995), p. 124; abstract of will of Alice Segrave, 13 October 1660 (RSAI, Elrington Ball MSS, vol xii, f. 40); Francis Elrington Ball, *Southern Fingal* ... (originally published 1920, reprinted Dublin, 1995), p. 99. **153** Abstract of will of Thomas Luttrell, 20 March 1633 (RSAI, Elrington Ball MSS, vol vii, f. 17); Francis Elrington Ball, *A history of the County Dublin ... part fourth* (originally published 1906, reprinted Dublin, 1995), p. 10. **154** Abstract of will of Walter Segrave, 9 March 1619 (RSAI, Elrington Ball MSS, vol xii, f. 27); Francis Elrington Ball, *Southern Fingal* ... (originally published 1920, reprinted Dublin, 1995), p. 92. **155** Will of Robert Arthur, 4 June 1648 (NAI, Prerogative will book, 1664–84, f. 274). **156** Abstract of will of Thomas Luttrell, 20 March 1633 (RSAI, Elrington Ball MSS, vol vii, f. 17); Francis Elrington Ball, *A history of the County Dublin ... part fourth* (originally published 1906, reprinted Dublin, 1995), p. 10. **157** Abstract of will of Alice Segrave, 13 October 1660 (RSAI, Elrington Ball MSS, vol xii, f. 40); Francis Elrington Ball, *Southern Fingal* ... (originally published 1920, reprinted Dublin, 1995), p. 99. **158** Abstract of will of Walter Segrave, 9 March 1619 (RSAI, Elrington Ball MSS, vol xii, f. 27); Francis Elrington Ball, *Southern Fingal* ... (originally published 1920, reprinted Dublin, 1995), p. 92. **159** Examination of George Bursan, 11 December 1641 (TCD, MS 809, f. 211). **160** Abstract of will of Matthew Cusack, 4 November 1667 (NLI, Fisher will abstracts, GO MS 290, p. 105). **161** Abstracts of wills of Richard Berford, proved 21 November 1662 and Bennett Arthur, dated 18 July 1673 (RSAI, Elrington Ball MSS, vol xi, ff 41and 43); Francis Elrington Ball, *Southern Fingal* ...

Watches appeared as bequests in a few instances. Matthew Cusack of Rush left one to John Hollywood of Lusk in 1667.[160] Although he was described as a gentleman, his other individual bequests suggest that he was not a particularly rich man. Richard Berford left a watch to William Warren in 1662, while Bennett Arthur of Cabragh left his 'great clock watch' to his son in 1673.[161] Since these bequests were of rather late date, it seems likely that watches and clocks, as personal possessions, were still rather rare in Fingal in the early seventeenth century.

The carrying of weapons was a normal feature of life in seventeenth-century Fingal and, just occasionally they appeared in bequests. Joseph Woolley, a Grangegorman yeoman, left his sword to his brother-in-law in 1650.[162] The wealthy Thomas Bourke bequeathed his 'black hilt sword and belt' to his nephew.[163] The rounding-up of suspects at the outbreak of the 1641 rising disclosed that many ordinary people, especially travellers going through Fingal on the way to Dublin, had weapons, often skenes (from *scian*) or knives, in their possession. Shane O'Mahon, a Tyrone drover, when apprehended, claimed that he had 'no weapons' but a little skene about him.[164] A more serious case was that of Richard Birt, possibly a conspirator, who was found drawing his sword in a tavern in Oxmantown.[165] Some weapons were officially sanctioned. The sentinels at the city gates were, not surprisingly perhaps, armed with muskets.[166] In January 1642 Thomas Sevier of Ballymadun reported that, while returning home from market he and his companions were attacked at Stormanstown by a group, 'all of them armed with half-pikes and one of them had a skene'.[167] These may have been rebels or they may simply have been highwaymen, but there is no doubt that those who assaulted and hanged Henry Mawdesley, clerk of the peace for the counties of Dublin and Louth, at the church of Clonmethan in September 1642 were rebels, 'being horsemen and armed with pistols and swords'.[168] Thomas Clitheroe, vicar of Balrothery, was wounded by one of his neighbours, Michael Murphy, with 'a dart, which he borrowed of ... Walter St Lawrence of Dubber'.[169] John Lukey, minister of Ballyboghil, managed to rescue himself from pursuing dogs with the aid of 'a knife and a small cudgel'.[170] Since the date of this incident is not recorded it is impossible to say if the clergyman normally protected himself with these weapons or if he was taking extra precautions because of the dangerous state of the country. During the Commonwealth period, tories and their pursuers were recorded as using a variety of weapons such as swords, fowling

(originally published 1920, reprinted Dublin, 1995), pp 25 and 27. **162** Will of Joseph Woolley, 10 July 1650 (NAI, Prerogative will book, 1664–84, f. 118). **163** Will of Thomas Bourke, 6 April 1669 (NAI, Prerogative will book, 1664–84, f. 166). **164** Examination of Shane O'Mahon, 6 November 1641 (TCD, MS 809, f. 118). **165** Examination of Henry Smith and Robert Caulfield, 8 November 1641 (TCD, MS 809, f. 134); examination of Nicholas Darcy, 8 November 1641 (TCD, MS 809, f. 140); examination of William Stowell, 8 November 1641 (TCD, MS 809, f. 145). **166** Examination of Henry Smith and Robert Caulfield, 8 November 1641 (TCD, MS 809, f. 134); examination of Laughlin Flood, 8 November 1641 (TCD, MS 809, f. 136). **167** Examination of Thomas Sevier, 29 January 1642 (TCD, MS 809, f. 232). **168** Deposition of George Cashell (copy only), 29 February 1644 (TCD, MS 810, f. 25). **169** Deposition of Thomas Clitheroe, 26 May 1642 (TCD, MS 810, f. 126). **170** Deposition of John Lukey, 2 March 1643 (TCD, MS 810, f. 168). **171** Examination of Richard Greg, 16 December 1652 (TCD, MS 810, f. 388); examination of Richard Raymond, 20 December 1652 (TCD, MS 810, f. 390); examination of John Talbot, 11 November 1652 (TCD, MS 810, f. 391); examination of Patrick Tankard, 27 May 1653 (TCD, MS 810, f. 395); examination of Richard Randall, not dated (TCD, MS 810, f. 399). **172** Purgatorium Hibernicum ..., *c.*1670 (NLI, MS 470, p. 80).

pieces and pistols.[171] There are few references to weapons in 'Purgatorium Hibernicum' since the anti-hero, Nees, 'never yet drew sword in anger'.[172] But even he buckled on his skene at one point in the narrative – suggesting that the carrying of weapons by men was the norm in early modern Fingal.[173]

The principal occupations of Fingallians were associated with agriculture. As already mentioned, a wide variety of farm animals was kept. Horses figured again and again in the depositions, with the type of horse seized, for example, nag, gelding, mare, colt, garron or ploughgarron often specified.[174] It is not possible to estimate the total number or value of the horses stolen, since only the total number and/or value of all types of animals appropriated is specified in most cases. However, a few examples will give some idea of the variation as between farmers. A single gelding, worth £5, together with other goods, was taken from James Smith of the Grallagh, five horses or ploughgarrons worth £10 sterling were seized from John Huxley of Rush, and three garrons worth £8 were removed from Thomas Lloyd, minister of Swords, by the rebels.[175] Thomas Benet of Johnstown, on the other hand, lost an unspecified number of horses worth 'three score pounds or thereabouts' and Huibart Cromphouts of Milverton reported that nine ploughgarrons valued at £31 10*s*. had been taken from him.[176] The large number of reports of horses stolen indicated both their importance in the economic life of the area and their attraction as military spoil. Not all the horses were taken by rebels. Thomas Waller of Finglas complained that he lost a mare and cart taken away by Captain Raleigh when the 600 'now lost' were going to Drogheda, his mare being pressed for that journey about 29 November 1641.[177] This was clearly a reference to the soldiers lost at the battle of Julianstown. Catholics as well as Protestants were forced to contribute to the needs of the rebel army, although in a somewhat different way. Contributions were levied by the rebel leaders on Catholic landowners and horses formed an important item in these assessments.[178]

173 Purgatorium Hibernicum ..., *c*.1670 (NLI, MS 470, p. 129). 174 Examination of Richard Dunn, 7 January 1642 (TCD, MS 809, f. 220); deposition of Thomas Smith, 20 January 1642 (TCD, MS 809, f. 224); examination of Thomas Sevier, 29 January 1642 (TCD, MS 809, f. 232); deposition of Mary Bucklie, 17 February 1642 (TCD, MS 809, f. 234); deposition of Nicholas Barry, 5 March 1642 (TCD, MS 809, f. 241); deposition of Thomas Benet, 26 February 1642 (TCD, MS 809, f. 243); deposition of Huibart Cromphouts, 2 March 1642 (TCD, MS 809, f. 268); deposition of Ann Foreside, 5 January 1642 (TCD, MS 809, f. 279); deposition of Christopher Hewetson, 5 March 1642 (TCD, MS 809, f. 280); deposition of John Husband, 11 March 1642 (TCD, MS 809, f. 281); deposition of Darby Lea, 25 January 1642 (TCD, MS 809, f. 288); deposition of Robert Benion (copy only), 25 July 1645 (TCD, MS 810, f. 62); deposition of James Smith, 26 April 1642 (TCD, MS 810, f. 104); deposition of Tabitha Eccles, 3 April 1642 (TCD, MS 810, f. 135); deposition of John Huxley, 21 May 1642 (TCD, MS 810, f. 158); deposition of Henry Mawdesley, 22 April 1642 (TCD, MS 810, f. 167); deposition of Richard Powell, 17 November 1642 (TCD, MS 810, f. 175); deposition of Thomas Waller, 29 March 1642 (TCD, MS 810, f. 187); deposition of Samuel Filgate, 8 January 1644 (TCD, MS 810, f. 232); deposition of William Fleming, 7 November 1643 (TCD, MS 810, f. 233); deposition of Thomas Williams, 10 January 1644 (TCD, MS 810, f.269); deposition of John Geny, 23 July 1645 (TCD, MS 810, f. 313); examination of Robert Boylan, 6 November 1652 (TCD, MS 810, f. 334); examination of Andrew Gyraght, 2 February 1653 (TCD, MS 810, f. 357); examination of Richard Greg, 16 December 1652 (TCD, MS 810, f. 388). 175 Deposition of James Smith, 26 April 1642 (TCD, MS 810, f. 104); deposition of John Huxley, 21 May 1642 (TCD, MS 810, f. 158); deposition of Thomas Lloyd, 18 June 1642 (TCD, MS 810, f. 165). 176 Deposition of Thomas Benet, 26 February 1642 (TCD, MS 809, f. 243); deposition of Huibart Cromphouts, 2 March 1642 (TCD, MS 809, f. 268). 177 Deposition of Thomas Waller, 29 March 1642 (TCD, MS 810, f. 187). 178 Deposition of Daniel Barwick, 23 May 1642 (TCD, MS 810, f. 114).

The presence of a large number of horses in the area gave rise to ancillary trades and industries. While the hearth money roll did not usually identify the occupations of taxpayers three forges are listed for the town of Swords, indicating that even in peace-time there was plenty of work for smiths.[179] There were also forges listed for Finglas (two), Skephubble (one), Kilshane (one) and Harristown (one).[180] All of these were situated in the central part of the area. Since the number of kilns specifically identified as such in the hearth money roll is far less than the number shown in the Civil Survey it seems likely that the number of forges was also understated. John Locke of Swords, who claimed that he had lost goods worth over £300 in December 1641 appears to have owned or operated a smithy, since his losses included smith tools worth £13 10*s.* 4*d.* and harness and other goods worth £20.[181]

Another interesting factor which emerges in particular from the depositions is that several landowners employed 'servants' who would be described as farm managers at the present time. Nicholas Barry, who deposed on behalf of his brother, Alderman Richard Barry of Santry, who also had a home in High Street, Dublin, gave evidence about tithes, rentals and debts while the alderman's servant, Robert Church, gave details about the farm losses suffered by his master 'by reason of the foresaid rebellion'.[182] The same pattern can be seen in the case of Henry Mawdesley, clerk of the peace for counties Dublin and Louth, who made a general deposition about his losses while his servant, Katherine Magee, spinster, detailed the goods stolen from his farm and listed the names of those believed to have taken part in the raid.[183]

The wide range of occupations closely associated with agriculture mentioned in the depositions illustrated the varied nature of the farming carried on in the area. While many of the drovers, cowherds and carters who travelled the roads of Fingal came from distant parts of the country, others were employed locally.[184] Butchers were also to be found, specifically at Finglas and Balscaddan.[185] A Dublin city butcher, John Geny, managed to combine two trades as he had a farm at Belgree, near Castleknock.[186] John Sephton of Jamestown near Finglas was a dairyman.[187] Two known millers, an unnamed man at Clontarf and Owen Hely at Chapelizod, were killed in 1641 and 1652, respectively.[188]

Other occupations noted in the depositions included servants and labourers, fishermen (at Clontarf), a pawnbroker (at Ballybough), a weaver, a carpenter, innkeepers,

179 'Hearth money roll for County Dublin, 1664' (second part), *Journal of the County Kildare Archaeological Society*, xi (1930–33), pp 418–20. 180 'Hearth money roll for County Dublin, 1664' (second part), *Journal of the County Kildare Archaeological Society*, xi (1930–33), pp 386 and 420–2. 181 Deposition of John Locke, 20 January 1642 (TCD, MS 809, f. 289). 182 Deposition of Nicholas Barry, 5 March 1642 (TCD, MS 809, f. 241); deposition of Robert Church, 5 March 1642 (TCD, MS 809, f. 241–2); Colm Lennon, *The lords of Dublin in the age of reformation* (Dublin, 1989), p. 230. 183 Deposition of Henry Mawdesley, 22 April 1642 (TCD, MS 810, f. 167); deposition of Katherine Magee, 22 April 1642 (TCD, MS 810, f. 174). 184 Examination of Tirlogue McMahon, 2 November 1641 (TCD, MS 809, f. 67); examination of Shane O'Mahon, 6 November 1641 (TCD, MS 809, f. 118); examination of Thomas Sevier, 29 January 1642 (TCD, MS 809, f. 232). 185 Examination of John Sephton, 15 November 1641 (TCD, MS 809, f. 176); examination of William Rowen, 19 November 1641 (TCD, MS 809, f. 188); deposition of Katherine Magee, 22 April 1642 (TCD, MS 810, f. 174). 186 Deposition of John Geny, 23 July 1645 (TCD, MS 810, f. 313). 187 Examination of John Sephton, 15 November 1641 (TCD, MS 809, f. 176). 188 Examination of David Powell, 14 December 1641 (TCD, MS 809, f. 214); examination of Richard Greg, 16 December 1652 (TCD, MS 810, f. 388). 189 Examination of David Powell, 14 December 1641 (TCD, MS 809, f. 214); examination of Thomas

a surgeon (at Tobersool, near Balscaddan), a postboy, a postmaster, a clerk of the courts, a clerk of the peace and a provost-marshal.[189] Accounts prepared in 1657 for repairing the church and the little stone bridge at Finglas noted the occupations of mason, plasterer, glazier, carpenter, joiner, carter and labourer in the list of payments made.[190] While it is not possible to be certain that all of these men were local people there is no indication in the accounts that they were brought in from outside the area. Finglas also had a constable at this period. The employment of constables and other public officials will be discussed further in chapter 4. The various lists of outlaws prepared during and after the 1641 rising, while listing occupations, are somewhat disappointing since most of those listed are shown as 'gentleman', 'esquire' or 'yeoman'. These lists, however, have identified a second surgeon, Nicholas Bellew, who lived at Balrothery and another miller, John Burley, who resided at Westpalstown.[191] Another source of information is the surviving Court book of the liberty of Saint Sepulchre which covered the period 1586–90.[192] Mentioned in this were cobblers or shoemakers in Kilreesk, Finglas and Lusk, a tanner in Swords, a fisherman in Portraine, a butcher in Lispopple, a glazier whose residence was not stated precisely but which appears to have been Swords and a lime-maker in Castleknock.[193] While the period covered by the court records is a little earlier than that covered by this study it is likely that the same occupations and perhaps even some of the same people were still to be found in the area after 1603. The day-to-day needs of the people for material goods and services appear to have been well catered for. In addition, many aldermen and merchants who lived or worked in Dublin city had homes or property in Fingal where they generated and provided employment for local people.

How did people travel about? Undoubtedly many of those who lived near the coast made short journeys by sea, but land travel along the roads in the area was the norm. Fynes Moryson, writing in 1617 about Ireland in general, pointed out that the roads were good and that there were few or no thieves robbing by the wayside.[194] He also pointed out that there were few or no coaches and that people rode for the most part upon their own horses.[195] This was still the general pattern in Fingal in the 1640s.

Sevier, 29 January 1642 (TCD, MS 809, f. 232); deposition of Francis Eccles, 17 January 1642 (TCD, MS 809, f. 277); deposition of Darby Lea, 25 January 1642 (TCD, MS 809, f. 288); deposition of Richard Price, 9 February 1642 (TCD, MS 809, f. 321); deposition of George Cashell (copy only), 29 February 1644 (TCD, MS 810, f. 25); deposition of Robert Benion (copy only), 25 July 1645 (TCD, MS 810, f. 62); deposition of Thomas Clitheroe, 26 May 1642 (TCD, MS 810, f. 126); deposition of Henry Mawdesley, 22 April 1642 (TCD, MS 810, f. 167); deposition of Katherine Magee, 22 April 1642 (TCD, MS 810, f. 174); deposition of Samuel Filgate, 8 January 1644 (TCD, MS 810, f. 232); deposition of Edward Leech, 18 March 1644 (TCD, MS 810, f. 244). **190** William Cotter Stubbs, 'Finglas, County Dublin, vestry books' in *Journal of the Royal Society of Antiquaries of Ireland*, xlvi (1916), p. 28. **191** John T. Gilbert (ed.), *History of the Irish confederation and the war in Ireland*, 1643–4 (7 vols, Dublin, 1882–91), iii, pp 344 and 349; R.C. Simington and John MacLellan, 'Oireachtas Library, List of outlaws, 1641–1647', in *Analecta Hibernica*, no. 23 (1966), p. 337. **192** *Court book of the liberty of Saint Sepulchre …*, ed. Herbert Wood (Dublin, 1930). I am grateful to Dr Raymond Gillespie for drawing my attention to this reference. **193** *Court book of the liberty of Saint Sepulchre …*, ed. Herbert Wood (Dublin, 1930), pp 7, 9, 37, 53, 59, and 66. **194** Fynes Moryson, *An itinerary …* (London, 1617), part iii, book 1, ch. 2, p. 29. **195** Fynes Moryson, *An itinerary …* (London, 1617), part iii, book 2, ch. 1, p. 62. **196** Examination of William Rowen, 19 November 1641 (TCD, MS 809, f. 188); examination of Edmund Archbold, 31 December 1641 (TCD, MS 810, f. 99).

However, by that time there were some coaches in the area, for example, those belonging to Sir Henry Tichborne and Mrs Barnewall (Countess of Tirconnell).[196] Cars and carts were frequently mentioned. The two women driven from Holmpatrick in December 1641 walked six miles, probably at least as far as the main road from the north, before they found a car to take them to Dublin.[197] Andrew Mainwaring, the wounded soldier who survived the battle of Julianstown, travelled hidden under straw in a car from Gormanstown to Dublin.[198] Twelve of the thirteen people who were expelled from Lambay in December 1649 travelled on foot from Howth to Dublin, 'having their goods at their backs and upon one car'.[199] The fact that Edward Leech mentioned that they travelled this distance suggests that such a journey on foot was rather unusual. Further evidence that Fingallians liked to travel even short distances on horseback is found in the deposition of William Rowen, who suggested to John Sephton that they should go to Santry to see if it was true that there was a large force of rebels there.[200] Sephton replied that 'if he had a horse he would bear him company for his own horse was fallen lame'. It is not surprising that their efforts to borrow a horse to travel the short distance from Finglas to Santry aroused the suspicions of the authorities about their motives in undertaking the journey. Both women and men were fond of riding, and the wealthier women, in particular, tended to ride in some style. Thomas Luttrell left his wife the horse he had appointed for her, together with three of his geldings to carry her waiting servants.[201] Alice Segrave left a horse to both her daughters 'to carry them on their journey and up and down'.[202] In 1660 Elizabeth Ussher bequeathed to her mother her long riding scarf and saddle cloth and cushion.[203] Travellers were accustomed to ride in groups or, if travelling alone, tended to join other groups of riders.[204] Another feature of seventeenth-century travel was that servants accompanying their masters might travel either on horseback or on foot. Tirlogue McGillarowe described how Lord Maguire, on his fateful journey to Dublin through Fingal in October 1641, was accompanied by five servants, three of whom travelled on horseback and two on foot.[205] An interesting insight into distances travelled was given by Francis McMurrohye, a thirteen-year-old boy, who was employed as a courier in 1641.[206] He travelled from Dundalk to the friary at Drogheda on a Tuesday. On the following day he went to Hollywood of Artaine with a letter which he had brought from Dundalk. On Thursday he travelled to the friary of Kildare with another letter. On Saturday

197 Deposition of Huibart Cromphouts, 2 March 1642 (TCD, MS 809, f. 268); deposition of Margaret Huiberts, 14 March 1644 (TCD, MS 810, f. 239). **198** Deposition of Andrew Mainwaring, 15 February 1642 (TCD, MS 809, f. 297). **199** Deposition of Edward Leech, 18 March 1644 (TCD, MS 810, f. 245). **200** Examination of William Rowen, 19 November 1641 (TCD, MS 809, f. 188). **201** Abstract of will of Thomas Luttrell, 20 March 1633 (RSAI, Elrington Ball MSS, vol vii, f. 17); Francis Elrington Ball, *A history of the County Dublin ... part fourth* (originally published 1906, reprinted Dublin, 1995), p. 10. **202** Abstract of will of Alice Segrave, 13 October 1660 (RSAI, Elrington Ball MSS, vol xii, f. 40); Francis Elrington Ball, *Southern Fingal ...* (originally published 1920, reprinted Dublin, 1995), p. 99. **203** Abstract of will of Elizabeth Ussher, 1 May 1660 (RSAI, Elrington Ball MSS, vol x, f. 29); Francis Elrington Ball, *Howth and its owners ...* (originally published 1917, reprinted Dublin, 1995), p. 116. **204** Examination of Redmond Maguire, 1 November 1641 (TCD, MS 809, f. 46); examination of Tirlogue McMahon, 2 November 1641 (TCD, MS 809, f. 67). **205** Examination of Tirlogue McGillarowe, 2 November 1641 (TCD, MS 809, f. 74). **206** Examination of Francis McMurrohye, 8 November 1641 (TCD, MS 809, f. 144).

he returned to a place 'he knoweth not' within five miles of Dublin and on Sunday he was apprehended in Dublin. Francis made his mark on the deposition, so it is probable that he could not write. He claimed he did not know the contents of the various letters he carried 'but only about the putting of a young friar into the house'. There is no mention of a horse in this deposition, and the journeys appear to have been too long to have been undertaken entirely on foot. It seems likely that the senders and recipients of the various letters arranged transport for him for part of the journey at least or that he managed to obtain lifts from carters. By the 1650s, travellers were no longer as safe as they had been when Fynes Moryson wrote his *Itinerary*. By then tories were a great threat, as the murders of Edward St Lawrence near Turvey, James Brandon, a hat-maker, at Ballymaguire and Owen Hely, miller, near Chapelizod show.[207]

There is very little local information available about the health of the people. Plague broke out in Ireland in October 1603 and lasted well into 1605.[208] Fingal was less affected than Dublin city and the court consequently moved to Howth.[209] Plague broke out again in Dublin in 1650 and lasted until 1652.[210] However these were abnormal events. There is little information about the medical practitioners who lived in Fingal during the period apart from the two surgeons already mentioned, George Cashell of Balscaddan and Nicholas Bellew of Balrothery. One well-known physician, Dr Thomas Arthur of Limerick, who practised in Dublin for many years, spent a great deal of his time treating Fingal patients. He listed in Latin the names of his patients (or the heads of households), dates of consultation and fees paid to him at his practices in Limerick and Dublin from 1619 to 1669 in an entry-book or fee-book.[211] The earlier section of this fee-book, dealing mainly with the Limerick practice, has been published.[212] The addresses of Dr Arthur's patients, particularly if they came from outside the cities of Dublin and Limerick, were occasionally noted. In some instances, particularly in the later years, the illness from which the patient suffered was also recorded. Almost all his patients came from well-known gentry families, and a large proportion of these were Fingal families, both Catholic and Protestant. The same names appeared over and over again and included such well-known names as Bolton, Bysse, Howth, Mainwaring, Mayart, Ussher and Ware among the Protestant families and Barnewall, Bath, Chamberlain, Delahide, Fagan, Hollywood, Hore, Luttrell, Segrave and Talbot among the Catholic families. While Dr Arthur's patients were mainly members of the aristocracy and gentry, just occa-

207 Examination of Arland Ussher, not dated (TCD, MS 810, f. 355); examination of Richard Greg, 16 December 1652 (TCD, MS 810, f. 388); examination of Giles Curran, 16 December 1652 (TCD, MS 810, f. 389); examination of Richard Raymond, 20 December 1652 (TCD, MS 810, f. 390); examination of John Talbot, 11 November 1652 (TCD, MS 810, f. 391); examination of Thomas Berry, 21 September 1653 (TCD, MS 810, f. 393); examination of Patrick Tankard, 27 May 1653 (TCD, MS 810, f. 395); examination of Thomas O Rannahie, 23 April 1653 (TCD, MS 810, f. 397); examination of Richard Randall, not dated (TCD, MS 810, f. 399). **208** *Cal. S. P. Ire., 1603–06*, pp 95, 111, 117, 142, 162, 245, 250 and 331–4. **209** *Cal. S. P. Ire., 1603–06*, pp 331–4; Francis Elrington Ball, *Howth and its owners …* (originally published 1917, reprinted Dublin, 1995), p. 92. **210** Joseph Robins, *The miasma: epidemic and panic in nineteenth century Ireland* (Dublin, 1995), pp 23–4. **211** Entry Book of Thomas Arthur, 1619–1669 (BL, Add. MS 31,885). **212** Maurice Lenihan, 'Ancient *Liagh*s and *Ollamh*s: the fee-book of a physician of the seventeenth century' in *The Journal of the Kilkenny and South-east of Ireland Archaeological Society*, vi (1867), pp 10–33, 139–176 and 239–248.

sionally he noted that a particular patient was the servant of a well-known client. There is one series of entries for a certain fisherman (*piscator*) of Malahide whom he attended three times in October and November 1633 at a fee of 5*s.* (a relatively modest fee) per consultation.[213] Perhaps there was something about this man's case which particularly interested Dr Arthur. He attended another (or perhaps the same) Malahide fisherman in March 1638, and a Malahide cook, called Bryan Michael, in September of the same year.[214] He clearly made several visits to Malahide but whether he had a special connection with the town or whether the Talbots of Malahide were particularly caring landlords is not known. While no apothecaries have been identified in Fingal, there is a possibility that the apothecary, Adrian Huybarts, who was admitted to the franchise in Dublin city in December 1639, was related to the Huiberts Verveer family, who lived in Holmpatrick.[215] There were, no doubt, other trained doctors, surgeons and apothecaries in the area. Practice in the medical profession called for a high level of competence and it was necessary for Catholic doctors, in particular, to go abroad for formal training. One such candidate was Nicholas Luttrell of Luttrellstown, who made his will in 1609 preparatory to his departure abroad to study medicine and who died not long afterwards.[216] Other occupations, which demanded specialized education and/or training, such as those of clergyman, lawyer and musician, will be considered in later chapters.

Some of those who became ill in the period were at the mercy of charlatans. The Capuchin historian, Nicholas Archbold, described how, when the notable preacher, Luke (Father Edward) Bath fell ill in 1634, 'among several remedies, he took a powder from a certain Scots mountebank whom he found at his sister's house, the viscountess of Ballygarth, taking upon him the office of extraordinarily curing of maladies. This powder, in lieu of prolonging his life, hastened his death'.[217]

Home remedies were also used. Luce Spell of Drogheda, together with her fellow-passengers, was taken prisoner when their barque from Liverpool was forced to land in Skerries in December 1641.[218] Her goods were seized and taken to Mathew Barnewall's house at Bremore and she was subsequently imprisoned in a number of places including John Passmore's inn at Balrothery, where she spent three weeks. She went on to say:

> And the said Passmore's wife complaining of a sore leg, this examinant told her that she had balsam amongst her goods at Bremore and would help her if she had it. Whereupon a messenger being sent thither the said messenger brought a box of balsam which the deponent saw and knew to be her own.

As well as relying on home medicine many people had a great faith in the efficacy of the water from holy wells which was used to treat a wide variety of ailments. As

213 Entry Book of Thomas Arthur, 1619–1669 (BL, Add. MS 31,885, f. 46). **214** Entry Book of Thomas Arthur, 1619–1669 (BL, Add. MS 31,885, ff 58 and 62). **215** *Anc. rec. Dublin*, iii, p. 365. **216** Abstract of will of Nicholas Luttrell, 22 June1609 (RSAI, Elrington Ball MSS, vol vii, f. 14). **217** Nicholas Archbold, The historie of the Irish Capucins, 1643 (Bibliothèque Municipale de Troyes, MS 1103, p. 94). **218** Deposition of Luce Spell, 5 February 1642 (TCD, MS, 834, f. 6); 'County Louth depositions, 1641', ed. Thomas Gogarty in *Journal of the County Louth Archaeological Society*, iii, no. 1 (1912), pp 71–2. **219** Caoimhín Ó Danachair, 'The holy wells of County Dublin' in *Reportorium*

Caoimhín Ó Danachair put it: 'Water from the wells was drunk and applied to sore eyes, ears and limbs, and in many cases the use of water for curative purposes continued after the saying of prayers at the wells had ceased.'[219]

This chapter has so far been concerned with material welfare and goods. How were these goods distributed amongst the population? Since many of the records which have survived have been concerned with the more affluent in society, it is difficult to discover just what level of poverty existed among the people. There are, however, occasional references, direct or indirect, to the poor, notably a reference in the Civil Survey to the sandy banks or hills of Rush 'on which common the poor fishermen and other inhabitants do graze their cattle for which a small sum or duty is paid'.[220] Even this does not suggest abject poverty since the men involved had an occupation – albeit precarious – possessed cattle and were able to pay a small duty. The probability that many people, particularly in the northern part of the area, were not even liable for the hearth tax is also an indication that poverty existed. There is little evidence of institutionalized help for the poor of Fingal although there is an intriguing reference to the 'poor house' of Corrstown (parish of Kilsallaghan) in the Civil Survey.[221] It is possible that some Fingallians obtained help in city institutions such as St John's Hospital, which, by the seventeenth century, had the character of a poorhouse.[222] It is not known if the bequest of £100 sterling left by Richard Nettervill of Corballis in 1607 to have a hospital built upon his land in Balrothery for the lodging of twelve poor men was used for that purpose since he gave his overseers discretion to employ the legacy for 'some other good and godly work'.[223] Individuals often made bequests designed to help the poor: Henry Burnell of Castleknock left £10 for charitable purposes in 1614;[224] in 1635, James Hussey, priest, of Smarmore, Co. Louth, left 10*s.* to the poor of Skerries and Holmpatrick, where he had expressed a wish to be buried;[225] Thomas St Lawrence, a relative of the lord of Howth, left a generous £100 in 1638 'to clothe the door-beggars' specifying that the poor of Howth were to be served first;[226] Sir James Ware left £30 to be distributed among the poor housekeepers in the city and suburbs of Dublin.[227] In 1607 Richard Nettervill wrote the following in his will: 'Item my will is that my funeral's month and year's mind or memory be kept in good sort for such friends as shall be there present and specially for the relief of the poor.' In a codicil dated 12 August 1636 to her will Cecily, dowager lady of Howth, directed her executrix to keep her month's mind and her year's mind according to the usual custom of the country and to bestow some alms

Novum, ii, no. 1 (1957–8), p. 68. **220** *Civil Survey, vii, county of Dublin*, pp 61–2. **221** *Civil Survey, vii, county of Dublin*, p. 237. **222** Charles McNeill, 'Hospital of S. John without the New Gate, Dublin' in *Journal of the Royal Society of Antiquaries of Ireland*, lv (1925), p. 64. **223** Will of Richard Nettervill, 11 April 1607 (NAI, Deeds and wills extracted from inquisitions, exchequer series, vol 1, Carlow and County Dublin, RC 10/1, pp 367–9.) **224** Abstract of will of Henry Burnell, 17 July 1614 (RSAI, Elrington Ball MSS, vol xi, f. 34). **225** L.P. Murray, 'The will of James Hussey of Smarmore, Co. Louth, "priest" (A. D. 1635)', in *The Journal of the County Louth Archaeological Society*, viii, no. 4 (1936), p. 304. **226** Abstract of will of Thomas St Lawrence, 27 March 1638 (RSAI, Elrington Ball MSS, vol x, f. 22); Francis Elrington Ball, *Howth and its owners ...* (originally published 1917, reprinted Dublin, 1995), p. 109. **227** Will of Sir James Ware, 10 August 1665 (NAI, Prerogative will book, 1664–84, f. 178). **228** Abstract of will of Cecilia, dowager lady of Howth, 1 August 1635 and codicil dated 12 August 1636 (RSAI, Elrington Ball MSS, vol ix, f. 94); Francis Elrington Ball, *Howth and its owners ...* (originally published 1917, reprinted Dublin, 1995), p. 78.

at those terms upon the poor.[228] This custom, if generally observed, must have resulted in the transfer of sums of money from rich to poor on a fairly regular basis and over an extended period. Bequests were sometimes made in kind. Elizabeth Ussher, widow of William Gough of Sutton, left three barrels of corn to be distributed among the poor.[229] The bequests of money to buy mourning made by Walter Segrave, Cecily, dowager lady of Howth, and Lady Bath have already been mentioned. This custom, while it gave an opportunity to display family wealth, may have been regarded as a considerate and tactful way of helping the poor since a service, namely, attendance at the funeral, was expected in return. Lady Bath's bequest gives an indication of where poverty was likely to be found, that is, among women, especially widows, and children. Apart from women and children, another group who suffered a great deal of poverty were discharged and wounded soldiers and others who supplied services to the government army for which payment was frequently delayed or not made at all. Mention has already been made of the case of Thomas Williams of Santry who complained that he had not been paid by the authorities for his army service.[230] Another sad story was told to the commissioners by Elizabeth, widow of Roger Parr, who had been one of the clerks in the court of exchequer and who had lost his employment:

> in the beginning of the present rebellion and by means thereof ... and having a charge of wife and three small children to maintain, he took up arms against the rebels and going out upon a party to the town of Swords was there slain in the way to the utter undoing of her and her poor infants, who are like to perish for want of means.[231]

Further confirmation of the existence of pockets of poverty is to be found in the earliest surviving Finglas vestry book which recorded the choice of four overseers for the poor of the parish and two persons to collect for the poor of the parish.[232] In the context of an attempt to determine the extent of poverty this is an important minute for the contemporary surveys suggest that Finglas was among the wealthiest parishes in the whole area. While the records cited here do not constitute a great deal of evidence for poverty, there is enough to show that such poverty as existed was not confined to any one part of Fingal. The general impression gleaned from the surviving documents is that, while there was some poverty in the area, the people of Fingal in general, except in times of epidemic or war, lived reasonably comfortable lives during the early seventeenth century.

The proximity of Fingal to Dublin city and to Drogheda as well as its numerous harbours (mentioned in chapter 1) ensured that it could be easily supplied with fuel and other material goods which otherwise might have been in short supply. Dublin city was, in fact, the nearest market town for much of the area.

229 Abstract of will of Elizabeth Ussher, 1 May 1660 (RSAI, Elrington Ball MSS, vol x, f. 29); Francis Elrington Ball, *Howth and its owners* ... (originally published 1917, reprinted Dublin, 1995), p. 116. **230** Deposition of Thomas Williams, 10 January 1644 (TCD, MS 810, f. 269). **231** Deposition of Elizabeth Parr, 7 January 1644 (TCD, MS 810, f. 237). **232** William Cotter Stubbs, 'Finglas, County Dublin, vestry books' in *Journal of the Royal Society of Antiquaries of Ireland*, xlvi (1916), p. 27.

3

The Hoar Stone and the Lady Bush

> '... she hath credibly heard that there was a stone set up upon the edge whereon was written Roman letters setting forth the meres between Diswellstown and the land of Stagob, and that she likewise heard that Justice Luttrell in the night time by moonlight did remove the said stone and cast it into some part of the Liffey but where she knoweth not'.[1]

This quotation, from the testimony of Ellen Hackett, widow, given in a suit taken by the dean and chapter of Christ Church against Simon Luttrell of Clonsilla, is a reminder of the intense attachment of the people of Fingal to their land. As Richard Stanihurst put it, in a passage already quoted, the race or sept of the English or strangers there were solely seized of that part of the island 'gripping with their talons so firmly that warm nest that ... the Irish enemy could never rouse them from thence'.[2] Any interference with the recognized boundaries of land was frowned on in this intensely traditional society. The story that Ellen Hackett heard may or may not have been true but she clearly believed it since she was prepared to include it as part of her sworn deposition in a suit against Simon Luttrell even though the proceedings did not affect her directly. Land formed the foundation of the seventeenth-century Fingal economy.

Because of the shortage of documentary sources it is difficult to obtain an overview of economic life in the early seventeenth century at a county or even at a national level. When one tries to do so at a sub-county level, the task becomes even more difficult. For example, the creeks and harbours of Fingal were all considered as part of the port of Dublin, a fact which makes the discussion of external trade particularly difficult. Writing about the sixteenth century, Raymond Gillespie pointed out that 'such evidence as does exist has not been fully sifted by historians'.[3] The same is true of the early seventeenth century. Because of the paucity of material for Fingal it is necessary to build up a picture, by using a series of case studies and by supplementing these with evidence from other sources which were not primarily intended for economic or fiscal purposes. For example, the papers relating to the suit

1 Deposition of Ellen Hackett, 16 April 1639 (RCBL, Christ Church cathedral records, Papers relating to the lands of Simon Luttrell and Dominic White, 1637–71, Interrogatory to be administered to the dean and chapter's witnesses together with their depositions, C6/1/26/15/5, f. 20). 2 Richarde Stanyhurst, *A treatise contayning a playne and perfect description of Irelande* ... in Raphaell Holinshed and Richarde Stanyhurst, *Holinshed's Irish chronicle* ..., ed. Liam Miller and Eileen Power (London, 1577, republished Dublin, 1979), p. 13. 3 Raymond Gillespie, *The transformation of the Irish economy, 1550–1700* (Dublin, 1991), p. 5.

against Simon Luttrell, and the Christ Church records in general, in the Representative Church Body Library, Dublin, are a fortunate survival and a rich source of information for an area of the country where estate papers and documents relating to the economy for the period 1603–60 are in short supply.

A study of land quality and land usage in Fingal as a whole led to tentative general conclusions that the Civil Survey data related to land potential rather than land usage and that livestock production was a far more important element in the rural economy of Fingal in 1641 than the Civil Survey figures for 1654–6, taken in isolation, might have suggested. In order to examine further the ownership and distribution of land two case studies were examined in detail. The first of these, relating to the Clonsilla area, demonstrated how the law and traditional practice were used to ensure the rights of proprietors over time while the second, a study of Glasnevin, highlighted the complicated leasing system which existed in the area.

In July 1637 Alson Luttrell, formerly St Lawrence, widow of Thomas Luttrell of Luttrellstown, petitioned the dean and chapter of Christ Church for a lease of the lands of Astagob (then known as Stagob) and Diswellstown for a period of twenty-one years.[4] These lands had been leased for sixty-one years to the Castleknock lawyer, Henry Burnell, on 25 October 1573 at an annual rent of £1 14*s*. 4*d*. Irish, 'in consideration of his giving the best council and advice in law'.[5] This lease was to come into effect on the expiration of an existing lease to Sir Thomas Luttrell. The Christ Church copy of the lease to Sir Thomas Luttrell appears to have been missing from the Christ Church records even in the seventeenth century. A list 'copied from the small old register' by the eighteenth-century copyist, John Lyon, included a lease made in the first year of the reign of Edward VI to Sir Thomas Luttrell of all the lands and tenements in Astagob for sixty-one years.[6] If the period of tenure was calculated from the actual date of the lease the lease would have been due to expire in the period 28 January 1608 to 27 January 1609, at which point the lease to Henry Burnell would have taken effect. In any event Henry Burnell, probably towards the end of the sixteenth century, transferred the tenancy to the Luttrell family since Alson Luttrell stated in 1637 that she and her late husband had 'continued possessors thereof this forty years'.[7] The dean and chapter had some misgivings about granting the lease to Alson since they conceived that Simon Luttrell, son and heir of Thomas Luttrell and Alson's stepson, 'claimeth some interest in the premises'.[8] They required him to produce two leases, one to Burnell and one to Sir Thomas Luttrell and, when he omitted to do so, they made a lease to Alson Luttrell at £10 sterling per annum 'and after eviction a lease for twenty-one years at the halfendeale of the value according to the statute'.[9] It transpired later that, when the lease to Alson Luttrell was granted, Simon Luttrell 'was sick and could not look out his writ-

4 Second chapter act book (copy) (RCBL, Christ Church cathedral records, C6/1/8/2, p. 60). 5 Abstract of lease to Henry Burnell, 25 October 1573 (RCBL, Christ Church cathedral records, C6/1/17/4, p. 112); *Christ Church deeds*, ed. M.J. McEnery and Raymond Refaussé (Dublin, 2001), no. 1337. 6 List of leases copied from 'the small old register' (RCBL, Christ Church cathedral records, C6/1/17/4, p. 107). 7 Second chapter act book (copy) (RCBL, Christ Church cathedral records, C6/1/8/2, p. 60). 8 Second chapter act book (copy) (RCBL, Christ Church cathedral records, C6/1/8/2, p. 60). 9 Second chapter act book (copy) (RCBL, Christ Church cathedral records, C6/1/8/2, p. 66); *Christ Church deeds*, ed. M.J. McEnery and Raymond Refaussé (Dublin, 2001), no.

ings'.[10] While the dean and chapter may have wished to use the opportunity to obtain a substantially increased rent from the property, the immediate cause for the setting up of a commission of investigation appears to have been Alson Luttrell's complaint that her stepson, Simon, had ploughed up one of the boundaries of the property *c.*1636.[11] There were two examinations of witnesses for the defendant, Simon Luttrell. On the first occasion (January 1638) the plaintiff was cited as Alson St Lawrence, but on the second occasion, in April 1639, the defence witnesses gave evidence against the dean and chapter of the cathedral church of the Holy Trinity as plaintiff.[12] It emerged during the course of the investigation that there was a difference of opinion about the boundaries between the estate of Simon Luttrell and the adjoining lands, which belonged to Christ Church cathedral, for which Alson Luttrell then held the lease. The quarrel hinged on whether two parcels of land, Ballystrowan and Tirmullen, were part of the Luttrell or of the Christ Church estate. The actual terms of the judgment are not known, but the Civil Survey listed 'Luttrellstown, Kellystown, Ballystrowan, Skirmullin' as a single denomination in the ownership of Simon Luttrell in 1641, which suggests that the decision was in his favour.[13] However, when, in July 1661, the dean and chapter of Christ Church finally granted a lease of Astagob and Diswellstown for twenty-one years to Thomas Luttrell, son of Simon, the terms were a fine of £5 and £10 rent yearly.[14] The Luttrells had secured the tenancy of the land but the dean and chapter had won for themselves a greatly increased rent.

The legal proceedings, which lasted from 1637 to at least 1640, represented a suit between two of the most powerful landowners in Fingal who were both in a position to call on the best legal advice and several witnesses. Although Alson Luttrell was the daughter and half-sister of lords of Howth she was probably a Catholic since she was adjudged 'innocent' in 1663.[15] Religion, therefore, does not appear to have been a major factor in the case but the large number of local witnesses on whom Simon Luttrell found himself able to call suggests that, indirectly, his Catholicism may have been of some advantage in the dispute with Christ Church. All in all, the documents relating to what was initially a disagreement about a relatively small piece of land, perhaps not more than twenty acres, affords a remarkable insight into landholding and rural life in southern Fingal during the early seventeenth century as well as illustrating how a family quarrel could escalate into a major dispute which demanded the attention of the lord deputy and council.

Simon Luttrell managed to summon eleven witnesses to speak on his behalf, of whom not more than two or three were tenants of his at the time of the hearing.[16]

1536. **10** Deposition of Thomas Howell, 16 April 1639 (RCBL, C6/1/26/15/5, f. 10). **11** Deposition of Alson Luttrell, 16 April 1639 (RCBL, C6/1/26/15/5, f. 18). **12** Papers relating to the lands of Simon Luttrell and Dominic White, 1637–71, Interrogatories to be administered to witnesses to be examined on the part and behalf of Simon Luttrell, Esq., defendant, against Alson St Lawrence, widow, plaintiff, January 1638 (RCBL, Christ Church cathedral records,, C6/1/26/15/6); Interrogatories to be administered to witnesses to be examined on the part and behalf of Simon Luttrell, Esq., defendant, against the dean and chapter of the cathedral church of the Holy Trinity, Dublin, April 1639 (RCBL, Christ Church cathedral records, C6/1/26/15/7). **13** *Civil Survey, vii, county of Dublin,* p. 230. **14** Second chapter act book (copy) (RCBL, Christ Church cathedral records, C6/1/8/2, p. 209). **15** 'Abstract of the decrees of the court of claimes for the tryall of Innocents' in Deputy keeper of public records in Ireland, *Nineteenth report* (Dublin, 1887), appendix, p. 43. **16** 'Fingal 1603–60', i, table 3.3,

Seven of these witnesses took part in the case taken by Alson Luttrell, while eight men (who included four of those who had deposed on the previous occasion) spoke in the case taken by Christ Church. They were of various ages and represented several walks of life. Several had Gaelic-Irish surnames. All appear to have been either natives of the area or to have resided there for some considerable time. Their depositions, as well as providing additional evidence for population movement between Fingal and Dublin city on the one hand, and Fingal and Meath on the other, also suggest that there was some population movement between the barony of Castleknock and that part of Co. Dublin lying south of the Liffey. The five witnesses for Christ Church included three (Alson Luttrell, George Hackett and his mother, Ellen) from the Sutton/Howth area, as well as one, Thomas Howell, the chapter clerk, who resided in Dublin and who may have been Welsh.[17] While the term 'of Stagob' was used to describe the residence of the Hacketts, Ellen Hackett herself tended to refer to her late husband as 'Hackett of Sutton'.[18] The only local Christ Church witness was the eighty-year old, Clonsilla-born, Richard Lock, whose testimony was hardly helpful to Alson Luttrell's cause.[19]

While the testimony of the defence witnesses was remarkably consistent regarding the estate boundaries there were, not surprisingly, given the fact that these men were speaking from memory about happenings many years previously, discrepancies in their ages and in some of their attempts at dating the merings, a fact which did not go unnoticed on the Christ Church side.[20] If, however, one makes the assumption that some witnesses were describing a sixteenth-century mering and others a second, early seventeenth-century mering, the evidence makes much more sense.

In the early-modern period, boundaries were not simply set down in writing. They were also 'trodden' in an elaborate ritual described by several of the defence witnesses. The boundaries between the lands of the Luttrells and those of Christ Church had an added significance. They were also the boundaries between the parishes of Clonsilla and Castleknock. Surprisingly, only one of the witnesses, Richard Braghall, collector for the barony of Castleknock and a local farmer, mentioned this fact. In what may have proved to be the clinching argument for the defence, he stated that the small and great tithes of Tirmullen and Ballystrowan (the areas in dispute) lay with the parish of Clonsilla and that the were not 'any part of the lands of Stagob nor of the parish where Stagob layeth' (Castleknock).[21] The fact that the disputed boundaries were parish boundaries may have been the reason for the elaborate mering ritual – one could almost describe it as a ceremonial – described by nine of the defence witnesses, three of whom had participated in it as small boys. The evidence suggests that there were within the memories of the witnesses at least two such merings of the same boundaries, the first of which took place 'in old Mr Simon Luttrell's time', that

p. 87. **17** 'Fingal 1603–60', i, table 3.2, p. 86; Raymond Gillespie, *Thomas Howell and his friends: serving Christ Church cathedral, Dublin, 1570–1700* (Dublin, 1997), p. 5. **18** Deposition of Ellen Hackett, 16 April 1639 (RCBL, C6/1/26/15/5, f. 19). **19** Deposition of Richard Lock, 16 April 1639 (RCBL, C6/1/26/15/5, ff 11–13). **20** Papers relating to the lands of Simon Luttrell and Dominic White, 1637–71, Notes of the evidence arising from records and the depositions of witnesses concerning the right of the church to said lands (RCBL, Christ Church cathedral records, C6/1/26/15/2). **21** Deposition of Richard Braghall, 22 January 1638 (RCBL, C6/1/26/15/6, ff 32–5); deposition of Richard Braghall, 16 April 1639 (RCBL, C6/1/26/15/7, ff 30–1).

is, before his death on 12 September 1596.[22] The second mering, remembered by the younger witnesses, appears to have taken place during the first decade of the seventeenth century.

The earlier mering was described by the elderly witnesses for the defence – Richard Malone, Nicholas Crenan (or Crynan) and William Maguire.[23] According to their accounts, Simon Luttrell's grandfather, also called Simon, was present together with the dean of Christ Church, 'Mr Burnell, the lawyer' (Henry Burnell of Castleknock), 'Mr Caddell, the lawyer' or 'Caddell of Mooretown' (probably John Caddell of Mooretown whose will was dated 28 March 1603 and who was closely related to many prominent Fingal families).[24] According to Richard Malone 'the meres were trodden by ancient men to the number of five or six'.[25] William Maguire corroborated the evidence that Simon Luttrell, the dean and the two lawyers were present, while Nicholas Crenan identified three of the ancient men as Nicholas Hunt of Kellystown, Nicholas Scanlon and Laurence Clarke.[26] Crenan's evidence is particularly interesting since he claimed that 'he was whipped at Hoar Stone upon mering of the said land with other boys in his parish when he was about ten years of age'.[27] Confirming this at the 1639 hearing he said that the mering had taken place 'forty-five years since' suggesting that the first mering took place about 1594.[28] The whipping of young boys also took place at the second mering which was described by James and Richard Braghall, John and Nicholas Coraghan, William Dollard and Patrick Mullen.[29] James Braghall deposed that 'Mr Burnell, the lawyer' had 'obtained a lease of the then dean of Christ Church of the dean's land in Stagob'.[30] Richard Braghall said that the events occurred 'upon a meeting of a mering upon a lease of reversion from the then dean of Christ Church unto Mr Burnell of Castleknock of the dean's land in Stagob'.[31] On this occasion the meres were trodden by Henry Burnell of Castleknock, Oliver Fitzgerald of Ashtown, Nicholas Hunt of Lucan, Henry Kerredan of Astagob, John Luttrell of Killeek, Thomas Luttrell (father of the defendant, Simon) and Nicholas Scanlon of Kellystown in the presence of Sir Christopher Plunket.[32] The participation of Henry Burnell, Nicholas

22 Deposition of Nicholas Crenan, 22 January 1638 (RCBL, C6/1/26/15/6, ff 29–30); Griffith, *Inquisitions*, p. 307. 23 Depositions of Richard Malone, 22 January 1638 and 16 April 1639 (RCBL, C6/1/26/15/6, ff 9–14 and C6/1/26/15/7, ff 5–9); deposition of William Maguire, 16 April 1639 (RCBL, C6/1/26/15/7, ff 13–16); depositions of Nicholas Crenan (or Crynan), 22 January 1638 and 16 April 1639 (RCBL, C6/1/26/15/6, ff 27–31 and C6/1/26/15/7, ff 23–6). 24 Abstract of will of John Caddell, 28 March 1603 (NLI, Fisher will abstracts, GO MS 290, p. 83). 25 Deposition of Richard Malone, 22 January 1638 (RCBL, C6/1/26/15/6, f. 12). 26 Deposition of William Maguire, 16 April 1639 (RCBL, C6/1/26/15/7, f. 15); deposition of Nicholas Crenan, 16 April 1639 (RCBL, C6/1/26/15/7, f. 25). 27 Deposition of Nicholas Crenan, 22 January 1638 (RCBL, C6/1/26/15/6, ff 29–30). 28 Deposition of Nicholas Crenan, 16 April 1639 (RCBL, C6/1/26/1/15/7, f. 26). 29 Deposition of James Braghall, 22 January 1638 (RCBL, C6/1/26/15/6, ff 22–7); depositions of Richard Braghall, 22 January 1638 and 16 April 1639 (RCBL, C6/1/26/15/6, ff 31–6 and C6/1/26/15/7, ff 29–33); deposition of John Coraghan, 22 January 1638 (RCBL, C6/1/26/15/6, ff 14–18); deposition of Nicholas Coraghan, 16 April 1639 (RCBL, C6/1/26/15/7, ff 17–20); deposition of Patrick Coraghan, 22 January 1638 (RCBL, C6/1/26/15/6, ff 7–9); depositions of William Dollard, 22 January 1638 and 16 April 1639 (RCBL, C6/1/26/15/6, ff 18–21 and C6/1/26/15/7, ff 20–23); deposition of Patrick Mullen, 16 April 1639 (RCBL, C6/1/26/15/7, ff 26–9). 30 Deposition of James Braghall, 22 January 1638 (RCBL, C6/1/26/15/6, f. 25). 31 Deposition of Richard Braghall, 22 January 1638 (RCBL, C6/1/26/15/6, ff 34–5). 32 Deposition of James Braghall, 22 January 1638 (RCBL, C6/1/26/15/6, f. 25); depositions of Richard Braghall, 22 January 1638 and 16 April 1639

Hunt and Nicholas Scanlon provided a degree of continuity from one mering to the other. Apparently some of the witnesses to the later mering were questioned about the presence of the dean of Christ Church since William Dollard, one of the younger witnesses, insisted that 'he saw not nor heard that the dean of Christ Church was at that mering or any other mering', implying that such merings were not unusual occurrences.[33] Speaking of another boundary, that leading from Astagob to Porterstown, one of the witnesses for the plaintiff, the thirty-six-year-old George Hackett, mentioned 'that he had seen it trodden out by ancient men within this few years as the true mere between the plaintiff's and defendant's several lands'.[34] The treading of boundaries was clearly something that happened fairly frequently, though not all merings may have been conducted as seriously and carefully as those which delineated the boundary between Astagob and Ballystrowan/Tirmullen as leading from the Lady Bush (in the highway between Diswellstown and Luttrellstown) to the Three Acres, from thence to the Hoar Acre and from there by an old ditch or trench to the Liffey. The Lady Bush was a focal point in the area, known to all witnesses on both sides, with the possible exception of the chapter clerk, Thomas Howell.

The mering ritual resembled the medieval English custom of the beating of the bounds which has been described as follows:

> A ceremony common in medieval England, and associated with the Rogationtide procession round the parish. When written maps, showing parish boundaries, were hardly known, this annual perambulation was a means of impressing these limits on the minds of the young. The bounds were solemnly beaten with willow rods, and on occasion boys of the parish were also beaten or bumped on the ground at the boundary. The custom is known to date back to the end of the 9th or beginning of the 10th cent. and lasted on long after the religious part of the procession was abolished under Elizabeth.[35]

In January 1638 William Dollard, the smith, stated that 'Sir Christopher Plunket and Mr Thomas Luttrell were then present and sent for this examinant and divers other children that were at school at Clonsilla and were whipped at the mering. But the cause of the mering he knoweth not'.[36] In his second deposition he made it clear that, while he may not have known the cause of the mering, he knew that he had been whipped 'to the end that he might take notice of the mering aforesaid'.[37] Nicholas Coraghan, who attended the second hearing, deposed that 'he, being at school at

(RCBL, C6/1/26/15/6, f. 34 and C6/1/26/15/7, f. 32); deposition of John Coraghan, 22 January 1638 (RCBL, C6/1/26/15/6, f. 16); deposition of Nicholas Coraghan, 16 April 1639 (RCBL, C6/1/26/15/7, f. 19); depositions of William Dollard, 22 January 1638 and 16 April 1639 (RCBL, C6/1/26/15/6, f. 20 and C6/1/26/15/7, f. 22); deposition of Patrick Mullen, 16 April 1639 (RCBL, C6/1/26/15/7, f. 28). 33 Deposition of William Dollard, 16 April 1639 (RCBL, C6/1/26/15/7, f. 22). 34 Deposition of George Hackett, 16 April 1639 (RCBL, C6/1/26/15/5, f. 32). 35 F.L. Cross and E.A. Livingstone (eds), *The Oxford dictionary of the Christian Church* (3rd ed., Oxford, 1997), p. 174. 36 Deposition of William Dollard, 22 January 1638 (RCBL, C6/1/26/15/6, ff 20–1). 37 Deposition of William Dollard, 16 April 1639 (RCBL, C6/1/26/15/7, f. 23).

Clonsilla, was brought to the said mering and was whipped thereat to the end that he should take notice thereof and that there was one William Dollard then also whipped and hath also seen and known what he deposeth to be true'.[38]

Merings were not confined to Fingal but were carried out also in other parts of the country where the common law prevailed. Richard Boyle, earl of Cork, noted merings in his diary on 1 July 1615 and 12 June 1621.[39] On the second of these occasions he recorded the occasion from the landowner's point of view:

> I was present when the bounds and meres between the lands of Affane, called Cooleeryn, and Coolgortbwy belonging to me, and the lands of Farnham belonging to John Fitzgerald of the same, were laid out and cleared, by fourteen of the ancient men and serjeants in those borders, and myself and the said John sworn on a book, to stand to those bounds so laid out, and agreed upon in both our presence, whereunto we did consent.[40]

Alson Luttrell's deposition, supported by those of Richard Lock, Ellen Hackett and her son, George, would have placed the disputed boundaries somewhat further to the west and would have thereby deprived Simon Luttrell of a considerable part of Tirmullen. Richard Lock described the mere as a 'bater (*bóthar*) or lane' running between the lands.[41] Alson Luttrell claimed that the mere ran from the Liffey to a waterway called Tobermatoule, from there to the Tirlagh Bush, from there to 'a new ditch cast up by Alderman Dowde upon the land of Porterstown' and from there to the Lady Bush.[42] Ellen Hackett also claimed that Tobermatoule was the boundary, while George Hackett admitted that he did not know the 'ancient meres and bounds'.[43] Much of the Christ Church case was based on issues relating to place-names, particularly that of Tirmullen, for which a knowledge of Irish was needed. The exact significance of the testimony is unclear since the defendant's lawyers' comments on the plaintiff's evidence are not available. Alson Luttrell clearly did not know Irish but the evidence suggests that the Hacketts, in particular, Ellen, had a competent knowledge of the language.[44] It is of interest that the lawyers for Christ Church assumed that the witnesses would be able to answer questions which required a knowledge of Irish.

Some evidence of land use emerges from the depositions in this case. The area had been mainly used for pasture for cattle and sheep and it was a change of land use to arable farming that sparked off the original complaint of Alson Luttrell when, about three years prior to her testimony (*c.*1636), a mere leading from Tobermatoule to the

38 Deposition of Nicholas Coraghan, 16 April 1639 (RCBL, C6/1/26/15/7, f. 20). **39** Richard Boyle, earl of Cork, *The Lismore papers (first series) viz. autobiographical notes, remembrances and diaries of Sir Richard Boyle, first and 'great' earl of Cork, never before printed*, ed. Alexander B. Grossart (5 vols, London, 1886), i, p. 77 and ii, pp 17–18. **40** Richard Boyle, earl of Cork, *The Lismore papers (first series) viz. autobiographical notes, remembrances and diaries of Sir Richard Boyle, first and 'great' earl of Cork, never before printed*, ed. Alexander B. Grossart (5 vols, London, 1886), ii, pp 17–18. **41** Deposition of Richard Lock, 16 April 1639 (RCBL, C6/1/26/15/5, f. 12). **42** Deposition of Alson Luttrell, 16 April 1639 (RCBL, C6/1/26/15/5, f. 15). **43** Deposition of Ellen Hackett, 16 April 1639 (RCBL, C6/1/26/15/5, f. 20); deposition of George Hackett, 16 April 1639 (RCBL, C6/1/26/15/5, f. 27). **44** Deposition of Ellen Hackett, 16 April 1639 (RCBL, C6/1/26/15/5, f. 24); deposition of George Hackett, 16 April 1639 (RCBL, C6/1/26/15/5, f. 30).

Tirlagh Bush was ploughed up 'by the defendant's servants and oats sowed therein'.[45] The general trend in agriculture in the early years of the seventeenth century was to change from arable farming to pasture.[46] The change in the opposite direction in Luttrellstown was probably prompted by the growing demand for food in the rapidly expanding city of Dublin. The earlier pastoral nature of farming in the area was shown by the response to one of the queries put by the lawyers when several witnesses spoke of the impounding of straying cattle. The young herds spent a good deal of time keeping sheep and cattle from encroaching on neighbours' land in circumstances where the fencing was bad. For example, Nicholas Kelly, speaking of one of the disputed areas called the Cargines, described how he had seen the Astagob tenants' cattle 'sundry times driven off the said Cargines by the defendant's father and grandfather their servants, and that the tenants of Stagob did endeavour to keep their cattle out of the said lands but could not for that there was no ditch between the said several lands to keep out their said cattle'.[47] The local tenants also knew how to exploit their familiarity with the local boundaries to outwit the law. Arguing that the Cargines belonged to Tirmullen (Simon Luttrell's land), Patrick Mullen described how

> about forty-five years sithence he saw the sheriff of the county of Dublin endeavouring to distrain upon the lands of Stagob for some arrears belonging to the church land but the tenants did remove their cattle from thence over the mere of Stagob as belonging to Tirmullen. And further than the mere between Tirmullen and Stagob the said sheriff did not follow the said cattle for he conceived the said lands did not belong to Stagob.[48]

The Fingal landowners took no chances when establishing the boundaries of their lands. In the days before map-making was generally practised, they made use of both eminent lawyers and traditional methods to ensure that the correct boundaries would be properly documented and known to the local community. But the merings had a deeper significance. They forged a bond of interdependence between the landlord and the community. While Simon Luttrell had leases to prove his entitlement to Astagob, he was dependent on those who had witnessed the merings to testify on oath to the precise boundaries to the land, which, to judge by the tone of their depositions, they were quite happy to do. These men were no doubt proud of their standing in the community, and there is no evidence of obsequiousness or a consciousness of subservience in their testimony as it has survived. The presence of a village school in Clonsilla in the early years of the seventeenth century doubtless contributed to their ability to migrate to take up employment elsewhere as adults while, at the same time, fostering a sense of loyalty to their home community. It does not seem altogether too far-fetched to suggest that the absence of Clonsilla names on the lists of outlaws drawn up after the rising of 1641, in which Simon Luttrell played

45 Deposition of Alson Luttrell, 16 April 1639 (RCBL, C6/1/26/15/5, ff 18–19). 46 Raymond Gillespie, *The transformation of the Irish economy, 1550–1700* (Dublin, 1991), p. 33. 47 Deposition of Nicholas Kelly, 16 April 1639 (RCBL, C6/1/26/15/7, ff 12–13). 48 Deposition of Patrick Mullen, 16 April 1639 (RCBL, C6/1/26/15/7, ff 28–9).

no active part, may be a further indication of community solidarity. Of those in Clonsilla parish who were outlawed, Edward Bermingham and Richard Ingle of Coolmine lived in a townland owned by the Protestant, Sir Edward Bolton, while the proprietor of Blakestown (Little Stahenny), where George Fleming, another outlaw, resided, was Mathew Barnewall of Bremore.[49]

Some further evidence of a close relationship between landlord and tenant in Clonsilla is found in one of the early 1641 depositions.[50] The precise circumstance in which the smith, William Dollard, was examined are not known, but he may have been suspected of having information about the rising because of his trade or he may even have volunteered to testify. No evidence has been found to suggest that he himself was involved in the rising, and his name does not appear on the lists of outlaws. On 30 December 1641 William Dollard

> being examined, saith that being in the house of one Richard Braghall of Clonsilla about the middle of this present month there came unto the said house Mr Edward Bermingham of Coolmine and one Best of Tullagh called Colonel Best, who there demanded of the said Braghall's wife what the reason was why her landlord, Mr Luttrell of Luttrellstown, did not ride in arms with the rest of the country gentlemen. And the woman making answer that the said Luttrell her master had reasons known unto himself for his forbearing that course; the said Bermingham and Best replied that he had better part with all he was worth than do as he did by giving up and restoring the king's arms which he once had in his hands. And they further said that the said Mr Luttrell was now making buttons for fear and durst not do as other men did which he would report him of.

Given the circumstances which existed in Fingal at the end of 1641 the answer given by Mrs Braghall to the rebels was highly circumspect. Despite having stood up to the rebels the Braghall family survived the rising. The name of Richard Braghall, gentleman, appeared as a titulado for Clonsilla in the so-called 'census of 1659'.[51] His death occurred before 17 April 1662.[52]

Despite the accusations of cowardice made by Bermingham and Best Simon Luttrell strove to maintain a neutral stance, which was not unhelpful to the rebels, during the conflict. A soldier, Daniel Conway, accused him of having prevented him entering the grounds of Luttrellstown in pursuit of a rebel who had sought refuge there.[53] This action may have contributed to the subsequent decision to transplant Thomas Luttrell, son of Simon, to Connaught, though, according to Francis Elrington Ball, the Luttrell family managed to remain in Dublin during the Commonwealth.[54] Neutrality was no insurance against transplantation. Another

49 R.C. Simington and John MacLellan, 'Oireachtas Library, List of outlaws, 1641–1647' in *Analecta Hibernica*, no. 23 (1966), pp 337 and 340; *Civil Survey, vii, county of Dublin*, pp 232–3. 50 Examination of William Dollard, 30 December 1641 (TCD, MS 809, f. 218). 51 *A census of Ireland* circa *1659* ..., ed. S. Pender (Dublin, 1939), p. 391. 52 Abstract of will of Richard Braghall, proved 17 April 1662 (NAI, Betham genealogical abstracts, prerogative wills, series I, vol 10, p. 156). 53 Examination of Daniel Conway, April 1642 (TCD, MS 810, f. 97). 54 Robert C. Simington, *The transplantation to Connacht 1654–58* (Dublin, 1970), p. 84; Francis Elrington Ball, *A history of the County Dublin ... part*

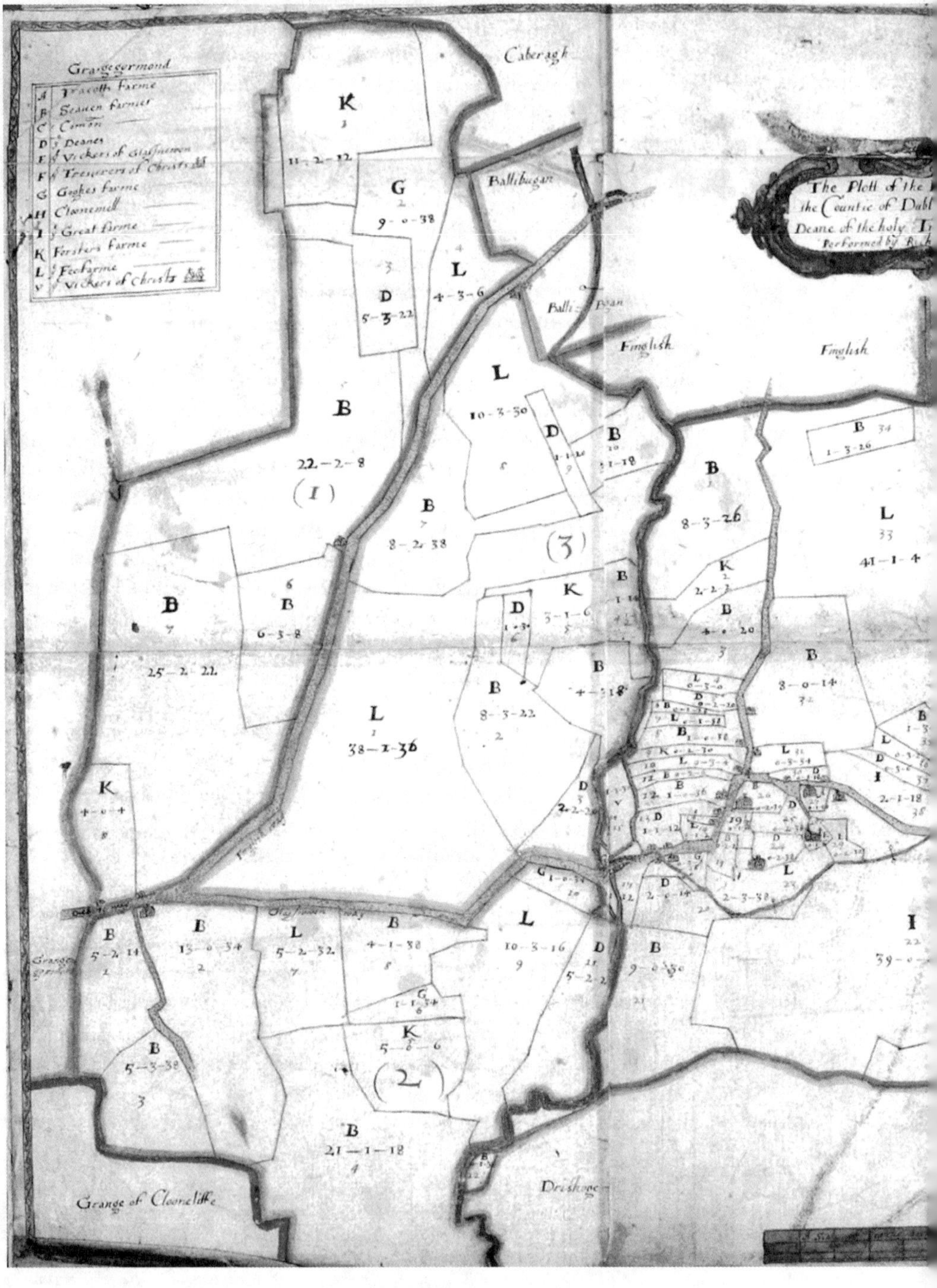

Fig. 3.1 Map of Glasnevin parish, 1640, by Richard Francis

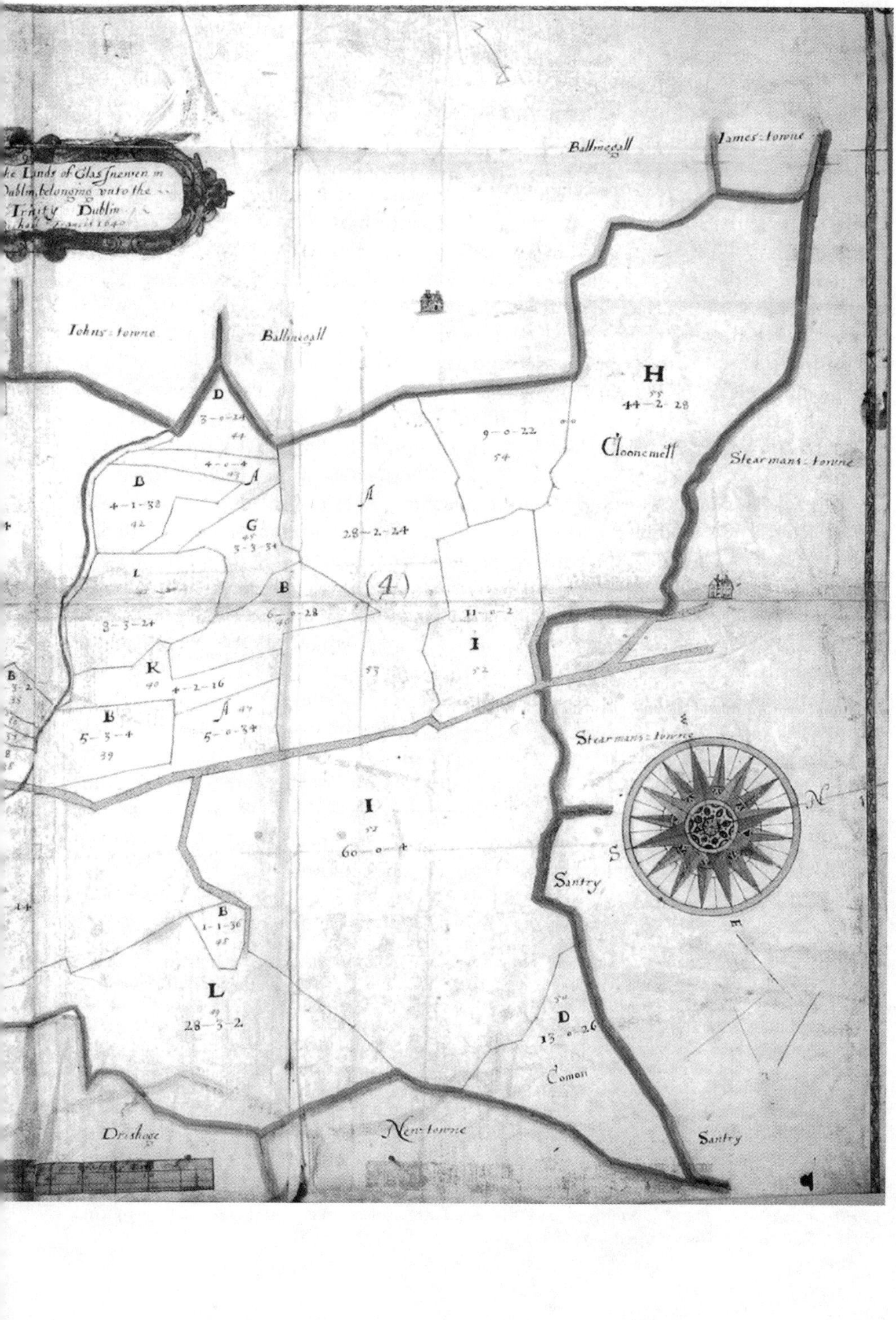
James: towne
Ballmegall
Johns: towne
Ballmegall
H
Cloonemett
Stearmans: towne
Stearmans: towne
(4)
I
I
L
K
Santry
Santry
Coman
New: towne
Drishoge

major Fingal landowner, the Catholic John Talbot of Malahide, whose demesne area remained relatively peaceful during the rising, was outlawed and transplanted to Connaught.[55]

At almost exactly the same time as the disputants in the Clonsilla/Castleknock area and their lawyers were using traditional procedures to resolve a dispute relating to landholding the Christ Church authorities were employing highly sophisticated methods to solve another problem in Glasnevin. The survey of the lands of Glasnevin carried out in 1640 by Richard Francis for the dean and chapter of Christ Church affords us another rare insight into the pattern of early seventeenth-century landholding.[56] This survey was almost certainly carried out in connection with a commission appointed to conduct of valuation of certain lands held by the cathedral.[57] It followed the leasing by the dean to Abraham Tilson, yeoman, of twelve acres of common of pasture in Glasnevin which had been enclosed by John Fagan, tenant to the dean, without his licence and against the covenants of his lease.[58] The Glasnevin lands to be valued included the Great Farm and Seven Farms held by John Fagan, Foster's Farm held by William Ball and the Glasnevin lands held by James Bath. In each of these farms, with the exception of the Great Farm which was situated north of the river, there were lands on both sides of the Tolka. The survey by Richard Francis was extended to include the whole parish of Glasnevin. The survey itself is very detailed and lends itself readily to analysis by means of a computer database. The accompanying map, a reduced copy of which is included as figure 3.1, has a set of alphabetic and numeric keys which facilitate reference to the manuscript tables. The orientation of this map is west-east instead of the more usual north-south. Figure 3.2 is a detail from this map which shows the village of Glasnevin.

The division of land by farm in the Richard Francis survey was compared with that shown in the later Civil Survey.[59] This showed certain discrepancies between the acreages given in the two surveys. The biggest discrepancy arose in the case of the Fee Farm held by James Bath. One possible explanation for this is that the jury contributing to the Civil Survey used a different measure of land from that used by Richard Francis in the case of James Bath's land. An insight into the problem of varying land measures was afforded in 1639 by the testimony of an eighty-year old

fourth (originally published 1906, reprinted Dublin, 1995), p. 13. 55 Joseph Byrne, *War and peace: the survival of the Talbots of Malahide 1641–1671* (Dublin, 1997), pp 37–47. 56 Richard Francis, A survey of the lands of Glassnwen in the county of Dublin belonging unto the deane of the holy trinity Dublin shewing the quantity of acres in every parcel of each severall farme thereof, with the tenantes names, and undertenantes holding the same with the contentes of the lands in their severall divisions, retaineing their true forme and situation in a plot annexed unto the end of this book, distinguished by colours, and letters particular unto each severall farme, with numbers referring unto the divisions thereof, and figures referring likewise unto each particular of the severall farmes therein contained, setting forth the highways and rivers thereof with the true forme of the towne and places of habitation, wth the bounding townes and lands of the bordering neighbours distinguished by their colours, 1640 (RCBL, Christ Church cathedral records, C6/3/1/2). 57 A commission 22 Feb. 15 Charles I [1640] for enquiring into the extent and value of some lands at Glasnevin, the great tithes of Brenanstown and Dalkey and ten acres in Salcock's Wood (RCBL, Christ Church cathedral records, Guard book 7, C6/1/26/7/24). 58 Abstract of lease to Abraham Tilson, 1 May 1639 (RCBL, Christ Church cathedral records, C6/1/17/2, p. 4a); *Christ Church deeds*, ed. M.J. McEnery and Raymond Refaussé (Dublin, 2001), no. 1539. 59 *Civil Survey, vii, county of Dublin,* pp 181–3; 'Fingal 1603–60', i, table 3.4, p. 98.

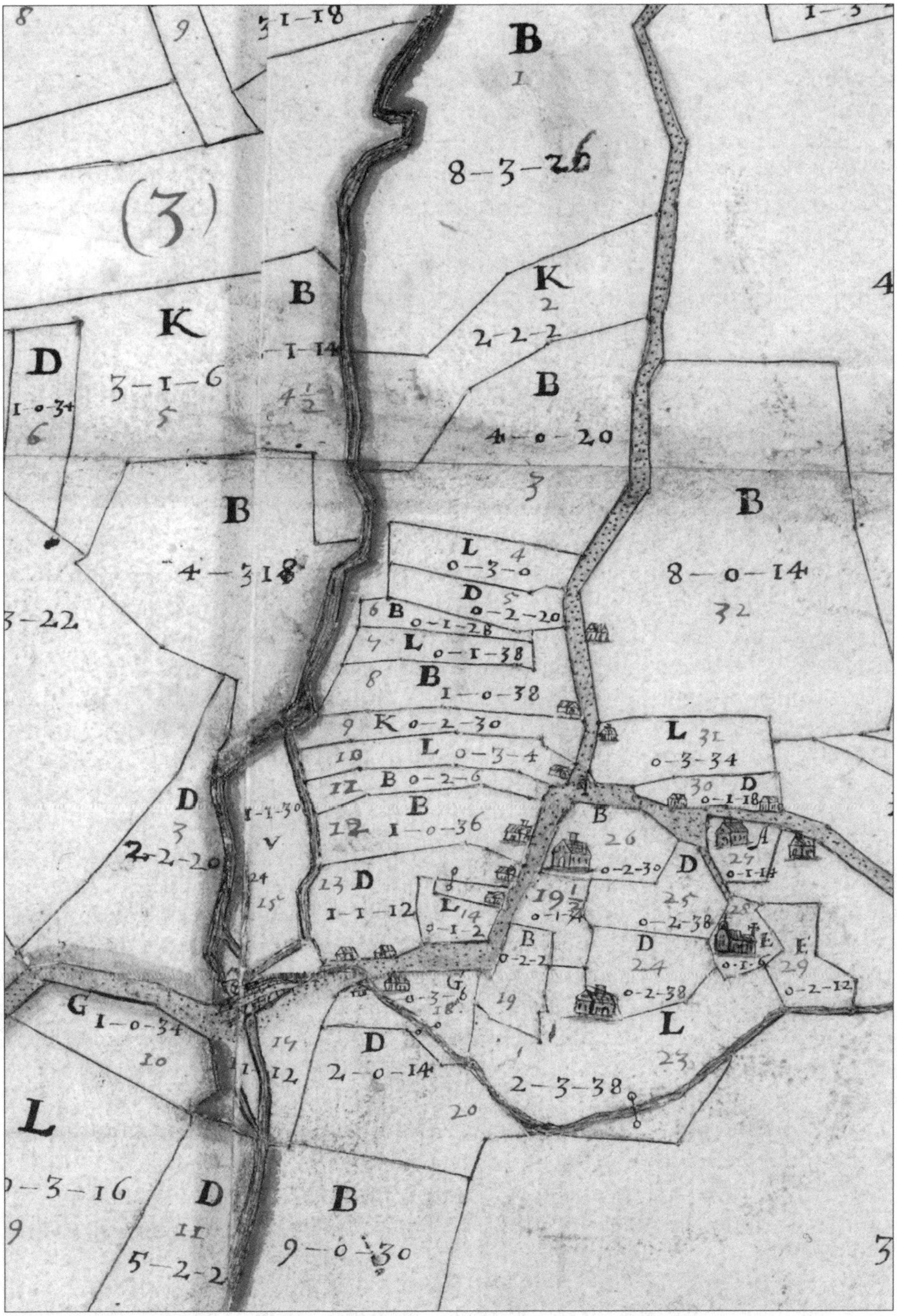

Fig. 3.2 Extract from map of Glasnevin parish, 1640, by Richard Francis showing Glasnevin village

Clonsilla witness, Richard Lock, in the case of Astagob already discussed, who deposed that 'the town and lands of Stagob aforesaid do contain six score acres of land but whether of English or Irish measure he knoweth not'.[60] With the exception of the Dean's Farm, each farm in Glasnevin was leased to a single person.

On the ground the situation was very different. Richard Francis gave each farm an alphabetic key and, as can be seen from his map (fig. 3.1) the parcels which made up the various named farms, with the exception of three of the four parcels which made up Draycott's Farm (A), the two Clonmel parcels (H), and the four parcels which formed the Great Farm (I), were widely scattered and interspersed with parcels which belonged to other farms. It is not possible to say for certain that a parcel was equivalent to a field but this seems likely. The central portion of the parish appears to have been originally composed of a series of strip fields linking the river Tolka with the main highway leading west towards Finglas. Most of the houses were situated on either side of this highway. The shape of some of these strips suggests that some of them may have been subdivided, perhaps to facilitate house building, at an earlier period. As one moved further from the centre of the village towards the parish boundaries the parcels, on the whole, became larger and more irregular in shape. Just beyond the centre of the village there was a fork in the road, as a second highway led north toward Stormanstown and Ballymun. At the southern end of the village, just west of the bridge over the Tolka, the river divided, forming a mill-race. The field enclosed by the river (Clerk's Meadow, V15) was the only area, apart from two small parcels of common land (C17 and C191/2), the churchyard (E28) and the mill land (F16), which was not sub-let. The mill stood just to the west of the bridge at the southern end of the town. The controversial holding which prompted the investigation was almost certainly the Dean's Common (D50) at the extreme north-eastern end of the parish. At the southern (Dublin) end of the parish a road forked east to the Grange of Clonliffe, while a second led west towards Finglas. This southern highway to Finglas by-passed Glasnevin village. Despite its small size, Glasnevin was the centre of a good communications network.

In his description of the survey Richard Francis claimed to have mapped the true form of the town and places of habitation. The houses in the parish can be classified into five groups, a single house on the eastern side of the parish, houses near the southern (Dublin) end of the parish, those on lands close to the church, houses at the western area of the village and those situated in the central area. The single house (L49) on the eastern side was shown in the rural area near the boundary with Santry parish.

At the southern (Dublin) end of the parish, which was also rural, on the eastern side close to the road leading to the Grange of Clonliffe, stood a house let to Robert Bath (B2). On the opposite side of the road there were two houses, one held by George Carruther (B7) and the other, at the parish boundary, on property held by William Ball (K8). William Ball inherited extensive lands, including those in Glasnevin, from his father, Robert, who was listed as proprietor of Ballygall (parish of Finglas) in the Civil Survey, although he had died in 1636 and had left the

60 Deposition of Richard Lock, 16 April 1639 (RCBL, C6/1/26/15/5, f. 13).

Ballygall property to his second wife, Margaret, for life.[61] According to the family history William Ball was living at Ballygall when his marriage to Ellinor, daughter of Christopher Bysse and sister of John, recorder of Dublin, and Robert, took place.[62] The date of this marriage is uncertain, but it certainly took place before August 1642.[63] If William Ball resided at Ballygall, who occupied his house in Glasnevin? This raises the more general question as to whether all the families or, indeed, all the houses in the parish have been accounted for by the survey and map. Two houses were situated on the southern highway to Finglas. One of these (L8), the most westerly house in the parish, was let to Edward Wickam, while Thomas Fleming was the occupier of a house (B1) on the southern side of the road about midway between Wickam's house (L8) and Carruther's (B7).

At the northern end of the village there were five house close to the church. One of these (L23), an isolated house on a parcel bounded to the south by a stream, was leased to, and almost certainly the residence of, Edward Wickam. This stream, which flowed from Ballygall and joined the Tolka near Glasnevin Bridge, forming a natural boundary for several parcels, was still to be seen on John Rocque's map of 1760.[64] The drawing of the house on the map suggests that this may have been a tiled house. Two other houses, on the eastern side of the road leading to Stormanstown, were held respectively by Jenico Preston (A27) and John Richards (I22). On the other side of the road Edward Wickam held two small buildings situated in the same parcel of land (D30).

There were four houses on the more northerly of the two roads leading west to Finglas. Those on the northern side of the road were held by Edward Wickam (L31) and John Coghlan (B32) while those on the southern side were let to Edward Wickam (L10) and Patrick Stronge (B8).

Within the central area of the village there were five houses on the western side of the highway and three to the east. Four of the houses on the western side (D13) were leased to Edward Wickam while the fifth was occupied by Patrick Stronge (B12). On the eastern side two buildings were held by the Widow Gough (G18). The third (B26), probably the largest house in the parish (if the houses were drawn to scale) and which appears to have had a loft, a tiled roof and a brick chimney, was occupied by Patrick Stronge. In fact, this was almost certainly his residence, since Richard Francis identified one of the parcels of common land (C191/2) as 'lying between the houses of Wickam and Stronge'. The second, smaller, parcel of common land (C17) was situated 'on both sides the ford by the mill'.

It seems clear that, despite the detail in Richard Francis's survey, he was concerned mainly with land and that not all the occupants of the houses were accounted for. The survey evidence suggests that Edward Wickam and Patrick Stronge were prominent men within the community who were sub-letting houses. It is also possible, though unlikely, that some houses were leased (separately from the adjoining

61 William Ball Wright, *Ball family records* (York, 1908), pp 24–8 and appendix, pp xx–xxi. 62 William Ball Wright, *Ball family records* (York, 1908), p. 29. 63 Abstract of will of Robert Bysse, junior, 20 August 1642 (NAI, Betham genealogical abstracts, prerogative wills, series I, vol 10, p. 138). 64 *The A to Z of Georgian Dublin: John Rocque's maps of the city in 1756 and the county in 1760*, ed. Paul Ferguson (Lympne Castle, Kent, 1998), p. 26Ca.

land) directly by Christ Church to tenants whose names are unknown. We are, however, faced with a problem. What happened to the two houses with their backsides which were leased directly by Christ Church to Abraham Tilson for 21 years on 3 March 1638?[65] The name of Abraham Tilson does not appear anywhere in Richard Francis's survey. As Henry Tilson held the office of dean in 1638 could this lease and the lease of the disputed Dean's Common have been purely technical or 'paper' leases to a relative, perhaps for legal reasons?

Apart from the church and the mill Richard Francis drew twenty-three buildings, probably all houses, in the parish of Glasnevin. For no apparent reason other than, perhaps, to put the Glasnevin houses into perspective, he also drew Sir James Barry's fine tiled two-storey house at Stormanstown (parish of Santry) on the right-hand side of the map and a second two-storey house, that of Robert Ball, further to the west in Ballygall (parish of Finglas). Robert Ball's 'stone house' was valued by the jury in the Civil Survey at £100 as was Sir James Barry's house, together with its 'one thatched house and some few cottages'.[66] There is no information about the Glasnevin buildings in the Civil Survey but, by 1664 there were ten occupiers only listed in the hearth money roll each assessed on a single hearth, but after a lapse of twenty-four years not one of the surnames identified by Richard Francis remained in the parish or, if they did, those who bore them were either very poor or were tax evaders.[67] In *Southern Fingal* Francis Elrington Ball gave some support to the latter interpretation. Using sources in the Public Record Office which no longer survive he commented:

> ... in 1667 the householders are stated to have increased to twenty-four, and three houses were rated for two hearths and an oven each, and three for two hearths each. For the former three Alderman Hutchinson was rated, but in the case of the latter three William Cooper, John Griffin, and John Allen are returned as the occupants.[68]

If the two sets of hearth money rolls represent a true reflection of the situation, Glasnevin must have undergone a remarkable transformation both in the quality and quantity of its buildings within the space of three years. It seems much more likely that the area was under-assessed in 1664 and that some small improvement in quality had taken place between 1640 and 1667.

Little further is known about those who lived or held property in Glasnevin in 1640 apart from William Ball, whose career has been documented and who died in 1649.[69] 'Richard Stronge of Glasnevin', who was probably the son of Patrick Stronge, was accused by Robert Benion of Dublin of being involved, together with other rebels, including the Longs of Abbotstown and the Freinds of Dunsink, in

65 Abstract of lease to Abraham Tilson, 3 March 1638 (RCBL, Christ Church cathedral records, C6/1/17/2, p. 4a); *Christ Church deeds*, ed. M.J. McEnery and Raymond Refaussé (Dublin, 2001), no. 1537. 66 *Civil Survey, vii, county of Dublin,* pp 146 and 200. 67 'Hearth money roll for County Dublin, 1664' (second part), *Journal of the County Kildare Archaeological Society*, xi (1930–33), p. 398. 68 Francis Elrington Ball, *Southern Fingal* ... (originally published 1920, reprinted Dublin, 1995), p. 128. 69 William Ball Wright, *Ball family records* (York, 1908), pp 26 and 28–30.

taking twenty English cows, one mare and a nag worth about £40 from him on Trinity Sunday 1642 and of participation in several other raids.[70] A much more serious accusation was made by Richard Swinson that, in January 1643 at Meakstown, several named rebels including 'Walter Clench and Richard Stronge, then both of Cappagh, farmers, but the said Richard Stronge now liveth with his mother at Glasnevin', had blinded him in one eye and later shot an Irishman and hanged three Englishmen at Piercetown leaving them unburied.[71] Richard Stronge's name does not appear on the lists of outlaws probably because the accusations were not made formally until 1645. Even worse was to follow. Richard Stronge was one of the ring leaders in the raid at the Forrest near Swords in 1650 in which several men, including the son and nephew of Justice Donnellan, were killed.[72] His fate is unknown. Patrick Stronge of Glasnevin, described as a 'farmer', died intestate in or before 1662.[73]

Three further residents of Glasnevin, Elizabeth Doyle, William Robban and Garrett Toole, who were outlawed at Kilmainham on 18 November 1643, have not been identified.[74] The name 'Garrett Toole' may provide a link with a James Toole who, according to the Christ Church deeds was resident in Glasnevin in 1572.[75] Other residents mentioned in the same deed had the surnames, Doyne, Webb, Quatermas, Swane and Man. A striking feature of early-modern Glasnevin is the turnover of surnames over a relatively short period. The surname, Toole, is a notable exception. This lack of continuity in family names suggests that the population actually resident in Glasnevin, especially at the lower levels of the social scale, was, if anything, even more mobile than that in Clonsilla.

The Richard Francis survey showed that the leasing pattern in general was extraordinarily complex and led to situations where the actual occupiers of the land were not those who had leased it from Christ Church.[76] Religion does not appear to have been a major factor in the leasing or sub-letting of land in Glasnevin before 1640.

Since Glasnevin parish belonged in its entirety to Christ Church, the land was classified in the Down Survey as 'unforfeited'.[77] Therefore no further information about land quality can be obtained from that source. It is, however, possible to form a picture of the economic life of the area by examining some of the Christ Church deeds. While many of the leases mentioned were drawn up in the sixteenth century, in most cases they extended into the seventeenth century. The shortage of timber in Glasnevin as in Fingal in general, was reflected in some of these deeds. For example,

70 Deposition of Robert Benion, 25 July 1645 (copy only) (TCD, MS 810, f. 62). 71 Deposition of Richard Swinson, 28 July 1645 (TCD, MS 810, f. 325). 72 Examination of Robert Boylan, 6 November 1652 (TCD, MS 810, f. 334); examination of Nicholas Bellew, 17 November 1652 (TCD, MS 810, f. 351); examination of Andrew Gyraght, 2 February 1653 (TCD, MS 810, f. 357); examination of Thomas Waltryn, 1 February 1653 (TCD, MS 810, f. 375); examination of John Confy, 1 February 1653 (TCD, MS 810, f. 377); examination of Patrick Maguire, not dated (TCD, MS 810, f. 379); examination of John Heard, 24 November 1652 (TCD, MS 810, f. 380). 73 Deputy keeper of public records in Ireland, *Appendix to the twenty-sixth report* (Dublin, 1894), p. 819. 74 R.C. Simington and John MacLellan, 'Oireachtas Library, List of outlaws, 1641–1647' in *Analecta Hibernica*, no. 23 (1966), pp 340, 343 and 345. 75 *Christ Church deeds*, ed. M.J. McEnery and Raymond Refaussé (Dublin, 2001), no. 1325. 76 For a full discussion see 'Fingal 1603–60', i, pp 103–12. 77 Map of the barony of Coolock, Down Survey parish maps … (NLI, MS 714).

even in the first half of the sixteenth century, a general lease of the manor constrained the dean to allow yearly to the tenants two ash-trees for making cartwheels.[78] In return the tenants were required to plant twenty ash trees every year in convenient places of the manor, none of which, or other great trees, were to be cut down without leave of the dean or his successors. John Raghty (or Raghter), a shearman, who received a lease for thirty-one years in 1585 for two houses and just two acres of land with pasturage rights on the common was required to 'set one hundred of ashes in the backside and about the said ground and premises within [the first] four years of this term'.[79] Richard Fagan who received a lease of the Great Farm in 1592 for 119 years was required to plant six ash-trees yearly.[80]

Tenants were also required to supply men to work for Christ Church on lands which were reserved and which had not been let. Giollachríost O Cane, a tailor, who had the lease of a property near Glasnevin bridge was required to supply two men to reap the dean's harvest for one day each year and to supply them with meat and drink.[81] The provision of men to work for the landlord at harvest either by contributing a certain number of days or by reaping one or more ridges was frequently specified in leases.[82] A variation on this practice is found in the archbishop's leases of land in Finglas. For example, in a lease dated 1 February 1594 to Robert Leycester it was specified that he should 'send unto the said lord archbishop and his successors at their pleasure to the manor of Tallaght six able men to reap corn one day in harvest every year during the said term if they be demanded'.[83]

The Christ Church authorities also prescribed some of the work that had to be carried out on the tenant's land in order that tillage might be maximized. Kerrol Doyne was required to sow his nine acres for three seasons so that tithes might grow to the vicar as had grown from them in times past.[84] When Richard Fagan received a lease of the Seven Farms in 1592 for ninety-one years he was required to plough and manure as much land as was then ploughed.[85] Provisions to ensure tillage were also made in 1594 in leases of Draycott's Farm and Foster's Farm for ninety-nine years to Arland Ussher and Alderman John Foster.[86] A more precise indication of the

78 Abstract of lease to Thomas, Alson and Oliver Stephens, 10 June 1542 (RCBL, Christ Church cathedral records, C6/1/17/2, p. 2). 79 Abstract of lease to John Raghty, 12 February 1585 (RCBL, Christ Church cathedral records, C6/1/17/2, p. 3); *The first chapter act book of Christ Church cathedral, Dublin 1574–1634*, ed. Raymond Gillespie (Dublin, 1997), p. 49; *Christ Church deeds*, ed. M.J. McEnery and Raymond Refaussé (Dublin, 2001), no. 1369. 80 Abstract of lease to Richard Fagan, 6 June 1592 (RCBL, Christ Church cathedral records, C6/1/17/2, p. 4); *The first chapter act book of Christ Church cathedral, Dublin 1574–1634*, ed. Raymond Gillespie (Dublin, 1997), p. 79; *Christ Church deeds*, ed. M.J. McEnery and Raymond Refaussé (Dublin, 2001), no. 1404. 81 Abstract of lease to Giollachríost O Cane, 10 October 1558 (RCBL, Christ Church cathedral records, C6/1/17/2, p. 2); *Christ Church deeds*, ed. M.J. McEnery and Raymond Refaussé (Dublin, 2001), no. 1256. 82 *Christ Church deeds*, ed. M.J. McEnery and Raymond Refaussé (Dublin, 2001), nos. 1263, 1355, 1358, 1369 and 1426. 83 Copy lease to Robert Leycester, 1 February 1594 (RCBL, Records of the archbishop of Dublin, D6/76/10/3). 84 Abstract of lease to Kerrol Doyne, 20 November 1581(RCBL, Christ Church cathedral records, C6/1/17/2, p. 3); *The first chapter act book of Christ Church cathedral, Dublin 1574–1634*, ed. Raymond Gillespie (Dublin, 1997), p. 39; *Christ Church deeds*, ed. M.J. McEnery and Raymond Refaussé (Dublin, 2001), no. 1358. 85 Abstract of lease to Richard Fagan, 12 February 1592 (RCBL, Christ Church cathedral records, C6/1/17/2, p. 4). 86 Abstracts of leases to Arland Ussher, 31 July 1594 and John Foster, 21 December 1594 (RCBL, Christ Church cathedral records, C6/1/17/2, p. 5); *The first chapter act book of Christ Church cathedral, Dublin, 1574–1634*, ed. Raymond Gillespie (Dublin, 1997), p. 89; *Christ Church deeds*, ed. M.J. McEnery and Raymond Refaussé (Dublin, 2001), nos. 1417 and 1426.

type of cereal produce grown can be found in the lease of the Great Farm to Richard Fagan for 119 years in 1592.[87] The great tithes of the farm were also demised to Richard Fagan but he was required to pay for them 'twenty pecks of good sound corn, viz., ten pecks of good sound wheat and bearmalt, and ten pecks of good sweet sound oatmalt of like measure as now they use to receive of other farmers ...'

The almost invariable inclusion in leases of a provision for the payment of watch hens at Christmas indicates the importance of poultry-keeping in the Glasnevin economy. In leases made in 1581 and 1638 to Laurence Enos and Abraham Tilson, yeoman, of the same two messuages and backsides, the tenants were required to pay yearly, in addition to the watch hens, four capons on Trinity Sunday.[88] Perhaps this reflected a specialization in poultry-keeping on this holding. While the keeping of other livestock was permitted it does not seem to have been encouraged except on the common land. In this respect Glasnevin differed considerably from the Castleknock/Clonsilla area.

The other major holdings of Christ Church in Grangegorman and Balscaddan displayed a similar pattern. There was a similar emphasis on the conservation of trees.[89] In Balscaddan geese and capons tended to be substituted for watch hens.[90] Many leases contained clauses which constrained tenants to find accommodation for men or boys and horses for one or two nights at Christmas.[91] This may suggest the lease of a tavern or alehouse but in no case has this been confirmed. Sometimes the demands made on tenants were more onerous. For example, in a fee-farm grant of Tobertown and other properties John Finglas of Tobersool (Balscaddan) was required to find meat drink and lodging for the dean and seneschal of Christ Church and their horses during such convenient time as they should come and remain there for keeping court twice a year.[92]

A high proportion of the land in Fingal was held by the established church. Raymond Gillespie has discussed the measures taken by the authorities of Christ Church Cathedral to tackle two economic problems which beset the authorities of the established church in the early seventeenth century, namely, long leases and low rents.[93] An attempt was made to analyze and quantify the position as regards church

87 Abstract of lease to Richard Fagan, 6 June 1592 (RCBL, Christ Church cathedral records, C6/1/17/2, p. 4); *The first chapter act book of Christ Church cathedral, Dublin 1574–1634*, ed. Raymond Gillespie (Dublin, 1997), pp 78–9; *Christ Church deeds*, ed. M.J. McEnery and Raymond Refaussé (Dublin, 2001), no. 1404. 88 Abstracts of leases to Laurence Enos, 1 July 1581 and Abraham Tilson, 3 March 1638 (RCBL, Christ Church cathedral records, C6/1/17/2, pp 4a and 13); *Christ Church deeds*, ed. M.J. McEnery and Raymond Refaussé (Dublin, 2001), nos. 1355 and 1537. 89 For example, copy of lease to Mathew King, 31 December 1543 (RCBL, Christ Church cathedral records, C6/1/26/1, f. 3); abstract of lease to George Taaffe, 10 February 1547 (RCBL, Christ Church cathedral records, C6/1/17/2, p. 41). 90 For example, abstract of lease to George Taaffe, 10 February 1547 (RCBL, Christ Church cathedral records, C6/1/17/2, p. 41); abstract of lease to John Kelly, 1 March 1559 (RCBL, Christ Church cathedral records, C6/1/17/2, p. 42). 91 For example, abstract of lease to John Raghty, 12 February 1585 (RCBL, Christ Church cathedral records, C6/1/17/2, p. 3); *The first chapter act book of Christ Church cathedral, Dublin 1574–1634*, ed. Raymond Gillespie (Dublin, 1997), p. 49; *Christ Church deeds*, ed. M.J. McEnery and Raymond Refaussé (Dublin, 2001), no. 1369. 92 Abstract of lease to John Finglas, 17 February 1575 (RCBL, Christ Church cathedral records, C6/1/17/2, p. 44); *Christ Church deeds*, ed. M.J. McEnery and Raymond Refaussé (Dublin, 2001), no. 1342. 93 Raymond Gillespie, 'The crisis of reform, 1625–60' in Kenneth Milne (ed.), *Christ Church cathedral, Dublin: a history* (Dublin, 2000), pp 200–1.

lands in Fingal.[94] This analysis was biased towards the Christ Church lands since more information has survived concerning these than exists for the other major clerical landholder in the region, the archbishop of Dublin. Much of the material relating to the Christ Church property is contained in the published volume of *Christ Church Deeds*.[95] This can be supplemented from other information in the Representative Church Body Library such as the summary extracts from a volume which no longer exists and which is referred to as 'the small old register'.

If, however, the leases are divided into those which were granted before the accession of James I and those granted after that date the position is even more stark.[96] On 28 February 1603 the lords of the council in England wrote to Lord Mountjoy and the Irish council expressing concern about 'the great wrong which hath been done unto the cathedral church of the blessed Trinity commonly called Christ Church in Dublin in the aliening and granting away, and long leasing, without the founders' consent or licence of a great part of the land and titles and duties thereof by the former deans and chapters'.[97] This marked the start of a change of practice as far as Christ Church was concerned. Whereas only 9 per cent of the leases in the sample granted during the Elizabethan period were for less than forty years, 79 percent of those granted during the Stuart period were for less than forty years. In fact, all but five of the leases granted during the Stuart period were for twenty-one years or less, and, of the five which exceeded twenty-one years four related to the archbishop's lands. This shortening of leases represented a diminution of security of tenure, not just for those immediately affected, but also for the many tenants whose leases were due to run out in what was for them the foreseeable future.

The position regarding rents is even more difficult to quantify since, not only were there few renewals but where these occurred, they did not always represent exactly the same properties. For example, the first lease may have been in respect of one particular farm but in the second lease the original farm may have been combined with a second farm for which earlier particulars no longer exist or cannot be identified with certainty. If, as was usual, the rents were aggregated on the second occasion it is not possible to compare like with like. For the purpose of ascertaining if there were significant rent increases in Fingal such grants have had to be discarded. This leaves a very small usable sample restricted to Astagob and Diswellstown (674 per cent increase), Glasnevin – Joye's holdings (55 per cent increase), Finglas – Kilshane (311 per cent increase) and Finglas – Barrett's Land (no increase).[98]

The tenant of Kilshane when the rent was raised was Richard Bellings, who later became secretary to the Catholic confederation.[99] Alson Luttrell, with whom the 1637 lease of Astagob and Diswellstown was concluded, was declared an 'innocent' in 1663.[100] Dudley Boswell, to whom the lease of Barrett's Land was granted, was prebendary of St John's.[101]

94 'Fingal 1603–60', i, table 3.13, p. 116. 95 *Christ Church deeds*, ed. M.J. McEnery and Raymond Refaussé (Dublin, 2001). 96 'Fingal 1603–60', i, table 3.14, p. 117. 97 Lords of the council in England to Lord Mountjoy and the council in Ireland, 28 February 1603 (RCBL, Christ Church cathedral records, C6/1/26/2/6). 98 'Fingal 1603–60', i, table 3.15, p. 118. 99 Second chapter act book (copy) (RCBL, Christ Church cathedral records, C6/1/8/2, p. 80). 100 'Abstract of the decrees of the court of claimes for the tryall of Innocents' in Deputy keeper of public records in Ireland, *Nineteenth report* (Dublin, 1887), appendix, p. 43. 101 *The first chapter act book of Christ Church cathedral, Dublin,*

The state papers listed the names of others affected by rent increases on the Fingal estates belonging to the archbishop of Dublin calculated *c.*1637.[102] The percentage rent increases ranged from 122 per cent to 1,500 per cent. An interesting feature of this list was that it contained the names of several persons subsequently outlawed for their part in the 1641 rising, namely, Laurence Bellings, George Blackney, John Finglas, Thomas Fitzsimons and Richard Jorden.[103] James Plunket was almost certainly the son of Sir Christopher Plunket of Dunsoghly.[104] Though he did not himself appear on the list of outlaws, his brother, Richard, who was a prominent officer in the confederate army, appeared on the list published by John Gilbert.[105] William Horish was granted a sixty-one year lease of parcels of land in Swords and Lusk in 1607.[106] These parcels have not been identified for 1641 in the Civil Survey. It is possible that William died before that date. Several members of the Horish family of Ballyboghil, though none with the Christian name, William, appeared on the list of outlaws.[107] Mary Taylor and Pat Kennedy have not been identified.

Given the low base of the rents set in the original leases, the rent increases shown in the foregoing tables may not have been unreasonable. However, in the eyes of those who had to pay them they must have appeared excessive and, taken together with the shortening of the length of Christ Church leases, they must have had a severe effect on the morale, as well as the standard of living, of tenants over a wide area of Fingal.

Tithes were another source of grievance to those who owned and worked the land. Prior to 1641, the overwhelmingly Catholic population of Fingal had to support two groups of clergy, the clergy of the established church and their own pastors. As the number of Catholic priests increased due to the success of seminaries on the continent as well as the missionary work of the regular clergy, the financial burden became even greater. Where the owners of the tithes were Catholics, they could use some at least of the proceeds to support their own clergy. The position as regards tithes in 1630 and 1654–6 was examined.[108] The 1630 data were derived from the report on Archbishop Bulkeley's visitation of 1630.[109] A striking feature of this report was the large number of parishes for which no information was available or, if available, was not stated. The Civil Survey returns of 1654–6 showed that Catholic proprietors had an interest in tithes in something over one-third of the parishes but in some of these cases the interest was shared with Protestant proprietors.[110] The conclusion is that, while tithes in general were a burden, they represented a significant drain on the resources of Catholics in about two-thirds of the parishes.

One of the most important benefits of the rich land of Fingal was the employment

1574–1634, ed. Raymond Gillespie (Dublin, 1997), p. 193. **102** 'A true note of the ancient rent received by the archbishop of Dublin and of the increase of rent upon composition by virtue of a reference of the lord deputy to the bishop of Derry, dated 17 Feb. 1637' 4 August 1637 in *Cal. S. P. Ire., 1633–47*, pp 165–6; 'Fingal 1603–60', i, table 3.16, p. 119. **103** R.C. Simington and John MacLellan, 'Oireachtas Library, List of outlaws, 1641–1647' in *Analecta Hibernica*, no. 23 (1966), pp 337, 338, 340 and 342. **104** Griffith, *Inquisitions*, pp 456–8. **105** John T. Gilbert (ed.), *History of the Irish confederation and the war in Ireland, 1641–3 ...* (7 vols, Dublin, 1882–91), iii, p. 376. **106** *The first chapter act book of Christ Church cathedral, Dublin, 1574–1634*, ed. Raymond Gillespie (Dublin, 1997), pp 121–2. **107** R.C. Simington and John MacLellan, 'Oireachtas Library, List of outlaws, 1641–1647' in *Analecta Hibernica*, no. 23 (1966), p. 341. **108** 'Fingal 1603–60', i, tables 3.17 and 3.18, pp 121–2. **109** 'Archbishop Bulkeley's visitation of Dublin, 1630', ed. M.V. Ronan in *Archivium Hibernicum*, viii (1941), pp 56–98. **110** *Civil Survey, vii, county of Dublin*, ed. R.C. Simington (Dublin, 1945).

which it provided. Apart from the occasional reference to 'servants' in the 1641 depositions, it is difficult to obtain any kind of picture of the level of employment. What, for example, was the ratio of permanent employees to seasonal workers? Did the pattern of employing seasonal workers from south Ulster at harvest time, which obtained in later centuries, exist in the seventeenth century? How dependent was the economy on the contribution of women and children? It has not been possible to arrive at answers to these questions. Just one indicator of how important people were to the land-based economy has been found for Fingal. A single document in the Representative Church Body Library lists the distribution of the effects of Henry Freind (or Frend) of Dunsink, who died in or prior to 1645.[111] This document raises a number of question, not least of which is how it found its way into the Christ Church papers. Henry Freind was not a proprietor in his own right in Fingal nor does his name appear as a proprietor in Esker parish in the Civil Survey.[112] It is possible that he rented land south of the Liffey from Christ Church although his name cannot be traced in the *Christ Church deeds.* He belonged to a well-known Dunsink family, whose members played a prominent part in the 1641 rising and were among the most frequently mentioned rebels in the 1641 depositions.[113] Two Christian names, Henry (gentleman) and Richard (yeoman), appeared on the list of outlaws, while two names, Lieutenant Richard and Nicholas (farmers), were mentioned in the depositions. In two of the depositions, the expression 'Freind of Dunsink' was deemed sufficient to identify the person referred to, and in one case there was a reference to 'Freind and his son of Dunsink, farmers', while in another deposition they were described as 'tenants to the honourable Sir George Wentworth'.[114] This is somewhat puzzling, as the Civil Survey designated Sir Robert Loftus as the proprietor of Dunsink.[115] The property may have been sub-let to Sir George Wentworth. Since Henry Freind was described as a 'gentleman', it seems likely that he was head of the household and that at least one of the two, Richard or Nicholas, was a son of his. The Civil Survey stated that there were five or six small cottages in Dunsink in 1654–6.[116] There was no mention of houses of office or of ruined buildings which might have suggested an off-farm enterprise. Had Henry or a member of his family had an occupation other than that of farmer, it is likely that it would have been mentioned in the list of outlaws. The evidence suggests that Henry Freind was no higher in the landed hierarchy than a sub-tenant, but nevertheless he employed at least ten people, some of whom may have been relatives.[117]

111 Account of the distribution of the effects of Henry Freind (RCBL, Christ Church cathedral records, C6/1/26/6/42, f. 42). 112 *Civil Survey, vii, county of Dublin,* p. 307. 113 Deposition of John Smith, 19 January 1642 (TCD, MS 809, f. 222); deposition of Thomas Smith, 20 January 1642 (TCD, MS 809, f. 224); deposition of Robert Cullen, 7 February 1642 (TCD, MS 809, f. 270); deposition (copy) of Robert Benion, 25 July 1645 (TCD, MS 810, f. 62); deposition of Thomas Waller, 29 March 1642 (TCD, MS 810, f. 187); deposition of Richard Swinson, 28 July 1645 (TCD, MS 810, f. 325); John T. Gilbert (ed.), *History of the Irish confederation and the war in Ireland, 1641–3* ... (7 vols, Dublin, 1882–91), iii, p. 361; R.C. Simington and John MacLellan, 'Oireachtas Library, List of outlaws, 1641–1647' in *Analecta Hibernica*, no. 23 (1966), pp 340–1. 114 Deposition of John Smith, 19 January 1642 (TCD, MS 809, f. 222); deposition of Thomas Smith, 20 January 1642 (TCD, MS 809, f. 224); deposition of Thomas Waller, 29 March 1642 (TCD, MS 810, f. 187); deposition of Richard Swinson, 28 July 1645 (TCD, MS 810, f. 325). 115 *Civil Survey, vii, county of Dublin,* p. 249. 116 *Civil Survey, vii, county of Dublin,* p. 249. 117 'Fingal 1603–60', i, table 3.19, p. 125.

Some of the agricultural produce of Fingal was consumed by the farmers, their families and their servants. Some was surrendered to the landlords or to holders of tithes. Some was exported. It seems reasonable, however, to suggest that the vast bulk of it was disposed of at the various fairs which took place occasionally or at weekly markets.

The rural economy of Fingal was traditional and highly complex. There is evidence not just of estates made up of widely-scattered holdings but also of large-scale sub-letting of property to such an extent that, in the Civil Survey, lay people were described as the 'proprietors' of what were clearly church lands. The success of the economy depended on mutual cooperation between landlord and tenant, supported by a system of manor courts, as well on as the availability of external markets. As Dublin city grew so did the prospects for greater economic prosperity for rural Fingal. Relationships between landlords and tenants were generally good where they were of the same religion. Where there was a difference it was usually possible to find a *modus operandi* as happened in Glasnevin but there existed an underlying tension which surfaced when the 1641 rising broke out. While the shortening of leases of church lands and the general raising of rents in the late 1630s was somewhat mitigated by the fact that few leases actually fell due for renewal during that period, the threat to security of tenure was enormous since many more proprietors than those immediately affected faced the prospect of rent increases within a short time. Tithes were a significant burden for Catholic tenants, in particular. However, the war which broke out in 1641 and the confiscations which followed interrupted the relatively peaceful coexistence between landlord and tenant families which had lasted for centuries in many cases. The outcome of the 1641 rising brought uncertainty in place of stability to Fingal.

4

'Neptune's neighbour'

> Whereas Edward Hollywood, customer of the country shambles, hath been an humble petitioner unto the said assembly, praying that the free butchers of this city that repair to the country shambles on market days to sell flesh, might be compelled to pay such customs as the country butchers do: it is therefore agreed, by the said authority, that all such free butchers as resort to the country shambles to sell any flesh shall pay all such custom as foreign butchers do ...[1]

This quotation from the Dublin assembly roll, 1622, one of the records of the meetings of the corporation of Dublin, is a reminder of the close relationship that existed between Dublin city and its hinterland in early modern Ireland. Fingal and Dublin city were interdependent. The city relied on supplies from Fingal and regulated its affairs in such a way as to accommodate the needs of farmers and others bringing goods from the countryside while Dublin city was one of the conduits through which goods as well as ideas from abroad reached Fingal.

As has been shown in chapter 2, Fingal towns were small by modern standards. Swords, Lusk and Balrothery were ancient towns, and by the seventeenth century Swords had borough status with the privilege of sending two members to parliament. Both Swords and Lusk were manor towns and came within the purview of the archbishop of Dublin. Apart from a seneschal who presided over the manor court on behalf of the archbishop the towns had a structure of officials to ensure that the law and civic regulations were enforced. The late sixteenth-century Court book of the liberty of Saint Sepulchre provides some insight into this structure. The following is a modernized version of an entry which appeared in the Court book for December 1587:

> Presented by Patrick Blackney, bailiff, that he, distraining a garron for the lord's rent arrear upon Francus's messuage, that William Maghery of Swords contemptuously did rescue the said distress from the bailiff and sergeant. The said Patrick called for aid to the portreeve, Robert Dowding, who likewise refused to assist him.[2]

While cooperation between the elected and appointed officials may have left something to be desired the turnover of personnel suggests that the corporation of the

1 Dublin assembly roll, 1622, *Anc. rec. Dublin*, iii, p. 148. 2 *Court book of the liberty of Saint Sepulchre* ..., ed. Herbert Wood (Dublin, 1930), p. 46.

borough of Swords was reasonably active. Only three years later, in April 1590, the portreeve (or mayor) of Swords was Thomas Bellings while the bailiff (or sheriff) was William Horish.[3] They were supported by six constables: John Gavin and Patrick Dowde for Swords, Nicholas Butrbey and Michael Fleming for the north of Swords and Richard Foster and Richard Motten for the south part. In 1586 two bailiffs, the 'churchon' (churchwarden?) and John Field, the younger, as well as two constables, John Gower of Rathluckstown (probably Rallekaystown) and John Dermot of the Rowans were listed for Lusk.[4] By April 1590 Lusk had four constables: James Humphrey and Richard Wade for the east side and Patrick Harford and Nicholas Donnell for the west side. James Humphrey and John Farnelle were listed as bailiffs of Lusk at another meeting of the manor court on the same day.[5] In April 1589 John Patrick was listed as constable of Finglas while at the same court session James Regan appears to have been appointed to replace him.[6] The constables of Clonmethan (Richard Quatermas) and Portraine (Martin Giblin) were present at the manor court in Swords on 27 April 1590. There was also a gaol in Swords but it is not clear if a gaoler was employed or if the office was discharged by one of the other functionaries.[7]

While the archbishop of Dublin was the ultimate proprietor of much of the town of Swords, the borough appears to have encroached on the lands of other proprietors by the seventeenth century, although the precise boundaries of this unwalled town have not been determined. Propertyholding within the town was at least as complex as that shown for Glasnevin in the previous chapter. Some idea of this complexity can be gained by examining details of contemporary maps (see figures 4.1 and 4.2).[8]

Even outside the lands that fell within the jurisdiction of institutions of the established church, local government in Fingal was no doubt influenced by the expertise provided by the many Dublin aldermen who had homes or property within the territory. Information on the Fingal lands owned by aldermen in the late sixteenth and early seventeenth centuries has been provided by Colm Lennon.[9] The names of those who held land in 1641 included Sir James Barry, Robert Arthur, Patrick Gough and Charles Foster.[10] During the period 1603–60 certain recorders (chief legal officers) or former recorders of Dublin city, such as Richard Bolton, William Dongan and John Bysse, also held land in the area. Newcomers to the area, such as English and Welsh Protestant clergymen, as well as Catholic priests returning from the Continent, in particular, the Jesuits and the Capuchins, brought with them rich and diverse experiences of urban life which they had acquired abroad, often in large

3 *Court book of the liberty of Saint Sepulchre ...*, ed. Herbert Wood (Dublin, 1930), p. 68. 4 *Court book of the liberty of Saint Sepulchre ...*, ed. Herbert Wood (Dublin, 1930), p. 4. 5 *Court book of the liberty of Saint Sepulchre ...*, ed. Herbert Wood (Dublin, 1930), p. 59. 6 *Court book of the liberty of Saint Sepulchre ...*, ed. Herbert Wood (Dublin, 1930), pp 51 and 54. 7 *Court book of the liberty of Saint Sepulchre ...*, ed. Herbert Wood (Dublin, 1930), p. 69. 8 The barrony of Nethercross in the county of Dublin (Down Survey baronial maps, 1657, reproduced Ordnance Survey Office, 1908, from the originals in the Bibliothèque Nationale, Paris); The plott of severall farmes in ye county of Dublin, Barrony Neithercross and parish of Swords called by the severall names of Fitzsimmons his farme, Gough his farme, Damgood Meade, Nevingstowne, with a Farme called Gillingstowne performed by John Tormer, 1656 (RCBL, Records of the archbishop of Dublin, D6, map no. 3). 9 Colm Lennon, *The lords of Dublin in the age of reformation* (Dublin, 1989), appendix 2, pp 223–76. 10 *Civil Survey, vii, county of Dublin*, pp 34, 59, 71 and 201.

Fig. 4.1 The barony of Nethercross in the county of Dublin, Down Survey, 1657 (detail)

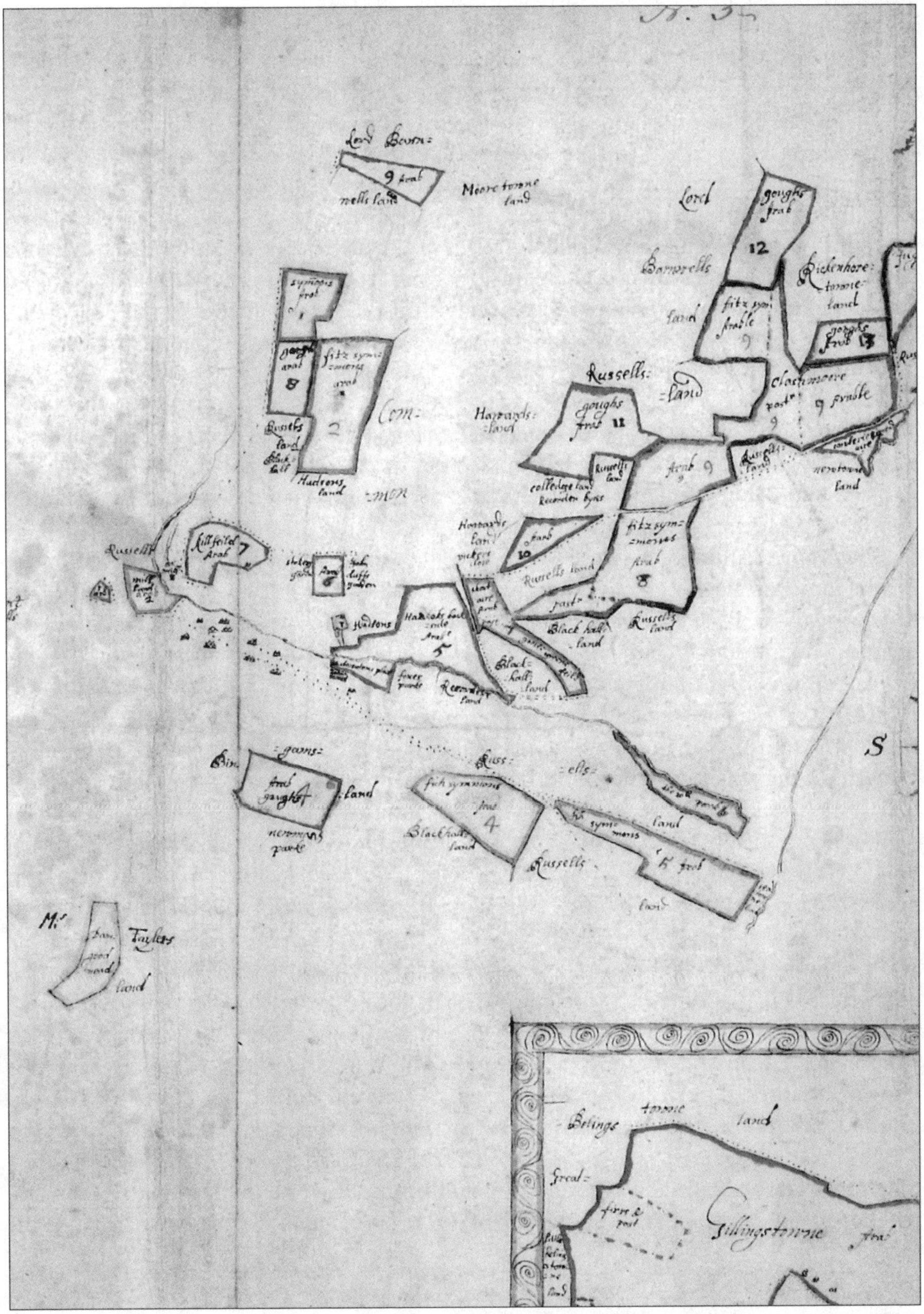

Fig. 4.2 Detail of map of part of the archbishop's lands in and near the town of Swords by John Tormer, 1656

cities. Many lay Protestants had been educated in English universities while members of the Catholic gentry had frequently studied in other countries or in the inns of court in London. While the records of local government for the area have been lost there is no reason to suspect that it did not function efficiently.

One of the functions of local government was to ensure the smooth operation of fairs and markets. A late (nineteenth-century) commission defined a market as 'an authorised public concourse of buyers and sellers of commodities meeting at a place, more or less strictly limited or defined, at an appointed time'.[11] A fair was described as a larger market. The commission considered that the specific differences between a fair and a market was that the fair was held less frequently, generally extended over a longer continuous period and was of a more miscellaneous character than a market. It also pin-pointed three characteristic and essential elements of both markets and fairs, namely, an authority conceded, a place more or less defined and a time specified. Market owners derived benefits from three sources – tolls (charges for bringing animals or goods into the market area), stallages (duties for the liberty of having stalls in a fair or market, or for removing them from one place to another) and rents (similar to stallages but applied where the accommodation was more fixed and substantial or where the hiring was for a more extended period).[12]

These fairs and markets were highly popular since, as well as providing an outlet for the local producers, they brought trade into a town or village. Just how important they were to the local economy and to the prestige of the local landlord can be judged from an angry letter sent by Robert Brian to the dean of Christ Church – St Doolagh's was part of the lands of Christ Church – protesting that his neighbour, John Bath of Balgriffin, had sent 'certain of his men here to St Doolagh's in arms to molest the fair of St Doolagh's' which had been held there 'in times out of mind'.[13] We learn from this letter that John Bath had enlisted his tenants to establish the fair 'partly in the king's majesty's highway and another part in the land of Balgriffin which is manifestly to be seen, which do appear by the places where these men lodge'. Robert Brian made it clear that, if necessary, he was willing to justify his claim before the lord deputy and council. It is clear from a postscript that the fair continued for two days and that Robert Brian was concerned 'to keep the possession of the fair and customs thereto belonging' in his possession. An interesting feature about this fair was that it was timed to coincide with the local patron (or Lughnasa festival).[14] Lammas Day fell on a Saturday in 1607 and no doubt exceptionally large crowds were expected on the Sunday (2 August). The outcome of Brian's protest is not known. Neither Balgriffin nor St Doolagh's figured among the fairs which were granted patents in the seventeenth century. Patents were granted for fairs in three Fingal centres – Garristown, St Margaret's and Swords during the period 1603–60.[15] The great fair at Swords was timed to begin on the feast of the local patron, as was the fair at St Margaret's. The parish of Garristown was dedicated to the Virgin

11 *Royal commission on market rights and tolls: final report of the commission*, H.C. 1890–1 (6268) xxxvii, 2. 12 *Royal commission on market rights and tolls: final report of the commission*, H.C. 1890–1 (6268) xxxvii, 44 and 47. 13 Robert Brian to the dean of Christ Church, 1 August 1607 (RCBL, Christ Church cathedral records, C6/1/26/2/8). 14 Máire Mac Neill, *The festival of Lughnasa* (Oxford, 1962), p. 640. 15 *Appendix to report of the commissioners appointed to inquire into the state of the fairs and markets in Ireland* (Dublin, 1853), H.C.1852/3 (1674), xli, 79–80 and 129–30; 'Fingal 1603–60', i, table 4.1, p. 133.

Mary, and the fair on the feast of the Assumption happily coincided with the Marian devotion of the Talbot family.[16]

The listing by the commissioners of a grant of fairs at Clonturk to Sir John Coghill in 1614 is somewhat puzzling, as the Coghill family came to Ireland after the Restoration.[17] It is quite possible, however, that there was already some type of fair at Clonturk since that property had been leased by Dublin corporation to John Bath, who was so keen to transfer the fair of St Doolagh's to Balgriffin.[18] The fair of St Doolagh's was one of the fairs that was not noted in the report of the nineteenth-century commission since there was apparently no trace of a patent. It is likely that there were many other such fairs in Fingal which, if granted patents at all, received them much later. During the second half of the seventeenth century patents were granted for fairs and markets in Ballyboghil (1669), Balrothery (1669), Clontarf (1675), Fieldstown (1684), Kilsallaghan (1669), Lusk (1700), Luttrellstown (1674 and 1696) and Swords (second patent, 1700) some or all of which may have been functioning at a much earlier date.[19] Fingal fairs and markets granted patents in the eighteenth century were Balbriggan (1766), Balrothery (1751), Finglas (1718), Garristown (additional fairs, 1776), Rush (1755) and Skerries (1788) and, possibly, also Clonturk.[20] While the late grants to Balbriggan and Skerries may be an indication of the spectacular rise in size and importance of the coastal towns during the eighteenth century some of the other grants may have been in respect of ancient fairs and markets. The later grants were less obviously associated with local religious festivals. There may have been practical reasons for this. Fieldstown (parish of Clonmethan) and Rush both had associations with St Catherine, whose feast was 25 November, while Kilsallaghan was dedicated to St David, whose feast was on 1 March. The preferred dates, particularly for single fairs, were the summer and early autumn. The earlier grant for Balrothery retained 29 June (feast of SS Peter and Paul) as one of the fair days but this was omitted in the later grant.[21] The fair-days cited in other late grants, for example, those in Balbriggan and Skerries, had no obvious connection with local religious festivals.

The relatively small number of local fairs and markets for which formal patents were granted during the early seventeenth century may be explained by the fact that Fingal fairs and markets had to compete with the large markets which were held in Dublin and Drogheda. There were certain risks in travelling to market in Dublin even in peace time. One drover, a Co. Tyrone man, Shane O'Mahon, described his experiences when driving cattle to Dublin during the week preceding the outbreak of the rising in October 1641.[22] His evidence, to which he appended his mark, was as follows:

16 Joseph Byrne, 'A rhapsody on the carved oak chimney-piece of the Assumption of the Blessed Virgin in the Oak Room at Malahide Castle' in *Archivium Hibernicum*, lii (1998), pp 24–9. 17 *Appendix to report of the commissioners appointed to inquire into the state of the fairs and markets in Ireland* (Dublin, 1853), H.C.1852/3 (1674), xli, 129; Francis Elrington Ball, *Southern Fingal* ... (originally published 1920, reprinted Dublin, 1995), p. 167. 18 Robert Brian to the dean of Christ Church, 1 August 1607 (RCBL, Christ Church cathedral records, C6/1/26/2/8); *Anc. rec. Dublin*, iii, p. 164. 19 *Appendix to report of the commissioners appointed to inquire into the state of the fairs and markets in Ireland* (Dublin, 1853), H.C.1852/3 (1674), xli, 79–80 and 129–30. 20 *Appendix to report of the commissioners appointed to inquire into the state of the fairs and markets in Ireland* (Dublin, 1853), H.C.1852/3 (1674), xli, 79 and 129–30. 21 *Appendix to report of the commissioners appointed to inquire into the state of the fairs and markets in Ireland* (Dublin, 1853), H.C.1852/3 (1674), xli, 129–30. 22 Examination of Shane O'Mahon, 6 November 1641 (TCD, MS 809, f. 118).

> The said examinant saith that he was born at Glan in the county of Tyrone upon the lord of Howth his land and lived there with his mother a poor widow woman and saith that he came to this city of Dublin upon Thursday was fortnight and saith that his business of coming to town at that time was that one Tirlagh McCarroll, a drover, hired him to help him to drive cattle to the Navan, and that he being at the Navan, a butcher that bought those cattle, whose name he knoweth not, hired him to drive the same beasts to Dublin and agreed to give him two shillings for his pains and saith that upon Wednesday he drove the beeves from the Navan within six miles of Dublin but the name of the place he knoweth not and that night the butcher drove the beeves to Dublin and left this examinant behind him and that next morning after, being Thursday was fortnight, this examinant came to Dublin after the butcher to seek his money but he knows not the butcher's name nor where he dwells and after he came to this town he was looking for the butcher until Saturday morning when he was apprehended having no weapons but a little skene about him.

While it is not possible to be certain where the meeting with the butcher took place it cannot have been far from Mulhuddart.

Local men were equally vulnerable. There was another market in Dublin on Saturday, 29 January 1642 to which Thomas Sevier and four named companions, all employees of Robert Preston of Ballymadun, travelled to sell corn.[23] Both the authorities in Dublin city and the landlords in Fingal, even at the height of an extremely difficult period were trying to maintain normal trading. How dangerous this was is shown by the fact that the men were attacked at Stormanstown while returning home by six men armed with half-pikes who took some money and five horses from them. The fact that Robert Preston was a Catholic was no protection against the attackers, but it may account for why, although the theft was reported immediately to Sir William Ryves, 'one of his majesty's justices of the court of king's bench', the names of those attackers who were recognized do not appear on the lists of outlaws.

Markets were needed not only to trade in meat, corn and agricultural produce but also, particularly in Fingal, to buy and sell fish. While it is clear that the sea was important to the Fingal economy, it is difficult to obtain a detailed and coherent picture of how exactly the maritime economy operated. This is not solely due to the loss of records although their disappearance is a significant factor. Part of the difficulty lies in the fact that the Fingal ports were part of the port of Dublin and maritime activities relating to Fingal tended to be included with those of the city.

The creeks and harbours of Fingal have been discussed in chapter 1. Here I summarize the situation with regard to the sea fisheries insofar as it is possible to do so. Newhaven, part of the denomination of Bremore in the parish of Balrothery owned by Mathew Barnewall, was described as 'a fishing town on the said land' in the Civil Survey and 'a considerable place of fishing' in the Down Survey.[24] In Holmpatrick the proprietor, who, for almost the whole period, was the earl of Thomond, was

23 Examination of Thomas Sevier, 29 January 1642 (TCD, MS 809, f. 232). 24 *Civil Survey, vii, county of Dublin*, p. 4; Down Survey parish maps ... (NLI, MS 714).

entitled to receive the 'tithe fish and custom fish, being the best of each boat'.[25] In Rush, the proprietor (the earl of Ormond) was entitled to the 'second best fish of each boat commonly called the custom fish' while there are two references to the 'poor fishermen'.[26] They had to pay a small sum or duty to graze their cattle on the common and pay a chief rent to the lord of the manor through fishes or 'caatts' (catches?), with twenty shillings or thereabouts as chief rent. If there was any interest in fishing in the barony of Nethercross, which contained Rogerstown, Portraine and the island of Lambay, it was not recorded in the Civil Survey, although the Down Survey noted the potential for fishing in the area.[27] In the barony of Coolock, Baldoyle had 'several fishing boats out of which the landlord [Alderman Preston by lease from the corporation of Dublin] at their coming in had his choice fish', while at Clontarf, where the proprietor was George King, there was 'a fishing belonging to the premises', and Malahide, whose proprietor was John Talbot, had 'a fishing harbour'.[28] The Civil Survey gave a fairly comprehensive description of the industry at Howth:

> There is upon the premises a harbour for small barques to which there belongs several fishing boats that take such fish as is usual on that coast, whereof the lord of Howth hath of every boat the choice fish which is called the lord's fish.[29]

The landlords who owned these fishing ports were likely to benefit in prestige as well as financially by running a successful fishery. The custom of the lord's fish was taken seriously. In July 1637 the corporation of Dublin, proprietors of Baldoyle, strenuously objected when 'Master Fitzsimons, of the Grange of Baldoyle, ... without any colour of right' detained the lord's fish from the city.[30] They prayed that it might be collected for the use of the mayor of the city towards the maintenance of hospitality and ordered 'Mr Recorder, Mr Alderman Foster and Mr Sheriff Smith' to go to Fitzsimons to demand possession of the lord's fish. He seems to have complied with this demand for, one year later, he was granted a lease of sixty-one years of Baldoyle and the Grange of Baldoyle at the yearly rent of £240 sterling together with 'one dozen of good large ling at Christmas, or, in lieu thereof, fifty shillings sterling'.[31] As in the case of Alison Luttrell's complaint about the meres of Astagob and the unauthorized enclosure by John Fagan of common land in Glasnevin there is a suspicion here that the demand for the 'lord's fish' may simply have been a ruse to facilitate the raising of the rent. Dublin corporation was less successful than Christ Church cathedral. By 1644 Thomas Fitzsimons had accumulated substantial arrears, failed to take up his new lease and was petitioning for a reduction in rent.[32] The corporation offered to consider his petition if he paid the arrears and took out his new lease. As he failed to comply the corporation then came to an arrangement with the new mayor, William Smyth, in whose debt the city then was, to lease him Baldoyle and

25 *Civil Survey, vii, county of Dublin*, p. 54. 26 *Civil Survey, vii, county of Dublin*, pp 61–2. 27 Down Survey parish maps ... (NLI, MS 714). 28 *Civil Survey, vii, county of Dublin*, pp 174, 176 and 195. 29 *Civil Survey, vii, county of Dublin*, p. 169. 30 *Anc. rec. Dublin*, iii, p. 332. 31 *Anc. rec. Dublin*, iii, p. 350. 32 *Anc. rec. Dublin*, iii, pp 422–3.

the Grange for seven years at a rent of £120, sterling, per annum.[33] Later, in the spring of 1654, five individuals, John Eastwoode, Samuel Weston, Richard Heydon, Thomas Springham and John Tottie, with whom the corporation had contracted for Baldoyle and the Grange, found they were unable to pay the rent and surrendered their interest.[34] When, it was brought to the attention of the corporation that the castle, town and lands of Baldoyle were lying waste and of no profit to the city and that George Surdevele, a tailor, wished to lease them at a yearly rent of £120, the corporation agreed to let him have them at a rent of £145 provided he paid £5 to the curate and provided one dozen and a half of ling to the mayor at Christmas.[35] In October 1656 it transpired that Surdevele's application had been made on behalf of Alderman John Preston who then applied to have the lease made out in his own name.[36] The corporation agreed to his request to alter the lease to ninety-nine years but refused to reduce the rent. The stability of the area and its fisheries had been disrupted not just by the war but also by the continuing attempts to raise rents.

Here and there one can find a hint that not all fishermen were as poor as those living in decayed dwellings at Rush. The Irish statute staple books recorded, for example, that Nicholas Bryan, a fisherman at Howth obtained security of £200 when he made a loan on 1 August 1637 while the fact that Thomas Lynam, a fishmonger, also of Howth, obtained security of £1,000 for a loan on 2 June 1630 suggests that the wider fishing industry was also prospering.[37] Nicholas Bryan held a thatched house with several houses of office, valued at 20*s*., in the town of Howth in 1641, indicating that he had gone into business in a big way.[38] Thomas Lynam appears to have been related to a prominent family of fishermen in Howth, the father and son, Thomas and Matthew White.[39] James Lynam, who received small legacies from both men was, apparently, married to Thomas's daughter, Alson, while Thomas Lynam was one of the witnesses to the will of Matthew, the other being the local Catholic priest, William Shergold, who also received small legacies from both men. The fishing industry, operated by Catholic fishermen, functioned successfully in the 1630s under the Protestant landlord, the lord of Howth. The main bequest in Matthew's will, made in 1633, was his 'great fishing boat with all things thereunto belonging' which he left to his son, Thomas.[40] Some fishermen clearly owned their own boats. However, in Skerries the situation was somewhat different since the local chief tenant, Dirrick Huiberts Verveer owned at least 'five fishing boats and the half of one fishing boat and all tackle and furniture to the same belonging to the value of one hundred pounds' which were seized during the rising of 1641.[41]

Another indirect piece of evidence of the success of the Fingal fisheries can be found in the records of Dublin corporation. At its meeting in January 1621 the commons 'prayed a speedy remedy for the preventing of the intolerable exactions used

33 *Anc. rec. Dublin*, iii, pp 428 and 434. 34 *Anc. rec. Dublin*, iv, pp 54–5. 35 *Anc. rec. Dublin*, iv, pp 55–6. 36 *Anc. rec. Dublin*, iv, p. 105. 37 *The Irish statute staple books, 1596–1687*, ed. Jane Ohlmeyer and Éamonn Ó Ciardha (Dublin, 1998), pp 73 and 120. 38 *Civil Survey, vii, county of Dublin*, p. 167; Francis Elrington Ball, *Howth and its owners …* (originally published 1917, reprinted Dublin, 1995), p. 114. 39 Abstract of will of Thomas White, 12 August 1629.(RSAI, Elrington Ball MSS, vol x, f. 2); abstract of will of Matthew White, 16 June 1633 (RSAI, Elrington Ball MSS, vol x, f. 2). 40 Abstract of will of Matthew White, 16 June 1633 (RSAI, Elrington Ball MSS, vol x, f. 2). 41 Deposition of Anthony Huiberts, 29 January 1642 (TCD, MS 809, f. 311).

by George King of Clontarf, who taketh of the free citizens of this city three pence, English, upon every barrel of herring, contrary to the statute . . .'[42] The corporation decided to pursue the matter. They took the somewhat drastic decision 'for the utility of the common wealth, to draw the herring fishing and the access of fishers and merchants' to Ringsend which was situated a little to the south of the city.[43] They made it clear that they hoped to make the facilities at Ringsend 'as convenient as Clontarf' which suggests that they believed that Clontarf had certain advantages. The regulations made to develop Ringsend specified some of the advantages that it was hoped would accrue to that area from the change; for example, 'strangers and merchants' would bring in additional coopers to the port area, particularly during the herring fishing season when the city merchants were unable to cope with the volume of work, bakers, butchers and cooks and their companies would sell bread and flesh and rent space to do so; and ships coming to the harbour would pay tithe fish.[44] There was an implication that Clontarf would lose out as a result of the move to Ringsend particularly as Ringsend would charge a quarter tithe as compared with the half tithe then charged by Clontarf.[45] This was clearly a threat to the livelihood of several people in southern Fingal.

Safe harbours and good seamen provided other opportunities for economic activity. Skerries, because of the quality and safety of its harbour was a recognized auxiliary port for Dublin in the eighteenth century.[46] The evidence suggests that this was equally true for the early seventeenth century after the quay had been repaired under the stewardship of the earl of Thomond.[47] In 1621 the small village of Skerries, even then described as a 'town', was granted a charter of the staple under the name of the 'Mayor, Constables and Society of the Merchants' Staple of the Town and Islands of Skerries'.[48] The members of the original body corporate, described by Victor Treadwell as 'officially inspired', were the earl of Thomond, then president of Munster, his son, Sir Barnaby O'Brien, Sir Francis Dudley, Sir Henry Power, Sir Thomas Roper, Sir Robert Newcomen, Sir Richard Bolton, solicitor-general, Egidius Rawlins, Francis White, Walsingham Cooke, Robert Cogan, William Massam, Henry Jones, Mathew de Renzi, Thomas Cave and Dirrick Huiberts Verveer.[49] Henry Jones was nominated as the first mayor and Thomas Cave and Dirrick Huiberts Verveer as the first constables of the staple at Skerries. The complete absence of members of the old Fingal families in the corporation is striking. Donough O'Brien, earl of Thomond and his son, Sir Brian (or Barnaby) represented the interests of the proprietors of the port. Several of the members of the company, in particular, Thomas Cave, Robert Cogan, Mathew de Renzi and William Massam, had associations with the customs.[50] Sir Robert Newcomen and his

42 *Anc. rec. Dublin*, iii, p. 132. 43 *Anc. rec. Dublin*, iii, p. 146. 44 *Anc. rec. Dublin*, iii, p. 147. 45 *Anc. rec. Dublin*, iii, pp 147–8. 46 Maighréad Ní Mhurchadha, *The customs and excise service in Fingal, 1684–1765: sober, active and bred to the sea* (Dublin, 1999), p. 22. 47 *A repertory of the inrolments on the patent rolls in chancery in Ireland; commencing with the reign of King James I*, ed. John Caillard Erck (2 pts, Dublin, 1846–52), i, part ii, pp 732–3. 48 *Irish patent rolls of James I*, ed. M.C. Griffith (Dublin, 1966), p. 498. 49 Victor Treadwell, *Buckingham and Ireland, 1616–1628: a study in Anglo-Irish politics* (Dublin, 1998), p. 52. 50 *Patentee officers in Ireland 1173–1826 including high sheriffs, 1661–1684 and 1761–1816*, ed. James L.J. Hughes (Dublin, 1960), pp 25 and 29; Victor Treadwell, *Buckingham and Ireland, 1616–1628: a study in Anglo-Irish politics* (Dublin, 1998), pp 51–2, 93, 95.

son-in-law, Francis White, were part of a family network of officials.[51] Sir Richard Bolton was then solicitor-general.[52] Walsingham Cooke was the son of Sir Richard Cooke, chancellor of the exchequer.[53] Sir Henry Power (at Chapelizod) and Sir Thomas Roper (at Dolphin's Barn) were involved in the cloth-making industry.[54] Earlier in 1614, William Massam had noted that Dirrick Huiberts Verveer had set up a venture in Cork which had drawn over forty Dutch cloth-workers to join him.[55] By 1621 Verveer was a merchant and chief tenant of the earl of Thomond at Skerries. There is little information about the mayor, Henry Jones. He may have been the Henry Jones who enjoyed a pension from the government and he was probably the Henry Jones, on whose behalf the king wrote to the lord deputy and council in 1627 'recommending Jones's petition to their care, that he may have an indifferent and speedy trial in the matter of 500*l.* which one Derrick Hubart [Dirrick Huiberts] owes him'.[56] Henry Jones of Dublin city, who used the Dublin staple to make six loans during the period 1613–25, was probably the same man.[57]

The reasons for the grant of this charter and that of New Ross at about the same time were stated to be as follows:

> that the wool and flocks in Ireland had not been properly worked up for the manufacture of cloth, but had been exported in a bad state to other countries, in foreign bottoms, or wrought into caddows, blankets, friezes, coarse rugs, and other fabrics of little value; and therefore, for the better manufacture of such wools and flocks, and for the encouragement of the people of Ireland, to breed and rear sheep, and to stock and depasture their waste lands therewith, and for the increase of shipping and sailors therein, the crown grants to said town the right of exporting and importing at said town and port, all kinds of wool, flocks, sheepskins, mortkins, woollen yarns, sherlings, pelts and lambskins ...[58]

Fingal was not noted as a wool-producing area. There may have been plans to export some of the cloth being made in Fingal through Skerries, though this could just as easily have been exported through Dublin or Drogheda but it would seem that the main reason for the setting up of the staple at Skerries was that it was intended to use Skerries as a recognized alternative port when, as happened fairly frequently, ships intending to land at Dublin or Drogheda were forced into Skerries by contrary winds. For example, the lord deputy, Sir Oliver St John landed at Skerries 'with much contrary wind' on 26 August 1616 and had to proceed from there to Dublin.[59]

51 Victor Treadwell, *Buckingham and Ireland, 1616–1628: a study in Anglo-Irish politics* (Dublin, 1998), p. 323, n. 18. 52 *Patentee officers in Ireland 1173–1826 including high sheriffs, 1661–1684 and 1761–1816*, ed. James L.J. Hughes (Dublin, 1960), p. 13. 53 *Cal. S. P. Ire., 1615–25*, pp 1 and 287. 54 *Civil Survey, vii, county of Dublin*, p. 223; *Cal. S. P. Ire., 1615–25*, p. 361; *Anc. rec. Dublin*, iii, p.251; Francis Elrington Ball, *A history of the County Dublin ... part fourth* (originally published 1906, reprinted Dublin, 1995), pp 153–4; Michael MacCarthy-Morrogh, *The Munster plantation: English migration to southern Ireland 1583–1641* (Oxford, 1986), p. 233; Victor Treadwell, *Buckingham and Ireland, 1616–1628: a study in Anglo-Irish politics* (Dublin, 1998), p. 53. 55 Michael MacCarthy-Morrogh, *The Munster plantation: English migration to southern Ireland 1583–1641* (Oxford, 1986), p. 234. 56 *Cal. S. P. Ire., 1615–25*, p. 447; *Cal. S. P. Ire., 1625–32*, p. 233. 57 *The Irish statute staple books, 1596–1687*, ed. Jane Ohlmeyer and Éamonn Ó Ciardha (Dublin, 1998), p. 113. 58 *Irish patent rolls of James I*, ed. M.C. Griffith (Dublin, 1966), p. 498. 59 *Cal. S. P. Ire., 1615–25*, pp 134–5; *Irish patent rolls of James I*, ed. M.C. Griffith

The port was already involved in the coastal trade for on 9 June 1615 Jasper Hurlston, the Drogheda merchant, brought 2 tons of French wine from Skerries and landed them in one of the Co. Louth ports (Drogheda, Dundalk or Carlingford).[60] He paid duty of £3 on the wine which would place the value of the cargo at £30.[61] The ship which carried the wine was the *Bryde* of Skerries and its master, whose name was not listed, was also from Skerries.[62] At the same period Dirrick Huiberts Verveer was already importing sack and muscatel into Dublin, or perhaps even into Skerries.[63] The various harbours and creeks in the port of Dublin were not listed separately but were treated as part of that port. Alderman Jasper Hurlston of Drogheda died *c.*1623 but the Dutch merchant, Dirrick Huiberts Verveer, went on to become a rich and successful businessman.[64] From the point of view of maritime history Verveer's connection with Lambay Island is of interest. In 1618, he was granted a licence to keep taverns and to sell wine and ardent spirits in Skerries and the manor of Holmpatrick and 2½ miles around the same (excluding Balrothery and Lusk) and in the island of Lambay.[65] Following the attack on his home in December 1641 he 'resolved to go to Lambay for succour' and in a report of his murder the lords justices and council in a letter to the earl of Leicester described him as 'the gentleman that held the island of Lambay'.[66] The proprietor of Lambay, which was situated in the parish of Portraine, was listed in the Civil Survey as Sir William Ussher.[67] In the absence of further evidence one must conclude that Verveer had either leased the island from Ussher or that he held some office perhaps that of constable or custodian of the castle there. In any event his position as chief tenant of Holmpatrick and his interest in Lambay placed him in an influential position in relation to shipping on the north Fingal coast.

Another indication that Skerries was already an important harbour can be found in the fragmentary accounts of the customs service that survive. In 1624 James I granted the office of 'customer, collector and receiver of all the customs, subsidies and imposts, great and small, within the ports of Dublin, Skerries, and Malahide, Dublin County, and within the port of Wicklow, and in all the bays, ports and creeks within same; with a fee of £10 annually' to Edward Bagshaw.[68] There may be some significance in the fact that Skerries and Malahide were described as ports. Similar terminology was used when Bagshaw was reappointed in 1626, together with John Bagshaw, with an annual fee of £40, and on the occasion of a further reappointment in 1627.[69] These were not the first nor the only occasions on which Skerries and

(Dublin, 1966), p. 307. **60** H.F. Kearney, 'The Irish wine trade, 1614–15' in *IHS*, ix, no. 36 (September 1955), p. 411. **61** H.F. Kearney, 'The Irish wine trade, 1614–15' in *IHS*, ix, no. 36 (September 1955), p. 408. **62** H.F. Kearney, 'The Irish wine trade, 1614–15' in *IHS*, ix, no. 36 (September 1955), p. 411. **63** H.F. Kearney, 'The Irish wine trade, 1614–15' in *IHS*, ix, no. 36 (September 1955), pp 408 and 410. **64** Arthur Vicars, *Index to the prerogative wills of Ireland, 1536–1810* (Dublin, 1897, reprinted 1997), p. 242; Maighréad Ní Mhurchadha, Skerries and the 'execrable Irish rebellion', December 1991 (Skerries Historical Society Archives, unpublished paper no. 161, pp 9–12). **65** *Irish patent rolls of James I*, ed. M.C. Griffith (Dublin, 1966), p. 362. **66** Deposition of Anthony Huiberts, 29 January 1642 (TCD, MS 809, f. 311); Historical Manuscripts Commission, *Calendar of the manuscripts of the marquess of Ormonde ...* (new series, 8 vols, London, 1902–20), ii, p. 33. **67** *Civil Survey, vii, county of Dublin*, p. 151. **68** *Irish patent rolls of James I*, ed. M.C. Griffith (Dublin, 1966), p. 591. **69** *Calendar of the patent and close rolls of chancery in Ireland of the reign of Charles the first: first to eighth year, inclusive*, ed. James Morrin (London, 1863), p. 266.

Malahide were described as ports. To quote just one other example Colley Phillipps and Richard Heathe were appointed to the office of searcher and gauger in the ports of Dublin city, Skerries, Malahide and Wicklow in 1613.[70] The appointment of Sir Edward Bagshaw was particularly interesting since he based himself, at least part-time, at Skerries and prepared some of the few extant reports of customs activities there during the period. On 4 February 1628 he wrote from Dublin to Secretary Nicholas seeking advice on a problem which had arisen:

> Eight days ago there arrived at the Skerries, twelve miles from this town, a ship of 80 tons (commander Roger Deane), with two prizes of French wines. Deane petitioned the deputy to be allowed to unload and sell one here, saying she was too leaky to go to England. The commissioners appointed to examine the matter (including Sir Beverly Newcomen and myself) found this to be the case with one. The other was a good Flemish ship, with French wine, but the four feet of chestnuts which covered the wine will make it sour, colourless, and unsaleable in a short time. The lord deputy gave leave to sell the ships, but I fear they will not be good prize unless they can be proved to be derelict, which there is some ground to expect ...[71]

It is clear, therefore, that in 1628 Skerries could handle, at the very least, three ships, one of which was of 80 tons. In a further letter dated 8 March from Skerries he gave some more information about the matter, indicating that there was considerable customs activity at Skerries:

> The two Dutch ships which were brought into Skerries were not sold there owing to the orders of the deputy, but were taken to Strangford, and there the goods and ships were sold to one Valentine Payne, his majesty's customer. He gave them £500 and provisions, and said they should have more, and a fair share of the purchase money. The wine was sent up by sea to Dublin to be sold, and passed by here [Skerries]. As it paid no tonnage I seized what came here and sent down an officer to do the same at Strangford.[72]

Another piece of evidence for the importance of Skerries harbour during the 1640s was the presence of a full-time waiter (a customs employee) in the 'creek at Skerries' in the summer of 1641.[73] When the rising broke out later that year, the harbour of Skerries was a hive of activity. The fishing boats owned by Dirrick Huiberts Verveer have already been mentioned. Early in December Luce Spell and several other Drogheda people in 'a barque of Liverpool with intent to land in the harbour of Drogheda were by contrary winds driven into the harbour of Skerries' and cast anchor there.[74] Christopher Hampton reported that he had run ashore at Skerries on

70 *Irish patent rolls of James I*, ed. M.C. Griffith (Dublin, 1966), p. 256. 71 *Cal. S. P. Ire., 1625–32*, p. 307. 72 *Cal. S. P. Ire., 1625–32*, p. 317. 73 *Journals of the house of commons of the kingdom of Ireland* ... (19 vols, Dublin, 1796–1800), i, pp 253 and 272. 74 Deposition of Luce Spell, 5 February 1642 (TCD, MS, 834, f. 6); 'County Louth depositions, 1641' ed. Thomas Gogarty in *Journal of the County Louth Archaeological Society*, iii, no. 1 (1912), pp 71–2.

5 December 1641.[75] Whether or not he was the master of the 'barque of Liverpool' or another vessel is unclear. Another ship carrying prisoners from Carlingford to Dublin was also driven into Skerries.[76] The presence of so many ships and boats in the vicinity of the harbour would have required skilled boatmen to service them since it is unlikely that all of them would have been small enough to land at the quay. Some idea of what was involved can be found in the examinations of Leonard Graves, a gabbardman of Dublin city, who operated with a second boatman, and of one of his passengers, William Shepherd.[77] These boatmen charged a fee to carry letters, goods and salesmen selling provisions, as well as passengers, to and from the ships anchored off shore.

According to Francis Elrington Ball, Howth was less used as a port during the seventeenth century than it had been previously.[78] But it remained popular with travellers. Like Skerries, Howth had an opportunity to welcome lords deputy during the period 1603–60. Lord Falkland arrived at Howth on 6 September 1622.[79] On 2 June 1636 Sir Thomas Wentworth (later earl of Strafford) left Howth in the *Ninth Whelp*, having knighted two men on his way from Dublin.[80] There are several references to the embarkation and disembarkation of family members at Howth in the diaries of Sir Richard Boyle, earl of Cork.[81] Howth had certain advantages. It was much closer to Dublin city than Skerries and its fishermen had acquired a reputation for seamanship.[82] This reputation enabled them to supplement their earnings. On 20 July 1630 Richard Boyle wrote a passage which noted that not all dangers encountered in the Irish Sea were due to the vagaries of the weather;

> White of Howth, being by me employed in his open boat, is from Howth to Holyhead to carry my letters to the earl of Kildare, and my son, expressing they should be very careful how they took their passage hither, for that the pirates were in the channel, delivered my letters there, brought me a certificate, and returned this day, to whom, Henry Staynes, his man, gave by my order £5 ...[83]

By 1633 the pirates were in the ascendant and there are vivid accounts of their activities which included the burning of a vessel off Howth, the *Tomine* of Hoorn, the flames of which were seen as far away as the centre of Dublin city in June of that

75 Examination of Christopher Hampton, 11 December 1641 (TCD, MS 809, f. 212). 76 Deposition of Roger Holland, 4 March 1642 (TCD, MS 834, f. 63); Thomas Fitzpatrick, *The bloody bridge and other papers relating to the insurrection of 1641 (Sir Phelim O'Neill's rebellion)* (first published Dublin, 1903, reissued New York and London, 1970), pp 22–3 and 170. 77 Examination of William Shepherd, 14 February 1646 (TCD, MS 810, f. 331); examination of Leonard Graves, 14 February 1646 (TCD, MS 810, ff 331–2). 78 Francis Elrington Ball, *Howth and its owners* ... (originally published 1917, reprinted Dublin, 1995), p. 88. 79 *Cal. S. P. Ire., 1615–25*, p. 345. 80 Richard Boyle, earl of Cork, *The Lismore papers (first series) viz. autobiographical notes, remembrances and diaries of Sir Richard Boyle, first and 'great' earl of Cork, never before printed*, ed. Alexander B. Grossart (5 vols. London, 1886), iv, p. 192. 81 Richard Boyle, earl of Cork, *The Lismore papers (first series) viz. autobiographical notes, remembrances and diaries of Sir Richard Boyle, first and 'great' earl of Cork, never before printed*, ed. Alexander B. Grossart (5 vols. London, 1886), iii, pp 47 and 84; iv, p. 46. 82 Francis Elrington Ball, *Howth and its owners* ... (originally published 1917, reprinted Dublin, 1995), p. 89. 83 Richard Boyle, earl of Cork, *The Lismore papers (first series) viz. autobiographical notes, remembrances and diaries of Sir Richard Boyle, first and 'great' earl of Cork, never before printed*, ed. Alexander B. Grossart (5 vols, London, 1886), iii, pp 44–5.

year.[84] Shortly before this incident took place, George Radcliffe had written to Viscount Wentworth: 'I hope this letter will come to your lordship: it is sent over by a boat of Howth, for no man else dares stir out.'[85]

Little is known about the harbour of Malahide. Like Skerries it was described as a 'port' in the patents appointing customs officers and Joseph Byrne has suggested that it contained a formal quayside.[86] It is not known if a serious dispute which arose between Dublin city and Malahide in 1609 and which was referred to the arbitration of the lord chancellor, related to the question of shipping or customs.[87] It was undoubtedly another instance of tension between Dublin city and Fingal.

In attempting to ascertain the type of tonnage the Fingal harbours could handle we find that a ship of 160 tons, the *Triall* of London, put into Clontarf in 1607.[88] The *Unicorne* of Clontarf, whose master was from Bristol, was one of the ships in which wine was imported in 1615.[89] The pillaging of a barque at Clontarf and the subsequent stealing, mainly by local fishermen, of any coals, salt and rope remaining on board, was one of the incidents which led to the burning of that town in 1641.[90] Clontarf also provided the only detailed account which has been found of maritime economic activity within Fingal at this period. The *Trinity* of Clontarf, owned by Christopher Browne, set out on a voyage in 1622.[91] In February of that year some goods, which had been loaded in the *Trinity* at Clontarf, were seized by local Cornish people when the ship ran aground near Padstow Bay. John Lynch, one of the ship's company, deposed as follows: (James Nugent and Adam Talbot, referred to in the deposition were Dublin merchants.)

> That about 1 February last the bark was laden with these several merchandizes, vizt. 422 salted cow hides, whereof 30 were great bull or ox hides, 112 tanned hides, 18 tanned hides of a smaller sort, 6 tanned hides of the smallest sort, 6 calf skins, 3 fardels of sheepskins wrought and tanned into white leather, 8 bags of feathers, 6 barrels of tallow, 12 barrels of beef, 1 box of candles, 6 sides of bacon, 1 new caddow, 1 flockhead, 1 half barrel of beef, 3 dozen neat's tongues, 12 fox cases, 3 checkers, 1 canvas tick, and 1 chest belonging to James Nugent. And also 407 salt hides, 1 trunk containing 1 cloak, 1 pair of hose, and 1 portmanteau with certain linens belonging to Adam Talbot. And 8 salt hides, 2 barrels of beef, and 1 barrel of herrings belonging to Christopher Browne.

84 The manuscripts of the Earl Cowper, KG, preserved at Melbourne Hall, Derbyshire, ii, in Historical Manuscripts Commission, *Twelfth report*, appendix, part ii (London, 1888), pp 10–11; *A calendar of material relating to Ireland from the high court of admiralty examinations, 1536–1641*, ed. John C. Appleby (Dublin, 1992), pp 213–14. **85** The manuscripts of the Earl Cowper, KG, preserved at Melbourne Hall, Derbyshire, ii, in Historical Manuscripts Commission, *Twelfth report*, appendix, part ii (London, 1888), p. 11. **86** Joseph Byrne, *War and peace: the survival of the Talbots of Malahide 1641–1671* (Dublin, 1997), p. 19. **87** Transcript of Monday Books, 28 January 1609 (Dublin City Council Archives, Gilbert Library, Dublin, MS 44). **88** *A calendar of material relating to Ireland from the high court of admiralty examinations, 1536–1641*, ed. John C. Appleby (Dublin, 1992), pp 116–17. **89** H.F. Kearney, 'The Irish wine trade, 1614–15' in *IHS*, ix, no. 36 (September 1955), p. 411. **90** Examination of David Powell, 14 December 1641 (TCD, MS 809, f. 214). **91** *A calendar of material relating to Ireland from the high court of admiralty examinations, 1536–1641*, ed. John C. Appleby (Dublin, 1992), pp 299–300.

The impression given by this list is that the merchants, or at least Adam Talbot, were travelling with the goods, which were predominantly the products of one or more tanneries. Christopher Browne of Clontarf, possibly the same man who been a ship-owner in 1622, was the master of a ship called the *Lion* of Fairlie, believed to have been built in Belfast in the 1630s, which was arrested at Portsmouth in 1640.[92] A dispute arose about the ownership of the vessel which had been engaged in the export of herrings and the import of malt. The general conclusion that one arrives at from the scanty evidence is that, rather surprisingly, given its proximity to the city, Clontarf, unlike Howth, specialized in the transport of goods rather than people. One of the minor Fingal ports, Portraine, is mentioned in the wine list as the port of registry for a ship called the *Saviour*, which brought sack into Carrickfergus in September 1615.[93] In general there is enough evidence to suggest that there was lively maritime activity in Fingal throughout the period, that each of the four main ports, Skerries, Malahide, Howth and Clontarf had its own character and that the sea supplied employment, directly and indirectly, to many people in the area throughout the year.

There is no evidence of large-scale industry, apart from agriculture and seafaring in Fingal. One small craft industry which was certainly carried on in the area was the building industry. The only clue which the Civil Survey gave to the existence of this industry at Chapelizod was the reference to 'one open quarry of stone'.[94] The industry may have declined by 1654–6, but it certainly flourished prior to 1641.[95] According to Francis Elrington Ball, the King's House at Chapelizod was erected by Lord Valentia but it is not known for certain if he used local builders.[96] It may have been built by Edmond Tingham, who operated a business there.[97] There is one account which throws light on the building industry in Fingal in the period 1603–60, namely, the repair of the church and the stone bridge at Finglas.[98] There had been considerable building activity in Finglas earlier in the century. A lease dated 1602 recorded that Lucas Challoner 'hath heretofore builded a strong stone house ... and hath already begun to build a stone castle upon the said land where none was ever formerly known to have to have been built'.[99] A note on another document in the Representative Church Body Library stated that Challoner's castle was destroyed in 1641 and that the stones were used afterwards to build the house of Colonel Bridges.[100] No doubt there was a great deal of rebuilding following the destruction of the town. In the case of the church and bridge, the work appears to have been supervised by the churchwardens rather than by a single master-builder, and the various tasks were contracted out to individual craftsmen and labourers. The surviving

92 *A calendar of material relating to Ireland from the high court of admiralty examinations, 1536–1641*, ed. John C. Appleby (Dublin, 1992), pp 275–6. 93 H.F. Kearney, 'The Irish wine trade, 1614–15' in *IHS*, ix, no. 36 (September 1955), p. 438. 94 *Civil Survey, vii, county of Dublin*, p. 223. 95 Francis Elrington Ball, *A history of the County Dublin ... part fourth* (originally published 1906, reprinted Dublin, 1995), pp 168–9. 96 Francis Elrington Ball, *A history of the County Dublin ... part fourth* (originally published 1906, reprinted Dublin, 1995), p. 167. 97 Francis Elrington Ball, *A history of the County Dublin ... part fourth* (originally published 1906, reprinted Dublin, 1995), p. 168. 98 Finglas parish combined vestry book and registers, 1657–1758 (RCBL, P.307/1/1, pp 4 and 6); William Cotter Stubbs, 'Finglas, County Dublin, vestry books' in *Journal of the Royal Society of Antiquaries of Ireland*, xlvi (1916), p. 28. 99 Copy lease to Luke Challoner, 10 June 1602 (RCBL, Records of the archbishop of Dublin, D6/76/10/11). 100 A lawyer's notes on the documents of title for Cardiff's Castle, etc. (not dated) (RCBL, Records of the archbishop of Dublin, D6/75/9).

accounts enable us to obtain some idea of the wage rates paid to tradesmen *c.*1657. Based on an arbitrary estimate of 250 working days a year to allow for absences on Sundays and holy days and for sickness the annual wage rates have been calculated at £12.50 for a labourer, £16.67 for a carter (including horse and cart), £20.83 for a joiner and £25.00 for a mason.[101] The tradesmen's names were also recorded in the vestry book.[102] John and Nicholas Chute were employed to carry timber from Dublin so they may not have been local men.[103] The names of the slater, John Rely (two chimneys), the smith, Peter Read (two chimneys and one forge), and the joiner, George Wadsworth (one chimney), appeared in the hearth money roll of 1664.[104] John Bochell who was assessed for one chimney may have been the labourer whose name is difficult to decipher in the vestry book. Some of the others had names which are not found in the hearth money roll for Finglas but which occurred in other parishes in Fingal which were reasonably near to Finglas. It seems likely, therefore, that the Finglas workforce was supplemented by travelling tradesmen from other parts of the area.

There were other small industries in Fingal in the period 1654–6. There was, for example, a tuck mill (or fulling-mill) in Chapelizod.[105] Nothing further is known about this mill, but it was probably no accident that Chapelizod was chosen by the duke of Ormond and the council of trade for the establishment of a linen, woollen and worsted factory there under Colonel Richard Lawrence during the Restoration period, since it is likely that the village had a suitable skills base.[106] This would not have been surprising, for Thomas Wentworth had commented when establishing a linen manufactory among his own tenants elsewhere in the country *c.*1635 that 'the women are all bred to spinning'.[107] Luttrellstown (parish of Clonsilla) also had a tuck-mill in use in 1654–6 which, no doubt, added to the reservoir of cloth-making skills in the barony of Castleknock.[108] It is not clear if the mill in Castleknock (the only mill listed in the town of Castleknock), described as a 'waste mill' in the Civil Survey, is identical with the 'Baron's Mill' listed in the hearth money roll for 1664 or if it was used for woollen manufacture prior to 1660.[109] According to Francis Elrington Ball, its owner in 1664, John Sprotton, who described himself as a clothier, was engaged in the woollen manufacture.[110] There is a suggestion here of a corridor of textile manufacture extending along the northern bank of the river Liffey. Perhaps at some future date more light may be thrown on the history of this part of Fingal by industrial archaeologists. There was also a tuck mill near the northern end of Fingal, close to the river Delvin at Westown (parish of the Naul).[111]

101 'Fingal 1603–60', i, table 4.2, p. 148. **102** 'Fingal 1603–60', i, table 4.3, p. 149. **103** Finglas parish combined vestry book and registers, 1657–1758 (RCBL, P.307/1/1, p. 3). **104** 'Hearth money roll for County Dublin, 1664' (second part), *Journal of the County Kildare Archaeological Society*, xi (1930–33), pp 420–1. **105** *Civil Survey, vii, county of Dublin,* p. 223. **106** Francis Elrington Ball, *A history of the County Dublin … part fourth* (originally published 1906, reprinted Dublin, 1995), p. 171. **107** Lord deputy to Sir Christopher Wandesford, 25 July 1636, in *The earl of Strafforde's letters and dispatches …* ed. William Knowler (2 vols, Dublin, 1740), ii, p. 19. **108** *Civil Survey, vii, county of Dublin,* p. 231. **109** *Civil Survey, vii, county of Dublin,* p. 242; 'Hearth money roll for County Dublin, 1664' (second part), *Journal of the County Kildare Archaeological Society*, xi (1930–33), p. 436. **110** Abstract of will of John Sprotton, 30 September 1670 (RSAI, Elrington Ball MSS, vol xi, f. 38); Francis Elrington Ball, *Southern Fingal …* (originally published 1920, reprinted Dublin, 1995), p. 23. **111** *Civil Survey, vii, county of Dublin,* p. 32.

Where the type of mill was not specified in the Civil Survey, it was assumed that the mill in question was a corn mill. As has been shown in chapter 1, there were many such mills in Fingal – reflecting the universal need for corn and flour. Occasionally mills were shown on contemporary maps as, for example, on the 1668 copy of a map of the archbishop's lands at Lusk originally drawn in 1656 (figure 4.3).[112] Neither of the windmills shown prominently near Ballough and Tyrrelstown on the map, the original of which was exactly contemporary with the Civil Survey, was mentioned in that document which prompts the question as to whether there were even more mills in the area than the large number listed in the Civil Survey. One windmill mentioned in the Civil Survey, at Knockdromin, was not shown on the map. Apart from the windmill at Knockdromin, an old mill (in use) at Gracedieu, a horse-mill (out of use) at Kenure and two watermills, at Whitestown and Corduff, were listed in the Civil Survey for the parish of Lusk.[113] No evidence of the practice of 'milling soke' (the feudal custom, by which, under common law, tenants were compelled to support mills set up by their landlords) has been found for early seventeenth-century Fingal. Since the custom was widely observed in Fingal in the eighteenth century it seems likely that it existed, in some areas at least, at an earlier date.[114]

One notable feature of seventeenth-century economic life was the level of money-lending by individuals. Nicholas Canny has drawn attention to the prevalence of money-lending by the clergy of the established church.[115] An attempt was made to analyze the situation which obtained among the Protestant clergy in Fingal.[116] The losses reported by nine clergymen in the 1641 depositions have been used for this purpose. Needless to say the reports did not follow any standard pattern so that the assignment of some of the losses to specific categories must be regarded as tentative. The amounts owing to Randall Dimmock (St Doolagh's and Clontarf), for example, were all from landowners with property in parishes in which he had an interest and for this reason are listed as 'tithes'.[117] On the other hand, the 'debts' for Thomas Lloyd (Swords) listed the names of some local residents and may, therefore, have included outstanding tithes.[118] None of the names of the nine deposing clergymen appeared in the list of creditors in *The Irish statute staple books, 1596–1687*.[119] The Irish statute staple books have also been examined to see if there was any evidence that other members of the clergy, while serving in Fingal, had engaged in lending money using the staple. Only one example, that of John Credland (or Credlan) of Coolock, has been found.[120] He obtained security on a small bond of £40 in respect

112 John Turmor, The plotts of Feilds farme, Humphrys farme, Walter Dermotts farme, Blackhall farme, the Stewards land, Charles Mease, Rathany, Terrels Towne, the gleabe land and the Burgage Cottages in Luske, in the Barony of Nethercross, Parish of Luske, and Con. Dublin, as also Knockdromin made in 1656, abstracted in 1668 by El. Arnoldi (RCBL, Records of the archbishop of Dublin, D6, map no. 12). 113 *Civil Survey, vii, county of Dublin,* pp 56, 61, 63 and 65. 114 Maighréad Ní Mhurchadha, The mills of Stephenstown, research project for the College Diploma in Local History, St Patrick's College, Maynooth, 1996 (Skerries Historical Society Archives, unpublished paper no. 203). 115 Nicholas Canny, *Making Ireland British, 1580–1650* (Oxford, 2001), pp 378, 388–9, 476. 116 'Fingal 1603–60', i, table 4.4, p. 154. 117 Deposition of Randall Dimmock, 1 March 1642 (TCD, MS 809, f. 276). 118 Deposition of Thomas Lloyd, 18 June 1642 (TCD, MS 810, f. 165). 119 *The Irish statute staple books, 1596–1687*, ed. Jane Ohlmeyer and Éamonn Ó Ciardha (Dublin, 1998), pp 56–161. 120 *The Irish statute staple books, 1596–1687*, ed. Jane Ohlmeyer and Éamonn Ó Ciardha (Dublin, 1998), pp 84 and 213. 121 Deposition of Francis Eccles, 17 January 1642 (TCD, MS 809, f. 277); deposition of Tabitha Eccles,

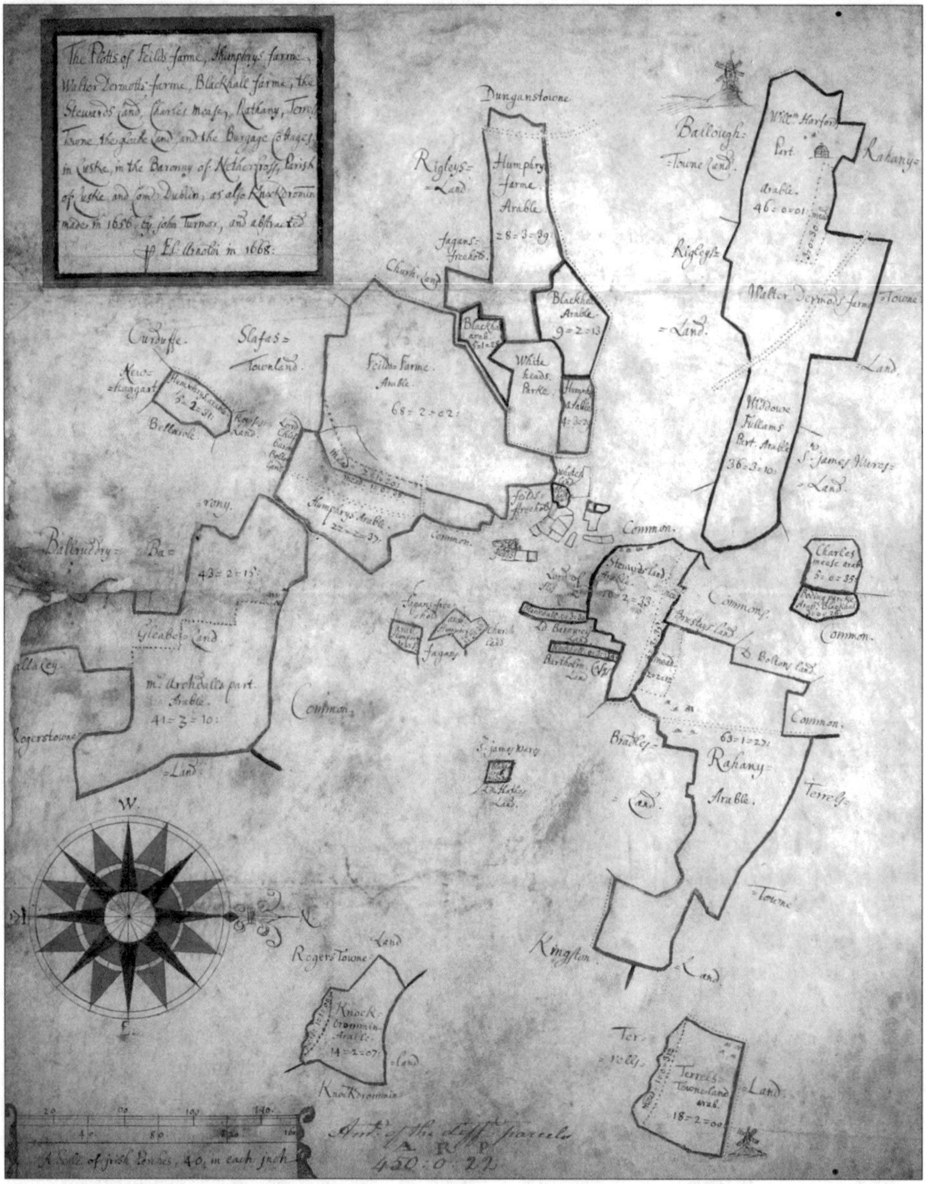

Fig. 4.3 Map of the archbishop of Dublin's lands at Lusk, abstracted by El. Arnoldi in 1668 from an original map of 1656 by John Turmor

of a loan to Richard English of Dublin in 1627. One must conclude, therefore, that, apart from the possible case of Thomas Lloyd, there is little evidence for widespread money-lending by clergy of the established church in Fingal in the early seventeenth century. Such fierce and widespread animosity as they aroused is more likely to have been caused by their demands for tithes, and in the case of church institutions, for rents and customs.

That money-lending was not a major problem associated with the clergy in Fingal is probably due to the fact that there were many other opportunities to acquire loans. At one end of the scale were the Ballybough pawnbrokers, Francis and Tabitha Eccles.[121] At the other end were those who were accustomed to use the staple, for example, prosperous local Catholic merchants and gentry such as Robert Arthur (22 loans, 1623–37), Philip Conran (18 loans, 1597–1613) and Philip Hore (17 loans, 1598–1609) or Protestant laymen with Fingal connections such as Richard Barry (10 loans, 1614–30), Robert Bysse (8 loans, 1616–30) and Chidley Coote (14 loans, 1653–78).[122] Many other Fingallians made use of the staple both as borrowers and lenders.

As far as one can judge from the scanty information at our disposal, trade and commerce flourished in the area. This was almost inevitable as the population of the city of Dublin continued to grow and to become more dependent on the fertile hinterland of Fingal. Fisheries and maritime trade prospered despite a major threat of pirates, and the Fingal ports took on a new importance. This was probably helped by new merchant families from Dublin city, such as the Fagans and the Arthurs, who purchased or leased land north of the Liffey. While most of the gentry families had lived in or near Fingal for several generations, the ordinary people were surprisingly mobile. There were a number of small industries in the area, based to a large extent on local raw materials and skills. It is noticeable, however, that many of the major entrepreneurs were English or Dutch. Coupled with the intellectual stimulus which local families, both Catholic and Protestant, received through widespread contact with the continent, the overall material prosperity of the area promised a bright future for Fingal.

3 April 1642 (TCD, MS 810, f. 135). **122** *The Irish statute staple books, 1596–1687*, ed. Jane Ohlmeyer and Éamonn Ó Ciardha (Dublin, 1998), pp 61, 65, 76, 81–3 and 110.

Part II

Expressing community values

5

'The race of the English'

> The word Fingal countervaileth in English, the race or sept of the English or strangers, for that they were solely seized of that part of the island, gripping with their talons so firmly that warm nest, that from the conquest to this day the Irish enemy could never rouse them from thence.
>
> Richard Stanihurst on the Fingallians (1577)[1]

In the words just quoted Richard Stanihurst, a member of a Fingallian family, set out, in general terms, his view of the history of Fingal. Who were the Fingallians? What kind of people were they? How did they regard themselves and how did their contemporaries view them?

It must be emphasized that Fingallians, like others, behaved differently in times of peace and in time of war. The various social and cultural groups in Fingal normally managed to control their differences by using the force of law. They lived together in relative harmony as long as the country was at peace. The underlying tensions between the sub-communities surfaced, however, when civil war threatened and, eventually materialized. In these circumstances, certain less attractive qualities such as cruelty manifested themselves.

Stanihurst was convinced that, after the Norman conquest, 'the empaled dwellers did sunder themselves, as well in land as in language from the Irish' bringing civility, good laws and loyalty to the Pale.[2] Later, in his view, with the infiltration of the Irish language to the Pale 'the canker took such deep root, as the body that before was whole and sound, was by little and little festered, and in manner wholly putrefied.' He clearly believed that a cultural change had taken place. In *Ireland under Elizabeth* published in 1621 Don Philip O'Sullivan Bear saw things rather differently.[3] Equating Fingal with the English province he stated that 'the majority of the inhabitants ... although they are Catholics, yet are not only of English descent, but also preserve the English laws and institutions and the English language, albeit in a crude and archaic form'. While he believed that the majority of the people of the Pale were

1 Richarde Stanyhurst, *A treatise contayning a playne and perfect description of Irelande* ... in Raphaell Holinshed and Richarde Stanyhurst, *Holinshed's Irish chronicle* ..., ed. Liam Miller and Eileen Power (London, 1577, republished Dublin, 1979), p. 13. 2 Richarde Stanyhurst, *A treatise contayning a playne and perfect description of Irelande* ... in Raphaell Holinshed and Richarde Stanyhurst, *Holinshed's Irish chronicle* ..., ed. Liam Miller and Eileen Power (London, 1577, republished Dublin, 1979), pp 13–14. 3 Philip O'Sullivan Bear, *Ireland under Elizabeth: chapters towards a history of Ireland in the reign of Elizabeth being a portion of the history of Catholic Ireland by Don Philip O'Sullivan Bear*, translated from the Latin by Matthew J. Byrne (Dublin, 1903, originally published Lisbon, 1621), p. 50.

Catholics who were also English in culture and outlook, it is not clear from this passage whether he regarded the minority as Catholics of Irish descent or as English Protestants.

Turning to modern historians we find that the views of the sixteenth and seventeenth-century writers have generally been accepted by them. Aidan Clarke wrote as follows:

> The seventeenth-century distribution of the descendants of these early colonists, both rural and urban, conformed of course to a pattern easily predictable in terms of the density of the original settlements and the vicissitudes of English rule in Ireland. Thus the greatest concentration was in the five counties of the Pale – Dublin, Meath, Louth, Kildare and Kilkenny – and in the counties of Westmeath, Wexford and Galway, while incidence in Ulster was confined to a handful on the Ards peninsula and a sprinkling in County Monaghan. Elsewhere they were present in proportionately significant numbers in every county except Clare and Leitrim ... To plot the distribution of the old English in this way, on the evidence of descent provided by surnames, is however, very largely to beg the seventeenth-century question, for by this stage membership of the group was polarized between two criteria: though the denotation of the term was demographic, historical and racial, its connotation was political and religious.[4]

An analysis of the surnames in the hearth money roll, *c.*1664 has led to the conclusion that those with a Gaelic-Irish background may well have been in the majority in the area.[5] The distribution of Gaelic-Irish surnames by parish has been mapped in figure 5.1. It is also possible to conclude from this analysis that there were two broad social groups in Fingal, a group which included officials and landed proprietors, who generally conformed to the traditional view of Fingallians as mainly 'Old English' and what might be termed an underclass of persons who had much in common with the Gaelic-Irish who lived outside the Pale. Fingal and Gaelic Ireland were linked by more than just roads. There were also ties of culture and relationships. But as these ties existed at the lower social levels of society they appear to have gone unnoticed, or at least unmentioned, until Sir William Petty and others initiated a more scientific approach to population analysis. But, by that time, as Mícheál Ó Siochrú succinctly put it: 'Place of birth, rather than blood, now provided the essential criterion for membership of the Irish nation'.[6]

An examination of Fingal surnames listed by Sir William Petty together with a classification of Christian names which appeared in the hearth money roll *c.*1664 also supports this view.[7]

While it is evident that a high proportion, perhaps even a majority, of the people of Fingal could be classed as 'Gaelic-Irish' by 1664, it is not possible to say how this came about. Many, such as the O'Casey family, were undoubtedly in the area since

4 Aidan Clarke, *The Old English in Ireland, 1625–42* (paperback ed., Dublin, 2000), pp 15–16. 5 For details see 'Fingal 1603–60', i, pp 156–61. 6 Mícheál Ó Siochrú, *Confederate Ireland 1642–1649* (Dublin, 1999), p. 240. 7 'Fingal 1603–60', i, pp 161–5.

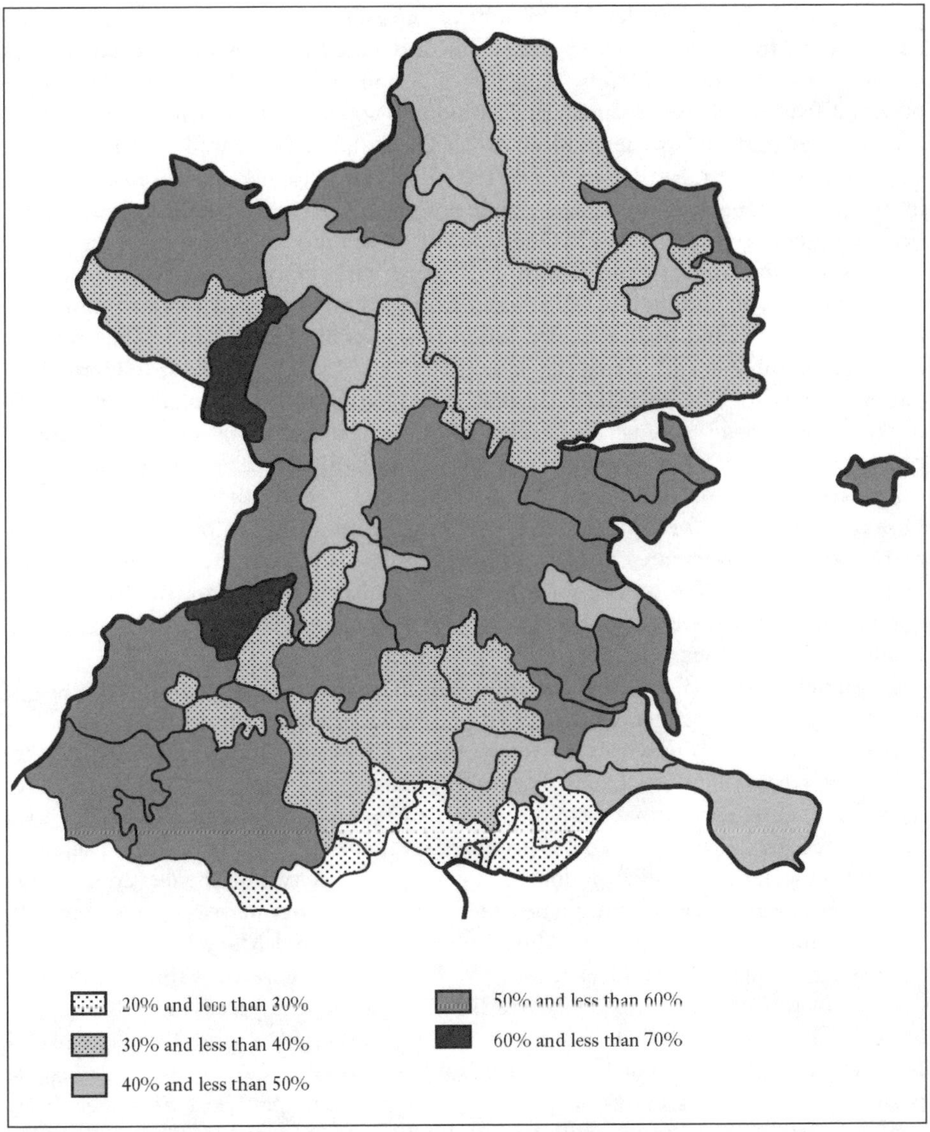

Fig. 5.1 Percentage of Fingal occupants with Gaelic-Irish surnames by parish, *c*.1664

pre-Norman times. Others may have moved in originally as labourers and perhaps married in the area. Yet others may have fled from Dublin city during the 1640s or perhaps left as a result of Dublin corporation's laws of 1657 against the Irish language and Irish dress.[8]

Other clues about the makeup of a community may be found in their marriage

8 *Anc. rec. Dublin*, iv, pp 118–9.

patterns. There is a considerable amount of information available concerning marriage among the élite groups in Fingal but a detailed analysis of such patterns is outside the scope of this study. However, a certain amount of information can be obtained from published primary and secondary sources. Donald Jackson analyzed the marriage patterns of the children of Sir Christopher Barnewall of Turvey (died 1607) and of his heir, Sir Patrick.[9] Thirteen of Sir Christopher's children contracted between them fourteen marriages while six of Sir Patrick's children contracted between them seven marriages.[10] One-third of these marriages were contracted with spouses within Fingal while almost half were with marriage partners from the adjoining areas of Dublin city, Meath and Kildare. Only one of the twenty-one marriages was contracted with a family which was possibly Gaelic-Irish. This was the marriage of Sir Patrick's daughter, Jane, to Roger Moore of Ballina, Kildare. This pattern seems to have been fairly typical of landed families in Fingal. Further evidence on marriage among the Fingal élite can be found in published funeral records.[11] These are not as satisfactory as genealogical records since they provided information only on children who had married before their parents' deaths. However, examples for Fingal provide even stronger evidence of the tendency to marry people from the area or from adjoining areas, at least in the case of older surviving children.[12] Of the twenty-six marriages contracted prior to the death of the parent twenty-three were to spouses with settler surnames and three to spouses with Gaelic-Irish surnames.

It is much more difficult to obtain information on the ordinary people as the single exclusively Fingal register which survives for the period is the Finglas Protestant register which covers only the last few years of the period under review.[13] The earliest entry, a baptism, dates from 1654 and the latest in the book, also a baptism, dates from 1684. Only eleven marriages are recorded for the period and all of these took place in the period 1666 to 1670. This suggests that there may have been a separate register for marriages which no longer survives. In only two of the eleven marriage entries are the addresses of the parties given. James Spooner married Anne Wagstaff, both of Finglas, in March 1667 while Robert Griffith and Mary Hawkins, both of 'Dunshaglin' (possibly Dunshaughlin, Co. Meath, but more probably Dunsoghly) married in July 1669.[14] Dunsoghly was listed as part of the parish of St Margaret's by the Civil Survey which cited the names 'Dunsaghlin' and 'Donsoughly'.[15] However, the civil parish of St Margaret's was regarded as part of the ecclesiastical parish of Finglas by Archbishop Bulkeley in 1630.[16] The parish of St Michan's lay partly within Fingal and partly within Dublin city. Most entries, even where addresses were given, stated simply the name of the parish. However, there were a few which gave information which is relevant to this study. For example, on 17 April 1654 Nicholas Doyle of Drumcondra (Clonturk parish) married Jane Flood of St

9 Donald Jackson, *Intermarriage in Ireland, 1550–1650* (Montreal, 1970), pp 31–4. 10 'Fingal 1603–60', i, pp 165–6. 11 Association for the Preservation of Memorials of the Dead, *Some funeral entries of Ireland* (Dublin, 1907–12). 12 'Fingal 1603–60', i, pp 166–7. 13 Finglas parish combined vestry book and registers, 1657–1758 (RCBL, P.307/1/1). 14 Finglas parish combined vestry book and registers, 1657–1758 (RCBL, P.307/1/1, pp 311 and 314). 15 *Civil Survey, vii, county of Dublin*, pp 209–10. 16 'Archbishop Bulkeley's visitation of Dublin, 1630', ed. M.V. Ronan in *Archivium Hibernicum*, viii (1941), pp 74–6.

Michan's.[17] Two further entries concerned the reading of banns but it is not possible to say if and where the couples were married. The first of these related to Edmond Brangan and Juhan Fitzharris, 'both of the barony of Balrothery', whose banns were read in St Michan's church in September and October 1654.[18] The second, which showed that marriage was a matter of public interest which concerned the whole community, read as follows:

> The banns of matrimony were published three several market days in the open market of Dublin by the register of Michan's parish between Christopher Dowdall and Jane Geragh, both of the town of Swords, vizt., on the twenty-seventh day of September 1656, and on the fourth and eleventh days of October next following.[19]

These entries suggest that young people sought their marriage partners locally but there is too little evidence to arrive at definite conclusions.

Little is known of the precise arrangements for betrothal and marriage that existed in Fingal. There are, however, one or two clues which suggest that, among the gentry at least, society gave firm control to the parents and those appointed by them to adjudicate in these matters. In 1644 Dr Thomas Arthur of Limerick, the eminent physician, wrote to his cousin, Robert Arthur of Hacketstown (parish of Lusk) as follows:

> Gentle cousin Robert, your son, John, came hither from Galway to see us, to whom he was heartily welcome, and being pleased to an affection upon my second daughter Dymphna, moved me and her mother earnestly in that behalf, to whose honest suit (though we had others nearer home) we are consented, as well in regard that both he now, and your son-in-law, Mr James Lynham, formerly persuaded us that the motion originally did proceed from you his parents, by consent of friends whom we always much loved and respected, as also for name's sake in hope that God be graciously pleased to raise us a hopeful posterity in them ...[20]

There were examples in Robert Arthur's will of how sanctions against marrying people whom the family considered unsuitable were imposed not just on children but also on servants.[21] He specified that bequests to his three unmarried daughters should be substantially reduced if they 'will not be directed and shall happen to marry any one contrary to the advice and good liking of my wife, my sons, John and Ignatius, and my said overseers, or the greater part of them ...' He left ten pounds to his servant, Catherine Walsh, on condition 'that she be ruled and demean herself

17 *The registers of the church of St Michan, Dublin, 1636–1685*, ed. Henry F. Berry (Dublin, 1907), p. 42.
18 *The registers of the church of St Michan, Dublin, 1636–1685*, ed. Henry F. Berry (Dublin, 1907), p. 44.
19 *The registers of the church of St Michan, Dublin, 1636–1685*, ed. Henry F. Berry (Dublin, 1907), p. 51.
20 J.D.H. Widdess, 'A notable Irish physician', in *The Irish Journal of Medical Science* (seventh series), no. 373 (Jan. 1957), p. 30. 21 Will of Robert Arthur, 4 June 1648 (NAI, Prerogative will book, 1664–84, ff 274–5).

as my wife shall advise her and especially if she shall marry such husband as my wife shall direct and think fit'. Joseph Woolley, a yeoman of Grangegorman, also placed some restrictions on the payment of legacies to his daughters if they married before reaching the age of twenty without the consent of their mother and brother.[22]

There is some evidence for the survival of the Gaelic practice of fosterage, or at least familiarity with it, in Fingal. Margaret Huiberts Verveer referred to 'a foster-brother of the said Alderman Arthur named Edward Walsh'.[23] Since she was a near neighbour of Robert Arthur, her testimony in this respect is likely to have been accurate. However, Robert Arthur, who had been brought up in Dublin city, was a relative newcomer to Fingal in 1641. A more pertinent example of the practice of fosterage was found in the case of Simon Corbally of Jordanstown (parish of Clonmethan) who left 48*s.* to his foster-son, James Preston, in his will which was proved in 1638.[24] There is a further reference in 'Purgatorium Hibernicum' to 'a troop of foster-brothers'.[25]

While the family was the principal vehicle for transmitting community values and norms the formal education system could also be employed for this purpose. Little is known about the type of education available within Fingal during the period 1603–60. However, Archbishop Bulkeley's visitation of the diocese of Dublin in 1630, although it was principally concerned with the state of the Protestant church, provided a considerable amount of information about the Catholic community in the diocese and even gave a glimpse of what the education system was like at that period.[26] The visitation report mentioned only four Catholic schools in Fingal together with a single school in the parish of St Catherine in Dublin city.[27] The Fingal schools were situated in Swords, Santry, Baldongan and Clonsilla. The schools in Swords and Baldongan were conducted by priests, Fathers Doyle and Clarke. The schoolmasters in Dublin city, Santry and Clonsilla were laymen – James Dunn, Patrick Drake and Thady Duffe. The four Fingal schools were, apparently, protected and supported by prominent local families – the Taylors of Swords, the Hollywoods of Artaine, the Fitzwilliams of Baldongan and the Luttrells of Clonsilla.

Even if there were no other elementary schools in the area, figure 5.2 shows that, assuming that schools could serve the population within a three-mile radius, there was wide coverage of the more populated areas, at least in theory. As there were chaplains in several great houses in the area, it is likely that other schools existed of which the authorities were unaware. It is also likely that, as the number of priests working in the area increased during the 1630s and 1640s, the number of Catholic schools also increased. Protestant children, apart from those living close to the city, were less well served. Since the Protestant population was low and almost non-existent in many areas it would have been difficult to sustain schools. It seems likely that private education was available, perhaps from the well-educated clergymen in

22 Will of Joseph Woolley, 10 July 1650 (NAI, Prerogative will book, 1664–84, f. 118). 23 Deposition of Margaret Huiberts, 14 March 1644 (TCD, MS 810, f. 238). 24 Abstract of will of Simon Corbally, proved 1638 (NLI, Fisher will abstracts, GO MS 290, p. 90). 25 Purgatorium Hibernicum …, *c.*1670 (NLI, MS 470), p. 5. 26 'Archbishop Bulkeley's visitation of Dublin, 1630', ed. M.V. Ronan in *Archivium Hibernicum*, viii (1941), pp 36–98. 27 'Archbishop Bulkeley's visitation of Dublin, 1630', ed. M.V. Ronan in *Archivium Hibernicum*, viii (1941), pp 61–4, 70 and 77.

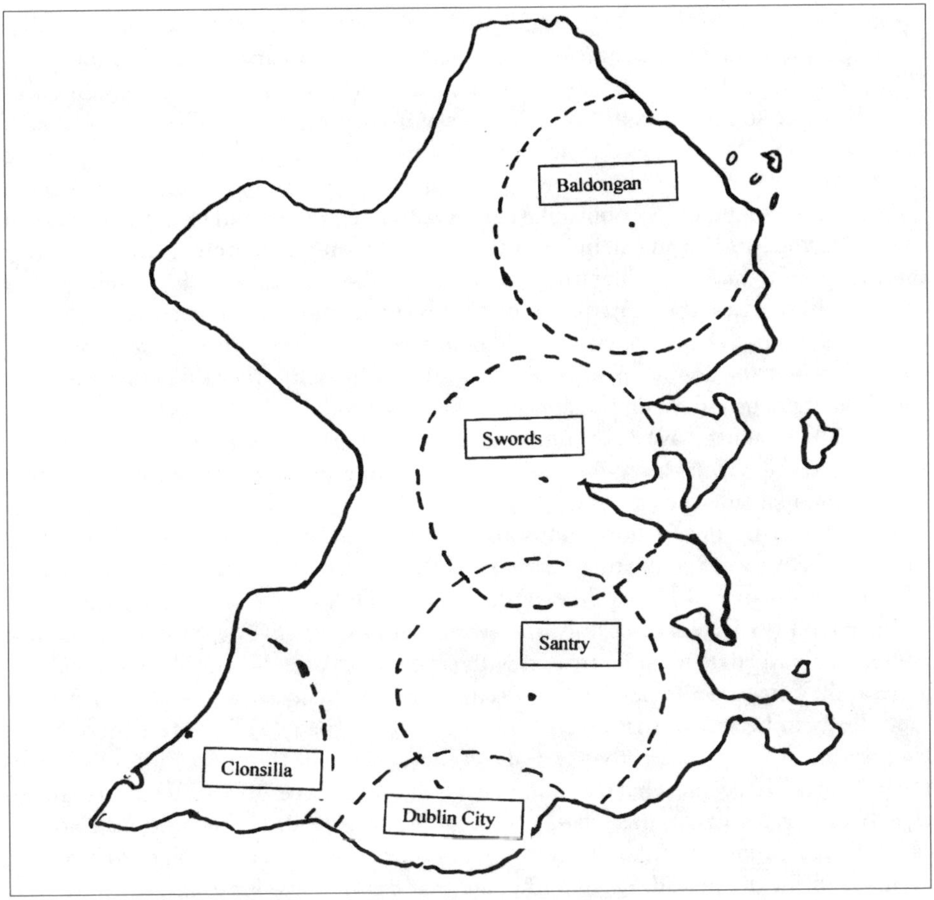

Fig. 5.2 Areas of Fingal situated within three miles of a known Catholic school, *c.*1630

the area, and there is evidence of a reasonably high literacy rate among Protestants. For those with access to Dublin city there was a choice of at least three schools, Christ Church Cathedral School, St Patrick's Cathedral School and the City Free School where arithmetic and writing were taught in 1608.[28] It is possible that Thomas Coffey, who taught in the Free School from 1643 to 1651 and who became minister of Finglas in 1654, took private pupils there.[29] William Hill, a former master at St Patrick's School, was known to have kept a private boarding school for the children of gentlemen at Finglas in the 1660s.[30]

It is difficult to gauge how effective this education system was. Since little private correspondence and few accounts, original wills or other similar documents have

28 Michael Quane, 'City of Dublin Free School' in *The Journal of the Royal Society of Antiquaries in Ireland*, xc, part ii (1960), p. 179. **29** Michael Quane, 'City of Dublin Free School' in *The Journal of the Royal Society of Antiquaries in Ireland*, xc, part ii (1960), pp 180–1. **30** Michael Quane, 'City of Dublin Free School' in *The Journal of the Royal Society of Antiquaries in Ireland*, xc, part ii (1960), p. 182.

survived for the area the only practical approach was to attempt to ascertain to what extent people signed documents or made their marks. This approach has limitations. While it is reasonable to conclude that those who were able to append their signatures were also able to read it is not possible to say if their writing skills extended much beyond signing their names. In the absence of any more reliable indicator an attempt was made to glean some information about literacy by examining the 1641 depositions for Co. Dublin (MSS 809 and 810) for those deponents and examinants known to have resided in Fingal (including three in suburban Oxmantown) before or after the rising up to and including 1653. Sixty-seven cases in all were identified in this category. In one case the signature or mark was indecipherable. In two cases the original depositions did not survive and it is impossible to determine from the copies whether or not the deponents signed the originals. In eight other cases the presiding commissioners or judges do not appear to have insisted on signatures or, if they did, the signatures must have been noted elsewhere. This leaves a sample of fifty-six usable cases of which thirty-four were signed, while in the other twenty-two cases the deponents made their marks.

An analysis by occupation/status has pin-pointed some rather surprising features.[31] Darby Lea, the postmaster of Balrothery, made his mark as did Katherine Magee, who managed Henry Mawdesley's farm. Of the five women whose names appeared in the fifty-six cases only one, Margaret Cooper of Oxmantown, signed her name. While the data must be treated with caution because the sample is so small, in general they suggest that ability to write increased with social status, that men were more likely to be able to write than women and that urban dwellers were more likely to possess writing skills than rural dwellers though the possibility that any rural/urban divide may have resulted from the existence of a different language (Irish) in rural areas, rather than a lack of writing skills, cannot be overlooked. Nevertheless an overall figure of more than 60 per cent who could sign their names seems high for the period. Despite the fact that examinants, for example, those who were suspected of plotting and those who had witnessed crimes, have been included, the preponderance of conventional deponents reporting losses gives an undue weighting to gentlemen and clergymen in the data. A certain amount of information on literacy can also be derived from the Finglas vestry books.[32] In 1661 three of the eight vestrymen present made their marks, while on 1 April 1662 five out of nine did so. Attendances were small in subsequent years but in 1667, when twelve attended, five vestrymen made their marks. While this is later than the period under review it seems to be a fair reflection of elementary education in what was probably the most prosperous area in Fingal in the pre-1660 period.

Higher education was a different matter. For Catholics who could afford it, there was by the year 1603 a network of Catholic colleges on the continent to which young men could be sent. However, most of the surviving published information concerns those who studied for the priesthood and, in particular, those whose names have been recorded by religious orders, a topic which will be examined in a later chapter. While

31 'Fingal 1603–60', i, pp 173–4. 32 Finglas parish combined vestry book and registers, 1657–1758 (RCBL, P.307/1/1).

education in Oxford or Cambridge had been available in earlier times, by the seventeenth century young Catholic men who wished for a good general education and, in particular, those with aspirations towards the professions, had to seek higher education on the Continent. The Protestant archbishop of Dublin and the bishop of Meath wrote in March 1604 to the council concerning the Catholics in their dioceses as follows:

> And they [the archbishop and bishop] now promise, if any order be taken that these people shall send their children to be taught by a religious schoolment and not to send their children out of the land to Dowa [Douai], and to Rhemes [Rheims], where their hearts are poisoned with idolatry, which is a thing easily done by the gentry of the Pale, both to provide and place a sufficient schoolment, and to maintain it according to the statute.[33]

One way in which the authorities could ensure that Catholic young men were educated in a Protestant environment in Ireland was by means of the court of wards. H.F. Kearney and Victor Treadwell have written about the activities of this court during the reigns of James I and Charles I.[34] Both historians concentrated on the administrative and financial aspects of the topic. As Treadwell has pointed out, the business of the wards was founded on the king's feudal tenures.[35] Those who held land by knight service, and this included many Fingal proprietors, were subject to a number of financial charges. Treadwell pointed out the particular difficulties which ensued when the heir was a minor.

> If the heir was a minor, the king assumed the wardship of his body and of his lands till he came of age. The heir then had to sue forth his livery of the lands from the king before he could enjoy his estate. According to the acts of supremacy of England and Ireland, he had also to take the oath of supremacy. If he failed to comply, his lands might be leased out to some other's profit.[36]

The impact of the educational provisions of the court of wards on Fingal does not appear to have been very great but it remained a threat. At least two local men, Thomas Bellings of Belinstown and Bartholomew Russell of Seatown were admitted to Trinity College.[37] In these two cases, the efforts of the authorities, in the long-term, were unsuccessful. In the Civil Survey Bartholomew Russell was listed as an 'Irish Papist' as was Laurence Bellings who had, according to the survey, inherited Belinstown.[38]

33 *Cal. S. P. Ire., 1603–06*, p. 153. 34 H.F. Kearney, 'The court of wards and liveries in Ireland, 1622–1641' in *Proceedings of the Royal Irish Academy*, lvii, section C, no. 2 (1955), pp 29–68; Victor Treadwell, 'The Irish court of wards under James I' in *IHS*, xii, no. 45 (March 1960), pp 1–27. 35 Victor Treadwell, 'The Irish court of wards under James I' in *IHS*, xii, no. 45 (March 1960), p. 2. 36 Victor Treadwell, 'The Irish court of wards under James I' in *IHS*, xii, no. 45 (March 1960), pp 2–3. 37 *A repertory of the inrolments on the patent rolls of chancery in Ireland, commencing with the reign of James I*, ed. John Caillard Erck (2 pts, Dublin, 1846–52), i, part ii, p. 356; G.D. Burtchaell and T.U. Sadleir, *Alumni Dublinenses: a register of the students, graduates, professors and provosts of Trinity College in the University of Dublin* (2nd ed., Dublin, 1935), pp 55 and 720. 38 *Civil Survey, vii, county of Dublin*, pp

Protestant young men in Fingal were in a particularly favourable position in the early seventeenth century. The new University of Dublin provided them with higher education on their doorstep. It is not clear how many actually availed of this facility since the records, where they gave any information about the place of an entrant's birth, tended to show it as 'Dublin' or 'County Dublin'.

One area of education in which both Catholics and Protestants mingled, at least at the start of the period was the law. Both confessional groups subscribed to the same legal system based on the common law. They met, not only in the higher courts, but also in the quarter sessions and manor courts which will be considered further in chapter 6. An interesting feature of these courts was that they were a means of bringing together the various social groups as well as people of different persuasions.

In 1970 Donal F. Cregan published detailed lists of Catholic Irishmen admitted to the English inns of court in the reigns of Elizabeth and James I.[39] Protestants were excluded from these lists. Colum Kenny has written an account of the King's Inns in Dublin which includes a detailed list of admissions during the period 1607–49.[40] With the help of the King's Inns admission papers and other lists of admissions it is possible to identify a number of members of Fingallian families and others who lived or had property in the area either before or after the date of their admission to one of the London inns or to the King's Inns.[41] It has also been possible to re-examine and extend these lists to cover the period to 1660 and to include Protestants known to have had associations with Fingal. The admissions during the reign of Elizabeth as well as those for the years 1603–60 were tabulated.[42] While the earlier list showed men who began their law studies prior to the period 1603–60, it is useful for a number of reasons. First, it showed a small number of students who were probably still in training in 1603. Secondly, it gave some idea of the number of trained lawyers in the area at the start of the period. However, a few of those listed had probably died before 1603, and at least one, William Bath of Drumcondra, had entered another walk of life, the priesthood. Thirdly, it provided a basis for comparison with the later list.

The strong traditional family associations with the law noted by Cregan was particularly obvious in the earlier (Elizabethan) list.[43] Almost all of those listed belonged to old Fingal families and, as has been pointed out by Colum Kenny, many of these families were related by marriage.[44] The later list showed a much greater variety.[45] It shows fewer representatives of the old families and a large number of Protestant newcomers to the area. The second list is probably incomplete. A few of the names

90 and 92. **39** Donal F. Cregan, 'Irish Catholic admissions to the English inns of court, 1558–1625' in *The Irish Jurist*, v. (n. s., 1970), pp 95–114. **40** Colum Kenny, *King's Inns and the kingdom of Ireland: the Irish 'inn of court' 1541–1800* (Blackrock, County Dublin, 1992), pp 275–81. **41** *Students admitted to the Inner Temple* (London, 1887); *The register of admissions to Gray's Inn, 1521–1889, together with the register of marriages in Gray's Inn Chapel, 1695–1754*, ed. Joseph Foster (London, 1889); *The records of the Honourable Society of Lincoln's Inn*, i, Admissions from A. D. 1420 to 1799 (London, 1896); H.A.C. Sturgess, *Register of admissions to the Honourable Society of the Middle Temple from the fifteenth century to the year 1944* (3 vols, London, 1949), i; *King's Inns admission papers, 1607–1867*, ed. Edward Keane, P. Beryl Phair and Thomas U. Sadleir (Dublin, 1982). **42** 'Fingal 1603–60', i, pp 177–9. **43** Donal F. Cregan, 'Irish Catholic admissions to the English inns of court, 1558–1625' in *The Irish Jurist*, v. (n. s., 1970), pp 99–101; 'Fingal 1603–60', i, p 178. **44** Colum Kenny, *King's Inns and the kingdom of Ireland: the Irish 'inn of court' 1541–1800* (Blackrock, 1992), p. 34. **45** 'Fingal 1603–60', i, p. 179.

of those admitted to the King's Inns in Dublin, particularly those of attorneys, corresponded to the names of Fingal tituladoes in the so-called census of 1659.[46] However, in the absence of details about residence in the *King's Inns admission papers, 1607–1867* it is not possible to be certain that those listed were, in fact, the Fingal tituladoes. The information available shows that there was a nucleus of highly-educated lawyers in Fingal in the early part of the seventeenth century, several of whom attained prominent positions in the legal system and in the administration. The restrictions on the practice of law by Catholics undoubtedly played a major part in the decline of representation in the profession by the older Fingal families.[47]

Little is known about the participation of Fingallians in other professions. The will of Nicholas Luttrell dated 22 June 1609 gives a tantalizing glimpse of how young men approached these matters. The extract from the will in the Elrington Ball papers reads as follows:

> Nicholas Luttrell of Luttrellstown in Co. Dublin, gent., having made a former will in perfect health and memory purposing to depart the realm of Ireland to apply his study towards Oxford, thereafter to the inns of court, though want of means altered his course, now purposing by the leave of God presently to go into other countries where he may attain the faculty of physic, in respect his means are short to accomplish the law, being at perfect health, wit and memory, makes his will . . .[48]

Since the will was proved less than a year later it is not possible to say how Nicholas would have prospered. The success of Dr Thomas Arthur of Limerick, referred to in chapter 2, suggests that well-trained Catholic doctors were in great demand.

A striking feature of Fingal in the early seventeenth century is the number of distinguished writers who lived at one time or another in the area. Many of the authors and their works were listed in Walter Harris's eighteenth-century compilation, *The whole works of Sir James Ware.*[49] Since this is an extensive topic which merits discussion in a separate study, only brief reference will be made to some of these writers and their works here. Many of them, though not all, were members of local families and some were probably natives of the area. Richard Stanihurst, historian and member of a Corduff family, and William Bath of Drumcondra, an authority on music and linguistics, were both priests living abroad at the beginning of the seventeenth century. Stanihurst's major works had already been published as had Bath's

46 *A census of Ireland circa 1659 . . .* ed. S. Pender (Dublin, 1939), pp 382–92. 47 Donal F. Cregan, 'Irish Catholic admissions to the English inns of court, 1558–1625' in *The Irish Jurist*, v (n. s., 1970), pp 95–114; Donal F. Cregan, 'Irish recusant lawyers in politics in the reign of James I' in *The Irish Jurist*, v, part ii (n. s., 1970), pp 306–20; Colum Kenny, *King's Inns and the kingdom of Ireland: the Irish 'inn of court' 1541–1800* (Blackrock, 1992), pp 70–139. 48 Abstract of will of Nicholas Luttrell, 22 June1609 (RSAI, Elrington Ball MSS, vol vii, f. 14); Francis Elrington Ball, *A history of the County Dublin . . . part fourth* (originally published 1906, reprinted Dublin, 1995), p. 8. 49 James Ware, *The whole works of Sir James Ware concerning Ireland, revised and improved*, ed. Walter Harris (2 vols, Dublin, 1764), ii.

works on music.[50] Bath's *Ianua Linguorum* was not published, until 1611 however.[51] His later works, in Latin and Spanish have been discussed by Seán P. Ó Mathúna.[52] James Ussher, archbishop of Armagh, a nephew of Stanihurst, who had somewhat more tenuous connections with Fingal, also wrote extensively. Sir Richard Bolton, a native of Stafford in England, who became recorder of Dublin in 1618 and lord chancellor in 1639 and who lived much of his life at Brazil near Swords, wrote an important book on law entitled *A justice of peace for Ireland*.[53] His near neighbour, Sir Samuel Mayart of Dubber, wrote a reply to 'A declaration setting forth how and by what means the laws and statutes of England, from time to time, came to be of force in Ireland' although this reply was not published for more than a century'.[54] The question of the real authorship of the original declaration (at one time attributed to Sir Richard Bolton) has been discussed by Aidan Clarke.[55] Sir James Barry of Santry, later chief justice of the king's bench, was another who contributed a legal work.[56] Sir James Ware, historian and antiquary, who had a home in Meakstown, Santry, wrote a number of books in Latin.[57] Catholic writers included Henry Fitzsimon, a Corduff Jesuit, who wrote two books.[58] Richard Bellings of Tyrrelstown, Mulhuddart, chronicled the recent history of the confederate wars in his *History of the Irish confederation and the war in Ireland*.[59] Another historian who had associations with Fingal was Nicholas Archbold of Mountainfoot (believed to be Shankill), son of the Baldoyle lawyer, George Archbold, a close friend and probably a relative of the Bath and Warren families of Drumcondra, who wrote two unpublished histories of the Capuchin mission to Ireland, including Fingal, in which he himself participated.[60] Another priest who was closely associated with the Bath family of Drumcondra and the Arthur family of Hacketstown, Walter Enos, was commis-

50 Richarde Stanyhurst, *A treatise contayning a playne and perfect description of Irelande* ... in Raphaell Holinshed and Richarde Stanyhurst, *Holinshed's Irish chronicle* ..., ed. Liam Miller and Eileen Power (London, 1577, republished Dublin, 1979); Richard Stanihurst, *De rebus in Hibernia gestis* (originally published Antwerp, 1584), translated from the Latin by Colm Lennon, in *Richard Stanihurst the Dubliner* (Dublin, 1981); William Bathe, *A briefe introduction to the true art of musicke* (London, 1584); William Bathe, *A briefe introduction to the skill of song, c. 1587*, introduced by Bernarr Rainbow (facsimile edition, Kilkenny, 1982). 51 William Bathe, *Ianua Linguarum, sive modus maxime accommodatus, quo patefit aditus ad omnes linguas intelligendas* (Salamanca, 1611). 52 Seán P. Ó Mathúna, *An tAthair William Bathe, C.Í., 1564–1614* (Dublin, 1980), pp 207–12. 53 Richard Bolton, *A justice of peace for Ireland* ... (Dublin, 1638). 54 Samuel Mayart, 'The answer of Sir Samuel Mayart, serjeant at law, and second judge of the common pleas in Ireland, to a book intitled, a declaration setting forth how and by what means the laws and statutes of England, from time to time, came to be of force in Ireland' in Walter Harris (ed.), *Hibernica or, some antient pieces relating to Ireland, never hitherto made publick (no. VI excepted)* (2 vols, Dublin, 1747–50), ii, pp 23–131. 55 Aidan Clarke, 'Patrick Darcy and the constitutional relationship between Ireland and Britain' in Jane H. Ohlmeyer (ed.), *Political thought in seventeenth-century Ireland: kingdom or colony* (Cambridge, 2000), p. 49. 56 James Barry, *The case of tenures upon the commission of defective title* (Dublin, 1637). 57 James Ware, *De scriptoribus Hiberniae libri duo* ... (Dublin, 1639); James Ware, *De Hibernia et antiquitatibus eius disquisitions* ... (London, 1654); James Ware, *Rerum Hibernicarum annales ... 1485–1558* (Dublin, 1664); James Ware, *De praesulibus Hiberniae commentarius* (Dublin, 1665). 58 Henry Fitzsimon, *The justification and exposition of the divine sacrifice of the Masse* ... ([Douai], 1611); Henry Fitzsimon, *Words of comfort ... letters from a cell ... and diary of the Bohemian war of 1620*, ed. Edmund Hogan (Dublin, 1881). 59 Richard Bellings, *History of the Irish confederation and the war in Ireland, 1641–3* ... ed. John T. Gilbert (7 vols, Dublin, 1882–91). 60 Nicholas Archbold, The historie of the Irish Capucins, 1643 (Bibliothèque Municipale de Troyes, MS 1103); Nicholas Archbold, The evangelicall fruict of the Seraphicall Franciscan order, centur 5, ab Anno Domini 1600, 1628, continued to 1645 (BL, Harleian MS 3888).

sioned by the papal nuncio, Rinuccini, to write a book presenting the case of the pro-Rinuccini faction in the Catholic Confederation.[61] The playwright, Henry Burnell of Castleknock, was the author of *Landgartha*.[62] Finally, it would be appropriate to include in this list of writers associated with Fingal the unknown author of 'Purgatorium Hibernicum' who contributed something rather unique to the history of the area in the form of burlesque.[63] While no authors in the Irish language have been identified the list of those who wrote in Latin, Spanish and English, and whose work survives, is impressive and testifies to the fact that, at the very least, an élite group of men in the area had access to a high standard of education. Not all of them left printed or even manuscript records. Nicholas Archbold paid the following tribute to the abilities of one of his colleagues, George Blackney of Rickenhore, whose baptismal name has not been identified:

> At our coming out of Germany to Charleville into France, by the general of the order's ordinance, Father George and Father Paul [Humphrey Warren] remained in Germany from whence afterwards they went to Rome the jubilean year of 1625. Whereunto did flock great numbers of pilgrims out of all parts of Christendom: for the receiving of whose confessions Father George, by papal authority, is ordained *penitentiary apostolicus*: having, so to say, the gift of tongues, for he heard confessions in the Irish, English, Latin, French, Spanish, Italian, Germanian and Flemish tongues.[64]

Luke Bath preached in French at Cologne.[65] The linguistic abilities of other Capuchin missionaries stood them in good stead when travelling to and from Ireland, particularly when they were forced to travel through England. Nicholas Archbold related how, on one occasion, Humphrey Warren pretended to be German and spoke Italian while in England and how he himself pretended to be French.[66]

The literary output of early seventeenth-century Fingallians was undoubtedly impressive but without more comprehensive research it is not possible to say that it was any richer than the work produced by natives or residents of other, particularly Irish-speaking, parts of the country. While the output in Fingal was varied there was a noticeable concentration on history and politics, reflecting perhaps the Fingallians' need to explain and come to terms with their own unique mixed culture during a time of change as well as their access to a variety of educational experiences.

No information has been found about the kind of education available to women. For ordinary women in the area public education seems to have been virtually non-existent. No doubt the daughters, as well as the sons, of the rich had the advantage of private tuition or were able to go abroad for education. It seems inconceivable that

61 Walter Enos, *A survey of the articles of the late rejected peace* ..., the first part (Kilkenny, 1646). 62 Henry Burnell, *Landgartha: a tragie-comedie, as it was presented in the new theatre in Dublin, with good applause, being an ancient story* (Dublin, 1641); Francis Elrington Ball, *Southern Fingal* ... (originally published 1920, reprinted Dublin, 1995), p. 21. 63 Purgatorium Hibernicum ..., c. 1670 (NLI, MS 470). 64 Nicholas Archbold, The historie of the Irish Capucins, 1643 (Bibliothèque Municipale de Troyes, MS 1103), p. 130. 65 Nicholas Archbold, The historie of the Irish Capucins, 1643 (Bibliothèque Municipale de Troyes, MS 1103), p. 94. 66 Nicholas Archbold, The historie of the Irish Capucins, 1643 (Bibliothèque Municipale de Troyes, MS 1103), p. 138.

less than seventy years after the suppression of the famous girls' school at Gracedieu, near Lusk, they were left entirely without education.

A common language helps to define a community. The evidence suggests that all of the people were able to speak English either as a first or second language. But as far back as 1577 Richard Stanihurst drew attention to the existence of an unusual dialect of English in Fingal which no doubt acted as a further distinguishing and unifying factor.[67] As Alan Bliss has shown, this dialect was spoken over a considerable period of time (written examples of the dialect date with certainty from *c.*1650 to 1689 but there is a high probability that works written as early as *c.*1596 and as late as 1705 were also written in Fingallian).[68] Bliss's definition of Fingal, which he extended to include the south-eastern part of Co. Meath, is somewhat wider than that used for the purpose of the present study. He defined the Fingallian dialect as a regional variety of Hiberno-English characterized by three features: 'rare words found also in the dialect of Forth, postponed stress in polysyllabic words, and a high proportion of Irish words and phrases'.[69] Bliss summarized the linguistic situation in Fingal as follows

> If we piece together all the evidence about Fingal and its dialect, we arrive at the following picture. Originally Fingal, at the heart of the English Pale, had been more completely English in language and customs than any other part of Ireland. Gradually it was penetrated by the Irish language, to such an extent that Stanihurst could be worried about the possible extinction of English. Subsequently, however, the English language underwent some revival; yet it remained so distinguished by the archaic character found also in Forth and Bargy, and by the survival of extensive Irish influence, that it could reasonably be described as a distinct language. What none of the writers specifically mentions is the existence of bilingualism in this area, and the ebb and flow of English and Irish is best explained in terms of a bilingual population preferring now one of their languages and now the other, as external influences made each of them more useful or acceptable.[70]

Some evidence, admittedly scanty, to support Bliss's argument for bilingualism in Fingal can be found in the 1641 depositions in Trinity College Dublin and in other sources. Just two direct references have been found in the depositions to support the argument that bilingualism occurred in Fingal. In the first of these Edward Leech vividly described his own experiences and those of his family and companions, who had been driven from Lambay in December 1641.[71] As they walked along the road 'by the sea-side' from Howth, where they had landed, to Dublin 'there were many of

67 Richarde Stanyhurst, *A treatise contayning a playne and perfect description of Irelande* ... in Raphaell Holinshed and Richarde Stanyhurst, *Holinshed's Irish chronicle* ..., ed. Liam Miller and Eileen Power (London, 1577, republished Dublin, 1979), pp 14–15. 68 Alan Bliss, *Spoken English in Ireland 1600–1740* (Dublin, 1979), pp 319–20. 69 Alan Bliss, *Spoken English in Ireland 1600–1740* (Dublin, 1979), pp 318–9. 70 Alan Bliss, *Spoken English in Ireland 1600–1740* (Dublin, 1979), pp 28–9. 71 Deposition of Edward Leech, 18 March 1644 (TCD, MS 810, ff 244–5).

the women of the villages thereabouts gathering cockles (as usually they do) who shouted aloud saying *Siggy Sassinagh, Siggy Sassinagh*, that is, there comes English ...' The second reference occurred in the Commonwealth examinations when Francis Dillon of Spricklestown in the parish of the Ward (barony of Castleknock) hailed a group of tories in Irish, calling to them to stand off.[72] The expectation that witnesses would be familiar with Irish place-names, which emerged in a suit concerning land boundaries in Clonsilla, has been noted in chapter 3. Perhaps the most telling pieces of evidence for the survival of Irish were those recorded by the Capuchins. The ability of the local Capuchin priest, George Blackney, to hear confessions in Irish in Rome in 1625 has already been mentioned.[73] During the Cromwellian period another Capuchin priest, Father Stephen, preached in Irish at Swords.[74] Some Irish words, for example, 'skene' (*scian*), 'garron' (*garrán*), 'tory' (*tóraí*) occurred from time to time in the depositions but since these words were not translated or defined in the text they may already have been assimilated into the Fingallian dialect of Hiberno-English or into Hiberno-English in general. Of more interest, perhaps, is the occurrence of the technical term 'slow begg' (*slua beag*), in a deposition made by a soldier, William Hollis, in April 1643.[75] He described how he went with his captain and the rest of his troop 'out of the town of Swords in the territory of Fingal upon a party to meet with and (if possible) to surprise the slow begg or small running army of the rebels then very frequent and dangerous to the king's loyal subjects in the country'. The deponent, or clerk, obviously found it necessary to explain the term, which suggests that it was not one familiar to most monolingual English speakers. Reference has been made in chapter 1 to the use of the words 'bater' and 'booter' in the Civil Survey and to the existence of a street known as the 'Irish Street' in Swords. As already noted, several typically Irish first names, for example, Donnogh, Teige, Phelim, are to be found in the hearth money roll for Co. Dublin.[76]

'Purgatorium Hibernicum' is particularly rich in Irish words.[77] These range from terms of endearment to the names of plants and birds. In some cases, the words were used as if they were English words, for example, with English plurals. In other cases complete Irish phrases were incorporated in the text. The fluency with which such words and phrases were used suggests a familiarity with the Irish language beyond that of a dilettante or learner. The later texts, based on the same theme, contained far fewer Irish words.[78] *The Irish Hudibras* was probably designed with the English market in mind and 'The Fingallian travesty' may well have been an earlier draft also intended for publication in England. The existence of a unique dialect no doubt helped to promote a sense of separate identity among the Fingallians, marking them

72 Examination of John Heard, 24 November 1652 (TCD, MS 810, f. 380). 73 Nicholas Archbold, The historie of the Irish Capucins, 1643 (Bibliothèque Municipale de Troyes, MS 1103), p. 130. 74 Nicholas Donnelly, *Short histories of Dublin parishes* (17 parts, Dublin, 1904–17), part xv, p. 73. 75 Deposition of William Hollis, 27 April 1643 (TCD, MS 810, f. 235). 76 'Hearth money roll for County Dublin, 1664' (second part), *Journal of the County Kildare Archaeological Society*, xi (1930–33), pp 386–466. 77 Purgatorium Hibernicum ..., c. 1670 (NLI, MS 470). 78 The Fingallian travesty: or the Sixt Book of Virgills Aenaeids A la mode de Fingaule (BL, Sloane MS 900); James Farewell (?), T*he Irish Hudibras or Fingallian prince, taken from the sixth book of Virgil's Aeneids, and adapted to the present times* (London, 1689).

off from both the Gaelic-Irish and from speakers of other forms of Hiberno-English. Although the dialect disappeared many years ago, the existence of traces of it in a few glossaries of locally-used words shows that up to the twentieth century there was a folk memory of the former distinctiveness of the area.[79] Some contributions from these sources have been included in recently published dictionaries of Anglo-Irish and Hiberno-English.[80]

In most cases people used conventional terms to describe time (reasonably precise dates and hours) and distance (miles). Sir Richard Bolton set out the official position on the citation of dates as follows: 'If it be Anno Domini 1599, the year shall be accounted after the computation of the Church of England and not *stilo novo*, as it is now at Rome, and other countries abroad'.[81] In *The whole works of Sir James Ware* the following paragraph appeared;

> Another measure was anciently in use in that part of the county of Dublin lying north of the river Liffey, which was called the Fingal measure. An act of parliament passed 13th Eliz., empowering Thomas Lancaster, archbishop of Armagh, to set some of his lands which lay out of the English Pale for any term not exceeding 100 years at 4*d*. an acre, according to the Fingal measure. This Fingal measure, was the English statute measure, containing 16 feet and half to the perch, which was introduced by the English, who planted themselves early in that country after the first English invasion.[82]

Some insight into the practices used by ordinary people is given in a series of depositions made in December 1652 in connection with the killing of the miller, Owen Hely, near Chapelizod by John Talbot of Belgard in February 1651. For example, Richard Greg, 'a husbandman aged twenty-three years or thereabouts' said that the incident took place 'one Sunday morning about Candlemas in the year one thousand six hundred and fifty' and mentioned that Knockvary was 'distant about a quarter of a mile from Chapelizod'.[83] The use of the term 'Candlemas' during the Commonwealth period is striking and suggests that there was little editing of the depositions. Giles Curran, also a husbandman, used a similar method of dating, 'about Candlemas last was a twelvemonth, upon a Sunday', but a more modern method of describing time and distance 'about eleven or twelve of the clock in the day time' and 'Knockvary, being about the distance of a quarter of a mile from the said Chapelizod'.[84] On the same occasion another deponent, Richard Raymond, a servant, used much the same method of dating but described Knockvary as 'being about the reach of musket shot from the said town of Chapelizod'.[85] John Talbot of

79 Patrick C. O'Neill, 'A north-County Dublin glossary' in *Béaloideas*, xvii (1947), pp 262–83; Patrick Halpin, 'English as we speak it in Skerries' (Skerries Historical Society Archives, unpublished paper no. 24, 1950); Patrick Archer, 'Gaelic and non-English words in use in Fingall' in *Fair Fingall* (2nd ed., Dublin, 1975), pp 129–42. 80 *A dictionary of Hiberno-English*, ed. Terence Patrick Dolan (Dublin, 1999); Diarmaid Ó Muirithe, *A dictionary of Anglo-Irish* (Dublin, 2000). 81 Richard Bolton, *A justice of peace for Ireland* ... (Dublin, 1638), part II, p. 17. 82 James Ware, *The whole works of Sir James Ware concerning Ireland, revised and improved*, ed. Walter Harris (Dublin, 1764), ii, p. 225. 83 Examination of Richard Greg, 16 December 1652 (TCD, MS 810, f. 388). 84 Examination of Giles Curran, 16 December 1652 (TCD, MS 810, f. 389). 85 Examination of Richard Raymond, 20 December 1652

Belgard, leader of the band of attackers, who was accused of the murder and who was probably a Catholic, said the incident took place 'in or about February 1650'.[86] This use of this method of dating suggests that the old style practice of denoting the year continued among all sections of the local population, not just the government authorities and Protestants. Evidence from other depositions shows that, at a time when watches and clocks were still luxuries, people often referred to time in a general way, for example, 'bedtime', 'early in the morning', 'falling of the night', 'about dinner time', 'till towards evening'.[87] Richard Swinson, who used a mixture of conventional and traditional dating methods, such as 'in harvest 1642' and 'on Friday at night next before the rebels were about to have taken the castle of Dublin', showed how major events impinged on the perceptions of the people.[88] Feast-days were used to denote dates by a number of deponents. As might have been expected, Christmas and Easter were mentioned.[89] Besides Candlemas (2 February) and Christmas day, fixed feast-days mentioned included St Luke's day (18 October, in a deposition made by Redmond Maguire of Enniskillen), St Thomas's Day (probably 21 December, in a south Co. Dublin deposition) and All-Hallows day (1 November).[90] More surprising, perhaps was the use of moveable feast-days (apart from Easter), such as Trinity Sunday, Shrovetide and Ash Wednesday.[91] As far as calculating distance was concerned the term 'musket shot' was used by a second deponent, in this case, Thomas O Rannahie, one of the accused, in his description of the attack on Edward St Lawrence near Turvey in 1651, which suggests that it may have been a normal way of measuring short distances.[92]

The 1641 depositions provide a few clues as to how the Fingallians saw themselves. Perhaps the most interesting is the account given by John Sephton of Finglas on 15 November 1641.[93] Part of his deposition reads as follows:

> This examinant saith that he knoweth Robert Davy of Jamestown aforesaid and that he and this examinant are sister's children and that he likewise knoweth William Rowan of Finglas and Bartholomew Walsh and John Copeland and Richard Delahide of Chapelmidway in the said county of Dublin and he further saith that William Rowen is a butcher and a papist and that Copeland is an Englishman, a Protestant, and Delahide is a gentleman and a papist but of what religion Walsh is he knoweth not but saith that his father hath cast him off by reason of his disobedience and lewd courses which

(TCD, MS 810, f. 390). **86** Examination of John Talbot, 11 November 1652 (TCD, MS 810, f. 391). **87** Examination of John Sephton, 15 November 1641 (TCD, MS 809, f. 176); examination of Richard Delahide, 19 November 1641 (TCD, MS 809, f. 198); deposition of Margaret Huiberts, 14 March 1644 (TCD, MS 810, f. 238). **88** Deposition of Richard Swinson, 28 July 1645 (TCD, MS 810, f. 325). **89** Deposition of Ann Cappar, 4 January 1642 (TCD, MS 809, f. 261); examination of John Coppinger, 4 May 1642 (TCD, MS 810, f. 199); deposition of William Hollis, 27 April 1643 (TCD, MS 810, f. 235); examination of Thomas Berry, 21 September 1653 (TCD, MS 810, f. 393). **90** Examination of Redmond Maguire, 1 November 1641 (TCD, MS 809, f. 46); deposition of Alice Poore, 23 January 1644 (TCD, MS 810, f. 248); examination of Patrick Tankard, 27 May 1653 (TCD, MS 810, f. 395). **91** Deposition of Robert Benion (copy only), 25 July 1645 (TCD, MS 810, f. 62); examination of Anthony Pile, 29 June 1643 (TCD, MS 810, f. 281); examination of Patrick Tankard, 27 May 1653 (TCD, MS 810, f. 395). **92** Examination of Thomas O Rannahie, 23 April 1653 (TCD, MS 810, f. 397). **93** Examination of John Sephton, 15 November 1641 (TCD, MS 809, f. 176).

> he followeth. And this examinant saith of himself that he is a dairyman and a Protestant and so hath been all his life and that he is tenant to Sir James Ware, knight …

During the early days of the rising this group of friends had been drinking together and discussing political affairs with the result that they had become suspects, even though there had been, as yet, no outbreak in Fingal. There are several interesting points about Sephton's description. All the surnames mentioned are settler names with the possible exception of 'Rowen', which may be either Gaelic or English. The socially-mixed group included men of different religions. The fact that Copeland was specifically described as an Englishman suggests that the others regarded themselves as Irish. Robert Church, servant to the Protestant alderman, Richard Barry of Santry, reported that some property had been burnt 'by the English'.[94] Robert Booth of Swords also had property burnt by 'the English army'.[95] Darby Lea, postmaster, of Balrothery, reported that 'English Protestants' had been murdered in the area.[96] Sarah Doughtie of Balcunnin described her neighbour, Dirrick Huiberts Verveer, as a 'Dutch man' even though he had been resident in nearby Skerries for many years.[97] It appears that the ordinary people, unlike some writers such as Richard Stanihurst and Richard Bellings and members of the gentry, were beginning to classify people by place of birth rather than by descent. However, they were becoming conscious of a conflict of identity which needed to be resolved. This was well expressed in the deposition of Susanna Stockdale, who gave the following account of her cousin, Nicholas Barnewall of Turvey, who had fled to Wales with 'the countess, his wife, and several priests and others of his family' when the rising of 1641 broke out.[98] Nicholas Barnewall had been potentially the most influential Fingallian of his age as he was descended from an old and respected line, he had extensive family connections, he was one of the largest landowners in the area, he had been a member of parliament and he was a Catholic. However, because of his departure to Wales at a critical time he remained a relatively minor figure in the history of Fingal. Susanna Stockdale met him while he was returning to Ireland in 1644 and, having 'asked him why those gentlemen of the gentlemen of the Pale, that were anciently descended of the English, could for pity rob and destroy the English Protestants as they did' he answered (according to Susanna's best recollection):

> that the poor Irish had the blame of all, but if the papists in England had but had as much power amongst themselves in England as the Irish had in Ireland, the English papists would have risen against the Protestants in England first, so as the poor Irish (as he called them) should not have been put to begin their quarrel there the first, further saying to this deponent the words: 'Do you think, cousin, that the Irish durst begin as they did, but that they conceived themselves sure of the like rising about the same time in

94 Deposition of Robert Church, 5 March 1642 (TCD, MS 809, f. 242). 95 Deposition of Robert Booth, 8 July 1642 (TCD, MS 810, f. 119). 96 Deposition of Darby Lea, 25 January 1642 (TCD, MS 809, f. 288). 97 Deposition of Sarah Doughtie, 20 January 1642 (TCD, MS 809, f. 275). 98 Deposition of Susanna Stockdale (copy only), not dated (TCD, MS 810, f. 94).

> England, according to the plot that the papists of both kingdoms had amongst them. So as there could come no aid or assistance out of England to the Protestants in Ireland' or to that effect. And then also the said Mr Barnewall seemed and expressed in word himself to be vexed for so leaving his countrymen and friends, the papists in Ireland, as he did, and going into Wales where he had spent so much money, further saying if he had stayed still in Ireland he might have done his countrymen, the papists of Ireland, more good there than he did by going into Wales and, besides, might have saved his own estates from the English, but said he: 'I feared because I lived as in the mouth of the state of Dublin. I should never have been quiet if I had stayed unless I should have been of the English Protestant party against my poor countrymen, the Irish, who were of my own religion and therefore I went away into Wales' or words to that purpose, to this deponent's now best remembrance.[99]

Can one derive any picture of the Fingallian character from the surviving evidence? Certain traits were alluded to in the records, but it is sometimes difficult to determine whether these traits were peculiar to Fingallians or whether they were typical of society in general in the early seventeenth century. When reading the 1641 depositions one cannot help but be struck by the reported cruelty of many of the inhabitants. The depositions were an important source of information but they were also generally one-sided and did not necessarily reflect the totality of normal human behaviour. The violence and cruelty which clearly emerged during and after 1641 may have been wartime manifestations of underlying tensions between neighbours and divisions within the community which had existed in peacetime and which boiled over under the pressure of war.

Eyewitness accounts survive of the killings of Henry Mawdesley and Dirrick Huiberts Verveer.[100] In the case of Verveer, the killing in December 1641 followed the stripping and robbing of his wife and sister when, in the words of his widow, the rebels 'compelled them to follow them, as they said, towards their colonel. And as they followed them, one of the said rebels, with a skene cut the said Dirrick in his head and stabbed him several times in his body till he fell dead down and when he departed he looked back to see if the said Dirrick did stir'.[101] The hanging of Henry Mawdesley in September 1642, witnessed by the young Balscaddan surgeon, George Cashell, was a much more deliberate affair and appears to have been in the nature of an execution. Having been brought first to the church of Clonmethan where he unsuccessfully attempted to send letters through Cashell to obtain ransom money, Henry Mawdesley was taken by the rebels to Mooretown, where 'they bade him prepare himself for he should die. But although the said Henry Mawdesley then and there begged earnestly for his life and told them that he had a wife and many small children, and done them no wrong nor hurt, yet the several rebels then and there present (by general consent amongst them), said he should be hanged, and instantly

99 Deposition of Susanna Stockdale (copy only), not dated (TCD, MS 810, ff 94–50). **100** Deposition of George Cashell (copy only), 29 February 1644 (TCD, MS 810, f. 25); deposition of Margaret Huiberts, 14 March 1644 (TCD, MS 810, f. 239). **101** Deposition of Margaret Huiberts, 14 March 1644 (TCD, MS 810, f. 239).

then and there most barbarously and without mercy hanged him accordingly'.[102] Cashell named twelve of the rebels and indicated that there were 'divers others whom he cannot name'. Despite his protestations Mawdesley and his servant, Katherine Magee, had made depositions about his losses some time earlier.[103] Katherine Magee had named twenty-eight rebels in her deposition though they were not, as far as can be ascertained, those involved in Mawdesley's execution.[104] One of those involved in Mawdesley's killing, Patrick Conran of Wyanstown, was, himself, later executed in Dublin.[105] The execution, if such it was, of Henry Mawdesley may have been part of a pattern. About 'harvest 1642' two ministers, a father and son, Ambrose and Robert Burton, who were travelling towards Drogheda, were captured near Skerries by what was later described as 'a company of tories'.[106] The two men were taken by a priest, Robert Passmore of Balrothery, a member of the troop of John Finglas (described by Passmore in his evidence under his later title of 'Lieutenant-Colonel') and brought to his commanding officer. The two ministers were taken to Mooretown where they were hanged on 20 August 1642 at a place called the 'English Green', apparently under Finglas's orders.[107] At Passmore's trial, which took place in 1653, witnesses to the capture and hanging gave evidence. There were certain similarities between the hangings of Mawdesley and the Burtons. They took place within a short time of each other. Both executions took place at Mooretown in the parish of Clonmethan, an area which was owned by the archbishop of Dublin, but which was leased to Luke Nettervill, leader of the Co. Dublin rebels in 1641.[108] Patrick Conran was involved in both captures. However, while the reason for Mawdesley's capture and execution was not clear, Passmore at his trial offered a plausible explanation for the capture of the ministers which was confirmed by another witness, Elizabeth Taylor.[109] He claimed that he had captured the Burtons in the hope that they might be used in an exchange of prisoners and also asserted that he was not present at their execution. Despite this plea he was found guilty of murder.[110]

Of the killings by tories which took place in the area somewhat later, those of the men killed at Forrest, near Swords, in 1650 and that of Owen Hely, the Chapelizod miller, took place in the course of skirmishes.[111] The death in 1651 of James

102 Deposition of George Cashell (copy only), 29 February 1644 (TCD, MS 810, f. 25). 103 Deposition of Henry Mawdesley, 22 April 1642 (TCD, MS 810, f. 167); deposition of Katherine Magee, 22 April 1642 (TCD, MS 810, f. 174). 104 Deposition of Katherine Magee, 22 April 1642 (TCD, MS 810, f. 174). 105 Deposition of George Cashell (copy only), 29 February 1644 (TCD, MS 810, f. 25). 106 Proceedings of the high court of justice held at Dublin and Cork in 1652, 1653 and 1654 (TCD, MS 866, ff 30–1). 107 Proceedings of the high court of justice held at Dublin and Cork in 1652, 1653 and 1654 (TCD, MS 866, ff 30–1 and 77). 108 *Civil Survey, vii, county of Dublin*, p. 157. 109 Proceedings of the high court of justice held at Dublin and Cork in 1652, 1653 and 1654 (TCD, MS 866, f. 31). 110 Proceedings of the high court of justice held at Dublin and Cork in 1652, 1653 and 1654 (TCD, MS 866, f. 31). 111 Examination of Andrew Gyraght, 2 February 1653 (TCD, MS 810, f. 357); examination of Thomas Waltryn, 1 February 1653 (TCD, MS 810, f. 375); examination of John Confy, 1 February 1653 (TCD, MS 810, f. 377); examination of Patrick Maguire, not dated (TCD, MS 810, f. 379); examination of John Heard, 24 November 1642 (TCD, MS 810, f. 380); examination of Richard Greg, 16 December 1652 (TCD, MS 810, f. 388); examination of Giles Curran, 16 December 1652 (TCD, MS 810, f. 389); examination of Richard Raymond, 20 December 1652 (TCD, MS 810, f. 390); examination of John Talbot, 11 November 1652 (TCD, MS 810, f. 391).

Brandon, the haberdasher or hat-maker, though probably premeditated and planned, also appears to have been swift.[112] The murder of Edward St Lawrence near Turvey in July 1651 was particularly brutal, involving humiliation and torture before the actual killing.[113] While the names of the perpetrators were given by the deponents, who included one of the accused, there was no mention of where they were from. They were described as a troop under the command of a Captain Francis Fleming. The attackers were under the command of a Patrick Dempsey, corporal of the troop, and numbered six or seven in all.[114] They may have been remnants of the confederate army. Two of the deponents stated that the corpse remained unburied, a fact also noted in the case of Dirrick Huiberts Verveer, whose body was left unburied from 'Thursday morning till Saturday night following ... for they denied him to be buried either in the church or churchyard' and in the case of three Englishmen, hanged in January 1643, possibly in Co. Meath, although the alleged perpetrators were from Fingal.[115] Richard Swinson of Meakstown, who described the latter incident, also stated that a fourth man, an Irishman, John Browne, had been shot, rather than hanged, and that he himself had been blinded in one eye and left for dead by the rebels.[116] As supporting evidence he claimed that he and others had found their bodies three or four months afterwards. It is not clear why the rebels should have made a distinction between the type of death penalty inflicted on Irish and English prisoners. A later incident, on this occasion clearly a military ambush by the rebels on a group of soldiers near Swords in March 1643, was described by William Hollis.[117] Following their capture two prisoners, William Murphy (probably an Irishman) and Henry Shelton were both hanged. Hollis himself escaped death 'earnestly pressing the rebels for the life they promised him upon his quarter'. Another of the eyewitness accounts concerned the murder in August 1642 of a man called Patrick, the servant of Samuel Filgate of Grangegorman, who described Patrick's death as well as the serious wounding of his maidservant, Margaret Boys.[118]

There were other accounts of murders in Fingal during the rising but some of these, at least, appear to have been based on hearsay evidence. Thomas Clitheroe, minister of Balrothery reported that he had been 'reliably informed that the rebels within the town of Balrothery aforesaid about that time most cruelly and barbarously murdered one, Mr Pardoe, a minister, and threw him into a dunghill water where he lay until the swine fed upon his head, and they also murdered one, Tom Rymmer, postboy for the packet'.[119] These alleged murders also appeared as hearsay evidence in the depositions of Darby Lea of Balrothery and Anthony Huiberts of Ballimad.[120]

112 Examination of Thomas Berry, 21 September 1653 (TCD, MS 810, f. 393); examination of Patrick Tankard, 27 May 1653 (TCD, MS 810, f. 395); examination of Peter Burnell, 23 June 1653 (TCD, MS 816, f. 302). 113 Examination of Arland Ussher, not dated (TCD, MS 810, f. 355); examination of Thomas O Rannahie, 23 April 1653 (TCD, MS 810, f. 397); examination of Richard Randall, not dated (TCD, MS 810, f. 399). 114 Examination of Thomas O Rannahie, 23 April 1653 (TCD, MS 810, f. 397); examination of Richard Randall, not dated (TCD, MS 810, f. 399). 115 Deposition of Margaret Huiberts, 14 March 1644 (TCD, MS 810, f. 239); deposition of Richard Swinson, 28 July 1645 (TCD, MS 810, f. 325); examination of Arland Ussher, not dated (TCD, MS 810, f. 355); examination of Thomas O Rannahie, 23 April 1653 (TCD, MS 810, f. 397). 116 Deposition of Richard Swinson, 28 July 1645 (TCD, MS 810, f. 325). 117 Deposition of William Hollis, 27 April 1643 (TCD, MS 810, f. 235). 118 Deposition of Samuel Filgate, 8 January 1644 (TCD, MS 810, f. 232). 119 Deposition of Thomas Clitheroe, 26 May 1642 (TCD, MS 810, f. 126). 120 Deposition of Darby Lea, 25 January

As well as the killings described previously, Richard Swinson alleged that in the autumn of 1642 the rebels murdered 'one Richard Synnott of Meakstown ... a Protestant, by cutting his throat'.[121] He also stated that that about July 1642 at Dubber they 'slew and murdered one, Patrick Mangan, that kept the cattle of Sir Samuel Mayart, knight, and others of the English'. The circumstances surrounding the death of Edward Cappar of Finglas are unclear.[122] His widow alleged that four members of Captain Barnewall's company murdered him. But it is not clear from her deposition that she actually witnessed the murder.

There were also allegations that victims had died as a result of the treatment meted out to them by the rebels. This is well documented in the case of Catherine Cromphouts, sister of Dirrick Huiberts Verveer.[123] James Smith of Grallagh claimed that he and his wife 'who, being very old, were also by the rebels stripped and robbed of their clothes, apparel and of their bedding whereby and by a wound which the rebels gave her in her throat, by cold and want, his wife died ...'[124] The depositions contain some reports of physical injuries inflicted by the rebels. John Lukey, minister of Ballyboghil, survived an attack by dogs which had been set on him.[125] Sarah Doughtie, widow of the minister of Lusk, having described the losses sustained as a result of the attack on her home at Balcunnin went on to say:

> And at the same time the said rebel whose name as she is informed was Cruise [of the Naul] drew his sword and held the same unto her breast swearing most horrid oaths that he would kill her unless she would deliver to him her money and threatened to kill her children unless they would cease to cry out. And also the said Cruise or some of his company hurt two of the deponent's servants very dangerously and turned her, and her four poor children out of the doors; since which time she and they are ready to starve were it not for the charity of well-disposed people.[126]

Several deponents reported death threats.[127] However, while many deponents described how they had been forcibly and cruelly deprived of their goods, few, apart from those already mentioned, cited specific instances of physical cruelty. During the early stages of the war the rebels, on the whole, appear to have been more interested in spoil than in revenge. The people of Fingal were inured to suffering as they were used to witnessing severe punishments for crimes. Hanging (including, in certain cases, drawing and quartering) for men and burning for women were the prescribed punishments for many crimes.[128] The rebels followed the same pattern as the author-

1642 (TCD, MS 809, f. 288); deposition of Anthony Huiberts, 29 January 1642 (TCD, MS 809, f. 311). **121** Deposition of Richard Swinson, 28 July 1645 (TCD, MS 810, f. 325). **122** Deposition of Ann Cappar, 4 January 1642 (TCD, MS 809, f. 261). **123** Deposition of Huibart Cromphouts, 2 March 1642 (TCD, MS 809, f. 268); deposition of Margaret Huiberts, 14 March 1644 (TCD, MS 810, ff 238–9). **124** Deposition of James Smith, 26 April 1642 (TCD, MS 810, f. 104). **125** Deposition of John Lukey, 2 March 1643 (TCD, MS 810, f. 168). **126** Deposition of Sarah Doughtie, 20 January 1642 (TCD, MS 809, f. 275). **127** For example, deposition of Ann Foreside, 5 January 1642 (TCD, MS 809, f. 279); deposition of Anthony Huiberts, 29 January 1642 (TCD, MS 809, f. 310); deposition of John Huxley, 21 May 1642 (TCD, MS 810, f. 158). **128** Richard Bolton, *A justice of peace for Ireland* ... (Dublin, 1638), book I.

ities. Randall Dimmock, minister of St Doolagh's, described how a gallows was set up in Swords in December 1641 to hang his son together with a Dutch man, 'yet they both escaped by God's providence'.[129] Daniel Barwick, commander of the pinnace, *The Swan,* was threatened with hanging during his imprisonment in Baldongan.[130] This threat was not carried out.

There were a few reports of help given by neighbours and others during the 1641 rising. Sarah Doughtie of Balcunnin was helped by the 'charity of well-disposed people'.[131] Ann Foreside of Coolock reported that, following death threats to her husband, he 'to shun the danger, hid himself in a ditch of water from twelve o'clock in the night till eight in the morning, by which he got a sickness which she thinks will kill him'.[132] She also reported that 'the rebels swore they would hang this deponent because they could not meet with her husband, and had done it as she thinks: but that some women, her neighbours, privately conveyed her away'. Thomas Williams, a labourer of Santry, told in 1644 that, though he had served against the rebels for two years, 'having been since sick and weak, got none of his pay or entertainment for near half a year last past: and now with his wife and children is like to starve, as they had done if the charity of good people had not relieved him'.[133]

Other characteristics have been noted that have, perhaps, less to do with the temporary influences of war. Richard Stanihurst wrote of the addiction to husbandry and the continual drudgery of the Fingallians as well as their expertise in agricultural matters.[134] An anonymous seventeenth-century writer described Co. Dublin, apart from the mountainous area to the south as 'rich and plenteous, the people of a stately port and garb, in genteel neatness and carriage surpassing all the rest of Ireland ...'[135] He also found Fingal 'very well husbanded' noting that 'this place discovers the idleness of the other counties, which would equally answer the industry of the labourer, if it were employed.'[136] The ability of Fingallians to work hard was well-attested but another side of their character appeared in the deposition of Revd George Creichton of Virginia in 1643.[137] Creichton certainly exaggerated when he said that 'all the inhabitants of the county of Dublin, Meath and Louth fled with all their goods into the county of Cavan'.[138] Most of the leaders he mentioned in his account were from Fingal and several of these were from the area around Swords. The refugees brought with them 'great droves of cattle of all sorts, great carts laden with trunks and all kinds of good household stuff, great store of wheat and malt'.

129 Deposition of Randall Dimmock, 1 March 1642 (TCD, MS 809, f. 276). 130 Deposition of Daniel Barwick, 23 May 1642 (TCD, MS 810, f. 115). 131 Deposition of Sarah Doughtie, 20 January 1642 (TCD, MS 809, f. 275). 132 Deposition of Ann Foreside, 5 January 1642 (TCD, MS 809, f. 279). 133 Deposition of Thomas Williams, 10 January 1644 (TCD, MS 810, f. 269). 134 Richarde Stanyhurst, *A treatise contayning a playne and perfect description of Irelande* ... in Raphaell Holinshed and Richarde Stanyhurst, *Holinshed's Irish chronicle* ..., ed. Liam Miller and Eileen Power (London, 1577, republished Dublin, 1979), p.13; Richard Stanihurst, *De rebus in Hibernia gestis* (originally published Antwerp, 1584), translated from the Latin by Colm Lennon, in *Richard Stanihurst the Dubliner* (Dublin, 1981), p. 143. 135 G.N., *A geographicall description of the kingdom of Ireland* ... (London, 1642), p. 14. 136 G.N., *A geographicall description of the kingdom of Ireland* ... (London, 1642), p. 17. 137 Deposition of George Creichton, 15 April 1643 (TCD, MS 832, ff 145–60; MS 833, ff 227–39); John T. Gilbert (ed.), *A contemporary history of affairs in Ireland from A. D. 1641 to 1652* ... (3 vols, Dublin, 1879–80), i, part ii, pp 525–46. 138 Deposition of George Creichton, 15 April 1643 (TCD, MS 832, f. 152); John T. Gilbert (ed.), *A contemporary history of affairs in Ireland from A. D. 1641 to 1652* ... (3 vols, Dublin, 1879–80), i, part ii, p. 536.

They were generous with their supplies and as Creichton went on to say: 'With these there came such plenty of corn that by God's providence we got some relief, the liberality of the deponent's own parishioners proving most scant and beggarly'. Creichton also said

> And this was most manifest in (almost) all the Pale gentlemen (and greater eagerness did show itself in the gentlewomen than in the men) that they were irreconcilable enemies to the English nation, for such were their words, they were sorry that they had let any English pass safe to Dublin. And in their discourse, speaking what number of English were killed in the several counties of the kingdom, the men of Fingal mentioned that they had killed far more than any other counties . . .[139]

This extract gives a rare insight into the attitudes of Fingal women as well as suggesting an unusual degree of arrogance in the men. Creichton commented further on this tendency to brag saying: 'And then they would brag what great matters they would do to the heavy heeled English, with stones and skenes, if ever they should see them come within their county, and yet how would they run away from their commanders upon a false alarum'.[140] Creichton also noted that the Fingallians tended to lie and to place little trust in outsiders saying:

> And why might not they as well lie in that, as in anything else, it being so common a thing, and so well known, that he perceived none of those people believed others what they said; at least the Pale people believed not the O'Reillys and the O'Reillys believed not the Pale.[141]

Creichton also commented on the Fingallians' ability to enjoy themselves, even in adversity. This aspect of their character will be considered in the next chapter.

The problem of attempting to define a seventeenth-century Fingallian is a daunting one. It is highly probable that the vast majority of the people who lived in the area in the period 1603–60 had been born there. The difficulty lies in establishing this fact in individual cases. Fingal then, as now, was a melting-pot. The concept of Fingallian has been broadened here to include not only people such as William Bath, Christopher Hollywood and Richard Bellings who, in all probability, were natives of Fingal but also those who, like Richard Stanihurst, belonged to Fingal families but were born elsewhere, those who, like James Ussher, spent a limited time in the area but displayed an affinity with and affection for it and newcomers such as Richard Bolton and Samuel Mayart, who had come from England to make their homes there.

139 Deposition of George Creichton, 15 April 1643 (TCD, MS 833, f. 236); John T. Gilbert (ed.), *A contemporary history of affairs in Ireland from A. D. 1641 to 1652 . . .* (3 vols, Dublin, 1879–80), i, part ii, p. 541. 140 Deposition of George Creichton, 15 April 1643 (TCD, MS 833, f. 237); John T. Gilbert (ed.), *A contemporary history of affairs in Ireland from A. D. 1641 to 1652 . . .* (3 vols, Dublin, 1879–80), i, part ii, p. 542. 141 Deposition of George Creichton, 15 April 1643 (TCD, MS 833, f. 237); John T. Gilbert (ed.), *A contemporary history of affairs in Ireland from A. D. 1641 to 1652 . . .* (3 vols, Dublin, 1879–80), i, part ii, p. 543.

Those just mentioned were writers, but the same interesting mix of natives and newcomers can be found in lists of lawyers, politicians and clergymen associated with the area. However, it must be emphasized that a great number of the people of Fingal, perhaps even the majority, had inherited and, to some extent, still shared a culture which predated that of the oldest settler families and which linked them to parts of Ireland with which the élite families in Fingal had little or no affinity.

6

'Drinking, piping and dancing'

> A sort of profane wretches, after they had chopped up their Mass in the morning, they spent all their time in playing at tennis (the deponent hath observed above 200 able men together) in drinking, piping and dancing . . .
>
> Revd George Creichton on the Fingallians (1643)[1]

In the quotation cited above Revd George Creichton, while showing a certain amount of sympathy for the plight of a group of Fingallian refugees, regarded them as a people who spent much of their time in vain pursuits. Was this a valid criticism of the people of Fingal? How did they generally interact with each other and with outsiders? This chapter explores social life and relationships in seventeenth-century Fingal.

The people of Fingal came together and interacted with each other in many ways. Perhaps the most important of these was the workplace. Certain aspects of the relationships between landlords and tenants have been discussed in chapter 3. As has been shown in chapter 4, farm workers met on their way to market and travelled together as much for company as for safety. The principal industries of the area, farming and fishing were labour-intensive and demanded a high degree of cooperation, particularly at certain times of the year, such as harvest in the case of farm labourers and Lent in the case of the fishermen. Forges, and there were several of them in Fingal, provided another setting for socializing in the course of a day's work. Markets and fairs, a topic examined in chapter 4, presented a pleasant opportunity for meeting others as well as for trade. A further activity which brought people together in an organized way was the repair of roads. In 1612 an act came into force which required the constables and churchwardens of every parish to call together a number of parishioners in Easter week to elect 'two honest persons of the parish, to be surveyors and orderers of the works for the amendment of the high ways, cashes, and paces in their parish, leading to any market town'.[2] Six days were to be set aside for the work between Easter week and the feast of St John the Baptist (24 June). Every person with specified land in the parish and every other person keeping a draught or plough was to supply one wain or cart, suitably equipped, together with two able men, while every householder, cottier and labourer of the parish, who was

1 Deposition of George Creichton, 15 April 1643 (TCD, MS 833, ff 236–7); John T. Gilbert (ed.), *A contemporary history of affairs in Ireland from A. D. 1641 to 1652 . . .* (3 vols, Dublin, 1879–80), i, part ii, p. 542. 2 An act for repayring and amending of high-ways and cashes, and cutting or clearing of paces, 11, 12 and 13 J.I, c.7, *Stat. Ire.* (1786), i, pp 444–8.

not a hired servant, had to take part in the work or arrange for someone else to substitute for him on each of the six days. Even the types of tools (shovels, spades, pickaxes, mattocks and axes) which the workers were required to bring with them were specified. Among the powers given to supervisors was permission to carry away rubbish or small broken stones from quarries and also underwood found within the parish, the owners to be compensated by the parish.[3] Given the number of highways leading to market towns this act was important for Fingal. In 1657, as the surviving Finglas parish vestry book recorded, the vestrymen selected William Johnson of Finglas and Nicholas Fitzpatrick of Broghan to act as 'supervisors of the highways within the said parish, and to see that the same be well and sufficiently repaired and amended and cleared of bushes and trees according to law'.[4] The same two men continued in office in 1658 and 1659.[5] It is interesting to note that the vestry used the term 'Midsummer Day' rather than the 'Feast of Saint John the Baptist' as the date by which the work should be completed in 1658. There are no records for 1660. It seems likely that, given the importance of the roads leading to Dublin, that the authorities would have enforced the 1612 act in relation to these roads, resulting in the coming together of a large number of men each year to carry out the work and, no doubt, to meet and drink in one of the Finglas alehouses when it had been completed.

The courts also provided an opportunity for people to meet. There were two types of court operating within the area, the quarter sessions, presided over by justices of the peace, and the manor courts which were operated by certain landowners or their deputies, who were known as seneschals. There are few surviving references to the practical operation of the legal system in Fingal in the period covered by this study. One indirect reference can be found in the deposition of Richard Delahide of Chapelmidway, dated 19 November 1641, which fell on a Friday.[6] This deposition was made before the lord chancellor, Sir Richard Bolton, and the lord chief justice of the common pleas, Sir Gerard Lowther, who would, no doubt, have been able to challenge any inaccuracy in Delahide's reference to the proceedings. He deposed that 'upon Thursday last was fortnight [4 November] upon the general sessions for the county of Dublin he, among others of the county, appeared upon the Abbey Green, where they continued until it was about the falling of the night and then repairing homewards in the way towards Finglas he met with William Rowen …'. The Abbey Green appears to have been the green adjacent to the former abbey of the Blessed Virgin Mary in Dublin, called 'the Abbey-green' and described in a grant of 1604.[7] It would seem that the sessions for Co. Dublin were held close to the city boundaries, were well attended and lasted all day.

The general question of the role of the justices of the peace and the quarter ses-

3 An act for repayring and amending of high-ways and cashes, and cutting or clearing of paces, 11, 12 and 13 J.I, c.7, *Stat. Ire.* (1786), i, p. 445. 4 Finglas parish combined vestry book and registers, 1657–1758 (RCBL, P.307/1/1, p. 1); William Cotter Stubbs, 'Finglas, County Dublin, vestry books' in *Journal of the Royal Society of Antiquaries of Ireland*, xlvi (1916), p. 27. 5 Finglas parish combined vestry book and registers, 1657–1758 (RCBL, P.307/1/1, pp 11 and 14). 6 Examination of Richard Delahide, 19 November 1641 (TCD, MS 809, f. 198). 7 *A repertory of the inrolments on the patent rolls of chancery in Ireland; commencing with the reign of King James I*, ed. John Caillard Erck (2 pts, Dublin, 1846–52), i, part i, p. 124.

sions, has been discussed, in relation to the early seventeenth century, by Raymond Gillespie and, in relation to the eighteenth century, by Neil Garnham.[8] Of particular interest for Fingal is the contemporary work, *A justice of peace for Ireland*, by the English-born chancellor, Sir Richard Bolton, who lived at Brazil, near Swords. He wrote concerning the commissions to a justice of the peace:

> These two commissions do somewhat differ in the second *Assignavimus*, for by that for the county of Dublin, the justices of the peace have power to hear and determine felonies, but in the other they have no power given them thereby to hear and determine of any felony, and the reason of this difference is twofold. First, because no justices of assize and gaol delivery go into the county of Dublin. Secondly, because at the quarter sessions of the peace there is always one or more of the judges or of the king's counsel present.[9]

All Fingal cases, apart from cases of treason, could be dealt with at local level. This resulted in the assignment of a wide range of powers to local justices. The names of a few of these justices of the peace are known. One such was James, son of Robert Bermingham of Ballough, who lived in the 1630s.[10] Another justice of the peace for Co. Dublin was Sir Robert Meredith who carried out several examinations in the period 1641–2.[11] Others mentioned in St Michan's parish register as justices of the peace for the city and county of Dublin were Captain William Ivery or Every, Alderman George Gilbert and Alderman Robert Mills.[12] Sir Richard Bolton gave a number of examples of documents showing how justices of the peace should operate in certain circumstances. While the names contained in these examples were almost certainly imaginary the proceedings they described were probably based on actual cases. Many of them mentioned Co. Dublin and some specified Swords.[13]

Of more immediate concern to the local people were the manor courts, consisting of courts leet and baron which were held in various parts of Fingal. A list of these courts derived from the published Civil Survey is probably incomplete.[14] No mention is made of the court known to have been held in the archbishop's manor of Finglas in the late sixteenth century.[15] At least two other courts were mentioned in grants, one of which was a grant of the lands of Saint Mary's abbey, which included Grangegorman and other areas in Fingal, to John Wakeman who was also granted a court leet.[16] The second was a grant of the lands of Hacketstown and various other lands to Theobald Bourke.[17] This grant mentioned a court leet and baron. It is not

8 Raymond Gillespie, *Colonial Ulster: the settlement of east Ulster 1600–1641* (Cork, 1985), pp 102–3; Neil Garnham, *The courts, crime and criminal law in Ireland 1692–1760* (Dublin, 1996), pp 81–2. 9 Richard Bolton, *A justice of peace for Ireland* ... (Dublin, 1638), book I, p. 14. 10 Association for the Preservation of Memorials of the Dead, *Some funeral entries of Ireland* (Dublin, 1907–12), p. 83. 11 For example, examination of Daniel Conway, April 1642 (TCD, MS 810, f. 97); examination of Edmund Archbold, 31 December 1641 (TCD, MS 810, f. 99). 12 *The registers of the church of St Michan, Dublin, 1636–1685*, ed. Henry F. Berry (Dublin, 1907), pp 41 and 43–4. 13 Richard Bolton, *A justice of peace for Ireland* ... (Dublin, 1638), book I, pp 285 ff. 14 'Fingal 1603–60', i, pp 202–4. 15 *Court book of the liberty of Saint Sepulchre* ..., ed. Herbert Wood (Dublin, 1930), pp 9, 54–6 and 70–1. 16 *A repertory of the inrolments on the patent rolls in chancery in Ireland; commencing with the reign of King James I*, ed. John Caillard Erck (2 pts, Dublin, 1846–52), i, part ii, p. 3. 17 *A repertory of the inrolments on the patent rolls in chancery in Ireland; commencing with the reign of King James I*, ed. John Caillard Erck (2 pts,

known if either of these courts was actually held in Fingal. Rather surprisingly two of the larger urban areas, Lusk and Balrothery, do not appear to have had separate manor courts. It is clear that the archbishop's tenants in Lusk attended the court in Swords.[18] By 1641 Balrothery lacked a dominant proprietor and the inhabitants may have attended courts elsewhere.[19] The wording in the Civil Survey suggests that the lord of Howth held separate courts in Howth and in the parish of Lusk and that the earl of Ormond held a separate court in Balscaddan for his Whitestown tenants.[20] The court at Reynoldstown appears to have originated as a court originally held by the Abbey of Kilmainham.[21] It adjoins the townland of the Naul where there was also a manor court.[22] Raymond Gillespie has pointed out that a large number of courts still survived in the barony of Balrothery in the mid-seventeenth century.[23] With two courts in Balscaddan parish and two in the Naul the extreme north of the barony was particularly well supplied. In addition the Balscaddan and Balrothery tenants of Viscount Gormanston may have been required to attend a court situated close by at Gormanstown in Co. Meath. Since a court leet was held on behalf of Lord Gormanston in Athboy in 1664, it is likely that he also held a court at Gormanstown.[24] However, neither court is recorded in the Civil Survey for Co. Meath.[25] Figure 6.1 shows the approximate location of the Fingal courts.

Joseph Byrne has provided a rare insight into the operation of a manor court, specifically a court baron, at Garristown in 1612.[26] Unfortunately little else is known about the workings of manor courts in Fingal during the period 1603–60. The initial grant of the manor of Holmpatrick on 20 June 1605 to the earl of Thomond empowered him 'to hold courts baron in the townland of Skerries aforesaid'.[27] The later, more comprehensive, grant of 1609 confirmed this grant but also included a general statement confirming his right to hold manor courts.[28] The relevant section reads as follows:

> Also, licence to said earl of Thomond, his heirs and assigns, to hold and enjoy, for ever a court-leet and view of frankpledge, and all things to court-leet and of frankpledge belonging, within the aforesaid respective manors of Clare, Bunratty, Clonrowan, Kilrush, Moy, Ibrackan and Danganbulke in County Clare; in the manor of Cowlenogonagh in counties Limerick and Tipperary; in the manor of Enniskeen in County Cork; in the manor of Carlow in County

Dublin, 1846–52), i, part ii, p. 126. 18 *Civil Survey, vii, county of Dublin,* pp 117–33. 19 *Civil Survey, vii, county of Dublin,* pp 13 and 15. 20 *Civil Survey, vii, county of Dublin,* pp 64, 73 and 169. 21 *Civil Survey, vii, county of Dublin,* p. 34. 22 *Civil Survey, vii, county of Dublin,* p. 30. 23 Raymond Gillespie, 'A manor court in seventeenth century Ireland' in *Irish economic and social history*, xxv (1998), p. 82. 24 John Ainsworth, 'Survey of documents in private keeping' in *Analecta Hibernica*, no. 25 (1967), pp 159–60; Raymond Gillespie, 'A manor court in seventeenth century Ireland' in *Irish economic and social history*, xxv (1998), p. 81. 25 *Civil Survey, v, county of Meath with returns of tithes for the Meath baronies*, pp 10 and 210. 26 Joseph Byrne, *War and peace: the survival of the Talbots of Malahide 1641–1671* (Dublin, 1997), pp 22–3: Joseph Byrne 'Garristown and the Talbots of Malahide' in Garristown Historical Society, *Olden times in Garristown* (Garristown, 2000), pp 19–20. 27 *A repertory of the inrolments on the patent rolls in chancery in Ireland; commencing with the reign of King James I,* ed. John Caillard Erck (2 pts, Dublin, 1846–52), i, part i, p. 221. 28 *A repertory of the inrolments on the patent rolls in chancery in Ireland; commencing with the reign of King James I*, ed. John Caillard Erck (2 pts, Dublin, 1846–52), i, part ii, pp 733 and 739.

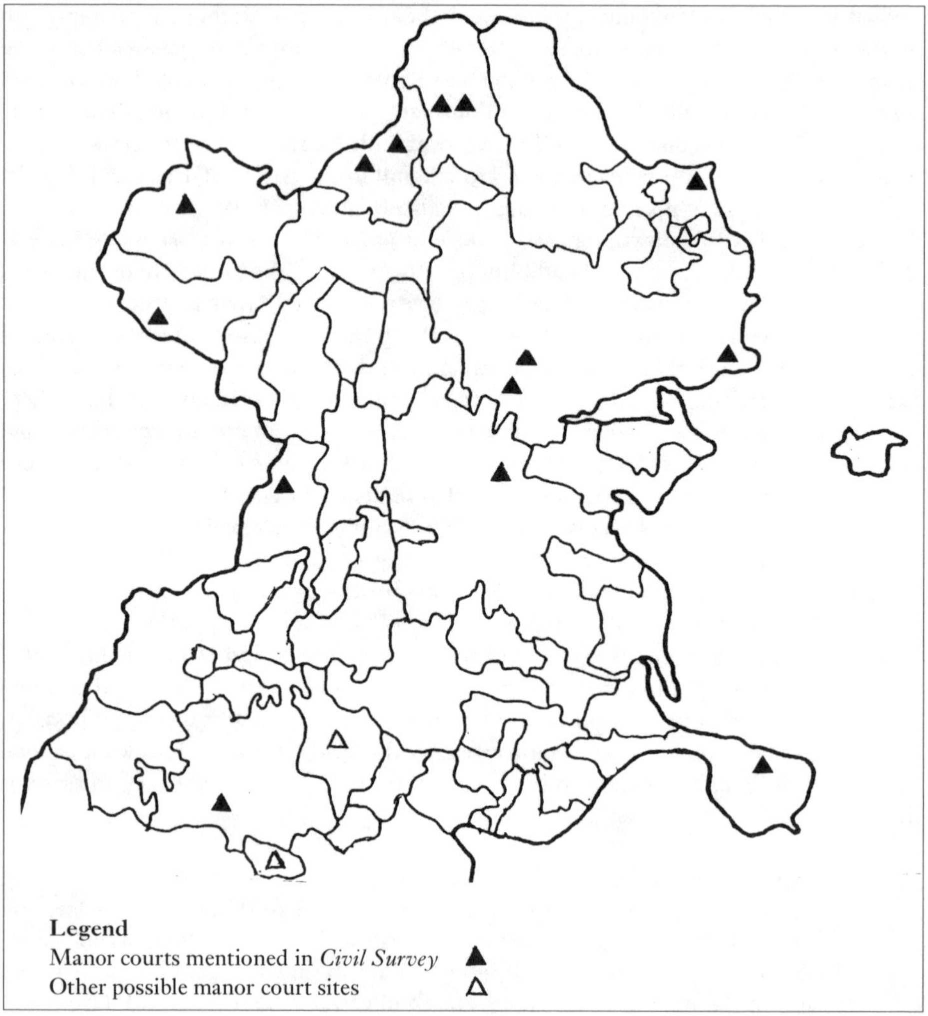

Fig. 6.1 Seventeenth-century manor courts in Fingal

> Carlow; and within the manors of Holmpatrick and Skerries, in County Dublin; to be held, twice in each year, for ever, before the seneschal or seneschals to be appointed, from time to time, by said earl, his heirs and assigns, according to the form of the statute in such case made and provided; with all jurisdictions, pre-eminences, privileges, liberties, perquisites, advantages, amercements, fines and emoluments thereto belonging.

Raymond Gillespie has published a charge given to the earl's seneschal for the manor of Croverghan and Kilrush which dates from *c.*1670.[29] Pointing out that not every-

29 Raymond Gillespie, 'A manor court in seventeenth century Ireland' in *Irish economic and social history*, xxv (1998), pp 86–7.

thing listed in the charge was applicable to every manor court, Gillespie went on to note that the court at Bunratty on the Thomond estate in 1667 'limited itself to dealing with suit and service to the court, heriots, mills, waste in woods, waifs and strays, alienations, hawking and hunting, concealed land and recovering arrears of rent from dead tenants'.[30] The activities mentioned were those which happened to occur in a particular year and, as might be expected, represented a much narrower range of activities than those listed in the charge, which, in addition, covered violent crimes and a large number of crimes likely to have been committed by merchants, retailers and tradesmen. It seems unlikely that the charge differed significantly from that given to the unknown seneschal at Holmpatrick.

Many of the types of crime mentioned in the Thomond charge of *c.*1670 appeared in the records of the court of Saint Sepulchre almost a century earlier. The *Court book of the liberty of Saint Sepulchre*, edited by Herbert Wood, provided information about courts within the jurisdiction of the archbishop of Dublin for the period, 1586–90.[31] Though this preceded the period covered by this study, taken together with the Garristown court baron and the Thomond charge, it gave some idea of what manor courts were like in the early seventeenth century. Wood described the seneschal's jurisdiction as follows:

> The seneschal's jurisdiction consisted in holding a court leet every Easter and Michaelmas, for the cognisance of criminal matters or pleas of the crown, when grand and market juries were sworn in and presentments made; for the view of frankpledge at which every freeborn man who had arrived at the age of fourteen had to produce neighbours to give security for his truth; and for the appointment of constables of the ward, clerk of the market, coroners and other officials. He also held a court baron, usually on the same day as the court leet, in which the homage jury enquired to see that their lord did not lose the services due to him but that the tenants made their suit of court. The chief business of this court was to administer the custom of the manor and to admit fresh tenants who had acquired copyholds by inheritance or purchase, and who had to pay, for so doing, a fine to the lord of the manor and do fealty ...

An attempt was made to quantify the participation of Fingal residents in these courts by comparing the total number of cases mentioned with the number in which one or more Fingal people took part.[32] Cases were defined arbitrarily. Appointments to office and straightforward cases concerning the appraisal of the value of goods were omitted. Inheritance cases were included. The number of cases shown as being those in which Fingal residents were involved must be regarded as a minimum, since place of residence was not always stated in the records. The data covered four years only (1586–7 and 1589–90). Records for the year 1588 are not available. The analysis showed that, at the very least, just under one fifth of all cases had one or more litigants

30 Raymond Gillespie, 'A manor court in seventeenth century Ireland' in *Irish economic and social history*, xxv (1998), p. 83. 31 *Court book of the liberty of Saint Sepulchre ...*, ed. Herbert Wood (Dublin, 1930). 32 'Fingal 1603–60', i, pp 207–8.

from Fingal. It also indicates that while there was a reasonably high participation rate in courts held in Dublin city there was little, if any, Fingal activity in courts held in the south county. These cases do not tell the whole story, however. The aspects of the court relating to the court baron, or manorial rather than criminal activities, showed that a number of Fingal residents held land in the south county and were required to do homage for their land at courts held there. The free tenants listed for the court held at Tallaght at Easter 1587 included such well-known Fingal family names as Chamberlain, Howth, Ussher, Fitzsimon, Taylor, Barnewall, Stanihurst, Luttrell and Russell.[33] A similar pattern has been observed in the royal court of Esker and Crumlin, although the number of Fingal proprietors holding land in that area was not as great.[34] There were also opportunities for the creation of networks of friends and acquaintances at a lower level of society. A jury listed for Saint Sepulchre's at Easter 1589 included six men from the city, one from Churchtown, three (Simon Cardon, Thomas Desmond and Tirlagh Dempsey) from Finglas and two (William Purple, perhaps Purfield, and Simon Regan) from Kilshane (parish of Finglas).[35] It appears, however, that jurors were usually recruited locally.

The sixty-four 'Fingal' cases were also broken down using five headings, 'debt and unjust detention of property' (twenty-five examples), 'trespass' (eleven examples), 'covenant' (four examples), 'death of a tenant' (three examples) and 'other' (twenty-one examples).[36]

A number of the cases labelled under the heading 'other' involved violence. One such was a memorandum of an incident which took place in 1582 when 'J.W. of Lusk, shoemaker' was accused of entering Swords within the cross and liberty with force and arms.[37] The court held at Finglas in May 1590 had to deal with a number of cases of affray and/or battery, several of which involved women.[38] One such was described as follows: 'It is presented by James Regan that Hugh Gormley and his wife, Ellen did make a fray by chiding, scolding and slanderous words unto the said James being constable'. A case of right of way was considered at the court held at Swords in April 1590 as was a case in which Nicholas O'Donnell of the Nevitt accused a neighbour, Patrick Kenna, of defaming and slandering him by calling him a thief and false knave.[39] The manor courts of the archbishop dealt with a wide range of problems, though perhaps few of those listed in the surviving court-book were of a very serious nature.

Punishment was also often administered in public and, no doubt, attracted many spectators. Mention has been made of the punishments for serious crimes in chapter 5. The place name, 'Gallows Hill' near Swords provided a constant reminder to local people about the threat of hanging.[40] The archbishop was permitted to retain pillories, tumbrels and thewen (an instrument of punishment for women) at Swords and

33 *Court book of the liberty of Saint Sepulchre ...*, ed. Herbert Wood (Dublin, 1930), pp 10–11. 34 'The court book of Esker and Crumlin, 1592–1600' ed. Edmund Curtis in *Journal of the Royal Society of Antiquaries of Ireland*, lix (1929), pp 45–64, 128–48 and lx (1930), pp 38–51, 137–49. 35 *Court book of the liberty of Saint Sepulchre ...*, ed. Herbert Wood (Dublin, 1930), p. 49. 36 'Fingal 1603–60', i, p. 209. 37 *Court book of the liberty of Saint Sepulchre ...*, ed. Herbert Wood, p. 37. 38 *Court book of the liberty of Saint Sepulchre ...*, ed. Herbert Wood, pp 54–6. 39 *Court book of the liberty of Saint Sepulchre ...*, ed. Herbert Wood, pp 58 and 69. 40 *Civil Survey, vii, county of Dublin,* p. 89.

Finglas.[41] At the Finglas vestry meeting of 13 April 1658 the following items of expenditure, suggesting that the stocks were frequently used, were recorded:

> More for a fair new pair of stocks with clock and a seat (?), the old being altogether decayed and unserviceable, was paid to the carpenter as by his acquittance produced, the sum of twenty-six shillings, ster. And more to Peter Read for fitting the old staple, hasp and hinges to the said new stocks and for a good padlock for the same for two shillings six pence.[42]

There were also stocks, guarded by a sentinel, close to St Michan's church with which the rural inhabitants of the parish would have been familiar.[43] As well as these public forms of punishment there were, of course, prisons, including one in the Plunket tower-house at Dunsoghly.[44] The castle at Baldongan also served as a prison during the 1641 rising.[45] A vivid description of the plight of prisoners is given in 'Purgatorium Hibernicum':

> And as a pair of Newgate guests
> that had a long time made their nests
> within a dungeon whose litter
> was bed and close stool too, together
> when once enlarged hence would prize
> the open air a paradise
> and though but to the gallows hurled
> would think them in another world.[46]

Alehouses, taverns and inns were important meeting places for Fingallians as they were for other Irish people, particularly those living in towns. Elizabeth Malcolm has pointed out that 'much popular recreation and ritual in Gaelic Ireland took place out of doors, while in the Pale and the port towns, dominated by settlers of English descent, there were already special indoor spaces set aside for drinking and the recreational activities that accompanied it'.[47] While the use of the word 'dominated' in relation to Fingal might have to be questioned, there is no doubt that social drinking and dining in company were very popular in the area. However, social drinking was not just an indoor activity which took place in specially designated areas such as alehouses. The people also participated in social drinking in their own homes, for example, at wakes and outdoors on special occasions such as patterns. A decree aimed at controlling drink shops was issued in 1611 and proclamations were published in 1620 and 1631, but by the 1630s alehouses were causing such problems to

41 *Court book of the liberty of Saint Sepulchre* ..., ed. Herbert Wood, p. viii. 42 Finglas parish combined vestry book and registers, 1657–1758 (RCBL, P.307/1/1, p. 13). 43 Examination of Henry Smith and Robert Caulfield, 8 November 1641 (TCD, MS 809, f. 134). 44 Harold G. Leask, *Irish castles and castellated houses* (2nd ed., 1944, revised 1946 and 1951, reprinted Dundalk, 1999), p. 121. 45 Depositions of Daniel Barwick, 21 and 23 May 1642 (TCD, MS 810, ff 112 and 114–5). 46 Purgatorium Hibernicum ..., *c.*1670 (NLI, MS 470, pp 131–2). 47 Elizabeth Malcolm, 'The rise of the pub: a study in the disciplining of popular culture' in J.S. Donnelly and Kerby A. Miller (eds), *Irish popular culture, 1650–1850* (Dublin, 1999), p. 55.

the authorities that legislation had to be introduced to curb them.[48] The nature of these difficulties is neatly summed up in the preamble to an act passed in 1635 which reads as follows:

> Forasmuch as it is found by daily experience, that many mischiefs and inconveniences do arise from the excessive number of alehouses, from the erection of them in woods, bogs, and other unfit places, and many of them not in townships, but dispersedly, and in dangerous places, and kept by unknown persons not undertaken for, whereby many times they become receptacles for rebels and other malefactors, and harbours for gamesters, and other idle, disordered and unprofitable livers, and that those that keep those alehouses for the most part, are not fitted or furnished to lodge or entertain travellers in any decent manner . . .[49]

To 'redress these inconveniences ... and to reduce those needless multitudes of alehouses to a fewer number, to more fit persons, and to more convenient places' the government introduced a licensing system based on the issue of annual licences. A number of conditions for the granting of a licence were specified. Those licensed were to be 'of good behaviour and report' and 'able to entertain travellers'. Their dwellings were to be 'in convenient places, as in market towns, in villages on roadways' or 'in towns, wherein are parish churches'. The making or uttering of 'unwholesome, bread, beer, ale, or victuals' was forbidden, and the licensee was required to keep at least two beds for the lodging of strangers. Drunkenness, excessive drinking, dicing, carding and unlawful games were forbidden, as was the harbouring of suspected persons, or any of ill behaviour or any of the neighbours' servants. No stranger was permitted to remain in the alehouse for more than twenty-four hours, except in case of sickness. One concession to the Irish custom of drinking in the open may be seen in the proviso that 'such persons as shall sell ale or beer only in places where the general assizes or quarter-sessions shall be kept, during the time of the assize or sessions, or at fairs during the time of the fairs, shall not be impeached for keeping the same without licence'.[50] It was also prescribed that the act should be published by public proclamation in every market town.[51] The act was not a success, at least as far as the Dublin area, was concerned. In 1640 the government had to introduce another act to punish offenders within the city and county of Dublin.[52] This extended the range of courts which might try offences as well as prescribing that, in the event of a successful prosecution, the informer responsible for it should have a third part of the fine. The following lines from Henry Burnell's play, *Landgartha*, spoken by one of two bumpkins on a visit to the city, which, despite the

48 Elizabeth Malcolm, 'The rise of the pub: a study in the disciplining of popular culture' in J.S. Donnelly and Kerby A. Miller (eds), *Irish popular culture, 1650–1850* (Dublin, 1999), pp 60–2. 49 An act for keepers of ale-houses to be bound by recognizances, 10 & 11 C.I, c.5, paragraph I, *Stat. Ire.* (1786), ii, p. 151. 50 An act for keepers of ale-houses to be bound by recognizances, 10 & 11 C.I, c.5, paragraph III, *Stat. Ire.* (1786), ii, p. 152. 51 An act for keepers of ale-houses to be bound by recognizances, 10 & 11 C.I, c.5, paragraph VI, *Stat. Ire.* (1786), ii, p. 153. 52 An act for punishing of offenders within the county of Dublin, and county of the City of Dublin, against the act for keepers of alehouses to be bound by recognizances, 15 C.I, c.8, *Stat. Ire.* (1786), ii, p. 202.

play's exotic setting, would have had some resonance for the Dublin audience of 1640, implied that the government's earlier efforts had been in vain:

> ... we are very near
> As good drinkers, as you be here in the city.
> For you see, when we come to town, we do
> Nothing but run from tavern to tavern;
> Oft to blind ale-houses, to visit the fine
> Wenches, of purpose there placed, to draw custom ...[53]

The outbreak of war in 1641 changed the context in which alehouses operated as did the introduction of an excise duty in 1643.[54]

It is not possible to calculate how many inns, taverns and alehouses there were in Fingal. The two acts of 1635 and 1640 would seem to imply that contemporaries had the same difficulty. It is likely that many of the houses of office listed in the Civil Survey were places where liquor could be obtained.[55] In April 1618 licences were granted to certain persons to keep taverns and to sell wine and ardent spirits, among whom was 'Dirrick Huiberts of Dublin city, gent., during the lives of Daniel Adrianson and Abraham Cornellison of Dublin, within the town of Skerries, and the manor of Holmpatrick and two and a half miles round the same, except Balrothery and Lusk, and within the island of Lambay'.[56] This suggests that, while the Skerries licence may have been new, there were already in existence licensed premises in Balrothery and Lusk. A small number of premises can be identified with certainty. In July 1635 Sir William Brereton on his way through Swords 'lodged at the sign of the Boot, a tavern, and were well used, and found far better accommodation in so mean a village than could be expected'.[57] He noted his satisfaction with the Boot once again in his summary of his journey through Ireland.[58] Patrick Browne of Corduff, innkeeper, made a will on 3 May 1677.[59] He was assessed for two hearths in the hearth money roll *c.*1664.[60] In some instances the existence of licensed premises can be inferred from the 1641 depositions. The losses of Darby Lea of Balrothery, described as a postmaster, suggest that he was also an innkeeper.[61] In addition to a quantity of drink he claimed for the loss of leases to various pieces of property including stables. Another Balrothery man, John Passmore, was listed among the rebels as an innkeeper by Thomas Clitheroe, the local minister, who would have been expected to know Passmore's status.[62] According to the deposition of Henry

53 Henry Burnell, *Landgartha: a tragie-comedie, as it was presented in the new theatre in Dublin, with good applause, being an ancient story* (Dublin, 1641), p. 19. 54 T.C. Barnard, *Cromwellian Ireland: English government and reform in Ireland 1649–1660* (2nd ed., Oxford, 2000), p. 28. 55 *Civil Survey, vii, county of Dublin,* ed. R.C. Simington (Dublin, 1945). 56 *Irish patent rolls of James I*, ed. M.C. Griffith (Dublin, 1966), p. 362. 57 William Brereton, *Travels in Holland, the United Provinces, England, Scotland and Ireland, M.DC.XXXIV–M.DC.XXXV*, ed. Edward Hopkins (Manchester, 1844), p. 136. 58 William Brereton, *Travels in Holland, the United Provinces, England, Scotland and Ireland, M.DC.XXXIV–M.DC.XXXV*, ed. Edward Hopkins (Manchester, 1844), p. 190. 59 Abstract of will of Patrick Browne, 3 May 1677 (NLI, Fisher will abstracts, GO MS 290, p. 51). 60 'Hearth money roll for County Dublin, 1664' (second part), *Journal of the County Kildare Archaeological Society*, xi (1930–33), p. 414. 61 Deposition of Darby Lea, 25 January 1642 (TCD, MS 809, f. 288). 62 Deposition of Thomas Clitheroe, 26 May 1642 (TCD, MS 810, f. 126).

Partington of Killelane, there were two men called John Passmore, both of whom were involved in the raid on his property.[63] They were John Passmore the elder and John Passmore the younger, who was described in his deposition as an innkeeper. Christopher Cruise of the Naul was described by Katherine Magee of Balscaddan, servant of Henry Mawdesley, who would also have had local knowledge, as an innkeeper.[64] Two taverns in Finglas, owned by John England and Patrick Browne, and one in Oxmantown, owned by Patrick McEnally, were mentioned in John Sephton's deposition.[65] As pointed out in chapter 2 the carrying off of quantities of malt from certain premises by the rebels suggests that there were alehouses in Lusk, Johnstown, Coolock, Killelane and Stormanstown.[66] Further confirmation of the existence of an alehouse in Lusk can be found in the deposition of the minister of Ballyboghil, John Lukey.[67] In the case of Johnstown the position is less clear. Thomas Benet submitted a large claim for losses amounting to £2,000.[68] He may, however, have been supplying malt rather than using it himself for brewing. The same applies to Ann Foreside of Coolock.[69] The description of the goods seized from Henry Partington of Killelane would indicate that he kept an alehouse.[70] William Fleming, late of Stormanstown, filed a short deposition describing how Simon Jorden of Barberstown took away his malt and other goods.[71] The relatively high valuation of the buildings in Stormanstown (£100) in the Civil Survey together with its situation straddling the main road to the Naul suggest that there may have been an inn or tavern there.[72] Alice Segrave left two houses to her daughters in 1660.[73] One of these was called Saracen's Head and the other the Horse Shoe but their location is not known. It is rather surprising that there is not more information available about inns in the coastal towns, particularly Malahide, Howth and Clontarf, where one would have expected to find inns serving travellers or alehouses for seamen and fishermen. One coastal village which almost certainly did have an alehouse or tavern was Baldoyle, to which the men engaged in hunting the hare retired at the end of the day.[74] The situation regarding drink shops, insofar as it could be verified or inferred, has been mapped in figure 6.2.[75]

While it is difficult to be certain where the Fingal taverns and alehouses were located it is possible to derive some information about the pattern of social drinking and dining out. Peter Clark, in his book *The English alehouse* has provided a picture of drinking in England at the period with which the Fingal situation may usefully be

63 Deposition of Henry Partington, 9 June 1642 (TCD, MS 810, f. 171). **64** Deposition of Katherine Magee, 22 April 1642 (TCD, MS 810, f. 174). **65** Examination of John Sephton, 15 November 1641 (TCD, MS 809, f. 176). **66** Deposition of Mary Bucklie, 17 February 1642 (TCD, MS 809, ff 234); deposition of Thomas Benet, 26 February 1642; (TCD MS 809, f. 243); deposition of Ann Foreside, 5 January 1642 (TCD, MS 809, f. 279); deposition of Henry Partington, 9 June 1642 (TCD, MS 810, f. 171); deposition of William Fleming, 7 November 1643 (TCD, MS 810, f. 233). **67** Deposition of John Lukey, 2 March 1643 (TCD, MS 810, f. 168). **68** Deposition of Thomas Benet, 26 February 1642 (TCD, MS 809, f. 243). **69** Deposition of Ann Foreside, 5 January 1642 (TCD, MS 809, f. 279). **70** Deposition of Henry Partington, 9 June 1642 (TCD, MS 810, f. 171). **71** Deposition of William Fleming, 7 November 1643 (TCD, MS 810, f. 233). **72** *Civil Survey, vii, county of Dublin,* p. 200. **73** Abstract of will of Alice Segrave, 13 October 1660 (RSAI, Elrington Ball MSS, vol xii, f. 40); Francis Elrington Ball, *Southern Fingal* ... (originally published 1920, reprinted Dublin, 1995), p. 99. **74** The Fingallian hunting of the hare (BL, Sloane MS 900, ff 54–5); Francis Elrington Ball, *Howth and its owners* ... (originally published 1917, reprinted Dublin, 1995), pp 119–20. **75** 'Fingal 1603–60', i, pp 214–6.

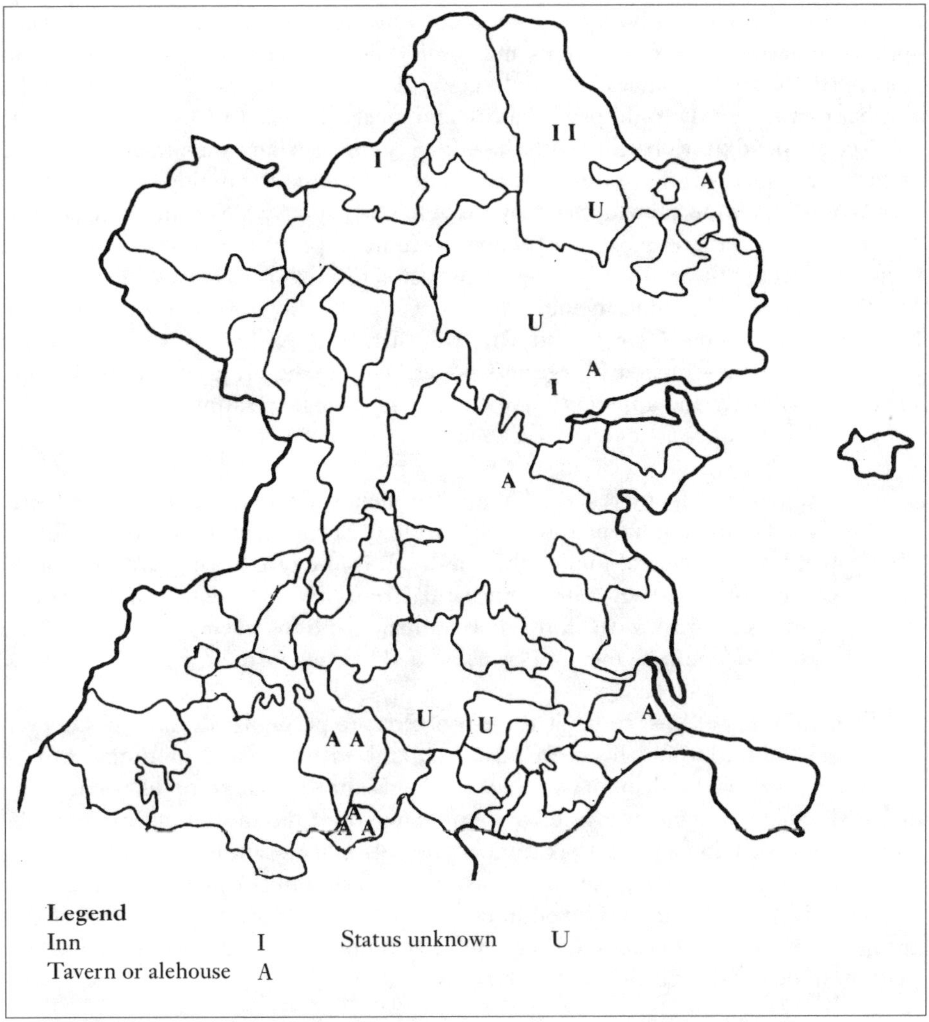

Fig. 6.2 Some inns, taverns and alehouses in seventeenth-century Fingal

compared.[76] Clark pointed out that, in England, women probably formed only a small proportion of alehouse customers.[77] That a similar situation existed in Fingal is suggested by the evidence which survives.[78]

Oxmantown, close to the Dublin city/Fingal boundaries, was a popular place of assembly. As well as Cooper's tavern in Oxmantown there were at least two other drinking house in the area, one at the sign of the White Horse in Stony Booter which

76 Peter Clark, *The English alehouse: a social history, 1200–1830* (London and New York, 1983).
77 Peter Clark, *The English alehouse: a social history, 1200–1830* (London and New York, 1983), p. 131.
78 Examination of John Sephton, 15 November 1641 (TCD, MS 809, f. 176); deposition of John Lukey, 2 March 1643 (TCD, MS 810, f. 168).

had facilities for stabling horses and another owned by Patrick McEnally.[79] Cooper's appears to have been a commodious and comfortable establishment with at least two storeys (there are references to people going downstairs into a lower room) and a number of rooms.[80] It could proved a fire and meals. The fact that the owner's wife was free to spend time chatting with the guests, some of whom were members of the gentry, suggests that other family members or servants were employed there. What was to prove an important supper took place in Cooper's on 7 November 1641. The composition of the group, some of whom were in all probability conspirators, who spent the evening there, is interesting. It consisted of Nicholas Darcy of Platten, Co. Meath, later a prominent member of the Confederation of Kilkenny, his son, Edward, two friends, George and Richard Birt, and Nicholas's servant, Oliver Darcy.[81] When they invited Margaret Cooper, wife of the proprietor to join them, she did so willingly and apparently joined fully in the conversation.

In *The English alehouse* Peter Clark stated:

> In the eyes of many respectable folk the alehouse posed a threat to the fabric of the family in four main ways: by attracting grown children and servants to spend their time and money there away from the tutelage of parents or masters at home; by separating husbands from wives; by encouraging family members to drink with all sorts of company; and by serving as a place where prostitutes could be met and casual sexual liaisons formed.[82]

Confirmation that at least some of these problems, in particular difficulties between parents and children and between husbands and wives, existed in Fingal can be found in the reports of drinking sessions in Finglas in which a group of friends participated. Some statements made by them about the time of the outbreak of the rising in the north in October 1641 came to the notice of the authorities and gave rise to the suspicion that some of them, at least, were conspirators though, naturally, this was denied. As has been mentioned in chapter 3 the social and religious mix of this group was described by one of them, John Sephton, during his examination. He went on to describe their drinking habits saying:

> that he, this examinant, divers times since the discovery of this present rebellion hath lain abroad out of his own house at the houses of one John England and Patrick Browne in Finglas and he saith that divers times when he, this examinant, lay out of his own house that said Rowen was in his company until bedtime and sometimes Patrick Dillon and Henry Merrick were with him, likewise until that time, and that Richard Delahide and John Copeland, Bartholomew Walsh and John England were also sometimes with him until bedtime. This examinant further saith that he lay out of his own house five

79 Examination of Tirlogue McMahon, 2 November 1641 (TCD, MS 809, f. 67); examination of John Sephton, 15 November 1641 (TCD, MS 809, f. 176). 80 Examination of Margaret Cooper, 8 November 1641 (TCD, MS 809, f. 138). 81 Examination of Margaret Cooper, 8 November 1641 (TCD, MS 809, ff 138); examination of Nicholas Darcy, 8 November 1641 (TCD, MS 809, f. 140). 82 Peter Clark, *The English alehouse: a social history, 1200–1830* (London and New York, 1983), p. 147.

> nights, two nights at John England's, two nights at Patrick Browne's and one night at Patrick McEnally in Oxmantown.[83]

John England, Patrick Browne and Patrick McEnally appear to have been keepers of taverns or alehouses. Robert Davy, William Rowen and Richard Delahide, who were also examined, confirmed the drinking pattern.[84] Delahide explained that, having attended the general sessions for the county of Dublin upon the Abbey Green until nightfall, he met Rowen on the way to Finglas and both called into England's house.[85] As in the case of Cooper's of Oxmantown, England's of Finglas had at least two storeys. According to Delahide's report there were at least two rooms available there for drinking, a 'room below' and 'an inner room' where the suspicious conversation took place. Thomas Waring, to whom John Sephton owed some money, also submitted a statement, saying that 'he heard the said John Sephton's wife say that of late, since the said John Sephton did keep continual company with William Rowen and such others, the said John Sephton did use her very hardly if at any time she refused to give him money to keep company with them'.[86] This statement, together with Sephton's account of Bartholomew Walsh's break with his father, supply evidence that, as happened in England, the pattern of excessive drinking was seen as having a detrimental effect on family life.[87] The alleged conspiratorial aspects of the meetings will be considered in a later chapter. At this point it is interesting to note that the friendship of the group crossed the social, religious and ethnic divisions of the period. There is other evidence of socializing which crossed these barriers if, indeed, they were perceived as such, prior to the outbreak of the war. John Lukey, a minister at Ballyboghil, in his deposition described how, 'nine months before the rebellion began' while he was at supper with Sebastian Finglas of the Murragh near Ballyboghil, Finglas 'being a wilful papist' tried to convert him to Catholicism.[88] He also told how William Bucklie, the clerk at Lusk, told him that he heard Mr Fitzwilliam of Baldongan say that 'he hoped shortly to see every minister's neck as long as his arm'. Interestingly, this conversation reportedly took place 'in an alehouse of Lusk'. William Bucklie or his wife may well have been proprietor of the ale-house as Mary Bucklie, 'widow and late wife to William Bucklie, bailiff of Lusk …, gentleman', reported that malt and drink worth 50*s.*, as well as several other items, had been taken away from her by the rebels about 1 December 1641.[89] These accounts supply evidence of cross-community social interaction, particularly in taverns and alehouses, in Fingal prior to the rising. They also suggest that there was a greater mixing of classes in Irish taverns and alehouses than in their English counterparts, perhaps because top-quality inns were harder to find.

While the partially controlled indoor drinking spaces which existed widely in Fingal are evidence of the permeation of English values into the area, drinking out

83 Examination of John Sephton, 15 November 1641 (TCD, MS 809, f. 176). **84** Examination of Robert Davy, 4 November 1641 (TCD, MS 809, f. 99); examination of William Rowen, 19 November 1641 (TCD, MS 809, f. 188); examination of Richard Delahide, 19 November 1641 (TCD, MS 809, f. 198). 85 Examination of Richard Delahide, 19 November 1641 (TCD, MS 809, f. 198). **86** Examination of Thomas Waring, 23 November 1641 (TCD, MS 809, f. 208). **87** Examination of John Sephton, 15 November 1641 (TCD, MS 809, f. 176). **88** Deposition of John Lukey, 2 March 1643 (TCD, MS 810, f. 168). **89** Deposition of Mary Bucklie, 17 February 1642 (TCD, MS 809, f. 234).

of doors, the norm in Gaelic Ireland, was also widely practised as was described by the Revd George Creichton of Virginia.[90] He noted that the Fingal people, unlike the Ulstermen who 'followed only drink', combined their drinking with other activities such as music, dancing and sport. Creichton, in another context, referred to an ale-house in Virginia but it seems highly unlikely, given the number of refugees in the town and the severe overcrowding which resulted, that the 'drinking, piping and dancing' referred to at the beginning of this chapter could have taken place indoors.[91] Although there are several allusions to drinking in 'Purgatorium Hibernicum', the consumption of drink was not specifically mentioned in the references to patterns at Lusk and Tubber Shane.[92]

One of the most popular meeting place for the Catholic community in seventeenth-century Ireland was the local holy well or pattern site. Fingal was no exception to this. Fortunately, as a result of the work of historians and others, and, in particular, by that of Caoimhín Ó Danachair in relation to Co. Dublin, it is possible to plot the distribution of traditional well sites.[93] As well as listing 'holy wells' Ó Danachair specified certain wells as 'doubtful wells', defining these as wells 'about which there is some doubt as to existence or location or sacred character'.[94] He also noted some other wells which could not be identified or about which vague traditions existed.[95] For the purpose of this study 'doubtful wells' and 'other wells' have been included where the dedication to a particular saint is known or where the prefix 'Tober-' is included in either the name of the well or of the townland in which it is situated. Also included in this analysis are a small number of wells not in Ó Danachair's list but which appear in the records of Dúchas – the Heritage Service.

The religious importance of wells and pattern sites will be considered in the chapter 8. Here we are concerned with these sites as meeting places. But can we assume that the wells listed by Ó Danachair in the mid-twentieth century were pattern sites in the seventeenth century? References to a small number of these sites can be found in contemporary or near-contemporary records. For the others we are dependent on tradition. While, in most cases, there is no absolute proof that these sites existed in the seventeenth-century there are two factors that strongly support the belief that most of these sites are ancient sites. In the first place holy wells were frowned on by church and state authorities from the seventeenth to the nineteenth centuries so that it is unlikely that many 'new' wells would have attracted public attention during this period. Secondly, none of the Fingal wells are dedicated to post-Tridentine saints, and in fact, many of them are very ancient dedications. One must, however, enter a caveat. It is possible that some more modern domestic wells became associated with popular early saints. The 'doubtful well' in Skerries (parish

90 Deposition of George Creichton, 15 April 1643 (TCD, MS 833, ff 236–7); John T. Gilbert (ed.), *A contemporary history of affairs in Ireland from A. D. 1641 to 1652* ... (3 vols, Dublin, 1879–80), i, part ii, p. 542. 91 Deposition of George Creichton, 15 April 1643 (TCD, MS 832, f. 152; MS 833, ff 233 and 236–7); John T. Gilbert (ed.), *A contemporary history of affairs in Ireland from A. D. 1641 to 1652* ... (3 vols, Dublin, 1879–80), i, part ii, pp 534, 536 and 542. 92 Purgatorium Hibernicum ..., *c.*1670 (NLI, MS 470, pp 133–6 and 150–1). 93 Caoimhín Ó Danachair, 'The holy wells of County Dublin' in *Reportorium Novum*, ii, no.1, pp 68–87 and ii, no. 2, pp 233–5. 94 Caoimhín Ó Danachair, 'The holy wells of County Dublin' in *Reportorium Novum*, ii, no.1, p. 71. 95 Caoimhín Ó Danachair, 'The holy wells of County Dublin' in *Reportorium Novum*, ii, no.1, p. 87.

of Holmpatrick), dedicated to St Patrick, is a case in point.[96] The distribution of wells and pattern sites has been mapped in figure 6.3.[97]

Twenty-eight of the forty-one parishes had at least one well site. Those in which no wells have, as yet, been identified are Baldongan, Baldoyle, Ballymadun, Chapelizod, Cloghran-huddart, Clonsilla, Glasnevin, Killeek, Killester, Killossery, Kilsallaghan, Naul and Westpalstown. One well, in the parish of Clonsilla, which has not been traced on the modern lists, is that of St Mochon at Kellystown. This well was mentioned by Meredith Hanmer in *The chronicle of Ireland in 1571*.[98] There are six Fingal townlands with names beginning with the prefix 'Tober-', which would suggest that any wells in those townlands were very ancient indeed. In four of these, Toberbunny (Cloghran), Tobergregan (Garristown) and Tobersool and Tobertown (Balscaddan) there are known wells. Wells have not been traced in Toberburr (Finglas) or Tobertaskin (Balscaddan). As noted in chapter 3 there was a placename, Tobermatoule, in the Astagob area of Clonsilla which did not rank as a townland. It is likely that other placenames with the prefix 'Tober-' remain unrecorded. Two parishes, in which no wells are listed, had pattern sites which may have been of a different type. There is an early eighteenth-century reference to the visit of an excise officer, Thomas Skellern, to a 'patron' at Stradbally on 2 March 1729.[99] The area then known as Stradbally was situated in the parish of Kilsallaghan at the time of the Civil Survey.[100] The Grand Jury presentment books for Co. Dublin for Easter 1817 mention the 'pattern-bank of Baldongan in the parish of Baldongan'.[101] The actual site of the pattern bank has not been identified with certainty. Baldongan is, however, situated on a low hill, with an extensive view of the countryside. It thus fulfils one of the conditions suggested by Máire MacNeill for a Lughnasa site, although it is not one of those listed in her study, *The festival of Lughnasa*.[102] Two well-known Fingal well sites, those at St Doolagh's and Grallagh have, however, been identified as traditional sites.[103]

Of the two pattern sites mentioned in 'Purgatorium Hibernicum' one is undoubtedly Lusk.[104] Ó Danachair did not specify the date of the pattern but the feast of the local patron, St Maccullin, fell on 6 September. The activities on 'patron's eve', described in the poem would, therefore, have taken place at harvest-time. The second pattern mentioned in 'Purgatorium Hibernicum', Tubber Shane, is more difficult to identify.[105] It may have been St John's Well located at Grallagh by Ó Danachair but placed at Cottrelstown in the parish of Palmerstown by Dúchas staff.[106] Another possibility is that it is the well called 'Church Well' in Kilshane in the western part of the parish of Finglas, which does not appear on Ó Danachair's list but which has

96 Caoimhín Ó Danachair, 'The holy wells of County Dublin' in *Reportorium Novum*, ii, no. 1, p. 74. 97 'Fingal 1603–60', i, pp 220–2. 98 Meredith Hanmer, *The chronicle of Ireland collected by Meredith Hanmer in the year 1571* (Dublin 1633, republished 1809), pp 81–2. 99 Minutes of the revenue commissioners, 7 March 1729 (PRO, Kew, CUST 1/21); Maighréad Ní Mhurchadha, *The customs and excise service in Fingal 1684–1765: sober, active and bred to the sea* (Dublin, 1999), p. 36. 100 *Civil Survey, vii, county of Dublin*, pp 236–7. 101 The Grand Jury presentment books for County Dublin, Easter 1817 (Fingal County Council Archives, pp 44–5). 102 Máire MacNeill, *The festival of Lughnasa* (Oxford, 1962), p. 67. 103 Máire MacNeill, *The festival of Lughnasa* (Oxford, 1962), p. 640. 104 Purgatorium Hibernicum . . ., *c.*1670 (NLI, MS 470, pp 133–6). 105 Purgatorium Hibernicum . . ., *c.*1670 (NLI, MS 470, pp 150–1). 106 Caoimhín Ó Danachair, 'The holy wells of County Dublin' in *Reportorium Novum*, ii, no.1, p. 74; Dúchas – the Heritage Service, County Dublin, file no. DU007–002.

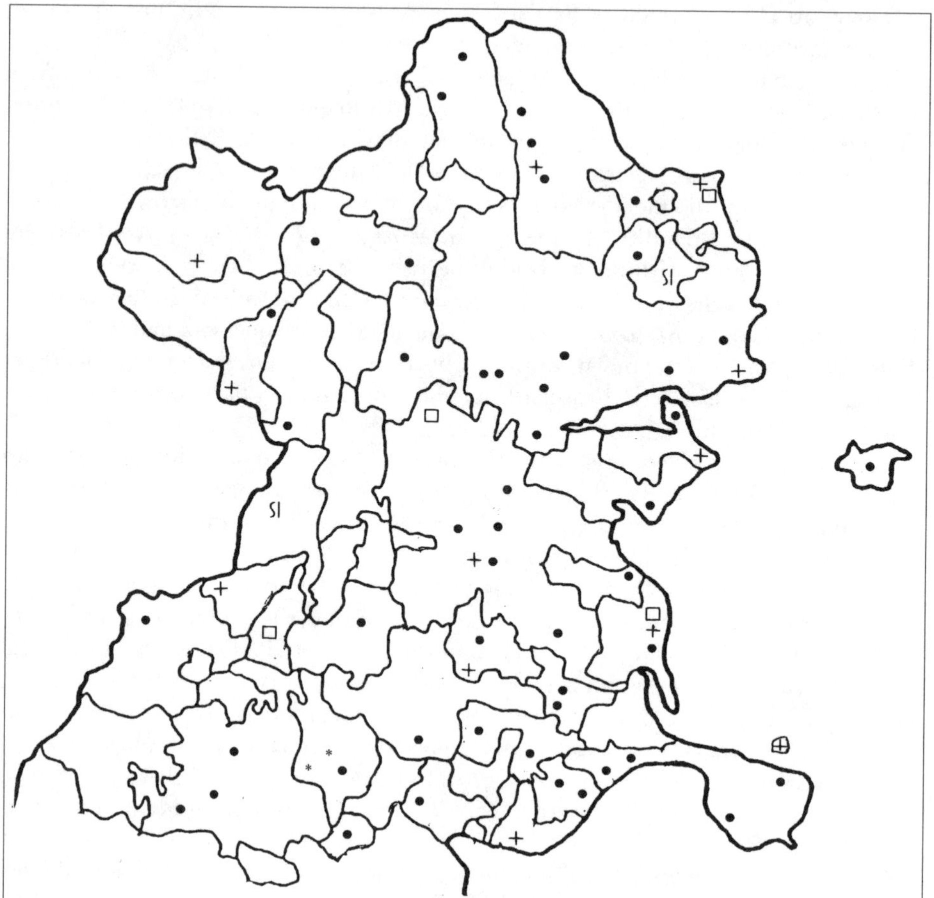

Fig. 6.3 Holy wells and other pattern sites in Fingal

been located by the staff of Dúchas.[107] The well is not shown on a plot of Kilshane drawn in 1656 though, as the buildings in the townland were also omitted, this may not be significant.[108] (See figure 6.4.) It is possible that further historical and/or archaeological research will unearth wells or other sites in parishes in which there are no known wells. It is also possible that the parish may not be the most appropriate unit to use when analysing the distribution of these very ancient sites and that the

107 Dúchas – the Heritage Service, County Dublin, file no. DU014–01203. **108** The plott of Killshane in the parish of Finglass, barony of Uppcross & county of Dublin, made by John Turmor, 1656, & abstracted El. Arnoldi, 1668 (RCBL, Records of the archbishop of Dublin, D6, map no. 13).

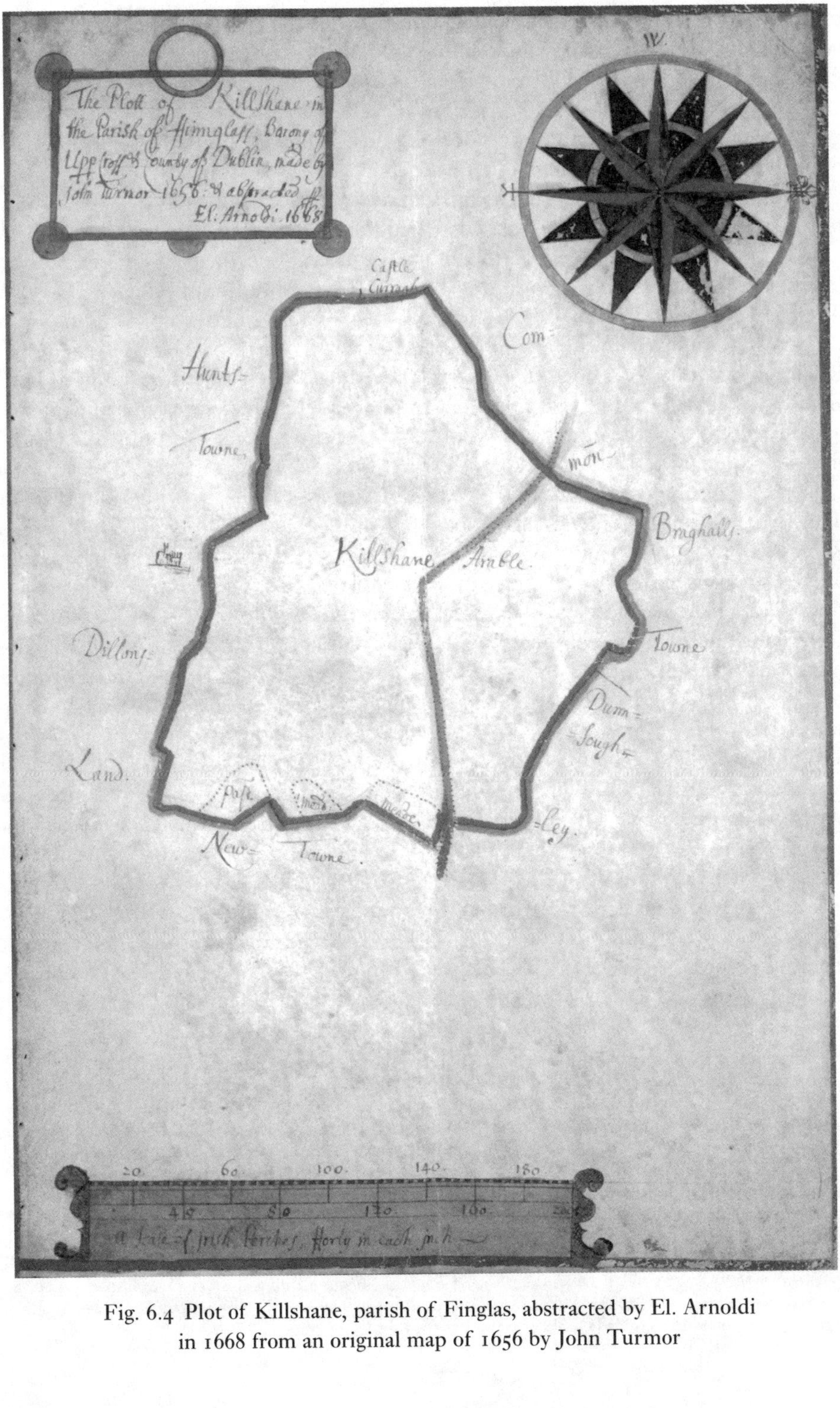

Fig. 6.4 Plot of Killshane, parish of Finglas, abstracted by El. Arnoldi in 1668 from an original map of 1656 by John Turmor

location of the sites themselves may, at some future date, give clues to ancient boundaries. In any event, even allowing for the fact that the list may not be complete, it is clear that everyone in Fingal lived within easy reach of a holy well, although, in general, the east of the district had rather more wells than the west.

Patterns may have been centred on religious ceremonies but they also provided opportunities for many leisure activities such as music, dancing and sport.

People in seventeenth-century Fingal enjoyed music. There was a strong church music tradition in Dublin city, particularly in the earlier part of the seventeenth century, which was exemplified in the music of the two cathedrals.[109] In 1606 the organist of St Patrick's Cathedral was Thomas Taylor, brother of Alderman Francis Taylor of the Swords family.[110] He was counted a 'skilful musician'. Dublin corporation also employed musicians during this period.[111] In 1598 Henry Fitzsimon, a Jesuit and member of a Swords family, had high mass celebrated in the house of a Dublin nobleman 'with full orchestra, composed of harps, lute, and all kinds of instruments except the organ'.[112] According to a contemporary account this was the first solemn mass celebrated for forty years.[113] It is noteworthy that Henry Fitzsimon was able to assemble a full orchestra and choristers in Dublin at that period. It seems likely that Fingal residents attended this and other services in Dublin city. References in 'Purgatorium Hibernicum' to the 'ceremonies of the Tenebrae', to the office of matins and to the chanting of *Salve Reginas* and *Kyrie Eleisons* suggest that they became increasingly familiar with the more elaborate rituals of the Catholic church during the period covered by this study.[114] Another Fingallian Jesuit who distinguished himself in the field of serious music was William Bath of Drumcondra (1564–1614) who published two books on music, *A brief introduction to the true art of musicke* and *A briefe introduction to the skill of song* in the late sixteenth century.[115] The lord of Howth kept a group of musicians who substituted on occasion for the Dublin corporation musicians under Mr Huggard.[116] The guild of tailors paid them 3*s.* in 1609 for standing in for Mr Huggard's group who were engaged at 'Mr Mayor's' and a further sum of 3*s.* in 1610 when the Corporation group was 'at the Circuit'. Henry Burnell's stage directions in the play *Landgartha* provided clues to musical taste in the early 1640s. A mask was performed to 'no music, or at most, to a single violin'.[117] Nymphs sang 'a song in four or five parts, to a pleasing tune' and the 'sweet solemn music of recorders' was heard.[118] This was the music of 'polite society' in Dublin and Fingal. Further evidence of the interest of the wealthier Fingallians in music is to be

109 Barra Boydell, 'The establishment of the choral tradition, 1480–1647' in Kenneth Milne (ed.), *Christ Church Cathedral Dublin: a history* (Dublin, 2000), pp 244–51. 110 Visitations, Dublin, 1607 (NLI, GO 48, p. 11). 111 For example, *Anc. rec. Dublin*, ii, pp 424, 427, 462, 464 and 502. 112 Edmund Hogan, *Distinguished Irishmen of the sixteenth century* (London, 1894)', pp 199 and 208–9. 113 Edmund Hogan, *Distinguished Irishmen of the sixteenth century* (London, 1894), p. 209. 114 Purgatorium Hibernicum . . ., *c.*1670 (NLI, MS 470, pp 59 and 61). 115 William Bathe, *A briefe introduction to the true art of musicke* (London, 1584); William Bathe, *A briefe introduction to the skill of song, c.1587*, introduced by Bernarr Rainbow (facsimile edition, Kilkenny, 1982); Seán P. Ó Mathúna, *An tAthair William Bathe, C.Í., 1564–1614* (Dublin, 1980), pp 195–207. 116 Extract from account book, Guild of Tailors, Dublin (RSAI, Elrington Ball MSS, vol x, f. 1). 117 Henry Burnell, *Landgartha: a tragie-comedie, as it was presented in the new theatre in Dublin, with good applause, being an ancient story* (Dublin, 1641), p. 20. 118 Henry Burnell, *Landgartha: a tragie-comedie, as it was presented in the new theatre in Dublin, with good applause, being an ancient story* (Dublin, 1641), pp 5, 21 and 33.

found in the will of Walter Segrave of Little Cabragh, made in 1619.[119] He listed a viol and a pair of virginals with a frame among the items which he wished to remain in his house after his death. Richard Berford of Blanchardstown also bequeathed a bass viol in 1662.[120] It is likely that other gentlemen and ladies in the area possessed musical instruments which were not listed separately in their wills. It must also be emphasized that few wills from north Fingal and mid-Fingal have been preserved. Therefore the surviving evidence concerning serious music comes from the wills of persons who could easily have participated in the musical life of Dublin city.

There is more widespread evidence for popular music, especially in the verse of the period. Music seems to have afforded the Fingallians an opportunity to express the Gaelic element in their culture. The Fingallian refugees who fled to Virginia after they were defeated at Kilsallaghan spent their time in 'drinking, piping and dancing', according to a deposition made to the commissioners in April 1643 by the local minister, Revd George Creichton.[121] The text of the play *Landgartha* contained references to the bag-pipe and to town-fiddlers.[122] 'Purgatorium Hibernicum' indicated that the Fingallians were familiar with a number of musical instruments. Nees carved a 'bag-pipe rampant on a fiddle' on MacShane's monument.[123] MacShane's death at the hands of a sneezing harper was mentioned.[124] Drums and trumpets were also referred to.[125] The instruments called 'melancholy knockles' on which the mourners tuned 'their doleful notes' have not been identified.[126] As the deposition of Revd George Creichton made clear, piping was also popular. This is confirmed at various points in 'Purgatorium Hibernicum'. As in the documented case in Virginia, piping was closely associated with dancing and the term 'sing' (as well as the terms 'whistle', 'blow' and 'play') appears to have been used frequently in connection with the playing of dance tunes.[127] Orpheus was described as playing a port (*port* or lilt) to raise the devil.[128] MacShane, the piper, went 'to sing a port in Purgatory.[129] The poem also provides the names of a number of dance tunes played by the piper:

> To improve his time could play Mageen,
> Whip of Dunboyne and Dance a Myeen
> and dance Balrothery. I that he
> could sing Portlaughrim and Bunratty
> and Machilmone …

119 Abstract of will of Walter Segrave, 9 March 1619 (RSAI, Elrington Ball MSS, vol xii, f. 27). **120** Abstract of will of Richard Berford, proved 21 November 1662 (RSAI, Elrington Ball MSS, vol xi, f. 41); Francis Elrington Ball, *Southern Fingal* … (originally published 1920, reprinted Dublin, 1995), p. 25. **121** Deposition of George Creichton, 15 April 1643 (TCD, MS 833, ff 236–7); John T. Gilbert (ed.), *A contemporary history of affairs in Ireland from A. D. 1641 to 1652* … (3 vols, Dublin, 1879), i, part ii, p. 542. **122** Henry Burnell, *Landgartha: a tragie-comedie, as it was presented in the new theatre in Dublin, with good applause, being an ancient story* (Dublin, 1641), pp 19 and 34. **123** Purgatorium Hibernicum …, *c.*1670 (NLI, MS 470, p. 53). **124** Purgatorium Hibernicum …, *c.*1670 (NLI, MS 470, p. 36). **125** Purgatorium Hibernicum …, *c.*1670 (NLI, MS 470, pp 39, 50, 135). **126** Purgatorium Hibernicum …, *c.*1670 (NLI, MS 470, p. 49). **127** Purgatorium Hibernicum …, *c.*1670 (NLI, MS 470, pp 34, 38, 39, 40). **128** Purgatorium Hibernicum …, *c.*1670 (NLI, MS 470, p. 29). **129** Purgatorium Hibernicum …, *c.*1670 (NLI, MS 470, p. 34).

Of the tunes mentioned it is evident from Fynes Moryson's fourth itinerary, written sometime before 1626, that 'Balrothery' and the 'Whip of Dunboyne' were the names of dances.[130] In *Landgartha* two of the comic characters, Hubba and Marsissa, danced 'the whip of Dunboyne' merrily.[131] This was followed by a 'grand dance', probably a more formal dance, in four couples.[132] 'Dance a Mween' (*Damhsa i mbuíon* ?) was almost certainly a dance tune and it seems probable that the other airs mentioned were also used for dancing. A further description of the musicians and their tunes can be found in the poet's comparison of the activities in the underworld with those in Lusk on 'patron's eve'. It read as follows:

> There was Mulrony with his trump too
> and Gillekelagh his brother plump too
> and old Tadhg dall and Hugh O'Darcy
> did sing all weathers at the clarsy,
> the Irish harp, whose airy mettle
> sounds like the patching of the kettle.
> Mageen, yea, and be he did play
> Whip of Dunboyne and Irish Hay
> Skipping of Gort, Tripping of Swords
> Frisk of Baldoyle, best he affords,
> and for variety cronnaans
> ports and portrinkas and strinkaans
> oraans and conies and gratulations . . .[133]

Once again we find an emphasis on dancing with some of the tunes having names associated with places in or near Fingal. While the rhyme suggests that the final line in the passage is missing the section which survives is of great interest. The use of several technical words adapted from the Irish language, such as *cronán* (a humming or drone), *port* (a lilt), *port rince* (a jig tune), *streancán* (a twang), *amhrán* (a song), suggests that the players at Lusk were in the mainstream of Irish popular music. The lines which follow the missing line,

> They had no anthems for to choose.
> Their Hallolujes were hul-lo-loos.
> And so, as merry as the day
> is long, they passed the time away.

give the impression of lack of restraint and perhaps even frenzy in the music.[134]

130 Graham Kew, *The Irish sections of Fynes Moryson's unpublished itinerary* (Dublin, 1998), p. 112. 131 Henry Burnell, *Landgartha: a tragie-comedie, as it was presented in the new theatre in Dublin, with good applause, being an ancient story* (Dublin, 1641), p. 22. I am grateful to Dr Raymond Gillespie for drawing my attention to this reference. 132 Henry Burnell, *Landgartha: a tragie-comedie, as it was presented in the new theatre in Dublin, with good applause, being an ancient story* (Dublin, 1641), p. 23. 133 Purgatorium Hibernicum . . ., *c.*1670 (NLI, MS 470, pp 135–6). 134 Purgatorium Hibernicum . . ., *c.*1670 (NLI, MS 470, p. 136).

There are some references to vocal music. Shela, the nun, was depicted as rising 'long before day ... to sing carols', suggesting that by the mid-seventeenth century the term 'carol' had taken on its modern meaning in Fingal.[135] The mourners at MacShane's wake sang cronans.[136] There are references to one, or possibly two, song-titles, 'Old Rose and Tory Rory'.[137] While this song has not been identified the title hints at a political ballad. The singing of a chorus in honour of St Patrick is also mentioned.[138] The reference to 'Beg Mac Dea and Iriell, that of their country sang so well' may be an allusion to an older form of singing and versification which would have survived in some areas during the lifetime of the poet.[139] The huntsmen who took part in the 'Fingallian hunting of the hare' ended their day's festivities by singing 'the hare's knell'[140] All in all, folk music, in both its instrumental and vocal forms, seems to have been cultivated widely in Fingal.

The popularity of dancing in seventeenth-century Ireland has been well documented. By 1625 Fynes Moryson had completed his itinerary.[141] He described the Irish attitude to dance as follows (spelling modernized):

> They delight much in dancing, using no art of slow measures or lofty galliards, but only country dances, whereof they have some pleasant to behold as Balrothery and the whip of Dunboyne and the dance about a fire (commonly in the midst of a room), holding withes in their hands, and by certain strains drawing one another into the fire and also the matachine dance with naked swords which they make to meet in divers comely postures ...[142]

Moryson went on to explain that he had seen the matachine dance in the houses of Irish lords. The impression given is that what he had seen were, in general, rather formal country dances which took place indoors. The hey or hay (*haie*), for example, is believed to have been 'a round dance in which men and women took part and which included figures in which the women wound in and about their partners'.[143] In *Folk music and dances of Ireland* Breandán Breathnach stated that dances of the Pale, such as Pacing the Whip, Trotting the Hey (or Hay), and Skipping of Gort, seemed

> tame affairs in comparison with the dances mentioned in an Irish poem of around 1670: *rince an ghadaraigh* (the withie dance), *rince an chlaidhimh* (the sword dance), *rince treasach re malartaibh ceolta* (a dance of ranks with change of music), and *rince fada re racaireacht ógbhan* (the long dance with the sporting of young maidens). Dances like these, which were traditional Irish

135 Purgatorium Hibernicum ..., *c.*1670 (NLI, MS 470, p. 26). 136 Purgatorium Hibernicum ..., *c.*1670 (NLI, MS 470, p. 49). 137 Purgatorium Hibernicum ..., *c.*1670 (NLI, MS 470, p. 100). 138 Purgatorium Hibernicum ..., *c.*1670 (NLI, MS 470, p. 140). 139 Purgatorium Hibernicum ..., *c.*1670 (NLI, MS 470, pp 140–1). 140 The Fingallian hunting of the hare (BL, Sloane MS 900, f. 55); Francis Elrington Ball, *Howth and its owners ...* (originally published 1917, reprinted Dublin, 1995), p. 120. 141 Graham Kew, *The Irish sections of Fynes Moryson's unpublished itinerary* (Dublin, 1998), pp 7 and 17 (note 5). 142 Graham Kew, *The Irish sections of Fynes Moryson's unpublished itinerary* (Dublin, 1998), p. 112. 143 Breandán Breathnach, *Folk music and dances of Ireland* (2nd ed., Cork, 1996), pp 37–8.

> forms of entertainment, suggest that more exciting amusements were to be found outside the Pale than in it.[144]

There are other descriptions of dancing in Ireland dating from the later part of the century by Thomas Dinely (1681), Sir Henry Piers (1682) and John Dunton (1699) which provide some additional information for that period.[145] The account of Sir Henry Piers, whose family owned property (part of the former monastic lands of Tristernagh) in the parish of Balrothery, is particularly interesting.[146] In his *Chorographical description of the county of Westmeath* he provided an general description of the manners and customs of the Irish people, emphasizing that he found 'little or nothing that can be said of this county [Westmeath] in this respect, that may not be said indifferently of all.'[147] Concerning dancing he wrote:

> On the patron-day in most parishes, as also on the feasts of Easter and Whitsuntide, the more ordinary sort of people meet near the ale-house in the afternoon, on some convenient spot of ground and dance for the cake; here to be sure the piper fails not of diligent attendance. The cake to be danced for is provided at the charge of the ale-wife, and is advanced on a board on the top of a pike about ten feet high; this board is round, and from it riseth a kind of garland, beset and tied round with meadow flowers, if it be early in the summer, if later, the garland has the addition of apples, set round on pegs fastened unto it; the whole number of dancers begin all at once in a large ring, a man and a woman, and dance about the bush, so is this garland called, and the piper, as long as they are able to hold out; they that hold out longest at the exercise, win a cake and apples, and then the ale-wife's trade goes on.[148]

John Dunton's account confirmed that such dancing sessions took place on Sundays and holydays in the afternoon, that the music was provided by a piper and that the dances were trials of endurance.[149] He provided the additional information that the sessions took place around large trees planted in the middle of villages and that the elderly people acted as spectators.

Turning specifically to Fingal we find that there is a considerable amount of material available on the Fingallians' attitude to dance. Dancing was listed by George Creichton as one of the pastimes in which the Fingallian refugees in Virginia

144 Breandán Breathnach, *Folk music and dances of Ireland* (2nd ed., Cork, 1996), p. 38. 145 Thomas Dineley, *Observations in a voyage through the kingdom of Ireland being a collection of several monuments, inscriptions, draughts of towns, castles, & c.*, ed. James Graves (Dublin, 1870), p. 19; Henry Piers, *A chorographical description of the county of Westmeath, written A. D. 1682* in Charles Vallancey, *Collectanea de rebus Hibernicis*, no. I (Dublin, 1770), p. 123; John Dunton, Letter no. 4, appendix B, in Edward MacLysaght, *Irish life in the seventeenth century* (2nd ed., Cork, 1950), p. 354. 146 'Calendar to fiants of the reign of Elizabeth' in *The Irish fiants of the Tudor sovereigns*, iii, 1586–1603 (Dublin, 1994), no. 5769, p. 198; *Civil Survey, vii, county of Dublin,* pp 14–5. 147 Henry Piers, *A chorographical description of the county of Westmeath, written A. D. 1682* in Charles Vallancey, *Collectanea de rebus Hibernicis*, no. I (Dublin, 1770), pp 103–4. 148 Henry Piers, *A chorographical description of the county of Westmeath, written A. D. 1682* in Charles Vallancey, *Collectanea de rebus Hibernicis*, no. I (Dublin, 1770), p. 122 149 John Dunton, Letter no. 4, appendix B, in Edward MacLysaght, *Irish life in the seventeenth century* (2nd ed., Cork 1950), p. 354.

engaged after the fall of Kilsallaghan.[150] 'The Fingallian Dance', a poem believed to date from the period 1650–60, suggests that the dancing at that period had become somewhat more sedate than it had been in earlier times.[151] As well as listing the several dance tunes already mentioned 'Purgatorium Hibernicum' provided additional information about dancing. Round dances were very popular in Fingal. 'Dancing and skipping in a ring' were some of the activities in which the people indulged in order to honour St Patrick.[152] There is a vivid account of ring dancing in the underworld:

> Those donny shoges that hop and scout
> from hill to plain and skip about
> like penny canes, as steeds of wattle
> drink dairies dry and stroke the cattle
> and pinch the maids until their flesh is
> of sable, hugs through keyholes sling
> toping and dancing in a ring.
> About the banks of Erryn they
> do keep their revels night and day.
> Eternal rings that drink and sot
> till what they are they have forgot
> and, all their former notions gone,
> to beasts and fiends transform anon.[153]

The hey, which appears to have been one of the more sedate dances, was danced at wakes.[154] The poet mentioned the whip and hay in connection with the dancing which preceded the betrayal of a garrison by Lacene although it is not known if this was merely a classical reference or if it was intended to reflect an actual incident which took place during the confederate wars.[155] The same dances were popular in *Limbo Patrum*.[156] A little later in the poem the shades of the underworld were compared to the people of Lusk at dusk on patron's eve, giving us a short but vivid picture of the dancing on such an occasion:

> Some frig and dance upon the grass
> and every *culleen* has his lass.
> Some dance in pairs, some in a ring
> some in a yoke and some a sling.
> Some bended dance, some dance astride,
> as maids of Duleek use to ride . . .[157]

150 Deposition of George Creichton, 15 April 1643 (TCD, MS 833, ff 236–7); John T. Gilbert (ed.), *A contemporary history of affairs in Ireland from A. D. 1641 to 1652* . . . (3 vols, Dublin, 1879–80), i, part ii, p. 542. 151 The Fingallian dance, c.1650–60 (BL, Sloane MS 900, f. 53); Alan Bliss, *Spoken English in Ireland 1600–1740* (Dublin 1979), pp 45–6 and 111. 152 Purgatorium Hibernicum . . ., *c.*1670 (NLI, MS 470, p. 140). 153 Purgatorium Hibernicum . . ., *c.*1670 (NLI, MS 470, p. 153). 154 Purgatorium Hibernicum . . ., *c.*1670 (NLI, MS 470, p. 50). 155 Purgatorium Hibernicum . . ., *c.*1670 (NLI, MS 470, p. 100). 156 Purgatorium Hibernicum . . ., *c.*1670 (NLI, MS 470, p. 133). 157 Purgatorium Hibernicum . . ., *c.*1670 (NLI, MS 470, p. 135).

Since only the first two lines of this description (modified slightly) were included in the published *Irish Hudibras*, it is hardly surprising that Breandán Breathnach underestimated the liveliness and vigour of the dances of the Pale.[158]

If music, and, to a lesser extent, dancing enabled the Fingallians to express the Gaelic element in their culture, games and sports, with one notable exception, reflected the settler influences on that culture. The exception was *camán* (hurling), which, according to 'Purgatorium Hibernicum' was one of the sports indulged in by the population on patron's eve at Lusk.[159] It may be useful to examine the context in which the people engaged in sport as official attitudes changed somewhat during the period. In its meeting on the second Friday after Easter in 1612 Dublin corporation decreed:

> It is further ordered and agreed, by the said authority that every apprentice, journeyman and every other of the age of fourteen years or upwards, which shall be found playing at stodball [*sic*], quoiting, tennis, cudgels, or any other unlawful games, within any street of this city or suburbs of the same upon Sundays or holydays, shall presently be taken by the aldermen, deputy aldermen, and constables of every ward, and be committed to the Newgate, there to remain for the space of twenty-four hours without bail ...[160]

As in the case of music those living in southern Fingal are likely to have taken part in the leisure activities of Dublin city. Since the ban of 1612 extended to the suburbs it is almost certain that it affected many Fingallians. The law was unsuccessful, however, since it had to be re-enacted a year later.[161] However, support for the beleaguered sportsmen came from an unexpected source. In 1618 King James I published his book of sports, extending the arrangements for the playing of games on Sundays and holydays after divine service to all his subjects. This was reissued with additional notes by Charles I in 1633.[162] 'Some puritan and precise people' in Lancashire had punished the 'good people, for using their lawful recreations and honest exercises upon Sundays and other holydays', and this had played into the hands of recusants.[163] It was also felt that banning of sports on Sundays and holydays (the only days on which ordinary people were free to participate) would render them unfit for army service. Lawful recreations, such as dancing for either men or women, archery for men, leaping, vaulting or any such harmless recreation, May games, Whitsun-ales, morris dances, maypoles and the carrying of rushes to church by women were to be permitted.[164] Unlawful games, such as bull and bear-baiting, interludes and bowling, among the 'meaner sort of people' were to continue to be prohibited. Recusants who did not attend divine service were to be prohibited from participation.

158 James Farewell (?), *The Irish Hudibras or Fingallian prince, taken from the sixth book of Virgil's Aeneids, and adapted to the present times* (London, 1689), p. 102; Breandán Breathnach, *Folk music and dances of Ireland* (2nd ed., Cork, 1996), p. 38. 159 Purgatorium Hibernicum ..., *c.*1670 (NLI, MS 470, p. 134). 160 *Anc. rec. Dublin*, iii, p. 20. 161 *Anc. rec. Dublin*, iii, pp 39–40. 162 James I, *Book of sports as set forth by K. Charles the I with remarks by the king* (London, 1633, reprinted 1710). 163 James I, *Book of sports as set forth by K. Charles the I with remarks by the king* (London, 1633, reprinted 1710), pp 1–2. 164 James I, *Book of sports as set forth by K. Charles the I with remarks by the king* (London, 1633, reprinted 1710), p. 3.

It is unlikely that the people of Fingal paid much attention to these restrictions, and they certainly paid none to the regulations regarding recusants. The deposition of the Revd George Creichton provides evidence that tennis was very popular among Fingallians.[165] Two hundred active male tennis players at one time seems an amazing number to have been recruited from the refugee population. Further evidence for the popularity of tennis can be found. An argument between Christopher, lord of Howth and Sir Roger Jones which took place on a tennis court in Dublin ended in tragedy in 1609 when a man called Barnewall, a kinsman of the earl was killed.[166] Bennett Arthur of Cabragh left 'three houses and a tennis court in Winetavern Street' in 1673.[167] Tennis is also mentioned in 'Purgatorium Hibernicum'.[168] The many games listed in this poem are generally of two kinds: wake games and pattern games. Most of the wake games are mentioned in the following passage:

Some play hot cockles,
some shoe the wild mare, some flea sheep,
some fast asleep and some bo-peep.
some heads and point, some turn up tail
and play a game called thrust a fail.
Some fling their caps and some throw darts
of rushes, engines to catch hearts.
Some squibs do throw and some throw clods.
Some play at even and some at odds.
Some stitch with artificial thread ...[169]

On the following page of the manuscript another wake game, noddy, is mentioned.[170]

It has been possible to identify some of these games. Bo-peep was a well-known nursery game.[171] Shoeing the wild mare has been described as a 'childish Christmas game'.[172] Blind-man's-buff was, according to Seán Ó Súilleabháin, 'a very popular type of parlour-game ... also played at wakes'.[173] Hot cockles appears to have been a rougher variant of blind-man's-buff similar to the game called *cluiche na gcochall*.[174] Noddy was a card game resembling cribbage.[175] Cat was also known as tip-cat, a game played by hitting a small piece of wood tapering at both ends with a cat-stick.[176] Heads and points was played with pins or nails.[177] Stitching with artificial thread may have been the game called 'box the tailor', described by Ó Súilleabháin as a game in which participants pretended to sew.[178] The flinging of caps and the throwing of

165 Deposition of George Creichton, 15 April 1643 (TCD, MS 833, ff 236–7); John T. Gilbert (ed.), *A contemporary history of affairs in Ireland from A. D. 1641 to 1652 ...* (3 vols, Dublin, 1879), i, part ii, p. 542. **166** Francis Elrington Ball, *Howth and its owners ...* (originally published 1917, reprinted Dublin, 1995), p. 101. **167** Abstract of will of Bennett Arthur, dated 18 July 1673 (RSAI, Elrington Ball MSS, vol xi, f. 43); Francis Elrington Ball, *Southern Fingal ...* (originally published 1920, reprinted Dublin, 1995), p. 27. **168** Purgatorium Hibernicum ..., *c.*1670 (NLI, MS 470, p. 134). **169** Purgatorium Hibernicum ..., *c.*1670 (NLI, MS 470, p. 49). **170** Purgatorium Hibernicum ..., *c.*1670 (NLI, MS 470, p. 50). **171** *OED*, ii, p. 409. **172** *OED*, ix, p. 363. **173** Seán Ó Súilleabháin, *Irish wake amusements* (translated by the author from the original Irish *Caitheamh aimsire ar thórraimh*, 1961, Cork, 1997), p. 117. **174** *OED*, vii, p. 426; Seán Ó Súilleabháin, *Irish wake amusements* (translated by the author from the original Irish *Caitheamh aimsire ar thórraimh*, 1961, published Cork, 1997), p. 117. **175** *OED*, x, p. 459. **176** *OED*, ii, p. 962. **177** *OED*, vii, p. 40. **178** Seán Ó Súilleabháin, *Irish wake amusements* (translated

darts, squibs and clods, as well as the game called 'thrust a fail' appear to have been part of the unruly behaviour associated in particular with the deaths of elderly people.[179] The wake games which have been identified were mainly, though not exclusively, indoor games which ranged from games suitable for children, through boisterous sports favoured by young adults, to card games which were, no doubt, popular with older people.

The second set of games in 'Purgatorium Hibernicum' were those in which the behaviour of the shades in the underworld was compared with that of people of Lusk on patron's eve. It reads as follows:

Some play at tennis, some at slurr,
at hurdles some and some at skirr,
some at *caman* and some do play
at fives and some bitty-bay.
Some play at this game, some at that,
at stoolball some and some at cat.
But those that lost their eyes with age
and in this rout dare not engage
are force(d) to play at blind man buff.
Some roast pattads and some grind snuff
by woods and bogs where store of fire is.
Some play at gammon, some at Irish,
for prayers and kisses and for beads,
for masses and for maidenheads.
Some trot the bogs and some swift hastle.
At cudgels some and some do wrestle ...[180]

We note that two of the games, cat and blind-man's-buff were also played at wakes. Gammon (backgammon), Irish and slurr were games played with dice.[181] No games of this type have been identified in the wakes list. Most of the other games listed were of the open-air athletic kind. The popularity of tennis in Fingal has already been mentioned. Fives was somewhat similar to modern handball.[182] In the absence of contemporary evidence hurdles is assumed to have resembled the modern version of the sport. Skirr was a throwing game.[183] Stoolball as played in England has been described as 'an old country game somewhat resembling cricket, played chiefly by young women or, as an Easter game, between young men and women for a "tansy" ... as the stake'.[184] Henry Burnell's *Landgartha* contained a reference to the playing of stoolball with young children.[185] The existence of stoolball in the area in the sev-

by the author from the original Irish *Caitheamh aimsire ar thórraimh*, 1961, published Cork, 1997), p. 46. **179** *OED*, v, p. 665; Seán Ó Súilleabháin, *Irish wake amusements* (translated by the author from the original Irish *Caitheamh aimsire ar thórraimh*, 1961, published Cork, 1997), pp 65–6. **180** Purgatorium Hibernicum ..., *c.*1670 (NLI, MS 470, p. 134). **181** *OED*, i, p. 865, vi, p. 350, viii, p. 77 and xv, p. 750. **182** *OED*, v, p. 980. **183** *OED*, xv, p. 621. **184** *OED*, xvi, p. 771. **185** Henry Burnell, *Landgartha: a tragie-comedie, as it was presented in the new theatre in Dublin, with good applause, being an ancient story* (Dublin, 1641), p. 31.

enteenth century may help to explain the extraordinary and continuing popularity of village cricket in rural north Fingal to the present day.[186] Wrestling, also listed as a pattern game, was a popular sport in Fingal, particularly in Lusk and other parts of north Fingal, until the late nineteenth century.[187] *Camán* was, of course, exceptional since it was a traditional native game. There is a brief reference to sport in the description of the people at Tubber Shane, but no details concerning particular games are given.[188] A rather surprising omission from the lists of games is football, unless, of course, it was played under another name. It may just possibly have been one of the games which have not been identified. Whether or not football was played it was certainly known in Fingal at this period. Sir Richard Bolton, discussing homicide by misadventure, stated that there was a difference of opinion as to whether 'playing at hand-sword, bucklers, football, wrestling and the like, whereby one of them receiveth a hurt and dieth thereof within a year and a day' constituted felony of death or not.[189] There is evidence that football was played in Fingal later in the century. In 1699 John Dunton wrote concerning the Irish that 'they do not play often at football, only in a small territory called Fingal near Dublin the people use it much, and trip, and shoulder very handsomely'.[190] By the early eighteenth century the game had become very popular in Fingal.[191]

Hunting and shooting were also popular pastimes, particularly among the gentry. The keeping of hounds and greyhounds was restricted to laymen having in lands 40*s*. per annum and priests and clerks having a 10*l*. living per annum.[192] The lord deputy, Sir Arthur Chichester, and the lord of Howth hunted a fox together in Balgriffin.[193] The poem, 'The Fingallian hunting of the hare', is a celebration of the sport.[194] The hunt described in this verse began in Howth and ended with a dinner in Baldoyle. While the hare and hounds were described in detail, it is not clear if the huntsmen rode or followed the hounds on foot. However, the mention of a saddle (as well as a fowling-piece) as a cherished possession in the will of one of the participants, John Radmore, suggests that the gentry normally hunted on horseback.[195] Hawking was also popular. Lewis Meredith reported that the friar Malone, who invaded Lambay Island on behalf of the 'Catholic army' in December 1641, asked him to carry a goshawk as a present to Luke Nettervill, the rebel leader, then in Swords.[196] This goshawk had been taken from Edward Leech who had been in charge of the castle of Lambay. That shooting was indulged in by persons lower down the social scale is

186 Joe Clinton, 'Cricket in Fingal' (Skerries Historical Society Archives, unpublished paper no. 176, 1994). **187** R.S. Duff, 'Some memories of Milverton' in *Time & tide*, iii (2001), p. 168. **188** Purgatorium Hibernicum ..., *c*.1670 (NLI, MS 470, p. 151). **189** Richard Bolton, *A justice of peace for Ireland* ... (Dublin, 1638), book I, p. 73. **190** John Dunton, *Teague Land* (1699), quoted in Andrew Hadfield and John McVeagh (eds), *Strangers to that land: British perceptions of Ireland from the reformation to the famine* (Gerrard's Cross, Buckinghamshire, 1994), p. 195. **191** Patrick Fagan, *The second city: portrait of Dublin 1700–1760* (Dublin, 1986), pp 79–81 and 186–98. **192** Richard Bolton, *A justice of peace for Ireland* ... (Dublin, 1638), book I, p. 46. **193** Edmund Hogan, *Distinguished Irishmen of the sixteenth century* (London, 1894), p.425; Francis Elrington Ball, *Howth and its owners* ... (originally published 1917, reprinted Dublin, 1995), pp 92–3. **194** The Fingallian hunting of the hare (BL, Sloane MS 900, ff 54–5); Francis Elrington Ball, *Howth and its owners* ... (originally published 1917, reprinted Dublin, 1995), pp 119–20. **195** Francis Elrington Ball, *Howth and its owners* ... (originally published 1917, reprinted Dublin, 1995), p. 119 (footnote 4). **196** Deposition of Lewis Meredith, 20 March 1644 (TCD, MS 810, f. 245).

suggested by an incident that occurred in December 1652, when Richard Greg, a twenty-three-year-old husbandman from Chapelizod, discharged a fowling piece against a group of tories in an effort to recover stolen garrons.[197]

Fynes Moryson noted the Irish in general and, in particular, the native Irish were fond of gambling.[198] An unusual instance of this occurred in Fingal early in 1642, when, in what appears to have been a draft deposition, Daniel Barwick, commander of one of the king's pinnaces, reported that, while a prisoner in Baldongan, he heard divers people say that the Dublin alderman, Robert Arthur of Hacketstown, 'would for 5*s.* give anyone 20*s.* if Drogheda was not taken by such a day'.[199] He went on to say that he 'heard the priest that liveth with the said Arthur say that he won 20*s.* of the said Arthur on those terms'.

There is evidence that the Fingallians were brash, sociable, outgoing and hospitable. These are qualities that one would particularly associate with the Gaelic-Irish element in their culture. Three references to coshering (*cóisireacht* – partying or friendly visits to the homes of neighbours) in 'Purgatorium Hibernicum' support this view.[200] There are also some interesting references to visiting the homes of friends and neighbours in the 1641 depositions. The visit of 'old Mr Fagan of Feltrim' to his friends in Carrickmines was mentioned in chapter 2.[201] Richard Duffe and his brother called to Gormanstown at Christmas 1641 and found there 'only the lord of Gormanstown, his lady and family, and Mr King of Clontarf and his wife'.[202] This suggests that the Kings were enjoying the hospitality of Lord Gormanston in the aftermath of the burning of their own home at Clontarf. Susanna Stockdale, a Protestant, who had also lost her home during the rising, was offered hospitality and a home by her Catholic cousin, Nicholas Barnewall of Turvey.[203] She refused this offer 'because she was confident that popish priests and rebels would haunt his house'. The Fingallians also showed that they had the ability to close ranks in the face of threats from outside. Simon Luttrell of Luttrellstown was one of those who remained aloof from the 1641 rising.[204] Yet in April 1642 a soldier, Daniel Conway, who had been engaged in pursuing a band of rebels towards Luttrellstown, reported that 'being very near unto two of the said rebels, one of them forsook his horse and strayed into the wood and the other, forsaking his horse likewise, got into the gate of the said Mr Luttrell's house, which gate was presently shut up and entrance denied unto him, this examinant'.[205] When dogs were set on the minister of Ballyboghil, John Lukey, in order to drive him out of the parish he went to two houses seeking help and on both occasions he was refused.[206] The same solidarity, or perhaps clannishness, was shown, when necessary, against the Ulster Irish. As George Creichton reported:

197 Examination of Richard Greg, 16 December 1652 (TCD, MS 810, f. 388); examination of Richard Raymond, 20 December 1652 (TCD, MS 810, f. 390). **198** Graham Kew, *The Irish sections of Fynes Moryson's unpublished itinerary* (Dublin, 1998), p. 39. **199** Deposition of Daniel Barwick, 21 May 1642 (TCD, MS 810, f. 112). **200** Purgatorium Hibernicum . . ., *c.*1670 (NLI, MS 470, pp 35, 58 and 108). **201** Examination of John Brackenbury, 27 May 1642 (TCD, MS 810, f. 198). **202** Examination of Richard Duffe, 2 May 1642 (TCD, MS 810, f. 210). **203** Deposition of Susanna Stockdale (copy only), not dated (TCD, MS 810, f. 95). **204** Examination of William Dollard, 30 December 1641 (TCD, MS 809, f. 218). **205** Examination of Daniel Conway, April 1642 (TCD, MS 810, f. 97). **206** Deposition of John Lukey, 2 March 1643 (TCD, MS 810, f. 168).

> The priest of the parish of Lurgan, Owen O'Linsey, did so hate the Pale people that he would not that any of their priests or friars should say Mass in his parish; and the Pale people did so hate him that they would not come to hear him, and they needed not, for many a priest they had of their own.[207]

The people of Fingal possessed no great cities, castles, palaces, theatres or cathedrals. Their towns, homes and churches were generally small. Undoubtedly, those who could afford to do so and who lived close to Dublin could enjoy the pleasures of the metropolis. But for many this was not an option. Yet enough evidence remains to show that Fingallians enjoyed a rich and varied social life, that they had many opportunities for contacts with their neighbours and with outsiders and that they were both faithful to old traditions and open to new ideas. They adapted elements of both Gaelic and foreign cultures and created something unique to themselves. Underpinning all of this were deep, though differing, religious loyalties. The different religious groups also provided opportunities for social interaction though the members of the various religious denominations generally met separately at services.

207 Deposition of George Creichton, 15 April 1643 (TCD, MS 833, f. 236); John T. Gilbert (ed.), *A contemporary history of affairs in Ireland from A. D. 1641 to 1652 ...* (3 vols, Dublin, 1879–80), i, part ii, p. 542.

7

Every house and hamlet a sanctuary

> Michael Fitz-Simon, Martyr, Dublinensis, cui dat optione, viuendi, si abiuraret religione, vel suum dominiu Forußi, Pseudoepiscopo Thomae Iohns, idque gratis, concederet: Ille preces, minas, morte pro Christo spreuit. In eius dominium Thomas Iohns statim inuolauit.
>
> Henry Fitzsimon, *c.*1611[1]

These words form one of the longer entries in the *Catalogus* or catalogue of Irish saints completed by Henry Fitzsimon, of the Society of Jesus, about 1611. He wrote, no doubt with great pride, of his kinsman, Michael Fitzsimon, of the Forrest (also known as Forrowes or Furrows), in the parish of Swords, who had been executed in May 1591 following the Baltinglass revolt.[2] Many of those living in Fingal when the catalogue was first published would certainly have remembered Michael Fitzsimon or would have heard his story from their parents. They might also have heard the allegation that Michael Fitzsimon 'was in one day indicted, arraigned, condemned and judged, and the next day executed, that his farm might be bestowed on the bishop of Meath' who was, at that time, Thomas Jones.[3] Some would have recalled the special inquiry about his property which took place at the Forrest following Michael's death and how his widow, Catherine Talbot, managed to spirit away nine heifers and three other large cows before the sheriff arrived.[4] There were allegations that other property, including some silver spoons, had been taken from the premises by persons unknown before the sheriff removed most of the valuables leaving 'a cupboard worth 20*s.*, a trestle table and benches worth 6*s.* 8*d.*, three wooden bedsteads worth 26*s.* 8*d.*, a chest worth 2*s.* 8*d.*, a tub worth 16*d.* and three other old bedsteads worth 4*s.*' at the Forrest in the custody of the bishop of Meath. It seems likely that, when Michael Fitzsimon's debts were paid, the bishop of Meath got rather less than he expected as a result of the execution. The *Catalogus* entry also gives an indication of the bitterness which Catholics felt towards Protestants in the early seventeenth century. The term 'pseudo-bishop' was one which was often used by Catholics when writing of bishops of the established church.

In this chapter it is proposed to explore the organization and membership of the various religious groups in Fingal. The sources are incomplete. At certain times during the period there were surveys which threw light on the strength of the var-

1 Henry Fitzsimon, 'Catalogus praecipuorum sanctorum Hiberniae' ... (Antwerp, 1621), pp 103–4. 2 *Cal. S. P. Ire. 1588–92*, p. 396; John Brady, 'Some Irish scholars of the sixteenth century', in *Studies*, xxxvii, no. 146 (June, 1948), p. 231; Colm Lennon, *The lords of Dublin in the age of reformation* (Dublin, 1989), pp 153–5 and 163–4. 3 *Cal. S. P. Ire 1592–6*, p. 272. 4 Griffith, *Inquisitions*, p. 286.

ious faiths, for example, Archbishop Bulkeley's visitation which took place in 1630 and which provided a considerable amount of the hard information which survives about both the Catholic and the established churches.[5] The Civil Survey and the '1659 Census' are also helpful.[6] Both the Catholic and established churches were organized by diocese. Fingal formed part of the diocese of Dublin which also included Dublin city, the remainder of Co. Dublin, most of Co. Wicklow and small areas in other adjoining counties. The Catholic archbishops were Matthew de Oviedo (1600–10), Patrick Mathews (1611–23) and Thomas Fleming (1623–51). James Dempsey was appointed vicar apostolic in 1657. The Protestant archbishops were Adam Loftus (1567–1605), Thomas Jones (1605–19) and Lancelot Bulkeley (1619–50). The established church was effectively disestablished in 1647. There was, therefore, no further appointment of a Protestant archbishop of Dublin until after the Restoration. During the Commonwealth the country was divided into precincts for the purpose of Protestant church organization. Fingal generally formed part of the Dublin precinct though for a short time in 1654 the Naul formed part of the Trim precinct.[7] Certain important sources are only available on a diocesan basis or, for the Commonwealth period, on a precinct basis. Some degree of caution must be exercised when extrapolating for Fingal from such sources since its fertile maritime plain and people who were predominantly Catholic, English-speaking and subject to influences from overseas, differed widely from both the mountainous and still largely Irish-speaking areas of south Dublin and Wicklow and from Dublin city with its substantial urban Protestant population.

A seventeenth-century visitor to Fingal, with a particular interest in religion, would probably have had his attention drawn first to the churches. Writing of the period 1590–1641, Alan Ford has stated that 'the symbol of pastoral failure in the Protestant church as a national church was the decay of the church fabric'.[8] As early as 1611 the deterioration was noted in a bitter denunciation of the Protestant clergy by the Jesuit, Henry Fitzsimon.

> And do not the naked churches, the glassless patent windows, the ruinous roofs, the razed monuments, the rotten lofts and unpaved floors belonging to God, compared to their own haughty habitation … demonstrate that their study is turned from the old to the new, from God to the belly, from devotion to dissolution, from charity to carnality?[9]

It is possible to extract some information about the state of the church buildings in Fingal from the reports of the royal visitation of 1615, Archbishop Bulkeley's visitation of 1630 and the Civil Survey.[10] These data suggest that, at most, only sixteen

5 'Archbishop Bulkeley's visitation of Dublin, 1630', ed. M.V. Ronan in *Archivium Hibernicum*, viii (1941), pp 56–98. 6 *Civil Survey, vii, county of Dublin,* ed. R.C. Simington (Dublin, 1945); *A census of Ireland* circa *1659* …, ed. S. Pender (Dublin, 1939). 7 Notes relating to the 'Ministers of the Gospel' … (RCBL, GS 2/7/3/20, p. 181). 8 Alan Ford, *The protestant reformation in Ireland, 1590–1641* (2nd ed., Dublin, 1997), p. 101. 9 Henry Fitzsimon, *The justification and exposition of the divine sacrifice of the Masse* … ([Douai], 1611), p. 16. 10 'Royal visitation of Dublin, 1615' and 'Archbishop Bulkeley's visitation of Dublin, 1630' ed. M.V. Ronan in *Archivium Hibernicum*, viii (1941), pp 1–55 and 56–98; *Civil Survey, vii, county of Dublin,* ed. R.C. Simington (Dublin, 1945).

of the forty-one parishes in 1615 and thirteen in 1630 had churches which could be used for divine service.[11] The position in 1654–6 is less clear. The only churches which were definitely described as being 'in repair' were those of Chapelizod and Lusk. In the case of Lusk there was an noticeable improvement on conditions in 1630 while the fact that Chapelizod was shown as being 'in repair' in both 1615 and 1654/6 suggests that it may have been omitted in error from the 1630 returns. The church at Clonmethan, though out of repair, may have been still usable in 1654–6.

The distribution of churches still available for use in 1615, 1630 and 1654–6, insofar as it could be ascertained from the surviving records, has been mapped in figure 7.1.

The churches which were in ruins in 1654–6 were, in general, those which had been in poor condition, that is, either in ruins or deteriorating, in 1630. However, four of the churches, Balscaddan, Donabate, Holmpatrick and Killossery, which were unavailable for use in 1654/5 had been in good or fair condition at the earlier date. Balscaddan, Donabate and Holmpatrick were situated in parishes in which parishioners played a significant part in the 1641 rising and the church buildings may have been damaged as a result of this. All of the seven churches listed in the Civil Survey, but for which no information was given on their condition, had been in ruins or, for practical purposes, extinct by 1630. Five of the eight churches, which were not mentioned at all in the Civil Survey, were also in ruins or extinct in 1630. This leaves three of these churches, Cloghran (Swords), Finglas and St Michan's, which were in good or reasonable repair in 1630. It is clear from other sources that St Michan's was being used during the 1654–6 period.[12] Assuming that Cloghran and Finglas were still suitable for service it appears that not more than about six churches, one of which was situated in Dublin city, were available to serve the members of the established church in Fingal in the mid-1650s. But as will be shown, one of these, Finglas, was badly in need of repair before it could be used as a meeting-house.

The Fingal churches were generally small. Some, indeed, were very small. However, there were some with striking features. Those at Lusk and Swords possessed ancient round towers which can still be seen. The ruined hill-top church of Baldongan, which still dominates the skyline of much of north Fingal, together with the neighbouring castle, which has now disappeared, would have emphasized the importance of local civil and ecclesiastical power. A somewhat different impression might have been obtained from the church in Finglas. George Carey, 'gentleman', founder of an important family in that parish, requested in his will in 1559 that he be buried before the picture of St Kevin (transcribed by Francis Elrington Ball as 'St Canice' – both saints had associations with the area).[13] This suggests that the church was brightly painted or, at least had some paintings, in the sixteenth century. However, almost a century later in 1657, when a vestry which contained a strong dissenting influence met to organize repairs to the church, the walls of the body of the church were white-washed.[14] One church, at least, had become much plainer by the

11 'Fingal 1603–60', i, pp 243–4; ii, appendix G, table G.1, pp 61–3. 12 *The registers of the church of St Michan, Dublin, 1636–1685*, ed. Henry F. Berry (Dublin, 1907). 13 Abstract of will of George Carey, 13 December 1559 (NLI, Fisher will abstracts, GO MS 290, p. 70); Francis Elrington Ball, *Southern Fingal* ... (originally published 1920, reprinted Dublin, 1995), pp 117–8. 14 William Cotter Stubbs,

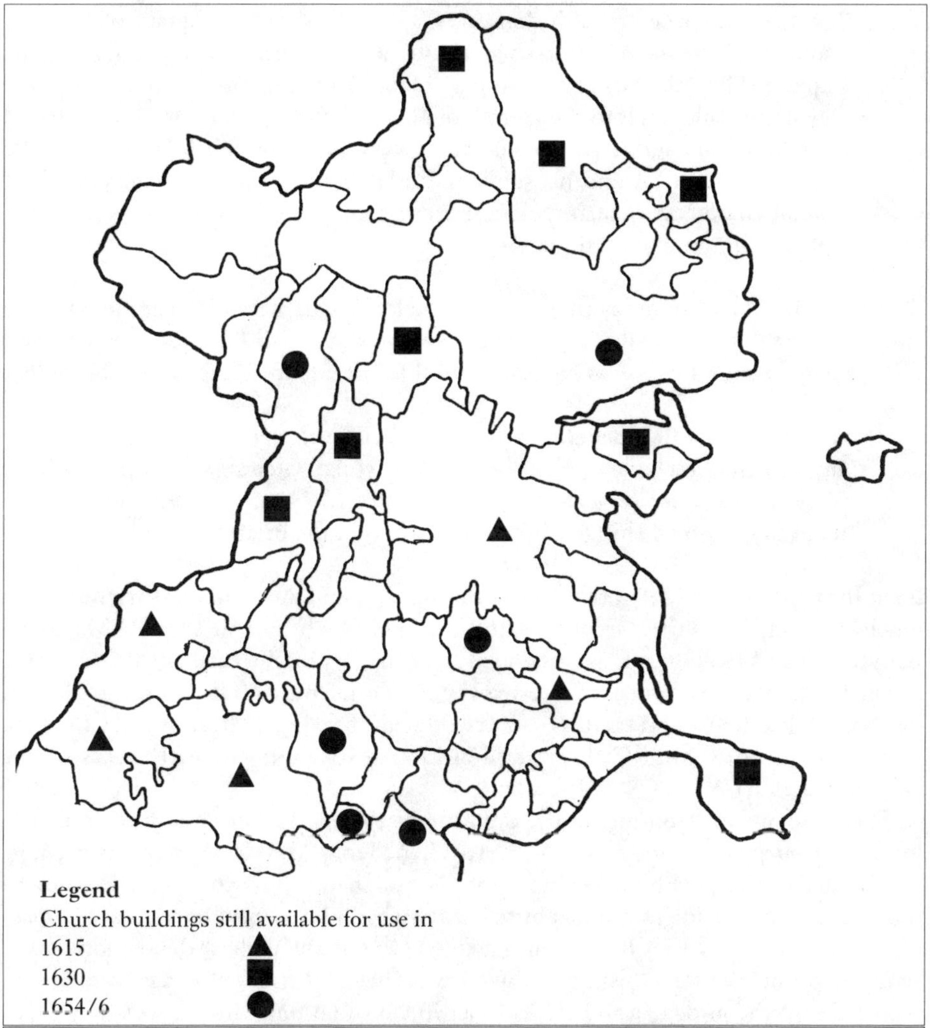

Fig. 7.1 Churches of the established church in Fingal still available for use in 1615, 1630 and 1654–6

end of the period under review. There are few contemporary accounts of the appearance of the churches, other than those which appear in the official surveys. However, the vicar of Balrothery, Thomas Clitheroe, made reference to one notable external feature of many Fingal churches, namely, the bells and belfries, in a deposition made in July 1642 as follows:

'Finglas, County Dublin, vestry books' in *Journal of the Royal Society of Antiquaries of Ireland*, xlvi (1916), p. 28.

> Thomas Clitheroe ... saith that one Captain Epsley, late captain of the garrison of Gormanstown (as this deponent hath been reliably informed by Captain Billingsley) did lately, under colour of the present rebellion and wars, go with his soldiers into the church of Balrothery and thence took and carried away four bells out of the steeple being very good and fair bells and that the said Captain Epsley and his soldiers did lately after enter into the church of Stamullen and there also took and carried away the bells and sent the same bells by shipping over the sea.[15]

When Finglas church was repaired in 1657 the local dissenters took care to have the old bell recast.[16] One possible explanation for the Fingallian fondness for bells and belfries may be found in the writings of a local Jesuit, Henry Fitzsimon, who stated:

> Among many other benefits wrought by bells, this is one witnessed by many authors, that if a hallowed bell be founded whilst witches be transported from place to place, the devils have no power to convey them further, but abandon them to their own shifts, leaving them often in the briars.[17]

Isaac Butler in 1744 noted a triple belfry in the ruined church of Portmarnock.[18] A nineteenth-century writer attributed the feature, which he had seen in Malahide, Ballyboghil and Hollywood, as possibly due to 'the art of the carillon player, which implied a knowledge of music and tested the player' talents'.[19] The church at Howth, too, had such a belfry, and the three inscribed bells, bearing dedications to Christ, St Mary and Nicholas Mun Cir were still at Howth Castle in the early years of the twentieth century.[20]

There are one or two hints in the depositions that particular churches were used for secular purposes by the rebels in 1641. When Henry Mawdesley was captured, he was brought to and held in the church of Clonmethan.[21] The church of Balrothery was plundered by soldiers.[22] The church at Ballyboghil was used to conceal the mastiff dogs that were set on Revd John Lukey.[23] One of the earliest depositions made after the outbreak of the rising in Fingal was that of Christopher Hampton, who reported that the lords of the Pale had met in consultation at the church of Duleek (Co. Meath) to which he had been taken as a prisoner prior to his release by Colonel Roger Moore.[24]

Information about the church buildings can be obtained from a variety of non-contemporary sources. Isaac Butler, who travelled through the area in 1744, paid a good deal of attention to the churches.[25] Austin Cooper, who visited Fingal in 1779,

15 Deposition of Thomas Clitheroe, 26 May 1642 (TCD, MS 810, f. 126). 16 William Cotter Stubbs, 'Finglas, County Dublin, vestry books' in *Journal of the Royal Society of Antiquaries of Ireland*, xlvi (1916), p. 30. 17 Henry Fitzsimon, *The justification and exposition of the divine sacrifice of the Masse* ... ([Douai], 1611), pp 4–5. 18 Isaac Butler, Journal of 1744 (Armagh Public Library, p. 2). 19 Robert Walsh, *Fingal and its churches* ... (Dublin, 1888), p. 59. 20 Francis Elrington Ball, *Howth and its owners* ... (originally published 1917, reprinted Dublin, 1995), p. 47. 21 Deposition of George Cashell (copy only), 29 February 1644 (TCD, MS 810, f. 25). 22 Deposition of Thomas Clitheroe, 26 May 1642 (TCD, MS 810, f. 126). 23 Deposition of John Lukey, 2 March 1643 (TCD, MS 810, f. 168). 24 Examination of Christopher Hampton, 11 December 1641 (TCD, MS 809, f. 212). 25 Isaac Butler, Journal of 1744

described many of them.[26] Robert Walsh wrote a comprehensive account of the condition of the buildings of the Church of Ireland in 1888.[27] However, before even Isaac Butler visited the area in 1744 much rebuilding and repair work had taken place, partly due to the prompting and encouragement of Archbishop William King. For example, Holmpatrick church, which was in ruins at the time of the Civil Survey, had been substantially repaired or rebuilt by 1721.[28] By the time Robert Walsh published his historical sketch in 1888, this rebuilt (possibly medieval) church was in ruins and had been replaced by a church completed in 1868.[29]

Even as early as 1654 action was being taken to improve the condition of certain church buildings. On 30 March Dr Daniel Rowles was appointed Commonwealth minister to Swords, the largest town in Fingal, at an annual salary of £100.[30] On 5 April it was noted that, as there was a necessity of repairing and fitting up a meeting-place at Swords, the commissioners of revenue at Dublin were to cause it to be repaired and to issue a warrant to the treasurer at Dublin to pay a sum of money for this purpose, not exceeding £40.[31] Within a short time it became clear that these measures were insufficient. On 26 June it was directed that: 'Upon consideration of the necessity for a meeting-place at Swords it be referred to the commissioners of revenue to cause the chancel and part of the church at Swords to be repaired for a public meeting-place. The cost is not to exceed £120, including £40 already advanced.'[32] About the same time (June-July 1654) Thomas Coffey, who had been appointed minister to Finglas in 1651 sought and received £10 to repair the house which he and his family lived in as it was 'much out of repair'.[33] It is not clear if he held meetings in his own home or if he used the church. However, in 1657 a determined group of vestrymen in Finglas set about repairing the church.[34] A detailed account of the repairs was entered in the new vestry book which still survives.[35]

The Finglas vestry book is the only Fingal vestry book which survives from the period. Although it did not commence until 1657 it enables us to supplement the work of antiquaries, in particular, that of the Revd Robert Walsh, who described Finglas church in *Fingal and its churches*, published in 1888.[36] It is thus possible to form some impression of the appearance of one Fingal church which was in use in the seventeenth century. The church of Finglas, which had been a ruin since 1843, had contained a chancel, 34 feet long by 22 feet wide, and a double nave, 48 feet long, divided into two aisles, one 28 feet, the other 16 feet wide, as well as a stone-roofed

(Armagh Public Library, pp 1–11, 22, 50–1). 26 *An eighteenth-century antiquary: the sketches, notes and diaries of Austin Cooper (1759–1830)*, ed. Liam Price (Dublin, 1942). 27 Robert Walsh, *Fingal and its churches* ... (Dublin, 1888). 28 *Civil Survey, vii, county of Dublin*, p. 54; Holmpatrick parish vestry book, 1720–1826 (RCBL, P.500/5/1), pp 1 and 3. 29 Robert Walsh, *Fingal and its churches* ... (Dublin, 1888), pp 247–9. 30 Notes relating to the 'Ministers of the Gospel' ... (RCBL, GS 2/7/3/20, p. 5). 31 Notes relating to the 'Ministers of the Gospel' ... (RCBL, GS 2/7/3/20, p. 5). 32 Notes relating to the 'Ministers of the Gospel' ... (RCBL, GS 2/7/3/20, p. 8). 33 Notes relating to the 'Ministers of the Gospel' ... (RCBL, GS 2/7/3/20, pp 8–9 and 75). 34 Finglas parish combined vestry book and registers, 1657–1758 (RCBL, P.307/1/1, p. 1); William Cotter Stubbs, 'Finglas, County Dublin, vestry books' in *Journal of the Royal Society of Antiquaries of Ireland*, xlvi (1916), p. 27. 35 Finglas parish combined vestry book and registers, 1657–1758 (RCBL, P.307/1/1, pp 1–4); William Cotter Stubbs, 'Finglas, County Dublin, vestry books' in *Journal of the Royal Society of Antiquaries of Ireland*, xlvi (1916), pp 27–8. 36 Finglas parish combined vestry book and registers, 1657–1758 (RCBL, P.307/1/1); William Cotter Stubbs, 'Finglas, County Dublin, vestry books' in *Journal of the Royal Society of Antiquaries of Ireland*, xlvi (1916); Robert Walsh, *Fingal and its churches* ... (Dublin, 1888), pp 221–2.

porch, 15 feet wide by 8 feet long.[37] The bell-turret had disappeared by 1888. The walls were described as being 'very thick and of plain rubble masonry'.[38] The accounts for the repair of the church in 1657 show that two gutters had been laid with hewn stone, the roof and walls of the body of the church had been repaired, stopped, plastered and white-washed and its windows glazed.[39] A pulpit and a 'great seat for strangers adjoining it, and the seat for the minister's family' were provided. The pulpit and the two special seats were provided with doors. The gable end of the church was closed. The chancel was also repaired. However, as one might have expected at this period, the emphasis was on the pulpit rather than on the altar. In summary, then, it is clear that, as far as the buildings of the established church in Fingal were concerned, the years 1603–60 represented a period of serious decline and destruction. However, an effort was already being made in the 1650s by dissenters, with the help of the government, to remedy the situation.

The Catholic church was faced with a much greater problem since it had lost its buildings to the established church following the Reformation. One of the striking features which emerged from Archbishop Bulkeley's survey is the degree to which it had become a 'domestic' church in Fingal. During the seventeenth century it operated almost entirely without purpose-designed churches. The 'great void house of nine couples [rafters] long covered with straw whereunto the parishioners do resort to hear Mass' in Garristown may have been an exception.[40] The 'common mass-house, frequented publicly since the proclamation in the town of St Margaret's', also appears to have been a purpose-designed building.[41] The Plunkets of Dunsoghly had a small private chapel built in 1573.[42] It is doubtful if this would have been large enough to accommodate the numbers wishing to attend Mass. It is more likely that the parishioners attended the 'common mass-house' at St Margaret's. It is, however, just possible that, occasionally, an ancient chapel was used for Mass and other services. There are many references to such chapels in the Civil Survey in addition to the references to ruined churches already considered. The walls of the old chapel associated with the pre-Reformation convent and girls' school at Gracedieu are mentioned as are those of the old chapel of ease at Whitestown.[43] Both of these were in the barony of Balrothery. In the barony of Coolock there was an old chapel at Artaine (parish of Finglas).[44] In the case of Howth the walls of a decayed chapel were mentioned as well as the parish church.[45] In the same parish the reference to 'a ditch leading to a chapel' as one of the boundaries of the townland of Sutton hints at a Mass-path.[46] In the barony of Castleknock the walls of an old chapel still stood at Abbotstown.[47] Swords was particularly rich in traditional religious buildings and placenames. The Civil Survey mentioned two of the old chapelries of Swords, the

37 Robert Walsh, *Fingal and its churches* ... (Dublin, 1888), p. 221. 38 Robert Walsh, *Fingal and its churches* ... (Dublin, 1888), p. 222. 39 William Cotter Stubbs, 'Finglas, County Dublin, vestry books' in *Journal of the Royal Society of Antiquaries of Ireland*, xlvi (1916), p. 28. 40 'Archbishop Bulkeley's visitation of Dublin, 1630', ed. M.V. Ronan in *Archivium Hibernicum*, viii (1941), p. 68. 41 'Archbishop Bulkeley's visitation of Dublin, 1630', ed. M.V. Ronan in *Archivium Hibernicum*, viii (1941), pp 75–6. 42 H.G. Leask, *Irish castles and castellated houses* (2nd ed., 1944, revised 1946 and 1951, reprinted Dundalk, 1999), p. 121. 43 *Civil Survey, vii, county of Dublin,* pp 56 and 63. 44 *Civil Survey, vii, county of Dublin,* p. 177. 45 *Civil Survey, vii, county of Dublin,* p. 169. 46 *Civil Survey, vii, county of Dublin,* p. 168. 47 *Civil Survey, vii, county of Dublin,* p. 245.

chapel of St Bride and St Finian's chapel which were still used as houses.[48] There were further intriguing references to a house called St Michael's, to St Colm's acre (perhaps the holy well site) and to St Patrick's acre. There were two very good reasons why ruined and ancient churches and chapels were remembered and cherished. First, they were frequently situated close to holy well sites and would have been often visited. Secondly, they were usually situated in burial grounds and would have been regarded as special holy places a point illustrated by the refusal to allow the Protestant dead to be buried in churchyards during the 1641 rising.[49] The fact that Protestant churches had formerly been used for Catholic services also remained in the folk memory. In December 1641, for example, Katherine Scanlon came to the home of Dirrick Huiberts Verveer in Holmpatrick and 'called him aside, telling him that she was sent to wish him and the rest to depart the house saying that the priest must come there to say Mass (it being an old abbey)'.[50] The hope that the Catholic church would recover its church buildings can be seen in the expectations expressed in the early days of the 1641 rising that Mass would be celebrated in Christ Church cathedral in Dublin.[51]

Catholics occasionally made bequests to build chapels or repair churches. Thomas St Lawrence of Howth left £100 to build a chapel dedicated to Our Lady at Howth, betwixt the College and the church, near the alley of the churchyard, 21 feet long and 12 feet broad, wherein his body should be buried, and £100 for a monument to himself.[52] A particularly interesting bequest because of its date (*c*.1650) was that of Alexander Aylmer of Knockdromin (now Beau) who left £10 to build the upper end of the chapel of Whitestown (Rush) called St Maur's Chapel and requested that a stone be place over him with the inscription 'I pray you all good Catholics to pray for the soul of Alexander Aylmer and Ann St Lawrence, his wife'.[53]

The main centres of assembly for Mass were private homes, which were generally, though not exclusively, those of the landed gentry. An attempt has been made to list and map the distribution of these mass-centres as they existed in 1630.[54] (See figure 7.2.) There were public or common mass-houses at Garristown, Lusk, Rush and St Margaret's which were probably fitted and furnished to resemble churches to the greatest extent possible in the circumstances. The gentry in Baldongan, Baldoyle, Balscaddan, Howth, Portmarnock, Malahide, Swords and Westpalstown opened their private homes to parishioners, and sometimes to others from outside the parish, for Mass. Mass was 'commonly said' in private houses in Artaine for Santry parish, in Cloghran (Swords) and in at least two homes in each of the parishes of Balrothery, the Naul and St Michan's. The exact meaning of the term 'commonly said' in this context is not clear but as the patrons in the rural parishes all belonged to prominent

48 *Civil Survey, vii, county of Dublin,* pp 92 and 111; Robert Walsh, *Fingal and its churches* ... (Dublin, 1888), p. 203. 49 Deposition of Margaret Huiberts, 14 March 1644 (TCD, MS 810, f. 238); deposition of Richard Swinson, 28 July 1645 (TCD, MS 810, f. 325). 50 Deposition of Margaret Huiberts, 14 March 1644 (TCD, MS 810, f. 238). 51 Deposition of Ann Cappar, 4 January 1642 (TCD, MS 809, f. 261); deposition of Edward Leech, 18 March 1644 (TCD, MS 810, f. 245). 52 Abstract of will of Thomas St Lawrence, 27 March 1638 (RSAI, Elrington Ball MSS, vol x, f. 22); Francis Elrington Ball, *Howth and its owners* ... (originally published 1917, reprinted Dublin, 1995), p. 108. 53 Abstract of will of Alexander Aylmer, July 1650 (NLI, Fisher will abstracts, GO MS 290, pp 7 and 11). 54 'Fingal 1603–60', ii, appendix G, table G.2, pp 64–7.

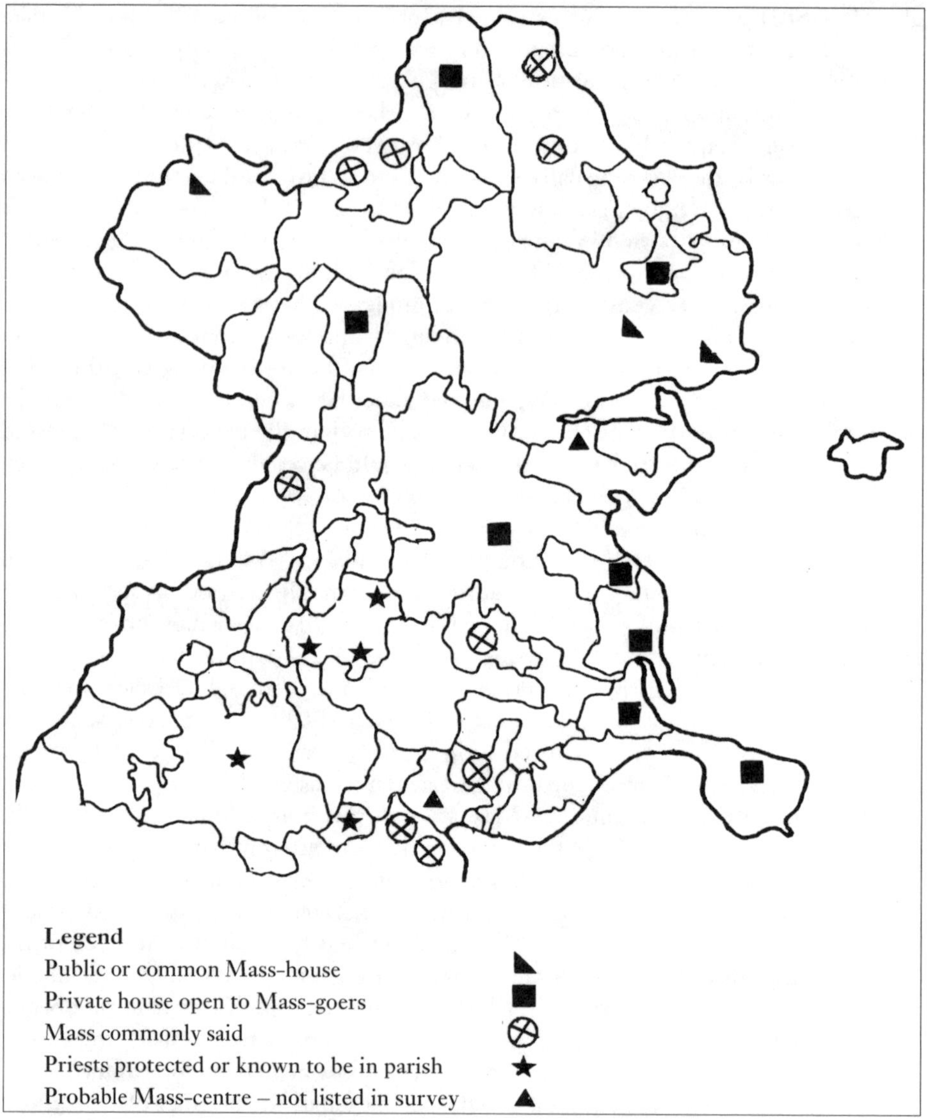

Fig. 7.2 Fingal Mass-centres in 1630

Catholic families it seems likely that their homes, too, were open to the public. The same was probably true of Kilsallaghan where the proprietor, Philip Hore kept away 'the glebe land from the vicar'. It may not have been necessary to open the houses at Dunbro, Dunsoghly, Harristown and Little Cabragh to the parishioners as they already had a 'common Mass-house' at St Margaret's. The position in Castleknock parish, where two priests were named, is not clear.

Some of the places for which there is little or no specific information may require comment. A surprising omission is the Donabate/Portraine peninsula. Under Donabate it was noted that 'Mr John Mooney, clerk, is vicar, whose wife is (as he himself hath certified under his hand) as rank and violent a recusant as any lives this day in Christendom. He hath not certified the value of that living nor the priest's name'.[55] M.V. Ronan suggested that 'some family, probably the Barnewalls', together with the vicar's wife, forbade the vicar to disclose this information.[56] This seems plausible. Susanna Stockdale, Nicholas Barnewall's cousin, told how he had fled to Wales with 'several priests' shortly after the outbreak of the 1641 rising.[57] On his return, she refused to go to live with him and his family in Turvey, although she had lost her own house, on the grounds that 'she was confident that popish priests and rebels would haunt his house'.[58] It seems very likely that Nicholas Barnewall was one of those who opened his house to Mass-goers. Mass was also said for the household at Corballis, the Nettervill home, also in the parish of Donabate, though whether it was open to the public at large is not known. The incident described by Sir Arthur Chichester, when Richard Nettervill had a curtain drawn between himself and the celebrant of the Mass 'that he might swear he saw no priest' almost certainly took place *c.*1606 in Corballis.[59] In a passage which showed how Fingallians were accustomed to accommodate themselves to the spiritual needs of their friends Nicholas Archbold began his account of the conversion of the young Protestant, Henry (later Father James) Warren, which took place in or before 1613 as follows:

> It happened on a certain Sunday at the Corballis of Donabate and the whiles the whole house was at Mass, he retired himself into a chamber alone, where finding the Resolution book he takes it of curiosity, and reads somewhat in it to pass over the time until his complices returned from Mass.[60]

Another who opened her home to the clergy was Lady Bath of Drumcondra. In her will she mentioned the priests, Walter Enos and her 'special friend', John Long.[61] She left Walter Enos silver to make a chalice, together with the vestments, stole and alb which he daily used. It seems likely that there were several other private Mass-houses in Fingal, particularly in parishes such as Killossery, Portraine, Clonmethan, Holmpatrick and Ballyboghil where all or most of the parishioners were known to be recusants.[62] In the early 1630s the Capuchins held missions at a number of Fingal sites, often returning to the same venue on several occasions.[63] Places mentioned in the records included not only known Mass sites such as Baldongan, Dunbro, Garristown, Lusk, Swords and Westpalstown, but also Finglas, Huntstown (parish of

55 'Archbishop Bulkeley's visitation of Dublin, 1630', ed. M.V. Ronan in *Archivium Hibernicum*, viii (1941), p. 63. **56** 'Archbishop Bulkeley's visitation of Dublin, 1630', ed. M.V. Ronan in *Archivium Hibernicum*, viii (1941), p. 63 (footnote 11). **57** Deposition of Susanna Stockdale (copy only), not dated (TCD, MS 810, f. 94). **58** Deposition of Susanna Stockdale (copy only), not dated (TCD, MS 810, f. 95). **59** *Cal. S. P. Ire, 1603–06*, pp 404–5. **60** Nicholas Archbold, The historie of the Irish Capucins, 1643 (Bibliothèque Municipale de Troyes, MS 1103, p. 69). **61** Abstract of will of Barbara Gough (Lady Bath), 23 February 1642 (RSAI, Elrington Ball MSS, vol xii, f. 188); Francis Elrington Ball, *Southern Fingal* ... (originally published 1920, reprinted Dublin, 1995), p. 164. **62** 'Archbishop Bulkeley's visitation of Dublin, 1630', ed. M.V. Ronan in *Archivium Hibernicum*, viii (1941), pp 64 and 68–71. **63** Nicholas Archbold, The historie of the Irish Capucins, 1643 (Bibliothèque Municipale de Troyes, MS 1103, ff 174–8).

Mulhuddart), Lispopple (parish of Ballyboghil) and Rickenhore (parish of Swords). The fact that parishioners in Balgriffin, Finglas and Killeek were prepared to attend Mass in other parishes suggests that the rationalization of the Catholic parishes in the diocese was already under way. An extract from Archbishop Fleming's *Relatio* of 1632, written just two years after Archbishop Bulkeley's visitation and quoted in part by Patrick F. Moran and M.V. Ronan, confirms this view. The archbishop wrote as follows;

> At the present time we enjoy some slight toleration, whilst exercising our religion in private houses; but to the great detriment of the Catholic faith all the public chapels and houses of the religious orders have been confiscated by the government. How long even the present slight toleration will be allowed us is a matter of great uncertainty. Our only hope is in God, in whose hands is the heart of the monarch, who of himself is well disposed and inclined to mercy, unless he be urged on by others to further persecutions ... There is no district in this diocese which cannot conveniently have a priest, who administers the sacraments, and on days of obligation offers up the holy sacrifice at which all the faithful can, without difficulty, assist, unless perchance through the violence of persecution the priests may be momentarily compelled to lie concealed. The religious orders strenuously cooperate with them in administering to the spiritual wants of the faithful – living as obscurely as possible according to their rule, and maintaining the regular discipline as far as the circumstances of the present times allow ...[64]

Alan Ford has described how the established church set up a trained ministry in Ireland.[65] Using official surveys and visitations he analyzed the regional impact of these newly-trained clergymen on the church in various part of Ireland and devoted a section to their influence on the church in the Pale.[66] He concluded that:

> the limitation of the pastorate of the ministry arose partly from financial considerations – in order to support themselves, preachers needed several benefices, often more than they could serve themselves. It also sprang from the origin and training of the ministers of the established church. In the Pale the majority, in Munster nearly all the preachers were of English origin, committed to an anglicising reformation, trained in English-style universities, and ill equipped to cope with or even to contemplate the proselytisation of the native parishioners.[67]

The main source for the database on which the Fingal analysis for the period 1603–60 was based was the diocesan succession list compiled by Canon James B.

64 Patrick F. Moran, *History of the Catholic archbishops of Dublin since the Reformation* (Dublin, 1864), p. 324; 'Archbishop Bulkeley's visitation of Dublin, 1630', ed. M.V. Ronan in *Archivium Hibernicum*, viii (1941), p. 56. 65 Alan Ford, *The protestant reformation in Ireland, 1590–1641* (2nd ed., Dublin, 1997), pp 63–87. 66 Alan Ford, *The protestant reformation in Ireland, 1590–1641* (2nd ed., Dublin, 1997), pp 99–105. 67 Alan Ford, *The protestant reformation in Ireland, 1590–1641* (2nd ed., Dublin, 1997), p. 102.

Leslie.[68] The data, which were summarized, must be treated with caution as certain assumptions had to be made in order to arrive at meaningful conclusions.[69] For example, if a clergyman was known to have been educated in England and had no obvious associations with Ireland, he was assumed to be English. If the name of a clergyman was reasonably uncommon and if it was found in one of the various university lists and the dates fitted he was assumed to have attended that university. Even when these assumptions are made the number whose origin and level of education remains unknown is disappointingly high. For those for whom information is available there is a discernible increase in the proportion of Irish-born and Irish-trained ministers in the period 1621–40 over the previous period. This seems to have decreased again in the troubled period 1641–60, probably due to the breakdown of church organization in the area and the influx of new Commonwealth ministers.

There was a considerable amount of movement from benefice to benefice within the established church. Some of those who served in Fingal moved to higher positions in other areas, particularly in Ossory and Ferns which were part of the Dublin province. Others, such as Luke Challoner, holder of extensive properties, and Meredith Hanmer, an antiquarian, obtained a great deal of influence within Fingal, though not necessarily or entirely because of church-related activities.

More detailed information can be obtained on the clergy who were responsible for the various parishes from the returns made in the years 1615 and 1630.[70] The returns for 1615 are of particular interest as they distinguish between 'preachers' and those 'reading ministers' who were not permitted to preach but simply read the service.[71] Figure 7.3 shows the extent of the areas for which some clergymen were responsible. Thirty-six of the forty-one parishes listed in the Civil Survey were under the care of a specified clergyman. Twelve parishes were under the care of eight preachers, a further sixteen were under the care of six reading ministers while the status of the ministers who held the remaining eight livings is unclear. Two reading ministers, Terence Ivers and John Rice, as well as one other minister, Patrick Beaghan, were responsible for four parishes each. Two clergymen, the preacher, Matthew Lee, and the reading minister, Nicholas Bacon, held three livings each. Five other clergymen were responsible for two parishes each. The only parishes in which more than one incumbent was noted were the combined parishes of Finglas, St Margaret's, Artaine and the Ward, though, as both clergymen had the surname 'Lee', there may have been only a single minister and the second Christian name may have been entered in error.

The information provided on the value of the livings and the presence or absence of books is too patchy to enable firm conclusions to be drawn. However it is clear even from the limited number of parishes from which data are available that the value of the livings ranged widely. For example, the figure for Swords was £67 while the clergyman in Ballymadun received only £10. The absence of books is also difficult

68 J.B. Leslie and W.J.R. Wallace, *Clergy of Dublin and Glendalough: biographical succession lists* (Belfast, 2001). 69 'Fingal 1603–60', i, pp 256–7. 70 'Royal visitation of Dublin, 1615' and 'Archbishop Bulkeley's visitation of Dublin, 1630' ed. M.V. Ronan in *Archivium Hibernicum*, viii (1941), pp 1–55 and 56–98; 'Fingal 1603–60', ii, appendix G, table G.4, p. 68. 71 Alan Ford, *The protestant reformation in Ireland, 1590–1641* (2nd ed., Dublin, 1997), p. 31.

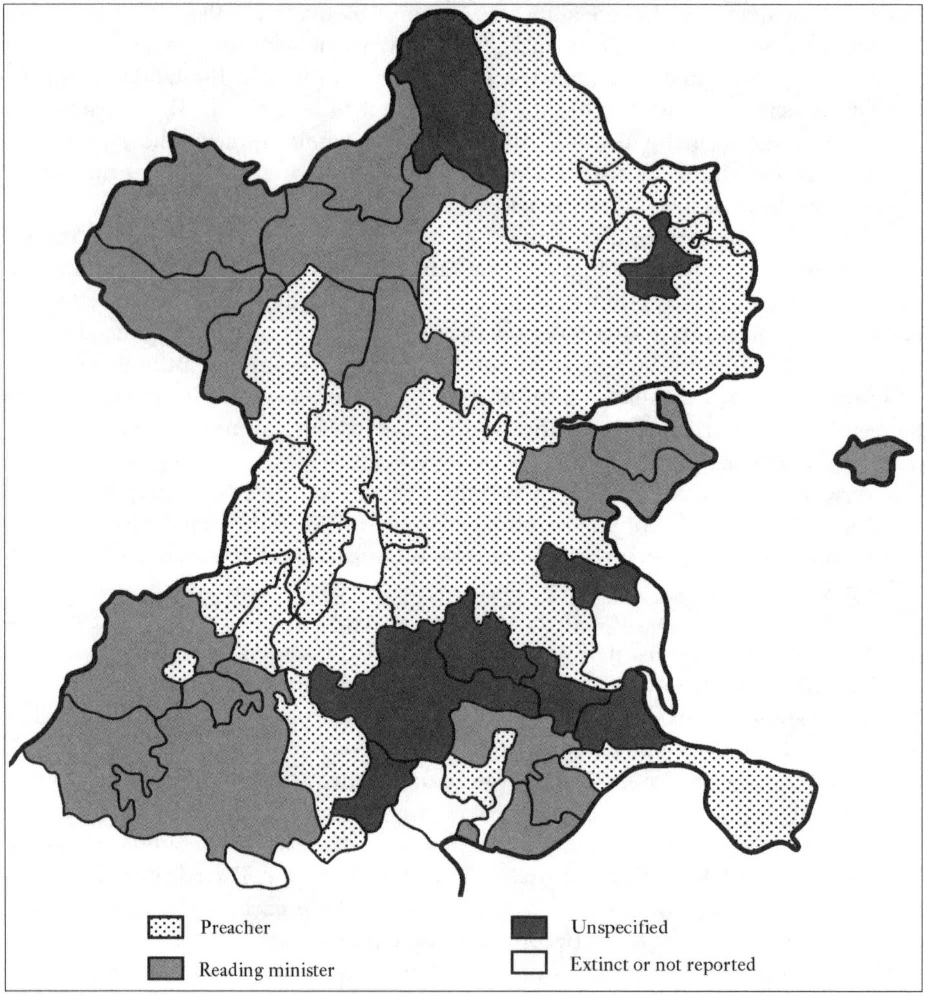

Fig. 7.3 Responsibility for parishes of the established church in Fingal, 1615, by status of clergyman

to assess since, in one case at least, a pluralist minister was reported as having no books in one of his parishes (Cloghran-huddart) although they were available in two others (Castleknock and Clonsilla).

Writing about the diocese of Dublin, Alan Ford stated:

> On the one hand were the English speaking university educated preachers, often dignitaries of one of the cathedrals, who held the most valuable livings, and served the parishes in the centre of the city, and the chief towns such as Athy and Wicklow, where substantial numbers of English lived. On the other hand were the poor reading ministers, usually local men, almost always plu-

> ralists. The various livings which they held were worth little, their parishes had few or no conformists, their churches were often ruined. Generally a Catholic priest was recorded as active in the parish, supported by prominent local gentry.[72]

While this was undoubtedly true in general, a caveat must be entered for the year 1615 in the case of the Fingal part of the diocese. As figure 7.3 shows, preachers were, on the whole, assigned to the larger parishes, including those with towns, such as Balrothery, Swords, Lusk, Howth and Finglas, but some smaller rural parishes such as Killossery, Kilsallaghan and Clonmethan also benefited from the presence of a preacher. Some Fingal parishes, notably Finglas, were already fragmented geographically and it could be argued that some of the plural assignments of contiguous parishes represented a sensible attempt to consolidate parishes that were too small to be viable rather than to increase the value of the livings of individual clergymen. There were, however, some exceptions which supported Alan Ford's argument. The assignment of Baldongan, where the church was completely ruined, to Thomas Hood, vicar of Balscaddan, made no sense geographically but the combination of the two livings provided him with a respectable £25 *per annum*.[73] While his status is not specified in the returns he may have been a Cambridge graduate.[74] Another clergyman, Patrick Beaghan, whose status is also unknown, had charge of the block of parishes of Baldoyle, Balgriffin and Cloghran (Swords) and also the separate parish of Malahide. However, if he was regarded as having some responsibility for the 'extinguished' parish of Portmarnock, contiguous to both Malahide and his main group of parishes, this combination would have made sense. On the whole, it would seem that the assignment of parishes in Fingal *c.*1615 represented a serious attempt to make the best possible use of available resources.

By 1630 the situation had changed.[75] (See figure 7.4). Archbishop Bulkeley's visitation provided information for thirty-four of the forty-one parishes listed in the Civil Survey.[76] The total number of clergymen had fallen to fourteen, of whom seven were university graduates, one who had attended university and was described as a 'preacher' and one other who had attended university but whose qualifications, if any, were not stated. The position in 1630 approximated much more closely to the general situation described by Alan Ford. While the larger parishes and groups of parishes were still under the care of trained ministers pluralism was much more evident. Eleven of the fourteen clergymen held more than one parish in the area. Nicholas Culme held the widely separated parishes of Balscaddan and Cloghran (Swords). While the parishes of Malahide, Portmarnock, Baldoyle and Balgriffin, now forming a block, was held by Richard Kelly, he also held another non-contiguous block consisting of the parishes of Killeek and Killossery. Virtually nothing is known about this Richard Kelly apart from the comment in Archbishop Bulkeley's return

72 Alan Ford, *The protestant reformation in Ireland, 1590–1641* (2nd ed., Dublin, 1997), p. 100. 73 'Royal visitation of Dublin, 1615', ed. M.V. Ronan in *Archivium Hibernicum*, viii (1941), p. 25. 74 James B. Leslie, Biographical succession list for the diocese of Dublin (RCBL, 61/2/4/1, p. 6). 75 'Fingal 1603–60', ii, appendix G, table G.4, p. 69. 76 'Archbishop Bulkeley's visitation of Dublin, 1630', ed. M.V. Ronan in *Archivium Hibernicum*, viii (1941), pp 56–98.

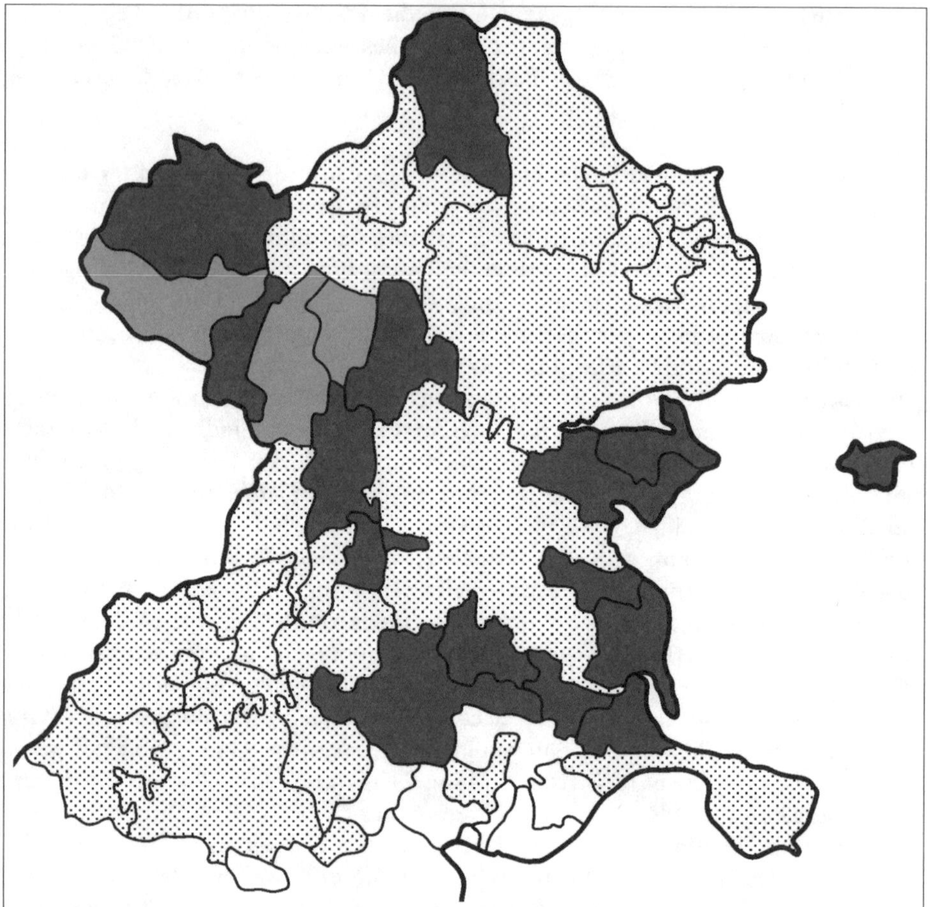

Fig. 7.4 Responsibility for parishes of the established church in Fingal, 1630

that he 'dischargeth the cure, and hath no certain allowance, only for these four years past, the right honourable, the lord chancellor allowed him xxv *libri*, part of which he is paid, the rest promised; but for the time to come he knoweth not what to have'.[77] The parishioners in the two blocks held by Richard Kelly were at that time almost exclusively Catholic.[78] In fact only one Protestant family, that of 'his majesty's solicitor, Mr Bolton', was identified in the six parishes. Kelly was a common Fingal surname and it may well be that Richard Kelly had Catholic connections, which made him acceptable to the Catholic landowners in the area. This was certainly true

77 'Archbishop Bulkeley's visitation of Dublin, 1630', ed. M.V. Ronan in *Archivium Hibernicum*, viii (1941), p. 67. 78 'Archbishop Bulkeley's visitation of Dublin, 1630', ed. M.V. Ronan in *Archivium Hibernicum*, viii (1941), pp 64–8.

of another clergyman, John Mooney, who, as already mentioned, was married to 'as rank and violent a recusant as any lives this day in Christendom' and who held the detached livings of Donabate, Garristown and Palmerstown.[79] While the name 'Etheridge' was unusual in Fingal, Gabriel Etheridge, who held Ballyboghil and Portraine, may well have been related to John Etheridge, who had held Donabate and Portraine in 1615. Two trained clergymen also held non-contiguous parishes. Robert Worrall held the widely-separated parishes of Balrothery and Kilsallaghan and Christopher Hewetson held the parishes of Swords and Howth.

The report on Archbishop Bulkeley's visitation also provided information on the relationship between tithes and clerical income in the case of some parishes. These data have been analyzed by deanery for the archdiocese as a whole by Colm Lennon.[80] At the level of the individual parish it was only possible to estimate the relationship for seven Fingal parishes.[81] While these may not have been altogether typical – in five of the seven cases they were supplied by a single minister, Richard Kelly, – they gave a good idea of the potential for profit which the farming of tithes permitted.

In general, then, while the numbers of clergy were probably adequate to serve the needs of the small and scattered Protestant population, they were totally insufficient to undertake meaningful missionary activity among a largely hostile Catholic population. They were generally poorly paid. The most striking thing about the clergy of the established church in Fingal was that they were outsiders. Richard Kelly and John Mooney, if indeed they were Fingallians, were exceptions. Not alone were the clergy outsiders. Very many of them were foreigners who came from England, Scotland or Wales. There is little or no evidence that clergymen from Fingal families went to work elsewhere though more detailed genealogical studies of Protestant Fingal families are needed to validate this. A possible exception was Archbishop James Ussher whose family had close connections with the area. In 1641 the Protestant clergy in Fingal suffered badly as a result of this lack of local support. Thomas Clitheroe (Balrothery) and John Lukey (Ballyboghil) were subjected to physical attack.[82] William Tedder (Garristown) claimed to have been forcibly driven out as well as robbed by the rebels.[83] Randall Dimmock (St Doolagh's and Clontarf) fled to Dublin following threats by the rebels.[84] Henry Pemberton, who had been presented to Baldongan by one of the most prominent rebel leaders, Thomas Fitzwilliam in 1640, listed £36 due from the same Thomas Fitzwilliam among his losses.[85] Robert Wilson (Finglas, later dean of Ferns), Thomas Lloyd (Swords) and Richard Powell (Clonmethan) claimed substantial losses and debts.[86] Robert Worrall,

79 'Archbishop Bulkeley's visitation of Dublin, 1630', ed. M.V. Ronan in *Archivium Hibernicum*, viii (1941), p. 63. 80 Colm Lennon, 'Mass in the manor house: the counter-reformation in Dublin, 1560–1630' in James Kelly and Dáire Keogh (eds), *History of the Catholic diocese of Dublin* (Dublin, 2000), pp 119–20. 81 'Fingal 1603–60', i, p. 263. 82 Deposition of Thomas Clitheroe, 26 May 1642 (TCD, MS 810, f. 126); deposition of John Lukey, 2 March 1643 (TCD, MS 810 f. 168). 83 Deposition of William Tedder, 25 January 1642 (TCD, MS 809, f. 332). 84 Deposition of Randall Dimmock, 1 March 1642 (TCD, MS 809, f. 276). 85 Deposition of Henry Pemberton, 25 May 1642 (TCD, MS 810, f. 180). 86 Deposition of Robert Wilson, 18 January 1642 (TCD, MS 810, f. 106); deposition of Thomas Lloyd, 18 June 1642 (TCD, MS 810, f. 165); deposition of Richard Powell, 17 November 1642 (TCD, MS 810, f. 175).

for many years vicar of Balrothery and Kilsallaghan resigned in 1641.[87] While the reason for his resignation is not clear it was probably due to the fact that he was accused by some local people of saying they were rebels, an accusation which was extended to the lord chief baron and his lady as well as by implication to the earl of Ormond whom, according to the allegations, Worrall accused of keeping of keeping a company of troops all of whom were rebels.[88] Henry Birch appears to have been curate at Holmpatrick from 1639–1643.[89] He was a son-in-law of Dirrick Huiberts Verveer who was murdered there in December 1641.[90] In May 1643, having by then been appointed minister of Newcastle Lyons, he made a short deposition claiming compensation for the robbery of goods and chattels and the profits of his church means but giving no details as to how or where this happened. The widow of a former rector of Holmpatrick and Baldongan, Sarah Doughtie, and her children were also threatened with death and driven from their home.[91] Nothing is known about the personal experiences of Henry Brereton (Santry), Edward Browne (Balscaddan), Thomas Chacentrell (Hollywood), Richard Foster (Donabate, Portraine and Killossery), Alexander Hatfield (Cloghran, Swords), George Hudson (Lusk), Richard Mathewson (Chapelizod and Castleknock), Eusebius Roberts (Howth) and Thomas Seele (Coolock and Raheny) during the rising as their depositions, if any, do not appear to have survived. It is possible that some of these ministers were protected by local Protestant patrons. Others may have been non-resident. However, the large number of attacks on ministers and their families emphasizes the deep-seated bitterness which many people felt against authority figures in the established church.

The Commonwealth brought a substantial change in the organization of the Protestant church in Fingal. Meeting houses were set up in the churches of Swords and Finglas and, at various times, Commonwealth ministers were based at these locations as well as at Lusk, the Naul, Clonsilla and Chapelizod.[92] There were also ministers based at centres just outside Fingal such as St Michan's, Lucan, Dunboyne and Stamullen, thus providing a reasonable spread of places of worship for dissenters and members of the established church who were prepared to attend services conducted by these ministers.[93] (See figure 7.5.)

In 1630 it had been reported that there were 'not above eight persons that frequent divine service' in the combined parishes of Hollywood, Grallagh and the Naul.[94] In February 1654 Thomas Busbetch, who had been appointed to Lisnaskea, was ordered to remove to the Naul 'where there are several Protestant English families, destitute of a minister to instruct them and other garrisons thereabouts'.[95] His

87 James B. Leslie, Biographical succession list for the diocese of Dublin (RCBL, 61/2/4/1, p. 14). 88 Examinations of Mathew Teeling, Christopher Teeling, Richard Carrick, Nicholas Ardagh, Hannibal Bagnall and Edward Dymmock, 25 January 1642 (TCD, MS 809, ff 228–9). 89 J.B. Leslie and W.J.R. Wallace, *Clergy of Dublin and Glendalough: biographical succession lists* (Belfast, 2001), p. 114. 90 Deposition of Henry Birch, 15 May 1643 (TCD. MS 810, f. 260). 91 Deposition of Sarah Doughtie, 20 January 1642 (TCD, MS 809, f. 275). 92 Notes relating to the 'Ministers of the Gospel' ... (RCBL, GS 2/7/3/20, pp 98 and 203–4). 93 Notes relating to the 'Ministers of the Gospel' ... (RCBL, GS 2/7/3/20, pp 12–3, 80 and 205). 94 'Archbishop Bulkeley's visitation of Dublin, 1630', ed. M.V. Ronan in *Archivium Hibernicum*, viii (1941), p. 69. 95 Notes relating to the 'Ministers of the Gospel' ... (RCBL, GS 2/7/3/20, p. 4).

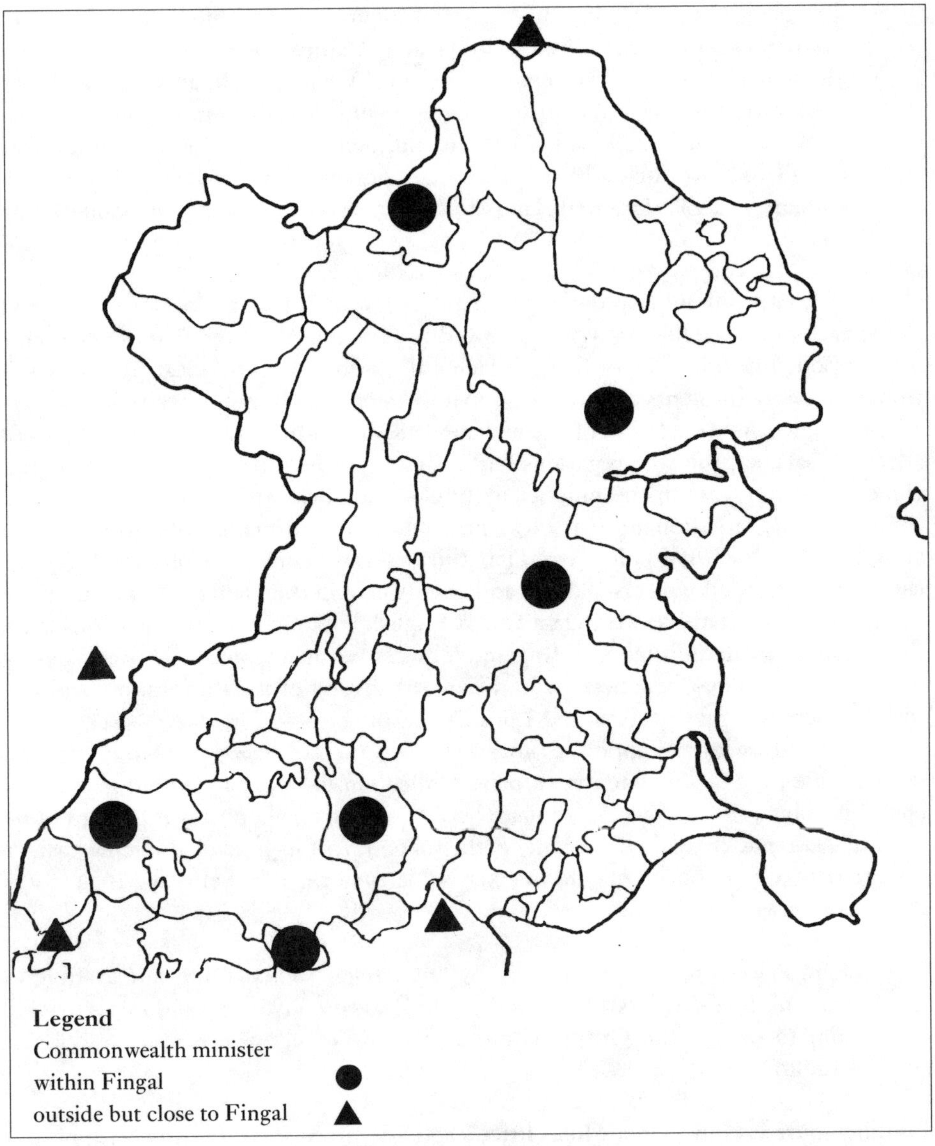

Fig. 7.5 Location of Commonwealth ministers in and near Fingal in the 1650s

appointment apparently did not take place until January 1656 when a certificate of fitness was issued by Dr Samuel Winter and Mr Mather.[96] His salary was fixed at £60 *per annum*. Busbetch was transferred to Ballyglass (Cork), *c.*1657 prompting the following comment in the records for March 1658:

96 Notes relating to the 'Ministers of the Gospel' ... (RCBL, GS 2/7/3/20, p. 11).

> The petition of Mr Timothy Avery and Lieut. Robert Whitefield on behalf of the parishes of the Naul and Hollywood, County Dublin. They have been altogether unsupplied since the removal of Mr Busbetch, and their auditory is now increased to a far greater degree than it was during his time, as many English families lately settled there, and some New England families now intend likewise their plantation there. They petition for James Symonds, a student in TCD. Granted. He is to have £80 *per annum* commencing the 25 March.[97]

James Symonds did not last long in the Naul. A few months later he was transferred to Saggart and the following year he moved to Graiguenamanagh (Co. Kilkenny).[98] This episode illustrates the difficulties facing the authorities. It is clear from this and from other appointments that the local members of the church exercised considerable influence in the choice of their ministers. It is also clear that, despite very attractive salaries, the congregations had difficulty in holding on to their preferred choices. The increase in the number of English families, while considerable in the context of the situation in 1630, was probably not considered substantial by the authorities. In the 1660 poll-tax returns thirty-seven people in Hollywood (17 per cent of the recorded poll-tax-payers) and twenty-two in the Naul (16 per cent of the recorded poll-tax-payers) were classified as English.[99] No information is available on the proposed plantation of New England families but it was probably overtaken by events. The main new beneficiaries in the area as a result of the Restoration land settlement were the duke of York and Lord Fitzharding.[100]

Dr Daniel Rowles was appointed to Swords at £100 *per annum* in March 1654 but it took some time before extensive repairs to the church were carried out in order to enable it to be used as a meeting-house.[101] Little is known about this minister but he was still acting as chaplain to Colonel Sadleir's regiment in June of the same year.[102] The repairs to the church may have taken some time since in February 1656 it was noted as follows:

> John Price is to get £10 towards buying a horse to assist him in travelling to such places as he from time to time finds most convenient and necessary for him to preach the Gospel either at Swords or elsewhere near the city of Dublin.[103]

Nothing more is known about John Price's activities in Swords. Dr Rowles appeared on the general list of ministers under the heading of Swords in 1654, 1655 and

97 St John D. Seymour, *The puritans in Ireland (1647–1661)* (Oxford, 1921), p. 208; Notes relating to the 'Ministers of the Gospel' ... (RCBL, GS 2/7/3/20, p. 99). **98** St John D. Seymour, *The puritans in Ireland (1647–1661)* (Oxford, 1921), p. 220. **99** *A census of Ireland circa 1659* ..., ed. S. Pender (Dublin, 1939), p. 387. **100** Books of Survey and Distribution for County Dublin (NAI, Quit Rent Office papers, pp 74–7). **101** Notes relating to the 'Ministers of the Gospel' ... (RCBL, GS 2/7/3/20, pp 5 and 8); 'Commonwealth state accounts: Ireland, 1650–1656' ed. Edward MacLysaght in *Analecta Hibernica*, no. 15 (November, 1944), pp 241 and 255–6. **102** Notes relating to the 'Ministers of the Gospel' ... (RCBL, GS 2/7/3/20, p. 8). **103** Notes relating to the 'Ministers of the Gospel' ... (RCBL, GS 2/7/3/20, p. 13).

1656.[104] By that time his abilities as a speaker had clearly impressed the authorities in Trinity College Dublin as he was chosen to offer the newly-arrived Henry Cromwell the 'congratulatory salutations' of the university at a solemn ceremony.[105] In a list of quarterly payments made for the second quarter of 1656, however, he was shown under Dublin city while John Cock was shown as minister of Swords.[106] Rowles was appointed to St Bride's sometime before 25 December 1657 as his salary was raised to £140 *per annum* from that date.[107] A special allowance was granted to ministers who were prepared to preach the Gospel in Irish in Dublin city and St Bride's had a partly Irish-speaking congregation.[108] If, indeed, Rowles had a knowledge of Irish – and no hard evidence to support this has been found – it may also explain his appointment to Swords, a district in which some Irish was still spoken in the 1650s.[109] Thomas Wilkinson, an Anabaptist, was appointed to Swords at a salary of £150 in June 1657.[110]

Thomas Coffey was one of the earliest appointees as Commonwealth minister in Fingal. He had been master of the free school in Dublin city and had been instrumental on two occasions in having the schoolhouse repaired at the corporation's expense.[111] He was appointed to Finglas in October 1651 'on the petition of the inhabitants of Finglas, stating that since the beginning of May ... [he] had preached among them'.[112] He was ordered to continue there at £30 *per annum*, a salary which was first raised to £40 and later to £50.[113] Once again he had building problems, on this occasion with his own residence, described as a 'mansion house', which was repaired at the expense of the authorities.[114] The fact that he was a graduate of Trinity College Dublin and a 'native' (presumably an Irish-speaker) may explain his move to Athlone *c.*1656 since Irish-speaking ministers were in great demand throughout the country.[115] His successor, the Presbyterian James Levingston, may also have worked in Finglas on a trial basis, prior to his formal appointment, as his salary, amounting to £100 *per annum*, was subsequently paid from 25 December 1657 although the appointment was not made until March 1658.[116] This appointment to the recently repaired meeting-house in the church of Finglas was marked by the insertion of a copy of the letter from the lord deputy and council in the vestry-book.[117] This letter, which stressed the care taken by the authorities in the appointment of ministers, as well as the willingness to consider the wishes of local church members, read as follows:

104 Notes relating to the 'Ministers of the Gospel' ... (RCBL, GS 2/7/3/20, pp 12, 181 and 186). **105** St John D. Seymour, *The puritans in Ireland (1647–1661)* (Oxford, 1921), p. 115. **106** 'Commonwealth state accounts: Ireland, 1650–1656' ed. Edward MacLysaght in *Analecta Hibernica*, no. 15 (November, 1944), p. 295. **107** Notes relating to the 'Ministers of the Gospel' ... (RCBL, GS 2/7/3/20, p. 203). **108** Notes relating to the 'Ministers of the Gospel' ... (RCBL, GS 2/7/3/20, pp 16, 47 and 78); St John D. Seymour, *The puritans in Ireland (1647–1661)* (Oxford, 1921), p. 114. **109** Examination of John Heard, 24 November 1652 (TCD, MS 810, f. 380). **110** Notes relating to the 'Ministers of the Gospel' ... (RCBL, GS 2/7/3/20, p. 203); St John D. Seymour, *The puritans in Ireland (1647–1661)* (Oxford, 1921), p. 110. **111** *Anc. rec. Dublin*, iii, pp 400 and 442. **112** Notes relating to the 'Ministers of the Gospel' ... (RCBL, GS 2/7/3/20, p. 75). **113** Notes relating to the 'Ministers of the Gospel' ... (RCBL, GS 2/7/3/20, pp 8, 75 and 181). **114** Notes relating to the 'Ministers of the Gospel' ... (RCBL, GS 2/7/3/20, p. 9). **115** Notes relating to the 'Ministers of the Gospel' ... (RCBL, GS 2/7/3/20, p. 203). **116** Notes relating to the 'Ministers of the Gospel' ... (RCBL, GS 2/7/3/20, p. 203). **117** Finglas parish combined vestry book and registers, 1657–1758 (RCBL, P.307/1/1, p. 9); William Cotter Stubbs, 'Finglas, County Dublin, vestry books' in *Journal of the Royal Society of Antiquaries of Ireland*, xlvi (1916), pp 28–9.

> Upon consideration of the report of the committee for the approbation of ministers dated the ninth day of March instant, to whom it was referred to confer with and examine the ability and fitness of Mr Levingston for the work of the ministry, whereby it appeared they have seen his certificates and testimonials from the Presbytery of Dunblane in Scotland fully approving him as to his gifts and conversation, and that they had also received good satisfaction as to his knowledge, tolerance and experience of a work of grace upon his own heart, and for as much as the inhabitants of the parish of Finglas near unto this city have by their humble petition presented unto this board desired he might be established amongst them, it is thought fit and ordered that the said Mr James Levingston be and is hereby chosen and appointed minister of the parish of Finglas aforesaid to preach the gospel to the inhabitants there until further order. Whereof all concerned are to take notice.

Following the Restoration this entry was ordered to be expunged as 'being derogatory to the ecclesiastical canon'.[118] In July 1660 James Levingston had been granted the tithes of Finglas, which were apparently disputed but no further information is available as the records were not transcribed before their destruction.[119] In any event, he died within a few months.[120]

John Archdall (or Archdale) was recommended for appointment to Lusk in May 1653.[121] His annual salary in 1654 and 1655 was £50 but by 1656 it had risen to £80.[122] Archdall was one of those who successfully made the transition into the ministry of the established church at the time of the Restoration when he was appointed vicar of Donabate.[123]

Andrew Wyke, an Anabaptist, was appointed to St Michan's in August 1651 but he left for Lisburn after just a few weeks.[124] He was succeeded at St Michan's by the Independent minister, John Murcot, who was ordered to preach there every Lord's Day.[125] The commissioners seem to have been particularly anxious to entice him to Ireland since he was granted £30 for the charge of bringing himself and his family to Ireland and, in April 1652, a further £20 to buy a horse for his journey with the commissioners into Munster.[126] During his brief career in Ireland – he died in the spring of 1655 – Murcot was under a great deal of pressure from the authorities, apparently because of his outstanding ability.[127] In October 1652 he was ordered to go to Cork and get a house there and received £20 for travelling expenses into

118 Finglas parish combined vestry book and registers, 1657–1758 (RCBL, P.307/1/1, p. 9); William Cotter Stubbs, 'Finglas, County Dublin, vestry books' in *Journal of the Royal Society of Antiquaries of Ireland*, xlvi (1916), p. 29. **119** Notes relating to the 'Ministers of the Gospel' ... (RCBL, GS 2/7/3/20, pp 135–6). **120** James B. Leslie, Biographical succession list for the diocese of Dublin (RCBL, 61/2/4/1, p. 142). **121** Notes relating to the 'Ministers of the Gospel' ... (RCBL, GS 2/7/3/20, p. 82). **122** Notes relating to the 'Ministers of the Gospel' ... (RCBL, GS 2/7/3/20, pp 186 and 192). **123** James B. Leslie, Biographical succession list for the diocese of Dublin (RCBL, 61/2/4/1, p. 106). **124** St John D. Seymour, *The puritans in Ireland (1647–1661)* (Oxford, 1921), p. 224. **125** Notes relating to the 'Ministers of the Gospel' ... (RCBL, GS 2/7/3/20, p. 80); St John D. Seymour, *The puritans in Ireland (1647–1661)* (Oxford, 1921), pp 64–5. **126** Notes relating to the 'Ministers of the Gospel' ... (RCBL, GS 2/7/3/20, pp 76–7). **127** Notes relating to the 'Ministers of the Gospel' ... (RCBL, GS 2/7/3/20, p. 70).

Munster.[128] In July 1654 he was sent to England for two months.[129] His salary is not known but he was not among the most highly paid ministers.[130] It would appear, however, that, because of his appointment to an important city ministry, he was paid more than most other Fingal ministers. After his death his widow and children were granted a pension of £100 *per annum* as well as the use of a house.[131] Daniel Neyland succeeded at St Michan's.[132]

South-west Fingal was catered for by the appointment of an Episcopalian, George Gunn, to Chapelizod in 1654 at an annual salary of £46 which was raised to £50 in 1657.[133] He had, apparently, a roving commission to preach in different areas. In 1657 the inhabitants of Balrothery petitioned for his appointment as their minister.[134] While this was referred to an examining committee no evidence has been found to suggest that any Commonwealth minister was appointed to the parish at that period. George Gunn was an elderly minister who had already served in the established church for many years. In 1646 he had been curate in Fingal (Cloghran, Swords).[135] In March 1661, following the Restoration, he was appointed vicar of Balrothery and Balscaddan as well as Ballyboghil and the Naul. Hugh Gunn was appointed to Chapelizod in 1655.[136] His salary was £80.[137] Edward Veale, an Independent minister, was transferred from Dunboyne to Clonsilla in 1659.[138] He was an associate of Dr Samuel Winter and had been appointed a fellow of Trinity College Dublin in 1655.[139]

The Independent minister, Dr Winter, was the most prominent of a group of ministers who were based in Dublin but who, like John Price and, perhaps, George Gunn, were not restricted to one particular district or meeting-house. Winter's career has been well documented.[140] In addition, his manuscript notebook survives in Trinity College Dublin while that part of it which formed an early register has been published by the Parish Register Society of Dublin.[141] This register, which tells us a little about the lives of the Fingal dissenters will be examined later.

The congregations of Fingal dissenters were exposed to a variety of religious influences, as the ministers contained Anabaptists, Independents, Episcopalians and

128 Notes relating to the 'Ministers of the Gospel' ... (RCBL, GS 2/7/3/20, p. 78). **129** Notes relating to the 'Ministers of the Gospel' ... (RCBL, GS 2/7/3/20, pp 85 and 90). **130** T.C. Barnard, *Cromwellian Ireland: English government and reform in Ireland 1649–1660* (2nd ed., Oxford, 2000), p. 136. **131** Notes relating to the 'Ministers of the Gospel' ... (RCBL, GS 2/7/3/20, pp 23–4 and 45). **132** St John D. Seymour, *The puritans in Ireland (1647–1661)* (Oxford, 1921), p. 218. **133** Notes relating to the 'Ministers of the Gospel' ... (RCBL, GS 2/7/3/20, pp 12, 181, 186, 192 and 204); St John D. Seymour, *The puritans in Ireland (1647–1661)* (Oxford, 1921), p. 213. **134** Notes relating to the 'Ministers of the Gospel' ... (RCBL, GS 2/7/3/20, p. 48). **135** James B. Leslie, Biographical succession list for the diocese of Dublin (RCBL, 61/2/4/1, pp 12, 15, 20 and 83). **136** St John D. Seymour, *The puritans in Ireland (1647–1661)* (Oxford, 1921), p. 213. **137** Notes relating to the 'Ministers of the Gospel' ... (RCBL, GS 2/7/3/20, pp 11, 186, 192 and 203). **138** Notes relating to the 'Ministers of the Gospel' ... (RCBL, GS 2/7/3/20, p. 98; St John D. Seymour, *The puritans in Ireland (1647–1661)* (Oxford, 1921), p. 222. **139** T.C. Barnard, *Cromwellian Ireland: English government and reform in Ireland 1649–1660* (2nd ed., Oxford, 2000), p. 203 (footnote 91). **140** J.W. *The life and death of the eminently learned, pious and painful minister of the Gospel, Dr Samuel Winter, sometime provost of Trinity College near Dublin in Ireland; together with some rare examples of God's gracious answer to his prayers, upon several occasions* (London, 1671); John Pentland Mahaffy, *An epoch in Irish history: Trinity College, Dublin, its foundations and early fortunes, 1591–1660* (London, 1903), pp 298–307. **141** Samuel Winter notebook (TCD, MS 805); *The registers of Provost Winter* ... (Dublin, 1907).

at least one Presbyterian in their ranks. Compared with those who preceded them the ministers were generally well-paid and enjoyed relative security. However, they were outsiders, they tended to remain in the area for just a short time and their opportunities for getting to know the people well were limited. T.C. Barnard has pointed out that 'the small number of ministers, and the very much smaller number competent to convert the native Irish, were a major disadvantage'.[142] However, as will be shown later, the vigour and ability of the lay dissenters in Fingal provided some compensation for the shortage of ministers.

Throughout the period the Catholic church in Fingal was the strongest single religious group yet little is known about its clergy. The church was a hidden church. Consequently, with the exception of the contemporary Capuchin records, few formal records, such as those which enabled the compilation of Canon Leslie's biographical succession list for the established church survive. There are three problems involved in conducting research into seventeenth-century Catholic clergy. The first is that of finding out the names of the priests who worked in the archdiocese of Dublin at that time. The second is that of discovering the baptismal names of those who were commonly known by their names in religion. This applied, in particular, to certain religious orders such as the Capuchins. The third is the identification of those who had particular associations with Fingal. The fact that the Catholic church was a universal, rather than a national or local, church and that Fingallian and other Irish priests worked abroad as well as at home must also be borne in mind.

There is, one important listing of secular priests for the archdiocese as a whole compiled by W.M. O'Riordan and published in *Reportorium Novum*.[143] The compiler cited a wide range of published sources used in the preparation of this list. Since its compilation some further sources have come to attention, for example, a manuscript in Trinity College Dublin, which listed priests and friars in 1613.[144] Other sources, which are associated with the 1641 rising, are the 1641 depositions and the various lists of outlaws.[145] As far as the regular clergy are concerned a number of lists of priests and student priests survive. Some of these related to religious orders and congregations while others were distilled from the records of colleges in continental Europe.[146] It is, perhaps, more meaningful in the case of the Catholic clergy to group the priests under various headings. One such group consisted of those who spent all

142 T.C. Barnard, *Cromwellian Ireland: English government and reform in Ireland 1649–1660* (2nd ed., Oxford, 2000), p. 182. 143 W.M. O'Riordan, 'A list of 17th century Dublin diocesan priests' in *Reportorium Novum*, ii, no. 1 (1958), pp 109–19, ii, no. 2 (1960), pp 257–68, iii, no. 1 (1962), pp 137–52. 144 List of priests and friars in 1613 (TCD, Papers relating to Roman Catholics in Ireland, MS 567, f. 35). I am grateful to Dr Raymond Gillespie for drawing my attention to this list. 145 1641 depositions (TCD, MSS 809 and 810); R.C. Simington and John MacLellan, 'Oireachtas Library, List of outlaws, 1641–1647' in *Analecta Hibernica*, no. 23 (1966), pp 317–67; John T. Gilbert (ed.), *History of the Irish confederation and the war in Ireland, 1641–3* ... (7 vols, Dublin, 1882–91), iii, pp 341–86. 146 For example, Edmund Hogan, *Chronological catalogue of the Irish members of the Society of Jesus, from the year 1550 to 1814* (no date); *Ibernia Ignatiana seu Ibernorum Societatis Iesu patrum monumenta*, ed. Edmund Hogan (Dublin, 1880); Edmund Hogan, *Distinguished Irishmen of the sixteenth century* (London, 1894); Brendan Jennings, 'Irish students in the University of Louvain' in Sylvester O'Brien, *Meascra I gcuimhne Mhichíl Uí Chléirigh* (Dublin, 1944), pp 74–97; Brendan Jennings, 'Irish names in the Malines ordination registers, 1602–1794' in *The Irish Ecclesiastical Record*, lxxv (1951), pp 149–162, lxxvi (1951), pp 44–8, 128–40, 222–33, 314–8, 399–408, 483–7, lxxvii (1952), 202–7, 366–9; John Brady, 'The Irish colleges in the Low Countries (a) Exhibitio Consolatoria' in *Archivium Hibernicum*, xiv (1949), pp 66–83.

or most of their priestly lives abroad. Examples were Richard Stanihurst, his two sons, both Jesuits, another Jesuit, William Bath of Drumcondra and the Capuchins, George Blackney and Nicholas Plunket.

A second group, which comprised both secular and regular clergy, was composed of those mentioned in the 1613 list.[147] It is difficult to be sure which of the priests named in this list had Fingal associations. Patrick Duffe, who was a *per obitum* appointee to the dissolved Priory of Holmpatrick in 1608, was certainly one of these. He appeared as pastor of Lusk and Rush in 1630.[148] Though little is known about him his name suggests that he was a local man. Christopher Hollywood, provincial of the Jesuits, was from Artaine and no doubt retreated there when the situation became difficult. An interesting entry is that of 'James Hussey, priest' who was almost certainly the parish priest of Smarmore, Co. Louth, at the time of his death in 1636.[149] A copy of his will, which has survived, provided a great deal of information about his life and times.[150] He asked to be interred in his father's sepulchre at Holmpatrick and made a bequest of 10*s*. to the poor of Holmpatrick and Skerries. A further bequest of 10*s*. to the poor of Corballis (parish of Donabate) and Ballygarth (Co. Meath) recognized the tenants of his Nettervill relatives. At the time of his death he held mortgages on Tobertown (parish of Balscaddan). The appearance of his name as a priest working in Dublin in 1613 helped to confirm his connection with Fingal. James Hussey was greatly admired by his nephew, Nicholas Archbold, as a writer and connoisseur of books.[151]

In his analysis of James Hussey's will L.P. Murray has traced part of the network of close family relationships which existed between many of the priests of the time in Fingal and Co. Meath.[152] According to Murray, Father Hussey's first cousins included the Jesuit, William Bath, and the Capuchin, Luke Bath, two brothers of Luke Nettervill, both priests, and Barnaby Barnewall of Crickstown, Co. Meath, who, following extensive missionary work in Fingal, 1627–33, was commissary-general of the Capuchin mission in the 1640s.[153]

A third group, which overlapped to some extent with the second, consisted of regular clergy, mainly Jesuits, who were active in Fingal during the period. Some of these probably acted as chaplains to Catholic landholders. Others were based in Dublin or other centres and conducted missions in Fingal. The lives of the priests, especially the Jesuits, who were educated and trained on the continent were, to some

147 List of priests and friars in 1613 (TCD, Papers relating to Roman Catholics in Ireland, MS 567, f. 35). **148** Nicholas Donnelly, 'The "*Per obitum*" volumes in the Vatican Archivio' in *Archivium Hibernicum*, i (1912), p. 29; 'Archbishop Bulkeley's visitation of Dublin, 1630', ed. M.V. Ronan in *Archivium Hibernicum*, viii (1941), p. 70. **149** Nicholas Archbold, The evangelicall fruict of the Seraphicall Franciscan order, centur 5, ab Anno Domini 1600, 1628, continued to 1645 (BL, Harleian MS 3888, f. 155). **150** L.P. Murray, 'The will of James Hussey of Smarmore, Co. Louth, "Priest" (A.D. 1635)' in *The Journal of the County Louth Archaeological Society* viii, no. 4 (1936), pp 303–21. **151** Nicholas Archbold, The historie of the Irish Capucins, 1643 (Bibliothèque Municipale de Troyes, MS 1103, p. 59); Nicholas Archbold, The evangelicall fruict of the Seraphicall Franciscan order, centur 5, ab Anno Domini 1600, 1628, continued to 1645 (BL, Harleian MS 3888, f. 9). **152** L.P. Murray, 'The will of James Hussey of Smarmore, Co. Louth, "Priest" (A.D. 1635)' in *The Journal of the County Louth Archaeological Society* viii, no. 4 (1936), pp 306–07 and 309–13. **153** Nicholas Archbold, The historie of the Irish Capucins, 1643 (Bibliothèque Municipale de Troyes, MS 1103, ff 175–8); Conrad O'Donovan, 'The Capuchins in Dublin' in *The Capuchin Annual* (1972), p. 178.

extent, documented. Particularly prominent among the Jesuits were Henry Fitzsimon, Christopher Hollywood and Richard Field.[154] The Cistercian priest, Patrick Barnewall of Bremore, became abbot of Mellifont abbey in Co. Louth.[155]

A number of men from Fingal, some of whom have already been mentioned, entered the Capuchin order in the early seventeenth century. Luke Bath, son of John Bath of Drumcondra and his second wife, Janet Finglas of Westpalstown, was a half-brother of the Jesuit linguist and musician, William Bath.[156] Luke's half-brothers, Henry and Humphrey Warren, sons of Sir William Warren and Janet Finglas, followed him into the Capuchin order.[157] Nicholas Plunket was a son of Sir Christopher Plunket of Dunsoghly and George Blackney (his baptismal name was not stated) was a member of the Blackney family of Rickenhore (parish of Swords).[158] Other Capuchins who had Fingal connections were Christopher (Father Nicholas) Archbold of Mountainfoot (Shankill), son of the Baldoyle lawyer, George Archbold, and a lay-brother, Patrick Dowde, son of Alderman John Dowde of Dublin, who leased property at Murdery (now Bettyville), parish of Lusk, in 1641.[159] Anselm Ball, whose baptismal name was John, was also a Fingallian.[160] He and another Capuchin, Stephen Hussey, worked in Howth and Swords during the Cromwellian period.[161] Anselm Ball was protected by the lord of Howth (a Protestant) and his family.[162] According to an eyewitness, the Capuchin, Brother Edward, Stephen Hussey, preached in Irish at Swords.[163]

A fourth group consisted of the secular clergy whose names appeared in Archbishop Bulkeley's visitation report, some of whom were probably educated in Ireland.[164] It is possible to piece together information about the lives of some of these priests from a variety of sources. 'Mr Clarke', the Mass priest and schoolmaster of Baldongan, may well have been a member of the Clarke family of the Bay (parish of Mulhuddart).[165] John Clarke of the Bay left 20*s.* to his nephew 'Father Clarke' in 1599.[166] Some secular priests working in Fingal in 1630 became notorious because of their participation in agitation against the regular clergy. Among these was Paul Harris, an Englishman, who was chaplain to the Luttrell family.[167] Peter Caddell, a

154 Edmund Hogan, *Distinguished Irishmen of the sixteenth century* (London, 1894), pp 163–82, 196 to 310 and 395 to 501. **155** Stephen B. Barnwell, 'The Barnewall family during the sixteenth and seventeenth centuries (part 6)' in *The Irish Genealogist*, iii, no. 11 (October 1966), pp 449–50; Colmcille Ó Conbhuidhe, *Studies in Irish Cistercian history*, ed. Finbarr Donovan (Dublin, 1998), pp 134 and 230. **156** Nicholas Archbold, The historie of the Irish Capucins, 1643 (Bibliothèque Municipale de Troyes, MS 1103, pp 27 and 93); Seán P. Ó Mathúna, *An tAthair William Bathe, C.Í., 1564–1614* (Dublin, 1980), pp 15, 26 and 32 (footnote 107). **157** Nicholas Archbold, The historie of the Irish Capucins, 1643 (Bibliothèque Municipale de Troyes, MS 1103, pp 69 and 133). **158** Nicholas Archbold, The historie of the Irish Capucins, 1643 (Bibliothèque Municipale de Troyes, MS 1103, p. 16 and 129). **159** Nicholas Archbold, The historie of the Irish Capucins, 1643 (Bibliothèque Municipale de Troyes, MS 1103, pp 16 and 85); *Civil Survey, vii, county of Dublin*, ed. R *c.*Simington (Dublin, 1945), p. 122. **160** Book of vestitians (Capuchin Archives, Dublin); *Notitia historica provinciae ordinis Fratrum Minorum Francisci Capucinorum in Hibernia* ... (Rome, 1859), p. 15. **161** Nicholas Donnelly, *Short histories of Dublin parishes* (17 parts, Dublin, 1904–17), part xv, pp 56 and 73. **162** Nicholas Donnelly, *Short histories of Dublin parishes* (17 parts, Dublin, 1904–17), part xv, p. 56. **163** Nicholas Donnelly, *Short histories of Dublin parishes* (17 parts, Dublin, 1904–17), part xv, p. 73. **164** 'Archbishop Bulkeley's visitation of Dublin, 1630', ed. M.V. Ronan in *Archivium Hibernicum*, viii (1941), pp 56–98. **165** 'Archbishop Bulkeley's visitation of Dublin, 1630', ed. M.V. Ronan in *Archivium Hibernicum*, viii (1941), p. 70. **166** Abstract of will of John Clarke, 25 November 1599 (NLI, Fisher will abstracts, GO MS 290, p. 71). **167** Nicholas Donnelly, *Short histories of Dublin parishes* (17 parts, Dublin, 1904–17), part viii, p. 170;

priest of the Meath diocese, who was appointed rector of Swords in 1625, was also involved in this controversy.[168] However, the agitation was centred mainly on the parishes of St Michael where Patrick Cahill, another Meath man, had been based in 1629, and of St Audeon in Dublin city.[169] The controversy developed into one which was not only a conflict between secular and regular priests and their supporters but also one between natives of Dublin and 'strangers' from Meath.[170] It was eventually resolved by the archbishop, Thomas Fleming, who was both a Franciscan and a native of Meath. One of those affected by the controversy was Edmund Doyle who had been working in Swords at the time of Archbishop Bulkeley's visitation and who was subsequently transferred to St Audeon's.[171] Echoes of the controversy can still be detected in the abstract of Edmund Doyle's will where he made the proviso that certain bequests could only be made if the recipients were natives of Dublin.[172] Another priest mentioned in Archbishop Bulkeley's report, Roger Begg of Westpalstown, must have been an elderly man when he was arrested, imprisoned and subsequently released under the Commonwealth in 1654.[173]

The fifth group consists of those priests whose names came to prominence during the 1641 rising. These are to be found in the 1641 depositions and lists of outlaws. Many of the names of the last group were not included in the *Reportorium Novum* list already mentioned. Among them was Robert Passmore who was identified by the vicar of Balrothery, Thomas Clitheroe, as the son of the local innkeeper, John Passmore, and one of the band whom he accused of 'maligning' him though he did not implicate him in the physical attack made upon him subsequently or in the robbery of his goods.[174] His name subsequently appeared on the list of outlaws.[175] In 1653 he was found guilty of murders committed in 1642 and 1645.[176] Another local priest whose name appeared on the list of outlaws was Laurence Rowen of Finglas.[177] The surname is not a particularly common one and it is possible that he was related to William Rowen, the Finglas butcher, who, with John Sephton and others, attracted the attention of the authorities even before the 1641 rising broke out in Fingal.[178] John and Thomas Smith of Finglas implicated 'Laurence Rowen, priest', in the attacks on their property during the early stages of the rising.[179] Christopher

Francis Elrington Ball, *Southern Fingal* … (originally published 1920, reprinted Dublin, 1995), p. 35. **168** W.M. O'Riordan, 'A list of 17th century Dublin diocesan priests' in *Reportorium Novum*, ii, no. 1 (1958), p. 115. **169** Patrick F. Moran, *History of the Catholic archbishops of Dublin since the Reformation* (Dublin, 1864), pp 372–80; Nicholas Donnelly, *Short histories of Dublin parishes* (17 parts, Dublin, 1904–17), part viii, pp 168–72. **170** Extract from letter from Thomas Fleming, archbishop of Dublin, 1 February 1631, quoted in Patrick F. Moran, *History of the Catholic archbishops of Dublin since the Reformation* (Dublin, 1864), p. 377. **171** 'Archbishop Bulkeley's visitation of Dublin, 1630', ed. M.V. Ronan in *Archivium Hibernicum*, viii (1941), p. 63; Nicholas Donnelly, *Short histories of Dublin parishes* (17 parts, Dublin, 1904–17), part viii, pp 171–2. **172** Abstract of will of Edmund Doyle, 25 April 1637 (NLI, Fisher will abstracts, GO MS 290, pp 140–1). **173** 'Commonwealth records' in *Archivium Hibernicum*, vi (1917), p. 198 and vii (1918–21), pp 24 and 50–1. **174** Deposition of Thomas Clitheroe, 26 May 1642 (TCD, MS 810, f. 126). **175** R.C. Simington and John MacLennan, 'Oireachtas Library, List of outlaws, 1641–1647' in *Analecta Hibernica*, no. 23 (1966), p. 343; John T. Gilbert (ed.), *History of the Irish confederation and the war in Ireland, 1641–3* … (7 vols, Dublin, 1882–91), iii, p. 377. **176** Proceedings of the high court of justice held at Dublin and Cork in 1652, 1653 and 1654 (TCD, MS 866, ff 31 and 77). **177** R.C. Simington and John MacLennan, 'Oireachtas Library, List of outlaws, 1641–1647' in *Analecta Hibernica*, no. 23 (1966), p. 344; John T. Gilbert (ed.), *History of the Irish confederation and the war in Ireland, 1641–3* … (7 vols, Dublin, 1882–91), iii, p. 378. **178** Examination of William Rowen, 19 November 1641 (TCD, MS 809, f. 188). **179** Deposition of John Smith, 19 January

Hewetson of Swords also accused Laurence Rowen and others of robbing and despoiling him.[180] Laurence Rowen was on active service for quite some time as William Hollis described how, in March 1642, he and six other soldiers, having left Swords were attacked by 'the rebels' captain, Oliver Walsh, a friar, Captain Finglas, Captain John Fottrell, Father Rowen, the priest and other priests in their company and divers other rebels, consisting in all of 100 horse and fifteen musketeers or thereabouts'.[181] Laurence Rowen's subsequent career will be examined in chapter 9. A Richard Fottrell, 'clerk', of Swords appeared on the list of outlaws but he may have been the same person as Richard Fottrell,'gentleman', of 'Westerbealingstown' whose name also appeared on the list.[182] West Belinstown was situated in the parish of Ballyboghil not far from Swords. In 1641 the proprietor, was Nicholas Barnewall of Turvey, and it is just possible that Richard Fottrell was one of his chaplains.[183] The *Reportorium Novum* list contains the following entry for Richard Fottrell: 'Chancellor of Dublin about 1668. Recommended by Dr Nicholas French, Bishop of Ferns, as suitable for appointment as Archbishop of Dublin. Dr Fottrell was then aged 74'.[184]

Similar uncertainty arises in the case of Patrick and Richard Travers of Ballykea.[185] The name of Patrick, 'clerk', appears on both the Oireachtas Library list of outlaws, the list in Armagh Public Library and that published by John T. Gilbert but Richard's name appears only on the Gilbert list. It is assumed that this entry for Richard was an error. However, it is not certain that all the priests on the list of outlaws actively participated in the fighting. George Talbot, a brother of John Talbot, proprietor of Malahide, was listed although the extent of his participation, if any, is not known.[186]

Three priests with local associations played an important part in the rising. They were Walter Enos, John Malone (or O'Molony) and Conor Donnogh. Walter Enos appears to have been chaplain to Lady Bath of Drumcondra since she left him silver to make a chalice together with the vestments, cloth and alb which he daily used.[187] His residence was given as 'Hacketstown' on the list of outlaws.[188] Hacketstown, near Skerries, was the home of Lady Bath's daughter, Catherine Gough, and her husband,

1642 (TCD, MS 809, f. 222); deposition of Thomas Smith, 20 January 1642 (TCD, MS 809, f. 224). 180 Deposition of Christopher Hewetson, 5 March 1642 (TCD, MS 809, f. 280). 181 Deposition of William Hollis, 27 April 1643 (TCD, MS 810, f. 235). 182 R.C. Simington and John MacLennan, 'Oireachtas Library, List of outlaws, 1641–1647' in *Analecta Hibernica*, no. 23 (1966), p. 340; John T. Gilbert (ed.), *History of the Irish confederation and the war in Ireland, 1641–3* ... (7 vols, Dublin, 1882–91), iii, pp 361–2. 183 *Civil Survey, vii, county of Dublin,* ed. R *c.*Simington (Dublin, 1945), p. 46. 184 W.M. O'Riordan, 'A list of 17th century Dublin diocesan priests' in *Reportorium Novum,* ii, no. 2 (1960), p. 264. 185 R.C. Simington and John MacLennan, 'Oireachtas Library, List of outlaws, 1641–1647' in *Analecta Hibernica*, no. 23 (1966), p. 345; John T. Gilbert (ed.), *History of the Irish confederation and the war in Ireland, 1641–3* ... (7 vols, Dublin, 1882–91), iii, p. 383. 186 R.C. Simington and John MacLennan, 'Oireachtas Library, List of outlaws, 1641–1647' in *Analecta Hibernica*, no. 23 (1966), p. 344; John T. Gilbert (ed.), *History of the Irish confederation and the war in Ireland, 1641–3* ... (7 vols, Dublin, 1882–91), iii, p. 382; Joseph Byrne, *War and peace: the survival of the Talbots of Malahide 1641–1671* (Dublin, 1997), pp 38–9. 187 Abstract of will of Barbara Gough (Lady Bath), 23 February 1642 (RSAI, Elrington Ball MSS, vol xii, f. 188); Francis Elrington Ball, *Southern Fingal* ... (originally published 1920, reprinted Dublin, 1995), p. 164. 188 R.C. Simington and John MacLennan, 'Oireachtas Library, List of outlaws, 1641–1647' in *Analecta Hibernica*, no. 23 (1966), p. 340; John T. Gilbert (ed.), *History of the Irish confederation and the war in Ireland, 1641–3* ... (7 vols, Dublin, 1882–91), iii, p. 360.

Alderman Robert Arthur. Walter Enos a native of Dublin, was appointed rector of the Irish Pastoral College in Louvain in March 1653.[189] Benignus Millett has made available in translation Enos's own account of his career in Ireland in an undated petition to the cardinals of the Sacred Congregation of the Propagation of the Faith in Madrid.

> He explains that he is a protonotary apostolic and was secretary to the assembly of clergy and prelates in Ireland; after imprisonment and the controversy caused by the publication by him of a book in English in 1644 refuting a Protestant book written by an apostate medical doctor and his conversion of the said apostate, he published, at the request of the clergy and supreme council, a famous book in 1645 on the justice of the Catholics' war, and in 1646 other books clearly demonstrating the injustice and invalidity of the peace then concluded; in 1647, though proposed by Father Scarampi and again by the nuncio himself, he frequently refused a bishopric; in 1648, as a result of the repeated written requests from the prelates and the nuncio, he agreed to the pleading of the assembly of bishops to vindicate the just cause of the Catholic clergy and of the censures published against those who sided militarily with the heretics; so he was hunted captured, imprisoned, and deprived of his property; he was rescued; in the later trials and tribulations he had to flee to Rome where he was kindly helped by the cardinals, and especially by Cardinal Chigi, now the Pope, and in 1653 he was made president of the Pontifical Irish Pastoral College in Louvain ...[190]

Much of the information contained in this autobiographical sketch can be confirmed from other sources. While it is not known when and how Enos was arrested he would appear to have been the man called 'Enos' released during an exchange of prisoners in the latter part of 1642.[191] His opposite number in the exchange, organized by Friar Anthony Nugent and others, was the minister of Virginia, George Creichton. Bishop Wadding possessed a copy of the first of his books.[192] His later writings were used extensively in the compilation of the *Commentaries of Rinuccini*, published later in Latin.[193] As a protégé of Nicholas French, bishop of Ferns, and, like the bishop, a

189 Cathaldus Giblin, 'Catalogue of material of Irish interest in the collection *Nunziatura di Fiandra*, Vatican archives: part 1, vols 1–50' in *Collectanea Hibernica*, no. 1 (1958), p. 89; Benignus Millett, 'Catalogue of Irish material in vols 370 and 371 of the *Scritture riferite originali nelle congregazioni generali* in Propaganda Archives' in *Collectanea Hibernica*, nos. 27 and 28 (1985–6), p. 54. **190** Benignus Millett, 'Catalogue of Irish material in vols 370 and 371 of the *Scritture riferite originali nelle congregazioni generali* in Propaganda Archives' in *Collectanea Hibernica*, nos. 27 and 28 (1985–6), pp 45–6. **191** Deposition of George Creichton, 15 April 1643 (TCD, MS 833, f. 234); John T. Gilbert (ed.), *A contemporary history of affairs in Ireland from A. D. 1641 to 1652* ... (3 vols, Dublin, 1879–80), i, part ii, p. 538. **192** Walter Enos, *Alexipharmacon, or a sovereign antidote against a virulent cordial composed the twenty-second of June 1644, by two druggists, the one an apostata, call John Loghan, a titular doctor of physick, the other a doctor of divinity of the pretended reformed gospel, called Edward Parry* (Waterford, 1644); James Ware, *The whole works of Sir James Ware concerning Ireland, revised and improved*, ed. Walter Harris (2 vols, Dublin, 1764), ii, p. 122; Patrick J. Corish, ed. 'Bishop Wadding's notebook' in *Archivium Hibernicum*, xxix (1970), pp 59 and 85. **193** Richard O'Ferrall and Robert O'Connell, *Commentarius Rinuccinianus, de sedis apostolicae legatione ad foederatos Hiberniae catholicos per annos 1645–49*, ed. Stanislaus Kavanagh (6 vols, Dublin, 1932–49).

strong advocate of the rights of the Catholic church, he fell foul of Richard Bellings, secretary to the supreme council of the Confederation of Kilkenny who wrote to the earl of Ormond on 18 February 1651 as follows:

> The bishop of Ferns [Nicholas French], Hugh Rochfort, father Giles Smith, that commanded the fort of Duncannon, and doctor Enos, do put to sea in the frigate [which] carries these. Their place of residence, as I am informed, will be in the Low Countries. How they are affected to your excellency is well known. It were well your lordship might find out their ways; they have busy bitter pens among them; and I am confident they will find a way to utter their malice in print ...[194]

An attestation by the Irish Franciscans of St Anthony's College, Louvain, in December 1663 gave a rather different account of the character of the man.[195] He lived frugally and maintained a strong discipline, he fostered study, spiritual exercises and prayer and he was 'a pious and exemplary man, skilled in administration' although inclined to become involved in law cases. In later life Walter Enos made many enemies and, following a turbulent career in Louvain in the post-Restoration period, he died in 1672.[196] The careers of two other priests, Conor Donnogh and John Malone, who had prominent military roles in the 1641 rising will be dealt with in a discussion of the war. Finally, mention must be made of the only priest in the area known to have been betrayed during the period 1603–60. In November 1655, the sum of £5 was paid to Thomas Baker, a soldier, for apprehending John Tobin, probably the Kilkenny Capuchin, Father Fiacre Tobin, in the barony of Balrothery.[197]

The priests with Fingal connections or who served in Fingal during the period 1603–60 identified in the course of this study probably represented just of fraction of the total number of those who lived or worked in Fingal in the period 1603–60. One feature which distinguished these clergymen from the clergy of the established and dissenting churches is that they were, in the main, local men. They were almost all from Fingal, Dublin city or, in a few instances, from the neighbouring diocese of Meath. Few, if any, came from the southern part of the diocese. A possible explanation for this is that Irish-speaking priests were needed for Wicklow and south Dublin while priests who did not speak Irish could, on the whole, operate successfully in Fingal. In any event the fact that the priests were local meant that they could stay among relatives and friends and could rely on the local gentry and people for help when it was needed. There was a long tradition of support for the clergy in the area.

194 Bellings to Ormonde, 18 February 1651 in John T. Gilbert (ed.), *History of the Irish confederation and the war in Ireland, 1641–3* ... (7 vols, Dublin, 1882–91), vii, p. 366. **195** Benignus Millett, 'Catalogue of Irish material in vols 370 and 371 of the *Scritture riferite originali nelle congregazioni generali* in Propaganda Archives' in *Collectanea Hibernica*, nos. 27 and 28 (1985–6), p. 51. **196** Benignus Millett, 'Catalogue of Irish material in vols 370 and 371 of the *Scritture riferite originali nelle congregazioni generali* in Propaganda Archives' in *Collectanea Hibernica*, nos. 27 and 28 (1985–6), pp 54, 56–7, 59–61, 63–76; Benignus Millett, 'Calendar of Volume 3 (1672–5) of the *Scritture riferite nei congressi, Irlanda*, in Propaganda Archives: part 1, ff 1–200' in *Collectanea Hibernica*, nos. 18 and 19 (1976–7), p. 63. **197** Book of vestitians (Capuchin Archives, Dublin); 'Commonwealth records' in *Archivium Hibernicum*, vi (1917), p. 175 and vii (1918–21), pp 21, 52 and 59; W.M. O'Riordan, 'A list of 17th century Dublin diocesan priests' in *Reportorium Novum*, iii, no. 1 (1962), p. 150.

Among the benefactors and friends mentioned by Henry Fitzsimon were George Blackney of Rickenhore, Thomas Fagan, William Nugent and his cousin, Michael Taylor.[198] The desire of the 'Pale people' to have their own, and only their own, priests was confirmed by the Revd George Creichton, minister of Virginia, in 1643.[199] It may be significant that the only known betrayal of a priest in Fingal during the Commonwealth period was perpetrated by a soldier.

There are some striking parallels between the operations of the two successful groups of clergy, the Catholic priests (prior to 1650) and the dissenting ministers (after 1650). Both groups approached their tasks with missionary fervour and with intent to change the *status quo*. Both groups operated with a mixture of settled and peripatetic clergy. In the case of the Catholics the parochial clergy and the chaplains to the gentry, who, in some instances, may have been the same persons, gave a degree of stability while the regular clergy often travelled around giving missions and supplying help to the secular priests when required. The dissenters also had (nominally) permanent appointees, often selected by their congregations, in fixed locations and their work was supplemented by ministers, such as Dr Samuel Winter, based in Dublin and, in one case, Chapelizod, who travelled about the precinct and thus added organizational flexibility. The other factor which applied in the case of both Catholics and dissenters was the strong support of the laity.

The vast majority of the members of each of the churches were lay-people. How were they divided up numerically between the various religious groups? The only known sources which provide information on the balance between Catholics and Protestants are the report, written in prose, of Archbishop Bulkeley's visitation in 1630 and Sir William Petty's summary figures derived from the poll tax returns for 1660.[200] At first glance it appears difficult, if not impossible, to make comparisons between the two sets of data. The poll-tax returns did not include children, for example. However, a careful examination of the visitation returns suggests that they, too, omitted small children and were concerned with those who attended church or, in some cases, Easter communicants. The visitation returns probably omitted those too old or frail to attend church and, in 1630, attending church would have involved travelling significant distances for some Protestants. If it is accepted that the term 'English' used in the poll-tax returns represented religion rather than ethnicity the two sets of returns may not be all that far apart. At the very least they offer a reasonable prospect of illustrating quantitively the extent of the religious divide and the way in which it changed in the second half of the period under review.

A comparison of the two sets of returns showed that, with the exception of the parish of Finglas (part of the archbishop's own estate in 1630) the figures suggested a remarkable increase in the number of Protestants in Fingal during the period 1630

198 Henry Fitzsimon, *Words of comfort to persecuted Catholics* … (Dublin, 1881), pp 251–2; Henry Fitzsimon, *The justification and exposition of the divine sacrifice of the Masse* … ([Douai], 1611), p. 361. **199** Deposition of George Creichton, 15 April 1643 (TCD, MS 833, f. 236); John T. Gilbert (ed.), *A contemporary history of affairs in Ireland from A.D. 1641 to 1652* … (3 vols, Dublin, 1879–80), i, part ii, p. 542. **200** 'Archbishop Bulkeley's visitation of Dublin, 1630', ed. M.V. Ronan in *Archivium Hibernicum*, viii (1941), pp 56–98; *A census of Ireland* circa *1659* …, ed. S. Pender (Dublin, 1939), pp 382–92.

to 1660.[201] Protestants were still a small percentage (20%) of the total population but potentially viable communities had been established in areas where there had been none such in 1630. Obviously there had been losses due to war and plague but these, as far as can be judged, affected both sides. The increase in some areas, for example Hollywood and the Naul, was due, at least in part to the presence of garrisons.[202] Nevertheless one can only conclude that, between them, the government authorities and the dissenting ministers had managed to bring about a remarkable change in the fortunes of Protestantism during the Commonwealth.

The growth of dissent in Fingal forms an interesting case-study. While this development may have owed something to the army this cannot be the complete explanation for its success. The earliest entry in the registers of Provost Winter was dated March 1649, before Samuel Winter actually arrived in Ireland, although it was made by him later.[203] It recorded the baptism of Joan Povey at Darndale by Thomas Seele, then vicar of Coolock and curate of Raheny.[204] Her parents' names were not given but her sureties (or godparents) were Elizabeth Br[own] for Lady Povey, Anne Kerdiff and Kit Hafenny (Halfpenny?). Elizabeth Povey (probably Joan's sister) was born on 1 July 1650. Her sureties were Sir Edward Povey, Mrs Margaret Ball and Mrs Elizabeth Brown. The children's father may have been John Povey, who was admitted to the King's Inns in April 1658.[205] The surnames, Povey, Kerdiff, Ball and Brown appear again in the register, the last three of them in connection with Finglas where there was a second and probably a larger group of dissenters.[206] Ales Povey, was, apparently, a widow (of a Mr Brown?) when she married Hierom (Jerome) Russell of Finglas. She may have favoured the more extreme form of dissent since Winter noted that her elder daughter, Joyce, had been 'christened after the new manner by Dr Lightburn' in 1656.[207] The place of Joyce's baptism was not stated but her sister, Margaret, was baptized in Finglas church in March 1660.[208] A churching ceremony followed. Jerome Russell was one of those appointed to audit the accounts of the church in 1658 and he was appointed churchwarden in 1659.[209]

A pivotal figure among the Finglas dissenters was the civil servant, Thomas Springham, who had been admitted to the King's Inns as an attorney in November 1639.[210] A fragment of his accounts, written in Roman numerals and bearing his signature, which survives among the 1641 depositions, shows that he was an impost master.[211] The Springham family had lived in Finglas since 1597 at least.[212] Thomas also had connections with the Springham family of Dublin city for he was a kinsman

201 'Fingal 1603–60', i, pp 282–4. **202** Notes relating to the 'Ministers of the Gospel' ... (RCBL, GS 2/7/3/20, p. 4). **203** *The registers of Provost Winter* ... (Dublin, 1907), p. 11. **204** James B. Leslie, Biographical succession list for the diocese of Dublin (RCBL, 61/2/4/1, pp 108 and 249). **205** *King's Inns admission papers 1607–1867*, ed. Edward Keane, P. Beryl Phair and Thomas U. Sadleir (Dublin, 1982), p. 407. **206** *The registers of Provost Winter* ... (Dublin, 1907), pp 17 and 23. **207** *The registers of Provost Winter* ... (Dublin, 1907), p. 17. **208** *The registers of Provost Winter* ... (Dublin, 1907), p. 23. **209** Finglas parish combined vestry book and registers, 1657–1758 (RCBL, P.307/1/1, pp 11 and 14). **210** *King's Inns admission papers 1607–1867*, ed. Edward Keane, P. Beryl Phair and Thomas U. Sadleir (Dublin, 1982), p. 459; Colum Kenny, *King's Inns and the kingdom of Ireland: the Irish 'inn of court' 1541–1800* (Blackrock, 1992), p. 281. **211** Thomas Springham, Receipts of the impost masters for four weeks beginning the 17th of September & ending the 14th of October 1647 (TCD, MS 840, f. 211). **212** Lease between John Carey, Luke Challoner and William Carey, 30 October 1597 (RCBL, Records of the archbishop of Dublin, D6/77).

of Walter Springham, a tanner, of New Row, whose will was proved in April 1650.[213] Thomas married Anne Barry, a daughter of Alderman Richard Barry of Dublin and thus became connected with some of the more important local families of the Commonwealth and Restoration periods.[214] Anne's sister, Margaret, married first Nicholas Kerdiff, sergeant-at-law, and secondly, Alderman Robert Ball, who died in 1636.[215] Another of Anne's sisters, Mary, who died in 1635, had married James Donnellan, who became a judge and resided at the Forrest, near Swords.[216] Provost Winter officiated at the baptisms of Anne Springham, daughter of Thomas, in February 1654, her sister, Katherine, who died shortly afterwards in May 1656, her brother, Thomas, in October 1657 and another sister, Katherine in May 1660.[217] Having played a prominent part in the rebuilding of Finglas church in 1657 Thomas Springham became one of the first two churchwardens appointed to it.[218] He died in 1668.[219]

More influential, though with fewer local connections, was the government auditor, Thomas Richardson, the second churchwarden appointed in Finglas in 1657. A relative newcomer, he had been invited to take up a post as auditor under the parliamentary commissioners in June 1651 at an annual salary of £200 together with an allowance of £20 a year 'for paper, books ink, pens, fire, candle and all other incidents belonging to his employment' and a further allowance of 20*s.* per week for two clerks.[220] However, it is just possible that he had some previous connections with this country for an attorney named Thomas Richardson had been admitted to the King's Inns in 1638.[221] He certainly had some legal training for he served as a member of the high court of justice in Dublin.[222] He became an alderman of Dublin, a member of Samuel Winter's congregation, and, having married Anne, daughter of Sir Edward Bagshaw of Finglas, settled in the area.[223] He was appointed senior churchwarden at the first vestry meeting recorded in the book which he presented in 1657.[224] His wife bestowed a pulpit cushion on the parish on the same occasion.

213 Betham genealogical abstracts, prerogative wills (NAI, series I, vol 58, pp 151–2). **214** Lord chancellor's order of dismiss in the case of John Mangan against Anne and James Springham, etc., 17 October 1671 (RCBL, Records of the archbishop of Dublin, D6/76/10/22). **215** William Ball Wright, *Ball family records* (York, 1908), p. 25; Colm Lennon, *The lords of Dublin in the age of reformation* (Dublin, 1989), p. 230. **216** Examination of Andrew Gyraght, 2 February 1653 (TCD, MS 810, f. 357); examination of Thomas Waltryn, 1 February 1653 (TCD, MS 810, f. 375); examination of John Confy, 1 February 1653 (TCD, MS 810, f. 377); examination of Patrick Maguire, not dated (TCD, MS 810, f. 379); examination of John Heard, 24 November 1652 (TCD, MS 810, f. 380); Francis Elrington Ball, *The judges in Ireland, 1221–1921* (2 vols, London, 1926), i, p. 337; Colm Lennon, *The lords of Dublin in the age of reformation* (Dublin, 1989), p. 230. **217** *The registers of Provost Winter* ... (Dublin, 1907), pp 14, 17, 19 and 23. **218** Finglas parish combined vestry book and registers, 1657–1758 (RCBL, P.307/1/1, pp 1– 10); William Cotter Stubbs, 'Finglas, County Dublin, vestry books' in *Journal of the Royal Society of Antiquaries of Ireland*, xlvi (1916), pp 27–9. **219** Betham genealogical abstracts, prerogative wills (NAI, series I, vol 58, p. 167). **220** 'Commonwealth state accounts: Ireland, 1650–1656' ed. Edward MacLysaght in *Analecta Hibernica*, no. 15 (November, 1944), pp 320–1; Aidan Clarke, *Prelude to Restoration in Ireland* (Cambridge, 1999), p. 185. **221** *King's Inns admission papers 1607–1867*, ed. Edward Keane, P. Beryl Phair and Thomas U. Sadleir (Dublin, 1982), p. 422; Colum Kenny, *King's Inns and the kingdom of Ireland: the Irish 'inn of court' 1541–1800* (Blackrock, 1992), p. 280. **222** Aidan Clarke, *Prelude to Restoration in Ireland* (Cambridge, 1999), p. 185. **223** T.C. Barnard, *Cromwellian Ireland: English government and reform in Ireland 1649–1660* (2nd ed., Oxford, 2000), p. 83 (footnote 170); Aidan Clarke, *Prelude to Restoration in Ireland* (Cambridge, 1999), p. 185. **224** Finglas parish combined vestry book and registers, 1657–1758 (RCBL, P.307/1/1, pp 1 and 10); William Cotter Stubbs, 'Finglas, County Dublin, vestry books' in *Journal of the Royal Society of Antiquaries of Ireland*, xlvi (1916), pp 27

Another lawyer whose name appeared in Winter's register was 'Thomas Browne, the attorney', who was godfather to Anne Springham in 1653.[225] He had been admitted to the King's Inns as an attorney in the same year as Thomas Springham (1639) but was later created a counsellor by royal letters patent.[226]

Apart from Darndale and Finglas baptisms were recorded at Newtown, Drumcondra, Clonshagh, Killeen, Piercetown, Coolock and Corballis.[227] Since the counties are not given in these cases it is possible that some of them may refer to baptisms outside Fingal. Winter and his collaborators were successful in establishing a small but influential network linking the members of the dissenting community in Fingal. Although the numbers are minuscule they represent just one of several dissenting congregations in the area. It is possible to distinguish a certain overlap between Winter's followers and other groups in society. The participation of a number of lawyers is striking as is the link with families that were associated with Dublin corporation. Among the women some of the older family names, such as Ball and Barry, emerge as being significant. Winter's congregation may not have been typical since he tolerated and even adopted many of the practices of the established church. As pointed out by the editor of *The registers of Provost Winter*, despite the fact that English Puritans always objected to the use of sponsors, Winter usually adopted the ancient custom of the Church of England in having three.[228] He also occasionally used the terms 'godfathers' and 'godmothers' (instead of 'sureties' or 'witnesses') as in the cases of Anne Springham of Finglas and John Foster of Clonshagh.[229] Churching ceremonies were noted following seven of the Fingal baptisms.[230] In one case Winter recorded that the ceremony took place on Ascension Day.[231] According to St John D. Seymour, Winter 'approximated closely to the Evangelicalism of the Irish Episcopalians, and so must have formed a connecting-link between the Low Church party and the Independents' as did John Murcot of St Michan's.[232] Some members of the established church attended ceremonies conducted by Winter. He preached at the baptism of Thomas Springham in Finglas church in October 1657.[233] On this occasion the sureties included Sir James Ware and his brother-in-law, Dr Dudley Loftus. While it is believed that Winter sometimes baptized the children of Catholic parents the position relating to Fingal is not clear. The names Lawrence Grace of Newtown and Carol McEnboy and Sarah McKely (or McKelly) of Drumcondra (assuming this was Drumcondra, Co. Dublin) raise certain questions.[234] The baptisms of John, son of Robert Scurlog and Margaret Dargan at Finglas in February 1658 (at which the sureties were Thomas Caroll, Edmond Nolan and Joan White), of Joan, daughter of John Brigly and Ellinor Laghlin (als. Lickin) at Coolock in June 1659 (at which the sureties were John Walsh, Joan Dermot and Margaret Ryan), and of Grace, daughter of Owen and Nora

and 29. **225** *The registers of Provost Winter* ... (Dublin, 1907), p. 14. **226** Colum Kenny, *King's Inns and the kingdom of Ireland: the Irish 'inn of court', 1541–1800* (Blackrock, 1992), pp 153–4, 158 and 281. **227** *The registers of Provost Winter* ... (Dublin, 1907), pp 14, 20, 22 and 23. **228** *The registers of Provost Winter* ... (Dublin, 1907), pp 5–6. **229** *The registers of Provost Winter* ... (Dublin, 1907), p. 14. **230** *The registers of Provost Winter* ... (Dublin, 1907), pp 19, 20, 22 and 23. **231** *The registers of Provost Winter* ... (Dublin, 1907), pp 6 and 23. **232** St John D. Seymour, *The puritans in Ireland (1647–1661)* (Oxford, 1921), p. 39. **233** *The registers of Provost Winter* ... (Dublin, 1907), p. 19. **234** *The registers of Provost Winter* ... (Dublin, 1907), p. 14.

Fullam at Finglas in April 1660 (at which the sureties were Gilligroomagt [*sic*], Margaret Martin and Joan White), while they do not provide conclusive proof, strongly suggest that the Independents may have had some success in attracting members from the local Catholic community by the end of the period.[235] The history of the decline of dissent in Fingal after 1660 remains to be written.

235 *The registers of Provost Winter* ... (Dublin, 1907), pp 20, 22 and 23.

8

'The holy company of heaven'

> In preaching he had such a spirit and efficacy of moving his auditors to compunction and tears that his fame and name went all over Ireland.
>
> Fr Nicholas Archbold on Fr Edward (Luke) Bath, *c.*1631[1]

Nicholas Archbold and Luke Bath were part of a Capuchin mission which began in 1616 and which was designed to regenerate the spiritual life of Catholics in Ireland. The two men, and in the early seventeenth century, the majority of their colleagues were members of distinguished Pale and, in several cases, Fingal gentry families. Yet, although they had been abroad for many years, had received a sophisticated continental education and were bringing a message of Tridentine reform that was unfamiliar to many, they managed to establish a remarkable empathy with their congregations, particularly in Fingal. As well as examining the traditional religious practices and beliefs of the people one of the tasks of this chapter will be to examine the degree to which these were comprehended by the reorganized structures of the Catholic church. Attitudes of Protestants to Catholics and of Catholics to Protestants will also be considered.

How did religion find its expression in the daily lives of the ordinary people? It is sometimes possible to find the private thoughts and beliefs of lay people in their letters and diaries. Unfortunately few of these survive for Fingal. There exists, however, among the 1641 depositions one remarkable letter, written by the Protestant Dublin lawyer, Robert Bysse, junior, in February 1642.[2] Robert had close associations with Fingal. He was the nephew of Robert Bysse of Pelletstown (Castleknock), and the brother to whom the letter was addressed, John, the recorder of Dublin, had several holdings in the area, some of which were inherited from his father, Christopher.[3] John was in England at the time the letter was written and it was, in effect, a plea to him to return home. While the letter is a valuable source of information on the progress of the rising it is also noteworthy for the many expressions of religious faith which it contained. These included a prayer that 'please God that the wind and weather serve' to bring good news of John.[4] The rebels at Drogheda were unable to press home their advantage 'with the permission of the good God'.[5] Having described how Captain Stutfield's ship had gone aground near Drogheda and the

1 Nicholas Archbold, The historie of the Irish Capucins, 1643 (Bibliothèque Municipale de Troyes, MS 1103, p. 94). 2 Robert Bysse, junior, to John Bysse, 16 February 1642 (TCD, MS 840, ff 7–10). 3 *Civil Survey, vii, county of Dublin,* pp 14, 40, 75–6, 114 and 208. 4 Robert Bysse, junior, to John Bysse, 16 February 1642 (TCD, MS 840, f. 7). 5 Robert Bysse, junior, to John Bysse, 16 February 1642 (TCD, MS 840, f. 7).

efforts made to defend her, he noted that 'by these means and God's good pleasure and mercy' she stayed then and came off the next tide.[6] Noting the ambiguous situation and the fears of Lady Bolton that she would be hurt by the English army, he commented that 'she may praise God for her husband and his good friends'.[7] He expressed the hope that 'in God's good time' they would have additional force at their disposal and that in time things 'with God's blessing' would settle.[8] Finally, he alluded to the uncertainty about the whereabouts of his sisters and friends. Unsure whether they were prisoners in the castle of Athlone or 'straightened in their own castle', he prayed that God would 'strengthen and comfort them all, and in his time deliver them and grant us a merry meeting and gathering together of the dispersed'.[9]

The expressions of religious belief found in the depositions were rather different. The occasions on which these were made were serious and solemn and offered less scope for the expression of inner feelings. The religious context of the evidence given at these enquiries was obvious, however, in that they were preceded by the swearing of an oath 'upon the holy Evangelist'.[10] As in the case of the letter written by Robert Bysse, junior, there were occasional references to God's providence as, for example, when the ship's captain, Daniel Barwick, was threatened with death if he did not help the insurgents to capture two ships lying near Ireland's Eye.[11] He reported to the commissioners that 'before the next day the said ships, by God's providence, loosed anchor and had wind that carried them away'. Elizabeth Russell, a widow and fishmonger, of St Michan's parish, who claimed in 1644 that, as a result of the activities of the English army, she was 'quite undone' and must depend 'next unto God unto the charity of her friends'.[12] As might have been expected some of the clergymen also referred to God's providence or pleasure.[13]

Some idea of the all-pervasive religious belief which existed among Catholic laypeople at the period can be found in the poem 'Purgatorium Hibernicum'. Written in a mixture of the Fingallian dialect and standard English, the speeches contained in the poem were permeated by religious feeling. There were many casual references to God and the saints both in English and Irish. When the English word 'God' was used it was often changed to 'good', perhaps for reasons of propriety, as in the phrase 'Good bless', but the original sometimes slipped into the text. Phrases with a religious connotation found in the poem included '*Grá Dé*', '*Fuil Dé*', 'by our Lady', 'God knows', 'as Christ would save her', 'Good bless thee' and 'God send thee better luck nor me'.[14] As death and the afterlife formed a major theme of the poem, prayers for the dead such as 'Good rest his soul and body', 'heaven rest his soul' and the somewhat ambiguous 'pray God reward him for 't' were interspersed in the text.[15]

6 Robert Bysse, junior, to John Bysse, 16 February 1642 (TCD, MS 840, f. 7). 7 Robert Bysse, junior, to John Bysse, 16 February 1642 (TCD, MS 840, f. 9). 8 Robert Bysse, junior, to John Bysse, 16 February 1642 (TCD, MS 840, ff 9–10). 9 Robert Bysse, junior, to John Bysse, 16 February 1642 (TCD, MS 840, f. 10). 10 Examination of Thomas Sevier, 29 January 1642 (TCD, MS 809, f. 232); deposition of Huibart Cromphouts, 2 March 1642 (TCD, MS 809, f. 268); deposition of Darby Lea, 25 January 1642 (TCD, MS 809, f. 288); deposition of Anthony Huiberts, 29 January 1642 (TCD, MS 809, f. 310). 11 Deposition of Daniel Barwick, 21 May 1642 (TCD, MS 810, f. 112); deposition of Daniel Barwick, 23 May 1642 (TCD, MS 810, f. 115). 12 Deposition of Elizabeth Russell, 6 July 1644 (TCD. MS 810, f. 300). 13 Deposition of Randall Dimmock, 1 March 1642 (TCD, MS 809, f. 276); deposition of Henry Pemberton, 25 May 1642 (TCD, MS 810, f. 180). 14 Purgatorium Hibernicum ..., *c.*1670 (NLI, MS 470, pp 16, 17, 19, 23, 26, 72, 88, 106, 109, 137, 148). 15 Purgatorium Hibernicum

Cursing was not unknown, as evidenced in the phrases 'the devil choke her', 'the devil may thy collar splice' and more elaborately as a punishment for sin in the lines

> And for that trick hungry [*sic*]and cold
> reward thee, for to be so bold,
> choking upon thy father's brood
> and let it never do thee good.
> A bad *sinkenagh* upon thee
> and strong *barlunagh* be thy fee,
> that without priest may be thy doom
> and no one weep upon thy tomb.[16]

The expressions 'blessing oneself' and 'crossing oneself' as well as 'coshirk' from *coisreacan* were used to denote the sign of the cross.[17] Several specific prayers were mentioned in the poem. The well-educated hero, Nees, for example, was able to say his *Pater Noster*, *Ave Maria*, Grace at table and Matins in Latin.[18] The *Pater Noster*, *Ave Maria* and *Salve Regina* were popular prayers.[19] No doubt this was due in no small part to their association with the rosary and the deep Marian devotion which existed throughout Fingal. The poem contained several references to the use of beads.[20] Also mentioned in it were the *Kyrie Eleison*, *Pias* and the *Oras*, perhaps because of their associations with litanies.[21] Nees was a particular devotee of St Patrick and he expressed his veneration in a long prayer, requesting temporal (military, political and economic) favours.[22] The poem is, of course, a burlesque. Nevertheless, the promises to dedicate an abbey to the saint and to hang his picture in the church, though perhaps somewhat exaggerated, were not untypical of the ambitions of some of the Fingal gentry, recorded in their wills, to be remembered by the erection of monuments in, or by the building and repair of, churches.[23]

The intensity with which many people prayed is conveyed in the following lines:

> But here the nun before she leads
> him further fall[s] unto her beads.
> For she had still, like cunning friends,
> her praying upon her fingers' ends.
> And, as she used to milk her sheep,
> thumping her dugs and in a deep
> sense of her *culpas* and her passion,
> she muttered out a learned oration.
> And so when she had done her praises,

…, *c.*1670 (NLI, MS 470, pp 28, 51 and 102). **16** Purgatorium Hibernicum …, *c.*1670 (NLI, MS 470, pp 58, 93 and 122). **17** Purgatorium Hibernicum …, *c.*1670 (NLI, MS 470, pp 2, 23 and 61). **18** Purgatorium Hibernicum …, *c.*1670 (NLI, MS 470, p. 2). **19** Purgatorium Hibernicum …, *c.*1670 (NLI, MS 470, pp 2, 13, 52 and 59). **20** Purgatorium Hibernicum …, *c.*1670 (NLI, MS 470, pp 13, 17, 59 and 134). **21** Purgatorium Hibernicum …, *c.*1670 (NLI, MS 470, pp 17, 59 and 61). **22** Purgatorium Hibernicum …, *c.*1670 (NLI, MS 470, pp 15–22). **23** Purgatorium Hibernicum …, *c.*1670 (NLI, MS 470, pp 20–1).

her *coshirks*, *Oras* and her graces,
new *Aves*, beads and all the ce-
-remonies of the *Tenebrae*,
and invocated every spirit
that in these regions did inherit . . .[24]

She went on to invoke a long list of Irish saints, whose names appear to have been selected for the sake of the rhyme rather than because of their local importance, though a number of them were, in fact, venerated in Fingal. The lines which follow this list hint at what seventeenth-century Protestants regarded as the excessive and unbridled devotion to the saints exhibited by Catholics:

She ceased, nor was there to be found
above, upon or underground
in all the register, not one
that she forgot to call upon
for to conduct her and her page
in subterranean pilgrimage.[25]

In an article entitled 'Catholic religious cultures in the diocese of Dublin, 1614–97', Raymond Gillespie has written that

> communities inherited from the middle ages a social parallel to their own world in a world of saints whose heavenly community mirrored their earthly one. This gave rise to communal devotions addressed to these holy men and women based on rituals performed at particular places validated by a hagiographic tradition. To reformers, both Tridentine Catholics and Protestants, this world of traditional religion was regarded with suspicion because it bore close comparison with superstition, and relied on rituals rather than a genuine interiorised spirituality.[26]

How true was this of Fingal? In an earlier chapter the importance of wells and other traditional pattern sites as venues for social intercourse has been discussed. The religious significance of these sites will now be examined. Of the sixty-nine holy wells identified in Fingal by Caoimhín Ó Danachair and by Dúchas the dedications of fifty-three have been recorded. A small number of wells have multiple dedications. This may indicate either a change in dedication, the existence of a second well which has now disappeared or perhaps some confusion in local tradition. Writing about the important well at Grallagh (parish of Hollywood) Caoimhín Ó Danachair pointed out that it was marked 'St Michael's Well' on the 6 inch Ordnance Survey map but that it was not known locally by this name but as 'St Maccullin's Well' and, by some,

24 Purgatorium Hibernicum . . ., *c.*1670 (NLI, MS 470, pp 61–2). 25 Purgatorium Hibernicum . . ., *c.*1670 (NLI, MS 470, p. 62). 26 Raymond Gillespie, 'Catholic religious cultures in the diocese of Dublin, 1614–97' in James Kelly and Dáire Keogh (eds), *History of the Catholic Diocese of Dublin* (Dublin, 2000), p. 128.

as 'St Patrick's Well'.[27] Another well which had two other possible designations is Sunday's Well at Malahide, which like that at Lissenhall (parish of Swords), was named for the Deity.[28] Caoimhín Ó Danachair gave St Sylvester (patron of the parish) as an alternative name for the well while Joseph Byrne mentioned a third (Marian) designation, namely, the 'Lady Well'.[29] St Margaret's Well in the parish of the same name had an alternative dedication to St Bridget.[30] There is no evidence, however, that the alternative name found in the files of Dúchas – the Heritage Service for the Lady Well in Stephenstown, namely, 'Mable's Well', had any religious significance.[31] In the case of St Dennis's Well at Clontarf Ó Danachair pointed out that the well was called 'St Dennis's' on one edition of the Ordnance Survey map but 'St Phillip's' on another.[32] He thought it probable that neither was the original name. Ó Danachair also carried out a detailed analysis of the wells and their dedications. The Fingal holy wells were tabulated and have been mapped in figure 8.1.[33] Three of the wells were dedicated to the Deity, nine to Our Lady, twenty-eight (involving twenty-one different dedications) to Irish saints and thirteen (nine different dedications) to other saints. Using the alternative names for the wells at Grallagh and St Margaret's would raise the number of wells dedicated to Irish saints to thirty and reduce those dedicated to other saints to eleven. A large number of the wells were dedicated to just three female saints, namely, at least nine to Our Lady, at least five to St Brigid and five to St Catherine. This may indicate an earlier goddess cult.

As mentioned in chapter 6 there are contemporary or near contemporary references to some of the wells. In his collection made in 1571 Meredith Hanmer mentioned St Pappin's Well at Santry, St Patrick's Well, presumably that at Finglas, and another well dedicated to St Mochan at Kellstown (Clonsilla) which is not included in the Ó Danachair and Dúchas lists or in figure 8.1.[34] Joseph Byrne has described the pilgrimage made by John Talbot of Malahide to St Marnock's well at Portmarnock in 1655.[35] There are several eighteenth-century references. In 1744 Isaac Butler described the condition of the well at St Doolagh's (one of the Lughnasa wells) as follows:

> There is ... a large raised tomb of black marble ... hither the devotees pay their orisons on the first of August, likewise at the well which was beautifully adorned with curious figures and an inscriptional stone importing the time when and by whom erected. It was wholly defaced, the carvings taken away,

27 Caoimhín Ó Danachair, 'The holy wells of County Dublin' in *Reportorium Novum*, ii, no. 1 (1958), p. 75. 28 Caoimhín Ó Danachair, 'The holy wells of County Dublin' in *Reportorium Novum*, ii, no. 1 (1958), pp 70, 78 and 81. 29 Caoimhín Ó Danachair, 'The holy wells of County Dublin' in *Reportorium Novum*, ii, no. 1 (1958), p. 78; Joseph Byrne, *War and peace: the survival of the Talbots of Malahide 1641–1671* (Dublin, 1997), p. 19. 30 John Rutty, *An essay towards a natural experimental medicinal history of the mineral waters of Ireland* (Dublin, 1757), p. 299; Caoimhín Ó Danachair, 'The holy wells of County Dublin' in *Reportorium Novum*, ii, no. 1 (1958), p. 78. 31 Dúchas – the Heritage Service, County Dublin, file no. DU005–002. 32 Caoimhín Ó Danachair, 'The holy wells of County Dublin' in *Reportorium Novum*, ii, no. 1 (1958), p. 69. 33 'Fingal 1603–60', i, p. 297; ii, appendix G, table G.5, p. 70. 34 Meredith Hanmer, *The chronicle of Ireland collected by Meredith Hanmer in the year 1571* (Dublin, 1633, republished 1809), pp 81–2, 84 and 185. 35 Joseph Byrne, *War and peace: the survival of the Talbots of Malahide 1641–1671* (Dublin, 1997), p. 46.

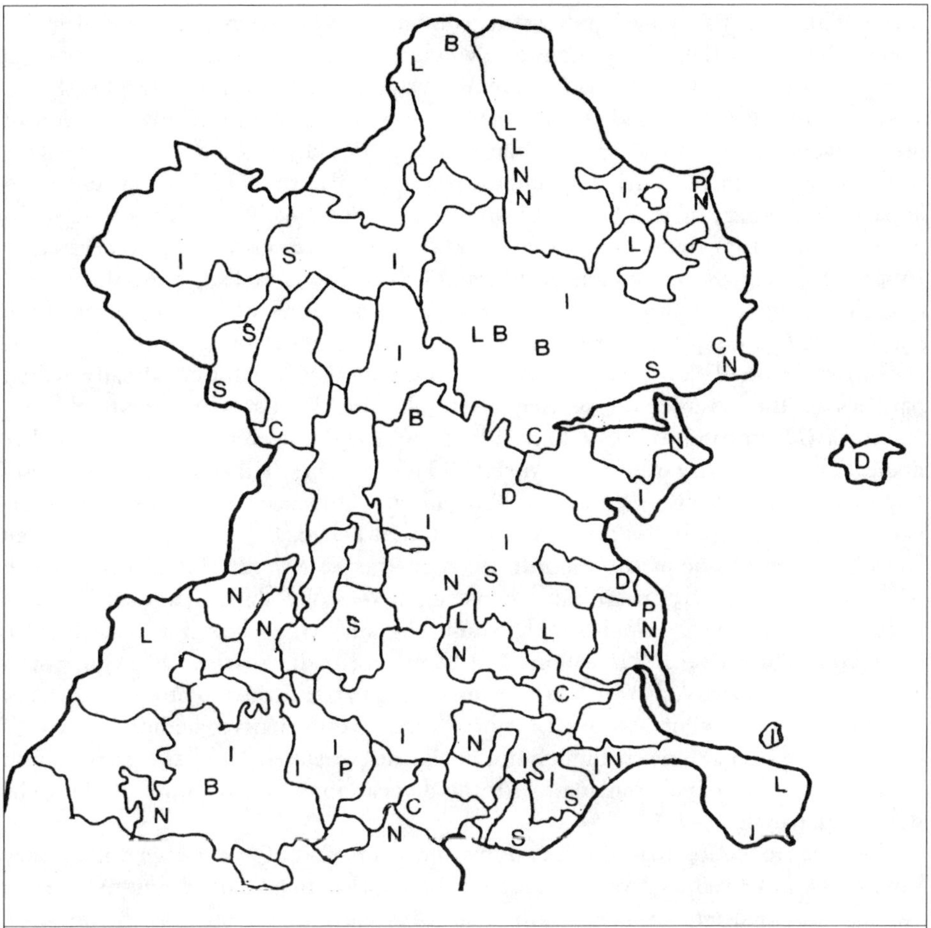

Well dedicated to

the Deity	D	St Catherine	C
Our Lady	L	Other Irish saint	I
St Patrick	P	Other saint	S
St Brigid	B	Not specified	N

Fig. 8.1 Dedications of holy wells in Fingal

> and inscriptional stone broke into many pieces by Sir Richard Buckley [Brickley ?].[36]

He also noted St Colmcille's well at Swords, 'a well of pure water encompassed with a square wall and covered with two large ash trees', and the well at Balrothery dedicated to St Peter 'on whose day they go to the said well and pay their orisons,

36 Isaac Butler, Journal of 1744 (Armagh Public Library, p. 1).

&c.'.[37] This was a particularly interesting comment as Ó Danachair's careful description of the well at Balrothery showed how much of this rich tradition had been lost by the twentieth century. It read as follows: 'A good well of clear water, lined with stone to ground level. Used for domestic supply. No tradition of any devotion or other practices. Legend: A woman named Biddy Boughy washed clothes in a holy well in Chapel Lane; this dried up and the present well appeared.'[38] Ó Danachair was apparently unaware of the dedication and, as in the case of St Mochan's well, it has been omitted from figure 8.1. Like St Peter there were other saints venerated in Fingal whose names did not appear in recent lists of known wells. An examination of church and chapel dedications has produced several names which do not appear in the well dedications. Not surprisingly St Nicholas figured twice in this maritime region, as patron of the parishes of Artaine and Kinsaley, which were already extinct parishes in the seventeenth century.[39] St John the Baptist was patron of both Clonturk (Drumcondra) and Clontarf.[40] There may, however, have been another dedication to St Margaret at Clonturk.[41] Three parishes, Killester, Killossery and Kilsallaghan, for which no wells were shown in the Ó Danachair listings, were dedicated to St Brigid (Killester and Killossery) and St David (Kilsallaghan).[42] St Finian was the patron of one of the subordinate chapelries of Swords.[43] Balgriffin church was dedicated to St Sampson but, when the parishes of Balgriffin and St Doolagh were amalgamated, St Doolagh, to whom the surviving church was dedicated, emerged as the patron.[44] The name of St Damnan (Rush, parish of Lusk) has been associated by Robert Walsh with Whitestown (alternative dedication to St Maurus or Maur) and by Bishop Donnelly with Kenure (alternative dedication to St Catherine).[45] In many cases, though not in all, the parish patron or the patron of an extinct parish or chapel coincided with the dedication of one or other of the wells within the parish.

There is no doubt that the 'heavenly community' of the seventeenth-century Fingallians was a rich and varied company. In addition to St Patrick and many Irish saints it included one archangel, a number of biblical saints, such as the apostles, Peter, James, Philip and, possibly, John the Evangelist, saints representing the early universal church (Sylvester, Nicholas, Catherine and Margaret), two saints from France (Dennis and Maurus or Maur), one from Wales (David) and one from England (Werburgh). This 'heavenly community' truly reflected the multi-cultural nature of the earthly community. But how was it regarded by the Tridentine reformers? The Jesuit, Henry Fitzsimon, in his *Catalogus* specifically associated three saints, all of whom were Irish, with Fingal, namely, St Doolagh, whose life survived at Malahide, St Canice, who was celebrated in Finglas and St Marnock, who

37 Isaac Butler, Journal of 1744 (Armagh Public Library, pp 4 and 11). 38 Caoimhín Ó Danachair, 'The holy wells of County Dublin' in *Reportorium Novum*, ii, no. 1 (1958), p. 74. 39 Robert Walsh, *Fingal and its churches* ... (Dublin, 1888), pp 227 and 237. 40 Robert Walsh, *Fingal and its churches* ... (Dublin, 1888), pp 223–4. 41 Francis Elrington Ball, *Southern Fingal* ... (originally published 1920, reprinted Dublin, 1995), p. 182. 42 Nicholas Donnelly, *Short histories of Dublin parishes* (17 parts, Dublin, 1904–17), part xiv, p. 13; Robert Walsh, *Fingal and its churches* ... (Dublin, 1888), p. 238. 43 Robert Walsh, *Fingal and its churches* ... (Dublin, 1888), p. 237. 44 Robert Walsh, *Fingal and its churches* ... (Dublin, 1888), pp 232–3. 45 Robert Walsh, *Fingal and its churches* ... (Dublin, 1888), p. 242; Nicholas Donnelly, *Short histories of Dublin parishes* (17 parts, Dublin, 1904–17), part xvi, p. 95.

was celebrated in Fingal.[46] His work contained the names of several other Irish saints, such as Brendan, Brigid, Kevin, Columba, Fintan, Maccullin and Mobhi, as well as the missionaries, Patrick and Sylvester, who had dedications in Fingal.[47] He was no doubt aware that two other saints in his list had connections with St Patrick's Island, off Skerries. Benin (Benignus) was associated with the folklore of the area while Malachy was a historical figure.[48] Henry Fitzsimon, writing about the use of holy water, said that 'therewith also did our St Malachy help and heal a woman in frenzy and divers others diseased'.[49] His use of the word 'our' to categorize a pre-Norman, albeit canonized, saint confirms that the Fingallian who had written: 'I am not an Englishman' was perfectly reconciled to his own Irish identity.[50] The evidence suggests that devotions to newer saints such as Ignatius supplemented rather than replaced the existing cults. The Capuchins, too, took part in the ancient practices. Father Barnabas interrupted a mission in Garristown to make a six-day pilgrimage '*in Connatiam*' to visit St Brigid's well.[51] Among others who travelled on pilgrimage outside Fingal was Thomas Luttrell's pregnant wife who died on a pilgrimage to Holy Cross early in the century.[52]

For the formal church regulations regarding the practice of religion it is necessary to consult the decrees of the synods. Alison Forrestal has examined these in detail.[53] There is no surviving record of any Dublin diocesan synod for the period 1603–60. The records of two provincial synods for the province of Dublin, held in 1614 at Kilkenny and in 1640 at Tyrchogir, have been published.[54] The records of a third synod held in 1632 are no longer extant.[55] An inter-provincial synod (provinces of Dublin and Cashel), in which the archdiocese of Dublin participated, was held in Kilkenny in 1629.[56] In relation to holy wells Michael Comerford summarized the decree made at the 1614 synod as follows:

> The ecclesiastical authorities were also charged to reform certain abuses and superstitious usages practised by ignorant persons assembling at wells and trees. If it appeared that there were any healing effects produced by such springs, whether proceeding from their natural properties or from the invocation and patronage of certain saints, access to the water was not to be

46 Henry Fitzsimon, 'Catalogus praecipuorum sanctorum Hiberniae' ... (Antwerp, 1621), pp 93, 98 and 102. 47 Henry Fitzsimon, 'Catalogus praecipuorum sanctorum Hiberniae' ... (Antwerp, 1621), pp 87, 89, 96, 102, 104, 110 and 113. 48 Henry Fitzsimon, 'Catalogus praecipuorum sanctorum Hiberniae' ... (Antwerp, 1621), pp 86 and 102; *Acta Sanctorum*, ed. Hippolytus Delehaye and Paulus Peeters, Tomus iv, vol 67 (Brussels, 1925) pp170–1; Dermot McIvor, 'In search of Saint Diomac' in *Journal of the County Louth Archaeological Society*, xiii, no. 3 (1955) pp 225–51; Dubhaltach Mac Firbishigh, *Chronicum Scotorum: a chronicle of Irish affairs from the earliest times to A.D. 1135: with a supplement containing the events from 1141 to 1150*, ed. William M. Hennessy (London, 1866) p. 345. 49 Henry Fitzsimon, *The justification and exposition of the divine sacrifice of the Masse* ... ([Douai], 1611), p. 115. 50 Henry Fitzsimon, *The justification and exposition of the divine sacrifice of the Masse* ... ([Douai], 1611), preface (no page number). 51 Nicholas Archbold, The historie of the Irish Capucins, 1643 (Bibliothèque Municipale de Troyes, MS 1103, f. 176). 52 PRO, SP 63/232/17. 53 Alison Forrestal, *Catholic synods in Ireland, 1600–1690* (Dublin, 1998). 54 Patrick F. Moran, *History of the Catholic archbishops of Dublin since the Reformation* (Dublin, 1864), pp 440–65; summary English translation in Michael Comerford, *Collections relating to the dioceses of Kildare and Leighlin* (3 vols, Dublin and London, 1886), i, pp 245–53. 55 Alison Forrestal, *Catholic synods in Ireland, 1600–1690* (Dublin, 1998), p. 195. 56 Alison Forrestal, *Catholic synods in Ireland, 1600–1690* (Dublin, 1998), p. 35.

prohibited but only abuses and superstitious practices in connection with them.[57]

There is little evidence that local celebrations were discouraged by the Dublin church authorities during this period. On the other hand, there was probably little active encouragement for such practices nor was there any need for encouragement. The wide-ranging panoply of saints venerated in Fingal, which included numerous Marian, Patrician and Brigidine dedications, and dedications of both churches and wells to other saints of the universal church, ensured that many of the local celebrations took place on official church holydays.[58] The people of Mulhuddart, whose well at Tyrrelstown was dedicated to Our Lady, took full advantage of this for they had days of devotion on 25 March, 15 August and 8 December as well as a pattern on 8 September.[59] There is no doubt that many of the patterns held to mark the festivals were great social as well as religious events. According to 'Purgatorium Hibernicum' the pattern or 'patron' was a two-day event and it appears that the secular events took place on the evening before the feast.[60] The brief reference to 'prayers' and 'beads' suggests a preponderantly lay celebration but the mention of 'Masses' indicates that the clergy also participated in the pattern. The following description of the pattern at *Tubber Shane* indicates that the pattern at that site was somewhat different.

Have you at *Tubber Shane* beheld
on patron day when Mass is held
to charm diseases at the plains
and valleys filled with numerous trains
of *crassies backaghs*, blind and lame,
and go away, even as they came?[61]

Although the use of the word 'charm' suggests superstitious practices, the implication here is that Mass was said at the pattern site to ask the almighty to heal the sick and disabled. In other words, the clergy participated fully in the ceremonies. Caoimhín Ó Danachair listed the cures associated with holy wells where these were known. Generally, the ailments listed were relatively minor and not life-threatening. Sore eyes, sore throats, toothache, headache, stomach disorders, coughs (including whooping cough), chilblains and warts were cited in the twentieth-century recollections recorded by Ó Danachair and in the Dúchas files already mentioned. An exception to the general pattern was the well at Tyrrelstown (parish of Mulhuddart) where sprains, cuts, bruises and rheumatism were the cures noted.[62] Legends survived in the case of fourteen of the wells described by Ó Danachair.[63] Five of these,

57 Michael Comerford, *Collections relating to the dioceses of Kildare and Leighlin* (3 vols, Dublin and London, 1886), i, p. 248. 58 Patrick F. Moran, *History of the Catholic archbishops of Dublin since the Reformation* (Dublin, 1864), p. 459. 59 Caoimhín Ó Danachair, 'The holy wells of County Dublin' in *Reportorium Novum*, ii, no. 1 (1958), p. 76. 60 Purgatorium Hibernicum …, *c.*1670 (NLI, MS 470, p. 133). 61 Purgatorium Hibernicum …, *c.*1670 (NLI, MS 470, p. 150). 62 Caoimhín Ó Danachair, 'The holy wells of County Dublin' in *Reportorium Novum*, ii, no. 1 (1958), p. 76. 63 Caoimhín Ó

Tobersool (Balscaddan), St Mobhí (Holmpatrick), Balrothery, Staffordstown (Lusk) and Sutton (Howth) were concerned with profanation of, or damage to, the well or the surrounding area. At Tobersool there was a legend, found elsewhere in the country, that 'Oliver Cromwell washed his feet in the well and it dried up; it was later restored by the prayers of a holy priest.'[64] This was the only legend recorded in Fingal which reflected quite specifically the religious divide and it probably surfaced some time after Cromwell's progress through the area in 1649. Other legends were associated with the saints who, according to tradition, caused the wells to spring up or with the associated cures. There was a legend associated with St Marnock's well at Portmarnock that 'a tree which overhung the well bent down at night to touch the water. This gave the well its curative powers and also foretold coming storms.'[65] This legend is purely concerned with natural phenomena and makes no mention of the saints or of Christian beliefs. Like the tradition at the Chink Well at Portraine, which told that 'the water remains sweet under the sea' and 'must be visited before sunrise to obtain a cure', the St Marnock's well legend hints at survivals from a religion that was older than Christianity.

Holy wells have always had a fascination for travellers, as well as for archaeologists and historians, but other local religious practices and beliefs have been less well recorded. There have been a number of fairly recent general works which dealt with religious beliefs and practice either at the national level or at diocesan level.[66] The attempt made here to record religious practise in early seventeenth-century Fingal is, of necessity, patchy, since it was often the very obvious which remained unrecorded. Prescriptive decrees of the synods, except where otherwise stated, can be taken as relating to the entire region covered by the synod, but decrees proscribing, suppressing or discouraging certain activities, while important in the national context, are of limited help when considering local practices. The archdiocese of Dublin contained a wide range of sub-cultures and those embraced by the province of Dublin were even more varied. Without corroborative evidence as, for example, exists in the case of the holy wells, it is not possible to say with certainty that a particular proscribed activity was or was not practised in Fingal or, indeed, in any other area.

Apart from the evidence contained in Provost Winter's register already discussed surprisingly little information exists about attitudes to the sacraments of baptism and matrimony. Mixed marriages were a problem for the Catholic clergy for reasons of security as much as anything else. Hinting that it was more serious for a Catholic woman to marry a Protestant man than vice versa, Henry Fitzsimon wrote in 1603: 'I have very often laboured to prevent Catholic women from marrying sectaries, and from thus being used as spies against ourselves; and in my efforts I have been

Danachair, 'The holy wells of County Dublin' in *Reportorium Novum*, ii, no. 1 (1958), pp 72–4, 76–8 and 80–2. **64** Caoimhín Ó Danachair, 'The holy wells of County Dublin' in *Reportorium Novum*, ii, no. 1 (1958), pp 71–2. **65** Caoimhín Ó Danachair, 'The holy wells of County Dublin' in *Reportorium Novum*, ii, no. 1 (1958), p. 78. **66** For example, Patrick J. Corish, *The Catholic community in the seventeenth and eighteenth centuries* (Dublin, 1981); Raymond Gillespie, *Devoted people: belief and religion in early modern Ireland* (Manchester, 1997); Colm Lennon, 'Mass in the manor house: the counter-reformation in Dublin, 1560–1630' and Raymond Gillespie, 'Catholic religious cultures in the diocese of Dublin, 1614–97' in James Kelly and Dáire Keogh (eds), *History of the Catholic Diocese of Dublin* (Dublin, 2000), pp 112–126 and 127–43.

generally successful'.[67] Others, however, were less successful and mixed marriages continued to take place. They did not surface as a specific problem for the synods until the post-Restoration period.[68] Little information survives to show how Catholics in Fingal managed to contract ecclesiastically-approved marriages at times such as the beginning and end of the period when there was an acute shortage of priests in the area. In a letter from Nantes dated 14 March 1656 Brother Edward (a Capuchin) stated that his fellow-Capuchin, Father Anselm, who worked in the Howth and Sutton areas had 'during the last couple of years (1654–1656) ... married more than eighty couples and baptized over 600 infants'.[69] Since this occurred during a period in which few priests remained at liberty in Fingal it may represent a population covering a much wider area than Howth parish. Nevertheless the numbers are impressive and help to put the work of Samuel Winter and his colleagues into perspective.

For Catholics the central event in their lives was the Mass. In 1611 Henry Fitzsimon wrote as follows in a preface to a major work on the subject:

> As for the Mass the most divine oblation not only in earth but in heaven, and not only that is presented to God, as containing Christ himself an holocaust to his father: the approved piety of our nation toward it, made me to justify and expound it according my best leisure and power. For beholding old and young, rich and poor to resort thereto in foulest weather; in certain danger of persecution; to places ten, fifteen, twenty miles distant; and of those divers with age and infirmities feebled; and being present in place of the propitiatory sacrifice to be so devout, so fervent, so admirably religious in hearty prayer, penitent purposes, inflamed defiers of amendment and the like virtuous affections: I then resolved, with first opportunity, to let them sensibly understand, that all such their piety was not without cause, but upon just and urgent desert, performed ...[70]

With these words, Henry Fitzsimon, while acknowledging the fervour of his people, hinted that they did not fully understand the basis for it. Ironically, the most detailed record of Mass attendance was contained in Archbishop Bulkeley's visitation in 1630 which has already been analyzed in connection with the attempt to gauge the relative strengths of the religious denominations and which showed that, almost twenty years after Fitzsimon wrote the lines quoted above, the people's enthusiasm for the Mass had not diminished.[71] While this enthusiasm was never specifically mentioned in the visitation reports there were occasional allusions to it, for example, in the case of Balgriffin and St Doolagh's where it was stated that all the parishioners were recusants and commonly resorted to Fitzsimon's Grange, Plunket's Grange and some to

67 Henry Fitzsimon to Father Aquaviva, 10 April 1603 in Henry Fitzsimon, *Words of comfort to persecuted Catholics* ... (Dublin, 1881), p. 56. 68 Alison Forrestal, *Catholic synods in Ireland, 1600–1690* (Dublin, 1998), pp 84–5 and 171. 69 Nicholas Donnelly, *Short histories of Dublin parishes* (17 parts, Dublin, 1904–17), part xv, p. 56. 70 Henry Fitzsimon, *The justification and exposition of the divine sacrifice of the Masse* ... ([Douai], 1611), preface (no page number). 71 'Archbishop Bulkeley's visitation of Dublin, 1630', ed. M.V. Ronan in *Archivium Hibernicum*, viii (1941), pp 56–98.

Howth, that is, they travelled some distance to hear Mass.[72] Again in Malahide all the parishioners were recusants 'and go to Mass now at Mr Talbot of Malahide's house, more usually than heretofore'.[73] Of Nicholas Fitzwilliam's house at Baldongan it was recorded that all the inhabitants round about resorted there to hear Mass.[74] As already mentioned the celebration of Mass in an old abbey or in Christ Church cathedral in Dublin was one of the great ambitions of the Catholics who took part in the 1641 rising as well as one of the threats feared by the Protestants.[75] In 1642 the Fingallian refugees in Virginia made sure that they attended Mass before they began their games and festivities.[76] When he invaded Lambay Island, the Friar Malone, also known as John O'Malony, used the Mass-book, rather than the New Testament, to swear an oath.[77] There are several references to the Mass in 'Purgatorium Hibernicum'.[78] Two of these have already been mentioned in connection with patterns at holy wells. Some are little more than casual references but others show that people believed in the efficacy of the Mass and of other prayers for the relief of the souls in Purgatory.[79] The lines

> Then did friar Conor, the old father,
> command a man to bear the lather
> to the road by which they went to Mass
> to make a bridge whereon to pass
> that every one, as he went by,
> might pray for his soul thereon did lie.

are a reminder of the custom of praying for the dead when passing a cemetery and may represent a variant of that custom.[80] The lines, however, may contain a veiled allusion to another practice described in Patrick F. Moran's *History of the Catholic archbishops of Dublin*:

> From time immemorial it had been the custom in Ireland to have an alms offered to the assisting priest at the monasteries or other places of burial: the heretics, however, having seized the monasteries and parochial graveyards, prevented the performance of the Catholic service, and claimed, moreover, the alms which might be offered by the friends of the deceased. To obviate this difficulty, the funeral, before arriving at the place of burial, halted at some convenient place, where the Protestant minister could put forth no claim, and there the prayers were recited and the alms offered to the assisting priest.[81]

72 'Archbishop Bulkeley's visitation of Dublin, 1630', ed. M.V. Ronan in *Archivium Hibernicum*, viii (1941), p. 67. 73 'Archbishop Bulkeley's visitation of Dublin, 1630', ed. M.V. Ronan in *Archivium Hibernicum*, viii (1941), p. 68. 74 'Archbishop Bulkeley's visitation of Dublin, 1630', ed. M.V. Ronan in *Archivium Hibernicum*, viii (1941), p. 70. 75 Deposition of Ann Cappar, 4 January 1642 (TCD, MS 809, f. 261); deposition of Margaret Huiberts, 14 March 1644 (TCD, MS 810, f. 238); deposition of Edward Leech, 18 March 1644 (TCD, MS 810, f. 245). 76 Deposition of George Creichton, 15 April 1643 (TCD, MS 833, ff 236–7); John T. Gilbert (ed.), *A contemporary history of affairs in Ireland from A. D. 1641 to 1652* ... (3 vols, Dublin, 1879–80), i, part ii, p. 542. 77 Deposition of Edward Leech, 18 March 1644 (TCD, MS 810, f. 244). 78 Purgatorium Hibernicum ..., *c.*1670 (NLI, MS 470, pp 13, 37, 52–3, 58, 112, 134, 150, 166 and 175). 79 Purgatorium Hibernicum ..., *c.*1670 (NLI, MS 470, pp 37 and 52–3). 80 Purgatorium Hibernicum ..., *c.*1670 (NLI, MS 470, pp 52–3). 81 Patrick F. Moran,

Respect for the dead manifested itself in various ways. For Protestants it usually meant a service and decent burial in a church previously selected by the deceased, as in the case of Robert Bysse of Pelletstown (Castleknock), or by the deceased's relatives, executors or overseers.[82] For many Catholics it meant the administration of the sacrament of extreme unction before death together with an arrangement to ensure not only decent burial in the church or churchyard of one's choice but also to arrange for prayers for one's soul after death and for some considerable time into the future. Wills, including their preambles, often tell a great deal about the religious beliefs of the individual and the community. Since very few wills have survived in their entirety for Fingal for this period, and as those which have survived mainly relate to the upper classes and gentry, it is impossible to construct a satisfactory picture. Abstracts made from wills generally omitted the pious preamble though they usually mentioned the place of burial where this was specified. Notwithstanding these deficiencies, those wills which have survived, in whole or in part, give us some indication of what was considered important in death as in life. The general introductory formula used by Catholics was generally short such as 'I bequeath my soul to Almighty God, my creator and redeemer' followed by an instruction about the place of burial as in the wills of Richard Nettervill (1607), Henry Burnell (1614), John Arthur (1666) and Christian Purfield (1666).[83] Robert Arthur, father of John, who made his will in 1648, omitted the preamble and began by appointing his executors and overseers.[84] He then went on to recommend his soul 'to God, my maker and redeemer' and asked that his body be buried in his parish church of Lusk. The preamble contained in the abstract of the will of Walter Segrave of Little Cabragh (1619), a very prominent Catholic, was as follows:

> In the name of the Holy Trinity, Father, Son and the Holy Ghost, three persons and one God, Amen. Walter Segrave of the Little Cabragh in the franchises and liberties of the city of Dublin, alderman, being in perfect memory and health of body, thanks be to God, considering with himself the shortness and uncertainty of man his life does make his last will and testament ...[85]

James Hussey, priest, of Smarmore, Co. Louth, used the following formula: 'first I bequeath my soul to Almighty God, the blessed Virgin Marie, and all the holy company of heaven. And my body to be interred in the sepulchre of my father at Holmpatrick'.[86]

History of the Catholic archbishops of Dublin since the Reformation (Dublin, 1864), p. 372. **82** Abstract of will of Robert Bysse, senior, 27 January 1643 (RSAI, Elrington Ball MSS, vol xi, f. 44); Francis Elrington Ball, *Southern Fingal ...* (originally published 1920, reprinted Dublin, 1995), p. 27. **83** Will of Richard Nettervill, 11 April 1607 (NAI, Deeds and wills extracted from inquisitions, exchequer series, vol 1, Carlow and County Dublin, RC 10/1, p. 353); abstract of will of Henry Burnell, 17 July 1614 (RSAI, Elrington Ball MSS, vol xi, f. 34); will of John Arthur, 4 October 1666 (NAI, Prerogative will book, 1664–84, f. 73); will of Christian Purfield, 23 April 1666 (NAI, Prerogative will book, 1664–84, f. 116). **84** Will of Robert Arthur, 4 June 1648 (NAI, Prerogative will book, 1664–84, f. 274). **85** Abstract of will of Walter Segrave, 9 March 1619 (RSAI, Elrington Ball MSS, vol xii, f. 26). **86** L.P. Murray, 'The will of James Hussey of Smarmore, Co. Louth, "Priest" (A.D. 1635)' in *The Journal of the County Louth Archaeological Society* viii, no. 4 (1936), p. 303.

The formula used by Protestants was generally longer and was often a profession of their view of salvation. Luke Challoner, clergyman of Finglas, wrote: 'first I leave my soul to the lord's gracious mercy in the mediation of his dear son in whom for my salvation I faithfully trust and my body to be buried as my executors shall think good'.[87] Anne Coote of Killester (1650) used the following formula:

> I bequeath my soul to God my maker hoping and expecting through the only merits of his son Christ Jesus by faith applied to me for a glorious and beatifical vision of my God, my saviour and my sanctifier, and of a happy resurrection of my body at the last day.

Sir James Ware (1665) bequeathed his soul to almighty God 'to be redeemed by the most precious death and mediation of my saviour, Jesus Christ' and asked to be buried with his parents, wife and some of his children in St Werburgh's church in Dublin.[88] Thomas Bourke (1669) commended his soul to Almighty God, 'hoping assuredly through the only merits of Jesus Christ my Saviour to be made partaker of life everlasting', and went on to request burial in the church of Raheny.[89] John Sprotton of the Red Mills near Chapelizod (1670) commended his soul 'to Almighty God, trusting in the merits and mediation of Jesus Christ'.[90]

The arrangements made by dying persons for the provision of clothing and mourning tokens, such as rings, for their relatives and friends has been adverted to in an earlier chapter. The treatment of death as a rite of passage, particularly in the context of religion, will now be examined. The poem 'Purgatorium Hibernicum' attempted to superimpose characters from seventeenth-century Fingal upon a story set in pre-historic Italy. While it was essentially a burlesque the basic theme of the original enabled it to give an elaborate picture of how the ceremonies connected with death and burial were carried out in the seventeenth century or, at least, how they appeared to the observer.

The vital importance of providing a proper burial and tomb was emphasized again and again in the poem. This may be due to the fact that the author was conscious of the fact that the wars of the mid-seventeenth century had, inevitably, caused a break in the tradition of due reverence to the dead. The refusal to allow the burial of the dead, especially the Protestant dead, had been a feature of that war in Fingal. Few funeral monuments from that period remain in the area and this may be due to the fact that such memorials were never erected. In the poem Shela explained that an unburied person 'may wander here [in the underworld] till he is weary and fast a hundred years, before he can be relieve[d] from Purgatory'.[91] Pillinure (*Pallinurus*) pleaded with Nees to bury his body in order that 'my poor bones may be at ease and with my fathers rest in peace'.[92] Nees promised to raise a tomb so that 'shall still

87 'Will of Luke Challoner, DD', in Newport J.D. White, *Four good men; Luke Challoner, Jeremy Taylor, Narcissus Marsh, Elias Bouhéreau* (Dublin, 1927), pp 22–4. 88 Will of Sir James Ware, 10 August 1665 (NAI, Prerogative will book, 1664–84, f. 178). 89 Will of Thomas Bourke, 6 April 1669 (NAI, Prerogative will book, 1664–84, f. 165). 90 Abstract of will of John Sprotton, 30 September 1670 (RSAI, Elrington Ball MSS, vol xi, f. 38). 91 Purgatorium Hibernicum …, *c.*1670 (NLI, MS 470, p. 73). 92 Purgatorium Hibernicum …, *c.*1670 (NLI, MS 470, p. 77).

endure the name of honest Pillinure' and the writer of the marginal notes to the poem identified this placename, now transposed to Kilmure (possibly Kilmore, parish of Coolock) as being in Fingal, five miles from Dublin. Later in the story Nees told another friend, Bryan Oge, whom he met in the underworld, that, unable to find his body, he had put up for him an empty bier to which Bryan replied

> I know
> how much I am beholden to
> thy own self then art do me all
> the reliquid of a funeral.[93]

The most detailed account of the ceremonies associated with death was given in connection with the death and burial of an ordinary man, the piper, MacShane. The sacrament of extreme unction was administered to dying Catholics. The following lines describe its administration to MacShane:

> There was the priest forgiving sins,
> busy as hen with two chickens,
> 'nointing his forehead, breast and nose,
> his drivers and his petty-toes,
> according method of his function
> with holy oil of extreme unction.
> But most his knees those twins of penance
> that to devotion were strict tenants.[94]

After death the corpse was washed and brought to a specially-built hut or mortuary where the wake was held.[95] After death the priest also had a function to fulfil at the wake.

> And in comes
> monk Conor too with all his trinkums,
> who, when he had his office paid,
> and for the dead a while had prayed,
> all ceremonies being ended,
> the mourners now are recommended
> to their own sports.[96]

Throughout the following night the mourners prayed, played and smoked – there was no mention of drinking at the wake – and on the following day they mounted MacShane's body on a bier 'with a white velvet overcast' and brought him for burial.[97] Having placed the corpse and personal possessions in the grave further

93 Purgatorium Hibernicum ..., *c.*1670 (NLI, MS 470, pp 98–9). 94 Purgatorium Hibernicum ..., *c.*1670 (NLI, MS 470, p. 36). 95 Purgatorium Hibernicum ..., *c.*1670 (NLI, MS 470, pp 45–8). 96 Purgatorium Hibernicum ..., *c.*1670 (NLI, MS 470, pp 48–9). 97 Purgatorium Hibernicum ..., *c.*1670 (NLI, MS 470, pp 49–51).

prayers and a Mass were said.[98] Two crosses were provided: the first of thorns, earth and broom was designed to protect the grave from marauding humans and animals; the second of grass was strewn by the priest over the body.[99] Finally, the priest gave the assembled throng his blessing.[100]

While this description of the funeral of an ordinary man suggests something rather different from the elaborate ritual planned by Lady Bath the common thread in Catholic funerals was the Mass and the accompanying prayers. The sombre ceremonies conducted at the funerals of some Protestants, such as Robert Bysse, senior, were very different.[101] Thomas Richardson, the Finglas dissenter, for example, asked to be buried in his tomb in St Werburgh's 'decently but not with pomp'.[102] An extreme case was that of Nicholas Loftus, who had married Margaret Chetham of Hacketstown and subsequently moved to Co. Wexford, who ordered 'that he should be buried in the night-time, without any ceremonies, assemblies, or mournings, but privately, as soon as he should be dead'.[103] He was buried in Fethard in 1666.

A few references to the sacrament of penance can be found in the records. The Capuchin, Brother Edward, writing in 1654, stated that his colleague, Father Anselm, would celebrate Mass in Howth 'in some secluded spot and during the night, and on each of these occasions would hear confessions and distribute Holy Communion among sixty, seventy, or even ninety individuals, all being over before daybreak; but at Easter time the number would reach nearly one thousand'.[104] A fellow-member of his order, Father Stephen, ministered to about twenty villages in Swords.[105] His work was mostly carried on by night and every Mass he offered was attended by a multitude of penitents and communicants. A lay perspective on penance is to be found in the burlesque 'Purgatorium Hibernicum'. The prince, Nees, had an personal confessor 'Father Brian', something which must have been difficult for ordinary people in Ireland at that time but the poet probably had a chaplain in mind.[106] The necessity of repentance for sin was understood.[107] Penance was a familiar concept and was mentioned several times in the poem.[108] One penitential practice which occupied the thoughts of seventeenth-century Fingallians was that of fasting. The practice of the people and, to some extent, the church regulations remained extremely strict in Ireland despite the changes which the papacy had introduced.[109] Patrick F. Moran pointed out that more than half the days of the whole year were days of fast and/or abstinence. Shela, who in the poem 'Purgatorium

98 Purgatorium Hibernicum ..., *c.*1670 (NLI, MS 470, pp 51–2). 99 Purgatorium Hibernicum ..., *c.*1670 (NLI, MS 470, pp 40–1 and 52). 100 Purgatorium Hibernicum ..., *c.*1670 (NLI, MS 470, p. 52). 101 Abstract of will of Robert Bysse, senior, 27 January 1643 (RSAI, Elrington Ball MSS, vol xi, f. 44); Francis Elrington Ball, *Southern Fingal* ... (originally published 1920, reprinted Dublin, 1995), p. 27. 102 Abstract of will of Thomas Richardson, 11 April 1668 (RSAI, Elrington Ball MSS, vol xii, f. 47). 103 John Lodge, *The peerage of Ireland or a genealogical history of the present nobility of that kingdom* (revised by Mervyn Archdall, 7 vols, Dublin, 1789), vii, pp 264–5. 104 Nicholas Donnelly, *Short histories of Dublin parishes* (17 parts, Dublin, 1904–17), part xv, p. 56. 105 Nicholas Donnelly, *Short histories of Dublin parishes* (17 parts, Dublin, 1904–17), part xv, p. 73. 106 Purgatorium Hibernicum ..., *c.*1670 (NLI, MS 470, p. 16). 107 Purgatorium Hibernicum ..., *c.*1670 (NLI, MS 470, p. 18). 108 Purgatorium Hibernicum ..., *c.*1670 (NLI, MS 470, pp 36–7, 84, 112, 118, 124, 127 and 156). 109 Patrick F. Moran, *History of the Catholic archbishops of Dublin since the Reformation* (Dublin, 1864), p. 271; Michael Comerford, *Collections relating to the dioceses of Kildare and Leighlin* (3 vols, Dublin and London, 1886), i, pp 250–1.

Hibernicum' represented the ordinary people, spoke of the principal devil in hell as one who 'eats fish on feasts or flesh on fast days' as if both practices were equally reprehensible.[110] Nees, the 'prince', on the other hand, who

of knowledge had no lack,
had in his pate an almanac,
knew by the motion of the sun
when 'twas a fast and when 'twas none

had a rather more sophisticated attitude to the regulations and found a way to get around them on his own terms.[111] In a long passage which enabled the author to explore the question of conscience, Nees, when offered a festive meal on a fast day, pretended ignorance 'for ignorance the Gods appeases' and determined 'to eat and say he forgot'.[112] Once having eaten he 'fell to't'. The severity of the fasts was such that Shela, although prepared to accompany him in a drink, 'of the butter would not taste, 'cause, as I said, it was a fast'.[113] The whole passage, although written in a light-hearted way, conveys the impression of a surprising degree of familiarity with the intricacies of church regulations on the part of lay people. Another example of how people managed to abide by the letter, if not the spirit, of the church's regulations is found in Shela's keeping a piece of beef throughout Lent to eat at Easter

which she indeed like frugal beef
within a clout till Lent was past
reserved till then to break her fast.[114]

The setting of the poem in the underworld gave the author ample opportunity to explore the topics of sin, punishment, hell and the devil. Among the sinners in hell from a wide range of professions and occupations Nees discovered priests, fanatics, clerks, curates and country vicars.[115] He specifically enquired about 'popes, cardinals and nuns' and was told that 'these fare as other spirits according to their deeds and merits'.[116] The reference to the 'numerous throngs of orphans got by friars and nuns i' abbeys and in monasteries and murdered by their votaries to cloak a venial sin' may reflect a folk memory since no abbeys, monasteries or convents are known to have existed in Fingal during the seventeenth century.[117]

As well as stressing the importance of the sacraments the Capuchin friars on the Irish mission placed a great deal of emphasis on preaching. Indeed, if the attention given to sermons in Nicholas Archbold's accounts accurately reflected the views of contemporary members of the order ability to preach was considered one of the more important attributes of a priest. As has already been mentioned, he and many

110 Purgatorium Hibernicum ..., *c.*1670 (NLI, MS 470, p. 112). **111** Purgatorium Hibernicum ..., *c.*1670 (NLI, MS 470, p. 120). **112** Purgatorium Hibernicum ..., *c.*1670 (NLI, MS 470, pp 118–22). **113** Purgatorium Hibernicum ..., *c.*1670 (NLI, MS 470, p. 122). **114** Purgatorium Hibernicum ..., *c.*1670 (NLI, MS 470, p. 26). **115** Purgatorium Hibernicum ..., *c.*1670 (NLI, MS 470, p. 126). **116** Purgatorium Hibernicum ..., *c.*1670 (NLI, MS 470, p. 126). **117** Purgatorium Hibernicum ..., *c.*1670 (NLI, MS 470, p. 85).

others regarded Luke (Father Edward) Bath of Drumcondra as an excellent example of a good preacher. Father Archbold left two accounts of one particular occasion in 1633 when Luke Bath preached at Lusk.[118] The more detailed account below described not only the power of the preacher but also the effects on his listeners.

> Father Edward, preaching once the passion on a holy Friday: when he came to these words '*Ecce Homo*' and showed a picture of that portraiture, the people (they were of a great number) were so moved and inflamed, what at the sight of the picture, what by the efficacy of his emphatical words, that melt into tears and contrition, they clapped their hands together and cried out a main '*Misericordia, misericordia*'; an accident the like of which, to my knowledge, never happened before in that [*sic*] parts. It happened in Lusk, in Fingal, or thereabouts, which kind of people use not to fall into such fevers: being otherwise of a cold blood, phlegmatic disposition, but as fire causeth cold water to boil, to leap up to fly out of its centre: so this seraphical, ignited preacher coming among such heavy, cold affectioned people; so inflamed them with heat of divine charity (the peculiar property of the seraphical order) that not able to contain themselves, they burst out; and flamed with tears of compunction and Christian zeal.
>
> This, their lacrimous clamour, endured for near the space of a quarter of hour, notwithstanding that Father Edward did what he could to have cut it short and appease them. After which they so affected the preacher that what for thirst and desire of the word, what for desire of discharging their consciences unto him by sacramental confession: they flocked in troops after him from village to village: giving him scarcely space to rest a little, and take his necessary food, a thing which hath often happened to others also, our missioners in Ireland.[119]

The narrative would suggest that the people of Lusk were unused to the type of religious picture used by Luke Bath and that such visual aids were an important component in the work of the missioners. It is also clear that though the sermon had a remarkably powerful effect on this occasion similar, if not so dramatic, successes by the Capuchins were by no means uncommon. Archbold also recognized the preaching ability of the controversial English secular priest, Paul Harris, who was chaplain to the Luttrell family at Clonsilla in 1630.[120] He stated that 'his sermons wanted not stuff and good matter, accompanied with curiosity and learning; his speech and delivery was correspondent'. However, he disapproved of the histrionic

118 Nicholas Archbold, The historie of the Irish Capucins, 1643 (Bibliothèque Municipale de Troyes, MS 1103, p. 96); Nicholas Archbold, The evangelicall fruict of the Seraphicall Franciscan order, centur 5, ab Anno Domini 1600, 1628, continued to 1645 (BL, Harleian MS 3888, f. 105). **119** Nicholas Archbold, The historie of the Irish Capucins, 1643 (Bibliothèque Municipale de Troyes, MS 1103, pp 96–7). **120** Nicholas Archbold, The evangelicall fruict of the Seraphicall Franciscan order, centur 5, ab Anno Domini 1600, 1628, continued to 1645 (BL, Harleian MS 3888, f. 106); 'Archbishop Bulkeley's visitation of Dublin, 1630', ed. M.V. Ronan in *Archivium Hibernicum*, viii (1941), p. 77; Nicholas Donnelly, *Short histories of Dublin parishes* (17 parts, Dublin, 1904–17), part viii, p. 170; Francis Elrington Ball, *Southern Fingal* ... (originally published 1920, reprinted Dublin, 1995), p. 35.

style of his sermons and of his 'odd conceits, quirks, composed phrases, verses, exotical proverbs and the like'. The established church had placed considerable emphasis on preaching ability in appointments in the Fingal area earlier in the century though what practical effect they had is not known but from 1616, when the Capuchin mission to Ireland began, the Catholic church was able to compete in this aspect of evangelization. As well as being employed to encourage people to frequent the sacraments, the sermon was also used as a vehicle for bringing other Tridentine ideas into Ireland.

Mention has been made in chapter 6 of the fact that Catholics and Protestants ate, drank and socialized together in early seventeenth-century Fingal. There were many marriages between people on either side of the religious divide, at least at the higher levels of society. There was, however, a deep-seated hostility between the two groups which caused tensions in society. These tensions found their expression in several ways but most clearly after the accommodations between the two groups had broken down after the outbreak of war in 1641. Catholics still hoped to recover the churches and priories, such as Christ Church cathedral and Holmpatrick priory, lost at the time of the Reformation. As already mentioned the celebration of Mass at these sites was one of the insurgents' great ambitions. Queen Elizabeth, too, had attracted opprobrium. 'Delahide of Rush', probably Thomas Delahide of Loughshinny, told Daniel Barwick, when he was a prisoner in Baldongan castle in 1642 that ' "he doth wonder that the Church of England should canonize Queen Elizabeth for a saint she being a damned whore" and other impious words against that blessed princess, not fit to be spoken or written'.[121] This was too much even for the commissioners for, in a longer and more formal version of the deposition drawn up two days later on 23 May 1642, Barwick's account was altered to read 'that one, Delahide of Rush aforesaid, gentleman, did, in this deponent's presence, give most base reports and words against the late Queen Elizabeth of famous memory; which he can, yet is ashamed to, express ...'[122]

One of the earliest indications of sectarian conflict during the rising came about when a Protestant named William Apsley, who when about to set out from Dublin early in November 1641 with others who were licensed to serve in Spain as soldiers under the command of a Colonel Barry, made a complaint to the authorities.[123] He stated that he (Apsley) had told his companions that he would like to have been with the rebels in the north in order to have surprised them. He accused his lieutenant, Luke Marriott, an English Catholic, who had been agent for the father of James Plunket of Dunsoghly, of saying that he, too, wished they had been with the rebels 'that then they would make some of the Protestants smoke and alleged that they (meaning the Protestants) had money enough and it were a good deed to cut their throats'. He went on to allege that Marriott 'did behave himself towards the examinant and such other Protestants as were ashipboard, under his command, very violent and bitter, not suffering them to go to prayers'.[124] Marriott was imprisoned

121 Deposition of Daniel Barwick, 21 May 1642 (TCD, MS 810, f. 112). 122 Deposition of Daniel Barwick, 23 May 1642 (TCD, MS 810, f. 115). 123 Examination of William Apsley, 7 November 1641 (TCD, MS 809, f. 127); examination of Luke Marriott, 8 November 1641 (TCD, MS 809, f. 128); petition of Luke Marriott, not dated, endorsed 6 November 1641 (TCD, MS 809, f. 130). 124 Examination

but denied these charges, made counter-charges against Apsley and appealed against his imprisonment to the lords justices and council.[125] While the outcome of this incident is not known it shows the potential for conflict that existed. On 23 November 1641 Thomas Waring made a deposition before Sir James Ware in which he stated that one of Ware's tenants, John Sephton of Finglas, a Protestant, who had aroused suspicions because of the company he kept, had told him 'that the enemies would be too strong for the Protestants and that they grew every day stronger and that he knew by divers papists whom he did usually recourse with that the Protestants would be destroyed'.[126] These reports and allegations made by Apsley and Waring show that there was considerable tension in the area associated with religion. Well before the rising took place Protestants in Dublin and Fingal were quite ready to believe, with some justification, that they would be forced to embrace Catholicism.[127] John Lukey, minister of Ballyboghil, reported that

> about nine months before the rebellion began, Sebastian Finglas of the Murragh, near Ballyboghil ... (being a wilful papist) wished this deponent divers times to turn to his religion for the papists should shortly universally reign in Ireland and he waited for the time every day and knew it would be very shortly: and then all Protestant ministers must become schoolmasters or mechanics. And ... about six weeks before the rebellion began one, William Bucklie, the clerk of Lusk, told this deponent that he heard one Mr Fitzwilliam of Baldongan, gentleman (in an alehouse at Lusk) say that he did hope shortly to see every minister's neck as long as his arms.

Needless to say the Protestant people of Fingal felt even more threatened after the rising broke out. On 11 December 1641 the inhabitants of Clontarf pillaged a barque 'and, when one, Evers, and a miller came to help to save the goods, they fell upon them and wounded the miller to death and caused Evers for fear of losing his life to turn papist'.[128] Susanna Stockdale, having refused her cousin's, Nicholas Barnewall's, offer of hospitality at Turvey 'because she was confident that popish priests and rebels would haunt his house' went on to depose that

> the countess, his wife, replied in some angry and scornful words: 'No, no, I am glad of it, for God would never bless the house if you were in it in regard of your religion, And then one, Father John, her popish priest or friar (being present) answered: "No, no, there can none work upon her, she hath been long enough in handling, but none could convert her" or to that effect.[129]

Protestants bitterly resented the attempts made by Catholics to convert them.

of William Apsley, 7 November 1641 (TCD, MS 809, f. 127). **125** Examination of Luke Marriott, 8 November 1641 (TCD, MS 809, f. 128); petition of Luke Marriott, not dated, endorsed 6 November 1641 (TCD, MS 809, f. 130). **126** Examination of Thomas Waring, 23 November 1641 (TCD, MS 809, f. 208). **127** Examination of Peter Fletcher, 11 December 1641 (TCD, MS 809, f. 210). **128** Examination of David Powell, 14 December 1641 (TCD, MS 809, f. 214). **129** Deposition of Susanna Stockdale (copy only), not dated (TCD, MS 810, f. 95).

Perhaps the most comprehensive account both of the fears of the Protestants and the ambitions of the Catholics in the area appears in the deposition of Edward Leech.[130] Leech was in charge of the castle of Lambay Island when it was invaded by a group of men from the Rush and Skerries areas, under the command of John O'Malony (a friar), more usually referred to in the depositions as the 'Friar Malone'. The relevant portion of the deposition reads as follows:

> Immediately upon the landing of the said friar in the island he sent to this deponent a letter without date offering this deponent quarter (if he would leave all to him) vowing by the Almighty, if he refused his gracious offer, to kill man, woman and child belonging to the said deponent. Soon after the said friar came up to the castle and told this deponent what he must trust unto. And this deponent being unable to resist (his own servants and the whole tenants of the island being papists leaving him) he submitted to the friar's pleasure ... He also saith that the said friar showed this deponent two commissions (which, as he alleged, were from the king of Spain) sealed with crucifixes which he said was to authorise him to do what he did. And the said friar took a Mass book out of his pocket and swore by the contents thereof, that he was the first man that drew the plot for the present rebellion in Ireland and that he himself in person had acquainted the pope and all the kings in Christendom therewith, except the king of England and the king of Denmark, and that some colonels in Dublin had had money of him, for to raise men for Spain and that he had kept them aboard for some time within the harbour of Dublin and that it was resolved by them, meaning the Catholic army, that not the spawn of an English Protestant should be left in Ireland very shortly ... He also said that they had both powder and ordnance making in Ireland, and when the deponent desired his Bible, which the said friar took from him with other books, he refused to give it, but told this deponent that he was sworn to burn all the Protestant Bibles that came to his hands. The said friar used many persuasions to this deponent and his wife to turn to their religion and promised them, that if they would so do, they should go with him to the house of Mr Barnewall of Bremore, and fair no worse than he did, and that if they would try, if they liked it not, he would leave them safe at the walls of Dublin, which this deponent refused ...

The deposition of John Huxley of Rush, described as a 'British Protestant', told that Malone displayed similar attitudes towards other Protestants:

> And this deponent further saith: that one Malone (who, as he heard, is a friar) and called himself the chaplain major to the Irish host, about the 6 of December last, 1641, said that he was the beginner of this rebellion, and that it cost him to bring it to pass three and twenty thousand pounds, the said Malone did say that this deponent and his wife should be both hanged by him,

130 Deposition of Edward Leech, 18 March 1644 (TCD, MS 810, ff 244–5).

> that there might be none of their breed left, but with much entreaty of a gentlewoman Mr James Russell's wife (falling upon her knees unto him to spare their lives) he was contented, but gave present order to take away all their corn and goods and to send it to the army called the Irish host.[131]

As the rising progressed the rift between Catholics and Protestants widened. In 1653 a servant, Mary Medowes, who was a witness at the trial of the Balrothery priest, Robert Passmore, for the murder of two ministers, Robert and Ambrose Burton, in 1642 told the court that John Finglas and others came to her master's house and told him 'that they had taken two black divils and were going to see them hanged'.[132]

Catholics as well as Protestants felt threatened. While enjoying an uneasy peace they had at intervals throughout the period leading up to 1641 witnessed at close quarters many traumatic events which reminded them that they were a subordinate group in society. Henry Fitzsimon was imprisoned for five years in the early years of the century.[133] Sir Patrick Barnewall and others were imprisoned in Dublin Castle and Henry Burnell, an old man, was placed under house arrest in 1605.[134] Robert Lalor, vicar-general of the archdiocese of Dublin, was arrested in 1606, attainted of *praemunire* for advancing foreign jurisdiction.[135] Cornelius O'Devany, bishop of Down and Connor, was hanged near Oxmantown in 1612.[136] Francis Taylor of Swords died in 1621 after seven years' imprisonment.[137] During the period 1629 to 1631 the government made a determined and generally successful, if temporary, effort to close Mass-houses and the houses of religious orders.[138]

Catholics also wanted to recover the status which they believed they had lost. In Fingal, at least, their hostility was directed against Protestants rather than against non-natives. Provided the Protestants embraced Catholicism they would be accepted. Many critical decisions were made on the basis of religious affiliation. The tenants of Lambay, when faced with a choice between supporting their landlord's agent or siding with their co-religionists, chose the latter course. In Rush, John Huxley's plough-holder took part in the raid on his property, while in Skerries it was alleged that two of Dirrick Huiberts Verveer's tenants were implicated in his murder.[139]

One way in which the tensions between Protestants and Catholics were perpetuated was through the tales that were told by clergymen about the opposing groups. Many of these stories were set in the locality or related to local families. For example,

131 Deposition of John Huxley, 21 May 1642 (TCD, MS 810, f. 158). 132 Proceedings of the high court of justice held at Dublin and Cork in 1652, 1653 and 1654 (TCD, MS 866, f. 31). 133 Edmund Hogan, *Distinguished Irishmen of the sixteenth century* (London, 1894), p. 232. 134 Documents of the seventeenth century, relative to the city of Dublin, transcribed by H.R. Hamilton, Esquire, from the originals in State Paper Office, London (Gilbert Library, MS 83, no. 9). 135 Richard Bolton, *A justice of peace for Ireland* ... (Dublin, 1638), book 3, pp 66–7; Patrick F. Moran, *History of the Catholic archbishops of Dublin since the Reformation* (Dublin, 1864), pp 219–20; Colm Lennon, *The lords of Dublin in the age of reformation* (Dublin, 1989), pp 185 and 214–15. 136 Patrick J. Corish, *The Catholic community in the seventeenth and eighteenth centuries* (Dublin, 1981), p. 30; Colm Lennon, *The lords of Dublin in the age of reformation* (Dublin, 1989), pp 197–8. 137 Patrick J. Corish, *The Catholic community in the seventeenth and eighteenth centuries* (Dublin, 1981), p. 30. 138 Aidan Clarke, *The Old English in Ireland, 1625–42* (paperback ed., Dublin, 2000), pp 61–2. 139 Deposition of Anthony Huiberts, 29 January 1642 (TCD, MS 809, f. 311).

Catholics must have been horrified at Henry Fitzsimon's account of 'Waller the murderer, under-minister of Swords, who in the year 1603, hanged on a gibbet the image of Christ crucified'.[140] Sometimes these stories were constructed so as to ensure that the readers or listeners were aware that there had been divine intervention to punish wrong doers (often Protestants). Henry Fitzsimon told that his rival's (the Revd Mr Rider's) son, when he attempted to pull down an image, was 'by God's judgement precipitated from a height and altogether crushed', and at the same time his servant was stricken with the plague.[141] Almost as vivid was the account given by another Jesuit, Christopher Hollywood, concerning an incident involving some Drogheda Catholics which took place off Skerries in 1606:

> On the feast of SS. Simon and Jude [28 October], while a Calvinist captain of a vessel was uttering blasphemies against these apostles of Christ, a north-east wind arose, and tore his vessel from its moorings off the Island of St Patrick, between Dublin and Drogheda and the crew had to run her against the shore in order to save their lives . . .[142]

The story told in 1607 by Henry Fitzsimon concerning the vision of Our Lady seen by Mrs Bellings, mother of Sir Henry Bellings, in 1580 and the subsequent miraculous appearance of a secret cellar designed to hide a priest, Patrick Nigram, from his pursuers was, no doubt intended to encourage the women of the area to continue to succour and protect their priests.[143] While religious beliefs and practices played a major part in raising the level of tension in seventeenth-century Fingal they were not the only factors. Economics also played a part. The established church was, itself, the owner of about half the land in the area. Tithes, which were exacted, at least in theory, to support the established church, were also an important element in economic life. Once the rising had taken place there was little hope for reconciliation between the religious factions. Local events, such as the massacre following the siege of Baldongan in 1642, left a mark on the people. Like other events in the area responsibility for this action would ultimately be associated with Cromwell in local folklore thus ensuring that the antagonism would be prolonged and perpetuated. Even when peace was restored the people of Fingal were still far from enjoying the 'merry meeting and gathering together of the dispersed' so longed for by Robert Bysse.

140 Edmund Hogan, *Distinguished Irishmen of the sixteenth century* (London, 1894), p. 236. **141** Edmund Hogan, *Distinguished Irishmen of the sixteenth century* (London, 1894), p. 236. **142** Fr. Christopher Hollywood to Fr. Aquaviva, 27 November 1606 in *Words of comfort to persecuted Catholics* . . . (Dublin, 1881), pp 148–9. **143** Henry Fitzsimon, *Words of comfort to persecuted Catholics* . . . (Dublin, 1881), p. 20.

Part III

Neighbours at war

9

'Universal desolation'

'... they pillage all the Pale as far as to Drogheda, till the two armies at Drogheda and Dublin could see each other, and rejoice for so doing: they burned all the lord's houses in the Pale and gentlemen's, and fired all the whole Pale ...'

March 1642[1]

'... The last night the country towards Drogheda seemed as one fire, there were above 200 fires counted by some who were on St Owen's [Audeon's] steeple ...'

Sir Maurice Eustace, November 1647[2]

The two extracts just quoted referred to different years and to different armies which had, however, a common purpose, the devastation of the Pale, particularly that part of it north of Dublin city towards Drogheda which included Fingal. The first extract described the devastation carried out by Ormond's troops in the immediate aftermath of the rising of 1641. The second, written while the fires were still burning, recounted the equally horrific destruction of the Pale by Eoghan Rua O'Neill following the defeat of the Leinster army at Dungan's Hill. In words which summed up the general experience of the ordinary people of Fingal during the 1640s and 1650s Sir Maurice Eustace wrote of O'Neill that 'he spareth none of what religion soever: all are alike to him'.[3] The tragedy of this second episode is compounded by the fact that there is evidence to suggest that O'Neill carried out the orders of the supreme council at Kilkenny with reluctance and went about his task unwillingly if efficiently.[4]

The history of the political élite during the period 1603 to 1660 in Fingal can be divided into two phases.[5] The first of these saw the emergence of strong and effective local Catholic leadership, lay and clerical, in the face of government opposition and even oppression, giving the impression of a close integrated traditional society where consensus was the norm. The second phase was marked, on the Catholic side, by the diffusion of leadership among several groups, by the growth of a militant

1 *April the first, 1642: a continuation of the tryumphant and couragious proceedings of the protestant army in Ireland* (London, 1642), p. 1 (NLI, Lough Fea pamphlet no. 109). 2 Sir Maurice Eustace to Ormond, 4 November 1647, in John T. Gilbert (ed.), *History of the Irish confederation and the war in Ireland, 1641–3 ...* (7 vols, Dublin, 1882–91), vi, pp 206–7. 3 Sir Maurice Eustace to Ormond, 4 November 1647, in John T. Gilbert (ed.), *History of the Irish confederation and the war in Ireland, 1641–3 ...* (7 vols, Dublin, 1882–91), vi, p. 207. 4 *The history of the warr of Ireland from 1641 to 1653 ...*, ed. Edmund Hogan (Dublin, 1873), pp 62–3. 5 For a detailed discussion of politics and leadership in Fingal in the period 1603–60 see 'Fingal 1603–60', i, pp 319–82.

clergy and, finally, by a failure in war that was probably as much due to geography – proximity to Dublin city – as anything else. On the Protestant side it was marked by a growth in self-confidence and a remarkable ability to survive and accommodate to the various political, religious and economic changes which took place. For a very brief period, in 1640–1, it looked as if the two sides might come together but this hope was shattered by the outbreak of war.

Writing about the approach of historians to the 1641 rising in an essay published in 1995, Nicholas Canny pointed out that 'the thrust of the scholarly endeavour has been to explain why 1641 occurred rather than to consider what happened'.[6] This chapter attempts to record, insofar as the sources will allow, what happened in Fingal and how the rising and its consequences affected Fingallians. There is a rich, if patchy, range of sources available, which include the 1641 depositions, a wide range of contemporary pamphlets, government papers, particularly those in the Ormonde and Egmont collections, and some near-contemporary histories, including those by John Temple and Richard Bellings of Mulhuddart and the *Commentarius Rinuccinianus*.[7] Some periods of the war, such as the first few months of the rising, are well covered for Fingal. Others, such as the early 1650s, in which several tory raids took place in Fingal, have much poorer surviving coverage, which is due, in part, to the loss of the Commonwealth records and, partly, to the paucity of Catholic sources at a period when few priests and religious managed to remain in the area.

One reason, perhaps, why historians in the past found it difficult to cope with the complexity of the period was the lack of tools to analyze the vast amount of material which has survived. There was no shortage of palaeographical skills as can be seen from the work of the many scholars who engaged in the controversies surrounding the 1641 depositions. Missing were those sophisticated data analysis tools which have become generally available in the recent past. It is only now becoming possible to compile the types of databases which, for all practical purposes, were unavailable to historians in the past. These facilitate the analysis of relationships and point up patterns which are not always obvious to us in the original narratives of those who participated in the rising, whether as activists, victims or observers, though no doubt, the participants themselves took these relationships and patterns for granted. When the various events which took place in the 1640s are listed it is striking, for example, to note the important part played by such mundane factors as the weather in the conduct of the war.

Since the depositions (sometimes in a highly selective form) have formed a high proportion of the source material available for the 1641/2 period the emphasis of commentators over the centuries, depending on their agenda, has fluctuated between condemnation (or justification) of the rebels and sympathy for their victims. Until

6 Nicholas Canny, 'What really happened in Ireland in 1641?', in Jane H. Ohlmeyer (ed.), *Ireland from independence to occupation 1641–1660* (Cambridge, 1995), p. 26. 7 TCD, MSS 809 and 810; Historical Manuscripts Commission, *Calendar of the manuscripts of the marquess of Ormonde* ... (new series, 8 vols, London, 1902–20); Historical Manuscripts Commission, *Report on the manuscripts of the earl of Egmont* (2 vols, London, 1905–9), i ; John Temple, *The Irish rebellion ... in the year 1641* (originally published London, 1646, reprinted London, 1746); Richard Bellings, *History of the Irish confederation and the war in Ireland, 1641–3* ..., ed. John T. Gilbert (7 vols, Dublin, 1882–91) i-ii; Richard O'Ferrall and Robert O'Connell, *Commentarius Rinuccinianus* ..., ed. Stanislaus Kavanagh (6 vols, Dublin, 1932–49).

recently, the interplay between attacker and victim has been somewhat neglected. While it is clear that an area of the size of Fingal is too large to enable the relationships between attackers and victims to be examined adequately some attempt will be made to examine this process for one part of the area by means of case studies.

Before examining in detail the events which took place in Fingal during the war some general comments may be in order. Once the leaders of the Catholic gentry of the Pale had formally decided to take part in the rising they organized their forces and their chains of command on an county basis and, as far as one can judge from the information available, within counties on a barony or regional basis. Initially, meetings, rather similar to hostings, were held at, for example, Swords in Co. Dublin, Knockcrofty and Tara in Co. Meath. and Tullyeskar in Co. Louth.[8] Although the rising in the Pale was initially organized on a county basis, and within counties, on a regional basis, it is impossible to describe its progress adequately by confining the analysis strictly to such boundaries. Precise details of the structure and organization of the rebel army are not available for Co. Dublin but it is possible to reconstruct them to some degree and to reach some general conclusions by analogy with the arrangements in counties Meath and Louth, by an analysis of background information relating to participants (where these are known) in some of incidents which took place and by examining some fragments of evidence which survive in the 1641 depositions. The evidence, such as it is, points to a strong local influence on the organization during the early stages of the war. This inevitably lessened as a formal provincial army structure developed under the Catholic Confederation and as large set-piece battles replaced sporadic raids on individual homes, farms and ships.

Another characteristic of the war in Fingal, though undoubtedly it was not unique to the region, was the speed with which a train of events, once set in motion, gathered momentum. While this is perhaps explicable in the case of a spontaneous popular uprising, it is less easy to understand in an environment such as that in which the Fingal gentry lived, where peace, support for the *status quo* and a general respect for the law had long been the norm and had survived many periods of pressure, particularly in regard to religion. As long as the people and the government were working in cooperation ease of access to Dublin, Drogheda and Britain was an advantage. When this relationship broke down Fingal, lying between two garrison towns and bounded by the sea on one side, was very vulnerable to attack from outside. Nevertheless those members of the gentry, who had assembled at the behest of Luke Nettervill, organized themselves quickly and showed an ability to react swiftly to unfolding events. This suggests that there had been a good deal of planning, or at least thinking, not just about how a military insurrection might be conducted but also on how to deal with the various eventualities which might arise.

Another feature of the war in Fingal was the non-emergence of any single dominant leader comparable to, say, Nicholas Preston, Viscount Gormanston, in Co. Meath. The reason for this probably lies in the fact that some landowners, for example, Lord Gormanston himself and the earls of Thomond and Ormond, were

8 Aidan Clarke, *The Old English in Ireland, 1625–42* (paperback ed., Dublin, 2000), pp 180–3; Harold O'Sullivan, *John Bellew, a seventeenth-century man of many parts* (Dublin, 2000), pp 31–2.

not resident within the territory and that the more important resident landowners such as the lord of Howth, Sir Henry Power of Valentia of Chapelizod, Nicholas Barnewall of Turvey, Simon Luttrell of Luttrellstown and John Talbot of Malahide, as well as the authorities of the established church, either took no part in the rising or supported the government side. This vacuum was filled in a number of ways. One rather surprising feature was the prominence of leaders from Co. Meath during the early stages of the popular rising in Fingal. On closer examination some of these men have been found to have been proprietors or lessees in Fingal. One such proprietor, Luke Nettervill, the nominal leader of the Co. Dublin gentry, organized the initial revolt of the gentry as well as the early military action. A number of priest-captains emerged as popular leaders in Fingal. One man who did not fit neatly into any category and perhaps the most unlikely leader of all was the talented young proprietor and former law student, John Finglas of Westpalstown, who was responsible for Fingal's unique military contribution to the war, namely, the highly mobile cavalry unit known as the *slua beag*.

Three main strands can be detected in the 1641 rising in Fingal. The first involved a small number of people acting on a national and international stage among whom Richard Plunket of Dunsoghly and Friar John Malone of Skerries were the most prominent in the early stages. The second included the gentry under Luke Nettervill together with those units under professional soldiers which later became part of General Thomas Preston's Leinster army and, eventually, the Confederate army. The third consisted of a number of bands of local people, organized and unorganized, sometimes under local leaders, including priest-captains, but occasionally apparently operating as unorganized mobs without any clearly-defined leadership.

A number of modern historians have considered aspects of the events immediately leading up to the outbreak of the rising of 1641.[9] In particular, Michael Perceval-Maxwell has made a detailed examination of the plots which led to the actual outbreak. He stated:

> There were, in all probability, two major plots, one devised by the Old English and the second by a combination of Irish leaders, including Rory O'More, most of whose estate lay in Armagh, Conor, Lord Maguire, of County Fermanagh, and the O'Neills of County Armagh. This second conspiracy was assisted by some elements of the Catholic church. In addition, there was a third plot, almost certainly inspired by Owen Roe O'Neill from the Netherlands. This included a plan to seize Dublin Castle and involved some of the colonels who were recruiting troops for Spain. Owen Roe also tried to persuade some of his relatives in Ulster to join a rising. By the end of August O'More's plot and that involving the colonels had become intertwined.[10]

9 For example, Aidan Clarke, *The Old English in Ireland, 1625–42* (paperback ed., Dublin, 2000), pp 153–61; Aidan Clarke, 'The genesis of the Ulster rising of 1641' in Peter Roebuck (ed.), *Plantation to partition: essays in Ulster history in honour of J.L. McCracken* (Belfast, 1981), pp 29–45; Raymond Gillespie, 'The end of an era: Ulster and the outbreak of the 1641 rising' in Ciaran Brady and Raymond Gillespie (ed.), *Natives and newcomers: essays on the making of Irish colonial society, 1534–1641* (Dublin, 1986) pp 191–213; Michael Perceval-Maxwell, *The outbreak of the Irish rebellion of 1641* (Dublin, 1994), pp 192–212. **10** Michael Perceval-Maxwell, *The outbreak of the Irish rebellion of 1641* (Dublin,

The first of these plots was overtaken by events. Perceval-Maxwell pointed out that the 'plan to use the Irish army, to seek another, and to assert independence from the English parliament could be set aside'.[11] As has been shown by Perceval-Maxwell and others, the details of the Ulster plot in the immediate run-up to the rising have been well documented. There is also a great deal of information about the involvement of Eoghan Rua O'Neill in the 'third plot'. A topic which remains to be examined is the clerical network both in Ireland and on the continent which linked these plots. Such an examination is beyond the scope of this study but it is clear that one figure whose actions merit further study was the Franciscan friar, John Barnewall, second son of Lord Trimleston of Co. Meath, who was provincial of the Franciscan order in Ireland from August 1638 to August 1641.[12] He later became guardian of the Franciscan house in Dublin.[13] He was a confidant of the Pale gentry, the colonels who had been recruiting troops for Spain and Conor, Lord Maguire.[14]

According to information given by several deponents a rising of some kind had been planned for a very long time. In a conversation with John Kerdiff in December 1641 John Malone (O'Malony), known generally as the Friar Malone, claimed that he had been 'fourteen years employed to bring this design to pass'.[15] However, despite the fact that he was to play a major part in the rising in the north-east of Fingal, no evidence has been found to suggest that the Friar Malone had any earlier connection with the area. One of the key figures in the 'third plot', Richard Plunket of Dunsoghly, told John Kerdiff at Armagh that he had been implicated in the plot for seven years.[16] If this was true, it would place the earliest known Fingallian involvement in the preparations for a rising as far back as 1634. Richard Plunket, a younger son of Sir Christopher Plunket of Dunsoghly, was a professional soldier.[17] As early as February 1632 he was in Spanish Flanders, where he was granted thirty crowns monthly as a captain in the regiment of the earl of Tirconnell.[18] Not long afterwards he sought further warrants to recruit men.[19] His companion in this enterprise was Thomas Preston of Gormanstown, later to become commander-in-chief of the Leinster forces. In January 1634 he was granted permission to go to Ireland to recruit for the earl's regiment which was 'weak in numbers' and in March 1636 he obtained a similar licence, this time to recruit for the regiment of Colonel Thomas Preston.[20] Two months later recruiting in Ireland was banned, and in November, Plunket's company together with others of Preston's regiment were ordered to be

1994), pp 199–200. **11** Michael Perceval-Maxwell, *The outbreak of the Irish rebellion of 1641* (Dublin, 1994), p. 203. **12** Brendan Jennings, 'Irish names in the Malines ordination registers, 1602–1794' in *The Irish Ecclesiastical Record*, lxxv, no. 2 (February, 1951), pp 154–5; Stephen B. Barnwell, 'The Barnewall family during the sixteenth and seventeenth centuries (part iv)' in *The Irish Genealogist*, iii, no. 8 (October 1963), p. 318. **13** Stephen B. Barnwell, 'The Barnewall family during the sixteenth and seventeenth centuries (part iv)' in *The Irish Genealogist*, iii, no. 8 (October 1963), pp 318–19. **14** John T. Gilbert (ed.), *A contemporary history of affairs in Ireland from A. D. 1641 to 1652 ...* (3 vols, Dublin, 1879–80), i, part ii, pp 498 and 504; Mary Hickson, *Ireland in the seventeenth century ...* (2 vols, London, 1884), ii, pp 344–5; Michael Perceval-Maxwell, *The outbreak of the Irish rebellion of 1641* (Dublin, 1994), p. 207. **15** Deposition of John Kerdiff, 28 February 1642 (TCD, MS 839, f. 4). **16** Deposition of John Kerdiff, 28 February 1642 (TCD, MS 839, f. 4). **17** *Cal. S. P. Ire., 1625–32*, p. 676. **18** *Wild geese in Spanish Flanders, 1582–1700 ...*, ed. Brendan Jennings (Dublin, 1964), entry 1194, p. 261. **19** *Cal. S. P. Ire., 1625–32*, p. 676; *Wild geese in Spanish Flanders, 1582–1700 ...*, ed. Brendan Jennings (Dublin, 1964), note to entry 1188, p. 570. **20** *Wild geese in Spanish Flanders, 1582–1700 ...*, ed. Brendan Jennings (Dublin, 1964), entries 1238, p. 266 and 1378, p. 288.

disbanded because of lack of manpower.[21] On 29 December 1636 Plunket, who had been in London since March, returned to Flanders 'unsuccessful and looking for money'.[22]

There were two Fingallians, Richard Plunket and Christopher Bellings of Mulhuddart, among the nine colonels granted permission to recruit regiments from Wentworth's disbanded army in 1641 for service in the Spanish army.[23] Bellings left in July with 1,000 men.[24] He played no further part in the history of Fingal. Richard Plunket, on the other hand, frustrated in his military ambitions, became deeply involved in the plans for the rising and, in particular, in the plan to seize Dublin Castle.[25] He was fortunate to escape 'over the river' from the city on the night of 22 October or early the following morning after the plot had been discovered.[26] He arrived at the house of a relative, Laurence Dowdall of Athlumney, Co. Meath, about midnight on 24 October and, having reassured his cousins, he departed, arriving in Virginia on 28 October.[27] Appointed by Sir Phelim O'Neill as lieutenant-general of Leinster in a commission dated 1641 he subsequently played an important part in the rising, though not primarily in Fingal where Luke Nettervill took command.[28] Plunket was typical of the small band of experienced professional soldiers, including Colonels Dillon and Byrne (who had been in contact with Eoghan Rua O'Neill), who, with Conor, Lord Maguire, planned a rising on a national scale in July 1641.[29] After the rising had broken out in Ulster other disparate groups initiated the movement within Fingal. Subsequent to the outbreak there were two, often overlapping, parties involved in the conflict on the Irish side in that area, a reasonably well-disciplined group of soldiers led by the local gentry and other more lawless bands, sometimes led by priests.

When reading the early examinations and depositions, and those later depositions which described the early days of the rising, it is often difficult to distinguish between fact and rumour. As the deposition of John Lukey of Ballyboghil showed, rumours of impending trouble were rife long before the outbreak though how significant these rumours were at the time they circulated is hard to judge.[30] Lukey stated:

> that about nine months before the rebellion began, this deponent being at supper with Sebastian Finglas of the Murragh, near Ballyboghil, gentleman: and the said Finglas and this deponent falling into some discourse concerning

21 *Wild geese in Spanish Flanders, 1582–1700 …*, ed. Brendan Jennings (Dublin, 1964), entries 1410, p. 291 and 1444, p. 295. 22 *Wild geese in Spanish Flanders, 1582–1700 …*, ed. Brendan Jennings (Dublin, 1964), entries 1455 and 1456, p. 296. 23 Aidan Clarke, *The Old English in Ireland, 1625–42* (paperback ed., Dublin, 2000), p. 154. 24 Aidan Clarke, *The Old English in Ireland, 1625–42* (paperback ed., Dublin, 2000), p. 154. 25 Aidan Clarke, *The Old English in Ireland, 1625–42* (paperback ed., Dublin, 2000), pp 157–8. 26 *The history of the warr of Ireland from 1641 to 1653 …*, ed. Edmund Hogan (Dublin, 1873), p. 11. 27 Examination of William Cadogan, 16 March 1644 (TCD, MS 816, f. 223); Deposition of George Creichton, 15 April 1643 (TCD, MS 832, f. 146; MS 833, f. 228; John T. Gilbert (ed.), *A contemporary history of affairs in Ireland from A. D. 1641 to 1652 …* (3 vols, Dublin, 1879–80), i, part ii, p. 527. 28 Deposition of George Creichton, 15 April 1643 (TCD, MS 832, ff 146–8; MS 833, ff 228–9; John T. Gilbert (ed.), *A contemporary history of affairs in Ireland from A. D. 1641 to 1652 …* (3 vols, Dublin, 1879–80), i, part ii, pp 527–9; Aidan Clarke, *The Old English in Ireland, 1625–42* (paperback ed., Dublin, 2000), p. 168; Pádraig Lenihan, *Confederate Catholics at war, 1641–49* (Cork, 2001), pp 33–4 and 198. 29 Michael Perceval-Maxwell, *The outbreak of the Irish rebellion of 1641* (Dublin, 1994), pp 208–9. 30 Deposition of John Lukey, 2 March 1643 (TCD, MS 810, f. 168).

> their religion: he, the said Finglas (being a wilful papist) wished this deponent divers times to turn to his religion for that papists should shortly universally reign in Ireland and he waited for the time every day and knew it would be very shortly: and then all Protestant ministers must become schoolmasters or mechanics. And further saith that about six weeks before the rebellion began one William Bucklie, the clerk of Lusk, told this deponent, that he heard one Mr [blank] Fitzwilliams of Baldongan, gentleman (in an alehouse at Lusk) say: that he did hope shortly to see every minister's neck as long as his arms.

Sebastian Finglas has not been identified, but he may have been a relative of the proprietor of the Murragh (parish of Westpalstown), the young John Finglas, who was later to play a prominent part in the war as lieutenant-general of horse.[31] Thomas Fitzwilliam of Baldongan leased Baldongan from the lord of Howth.[32] A son of Nicholas Fitzwilliam, he was related to the major families of Howth, Gormanston and Fitzwilliam of Merrion.[33]

All those travelling from Ulster to take part in the planned attack on Dublin Castle on 23 October 1641, unless they chose a very circuitous route, would have had to travel through Fingal. Since 23 October fell on a Saturday, market day, there were also many uninvolved travellers in the city. One such was the thirteen-year-old Francis McMurrohye of Dundalk who, if his story can be believed, was simply acting as a courier for Franciscan friars.[34] One of the places he visited during the week preceding the outbreak of the rising was the home of Hollywood of Artaine whose family was deeply implicated in the subsequent fighting.[35] The unease which existed in the area is well exemplified in the series of incidents, already mentioned, involving the drinking companions, both Catholic and Protestant, in Finglas.[36] Two of those who conducted their examinations, Sir Richard Bolton, the chancellor, and Sir James Ware, held considerable amounts of property in Fingal (though the Civil Survey listed much of Bolton's estate as the property of his son and heir, Sir Edward Bolton), while the third, Sir Gerard Lowther, leased a small amount of land in Finglas.[37] They were well equipped to assess the importance of the information which was being presented to them. The first of these examinations was conducted by Sir James Ware as early as Thursday, 4 November 1641.[38] Robert Davy of Jamestown, one of the properties leased by Ware, reported that 'about the five and twentieth of October last ... very early in the morning' John Sephton, also of Jamestown, with William Rowen and others had resolved to 'go to the army of the enemies to see in what state they stood'. There is a somewhat puzzling reference to

31 *Civil Survey, vii, county of Dublin,* pp 42–4. 32 *Civil Survey, vii, county of Dublin,* p. 67. 33 Francis Elrington Ball, *A history of the County Dublin: the people, parishes and antiquities from the earliest times to the close of the eighteenth century: part second* (originally published 1903, reprinted Dublin, 1995), p. 10. 34 Examination of Francis McMurrohye, 8 November 1641 (TCD, MS 809, f. 144). 35 Robert Bysse, junior, to John Bysse, 16 February 1642 (TCD, MS 840, ff 8–9). 36 Examination of Robert Davy, 4 November 1641 (TCD, MS 809, f. 99); examination of John Sephton, 15 November 1641 (TCD, MS 809, f. 176); examination of William Rowen, 19 November 1641 (TCD, MS 809, f. 188); examination of Richard Delahide, 19 November 1641 (TCD, MS 809, f. 198); examination of Thomas Waring, 23 November 1641 (TCD, MS 809, f. 208). 37 *Civil Survey, vii, county of Dublin,* pp 81, 163, 218 and 254 (indexes). 38 Examination of Robert Davy, 4 November 1641 (TCD, MS 809, f. 99).

'the troop which was about Santry [which] was taken up to his majesty's use' and to Sephton's alleged remark that 'if they had not been taken up when they were, they had been taken another way'. While this reference is somewhat unclear it may refer to one of the bands of disbanded soldiers roaming in the vicinity of the capital during this period.

While the notoriously hard-drinking Sephton appears as the central figure in this and subsequent examinations it may be more useful to focus on the role played by William Rowen. The surname 'Rowen' has not been found in the hearth money roll for Fingal compiled *c.*1664.[39] The only entry for a similar name is that of 'John Rone' who lived in the Grange of Portmarnock.[40] Bearing in mind the fact that impoverished people and tax-evaders did not appear on the hearth money roll, it nevertheless seems reasonable to conclude that the name was unusual in Fingal. It is likely, therefore, that there was some relationship between William Rowen and Laurence Rowen of Finglas, one of the most notorious of the priest-captains to emerge in Fingal, whose exploits will be described later. According to the story told by Sephton to Robert Davy, Rowen and others had promised on Saturday, 30 October, to give Sephton 'as good a horse as any was about Finglas to go with them to help the enemy'.[41] Eleven days elapsed before the examination of John Sephton on Monday, 15 November.[42] In a series of descriptions of his friends Sephton described Rowen as 'a butcher and a papist' but denied that he or anyone else had promised to give him a horse if he would go with him to help the enemy. Rowen himself was examined by Bolton and Lowther on Friday, 19 November, but his testimony did not add much to the story of a plot since, while admitting that he had been drinking with his friends 'upon Thursday last was fortnight' (4 November), he said that he did not remember that 'at that time or at any other time they had any discourse touching the rebellion in the north'. He also denied all knowledge of 'any plot or conspiracy for the taking or burning of the town of Finglas' and explained his visits to Santry and Swords as part of a search for a lost cow, which probably sounded plausible since he was a butcher.[43] Richard Delahide was interviewed on the same day by the same interviewers.[44] Like Rowen he admitted being present at the drinking session on 4 November but while he denied knowledge of any conspiracy to take Finglas he admitted that the rising in the north had been discussed by the group. Finally, Thomas Waring, who was not one of the group and to whom Sephton, a fellow-Protestant, owed money, made a short deposition before Sir James Ware in which he quoted Sephton as saying that 'this was a troublesome time and that the enemies would be too strong for the Protestants and that they grew every day stronger and stronger and that he knew by divers papists whom he did usually converse with that the Protestants would be destroyed'.[45] The outcome of these examinations is not known. They do, however, show how nervous the people were and how willing the

39 'Hearth money roll for County Dublin, 1664' (second part), *Journal of the County Kildare Archaeological Society*, xi (1930–33), pp 386–466. 40 'Hearth money roll for County Dublin, 1664' (second part), *Journal of the County Kildare Archaeological Society*, xi (1930–33), p. 390. 41 Examination of Robert Davy, 4 November 1641 (TCD, MS 809, f. 99). 42 Examination of John Sephton, 15 November 1641 (TCD, MS 809, f. 176). 43 Examination of William Rowen, 19 November 1641 (TCD, MS 809, f. 188). 44 Examination of Richard Delahide, 19 November 1641 (TCD, MS 809, f. 198). 45 Examination of Thomas Waring, 23 November 1641 (TCD, MS 809, f. 208).

government authorities were to spend a great deal of time investigating rumours of any description. It is noteworthy that none of the local men, who were, within a matter of days in some cases, to be recognized as captains of the rebels, were mentioned. While some of the early raids in Fingal were undoubtedly spontaneous the involvement of some important members of the local gentry, the rapid momentum with which the armed movement developed even prior to the formally-convened meeting which took place at Swords from 7–10 December and the careful selection of targets for attack suggest that some degree of local planning had taken place. If, indeed, such planning occurred, the secret was well kept.

The authorities apparently also failed to recognize the signals of forthcoming trouble which were evident in the reports of the fracas which took place following a drinking session at Cooper's Tavern in Oxmantown on 7 November 1641, when a sentinel was obstructed and threatened and, later that night, at the Dublin home of Nicholas Darcy of Platin.[46] Nicholas Darcy, a member of the Co. Meath gentry, was addressed in the tavern by another, Richard Birt (Brett ?), in the following terms: 'Marshal, spare this woman [Margaret Cooper, the vintner's wife] and her husband and do not cut their throats nor hang them for they are special friends of mine.'[47] Margaret Cooper noted that Birt addressed Darcy as 'marshal' and questioned them about this. She also observed that Darcy was very anxious to obtain her opinion on the military strength of the suburbs. Once again the outcome of the case is not known, though it would appear from the examinations that Darcy managed to restrain Richard Birt, the principle trouble-maker, sufficiently to maintain some credibility with the examiners who, once again, were Sir Richard Bolton and Sir Gerard Lowther.

The difficulties caused to and by disbanded soldiers and recruits waiting to be shipped abroad was documented in a number of the examinations.[48] Fearing mischief, the authorities made every effort to ensure that those already on board ship would be prevented from landing but, when they were threatened with starvation, 'the lords, having no means to victual them aboard, gave them leave to land, having first taken order they should not come into the city'.[49] While it cannot be said with certainty that any of these were involved in the rising it seems highly probable that, as they were banned from entering the city, many of them took part in the subsequent fighting in Fingal.

The response of the government to the events of 22 and 23 October in Dublin and the rising in Ulster was to arm selected prominent individuals with a view to protecting the Pale. This happened quickly as the action taken was reported by the lords

46 Examination of Henry Smith and Robert Caulfield, 8 November 1641 (TCD, MS 809, f. 134); examination of Laughlin Flood, 8 November 1641 (TCD, MS 809, f. 136); examination of Margaret Cooper, 8 November 1641 (TCD, MS 809, f. 138); examination of Nicholas Darcy, 8 November 1641 (TCD, MS 809, f. 140); examination of William Stowell, 8 November 1641 (TCD, MS 809, f. 145). 47 Examination of Margaret Cooper, 8 November 1641 (TCD, MS 809, f. 138). 48 Examination of Connor McCaffrey, 6 November 1641 (TCD, MS 809, f. 116); examination of William O'Murrohye, 6 November 1641 (TCD, MS 809, f. 125); examination of William Apsley, 7 November 1641 (TCD, MS 809, f. 127); examination of Luke Marriott, 8 November 1641 (TCD, MS 809, f. 128). petition of Luke Marriott, not dated, endorsed 6 November 1641 (TCD, MS 809, f. 130); examination of Edmund O'Murrohye, 8 November 1641 (TCD, MS 809, f. 146). 49 John Temple, *The Irish rebellion … in the year 1641* (originally published London, 1646, reprinted London, 1746), pp 83–4.

justices and council to the lords of the council in England on 5 November.[50] According to this account, the decision to allocate arms was taken at the request of the lords and gentry of the Pale. The choice as governor and commander for Co. Dublin fell on Nicholas Barnewall of Turvey, a prominent landowner, a long-standing member of parliament and a staunch Catholic.[51] His son-in-law, Viscount Gormanston, was selected for Co. Meath. The commissions granted to these and to prominent men in other counties required and authorized them to levy forces of horse and foot and 'with the said forces to resist, pursue, follow, apprehend, and put to death, slay and kill, as well by battle as other ways ... conspirators, traitors and their adherents'.[52] The government was short of arms with the result that the total number distributed was quite small. Barnewall received arms for only three hundred men for the county of Dublin.[53] It is not known whether Barnewall actually appointed officers or armed them. The speed with which the 'Catholic army' organized itself in Fingal, even before the formal appointment of captains at Swords during the period 7 to 10 December, would suggest that some kind of military structure had been put in place even though Barnewall himself took no part in the rising. Much later, in July 1654, Barnewall claimed:

> At the breaking out of the late rebellion his neighbours generally joined the enemy, and being unable to defend himself there, he retired to Dublin, where he shared the sufferings of the loyal. Shortly afterwards, having secured a garrison of Protestants and English for his house, which he maintained, he crossed to Wales with his family and lived there among his Protestant friends. The lords justices and council gave him letters saying he was a person deserving of favour.[54]

It is not clear if the garrison mentioned by Barnewall consisted of men levied by him in early November 1641. If it did, it seems rather surprising that there appears to be no record of either an attack on them by the rebels nor any attempt by them to suppress the rising.

Before reviewing the events at Swords and their consequences it is necessary to examine a series of incidents which began somewhat earlier. The robberies and appropriations carried out by the rebels from the commencement of the 1641 rising could have been interpreted and explained by contemporaries in a variety of ways. Their victims and the government clearly regarded them as criminal acts. However, this was not necessarily the way they were seen by the rebels though there were, no doubt, some persons among them who were simply interested in plunder. In many cases the seizures were organized and levied in order to support the army. Catholics contributed, sometimes willingly, sometimes grumblingly, sometimes under threat of

50 Lords justices and council to the lords of the council, 5 November 1641, in Historical Manuscripts Commission, *Calendar of the manuscripts of the marquess of Ormonde ...* (new series, 8 vols, London, 1902–20), ii, p. 9. 51 John Temple, *The Irish rebellion ... in the year 1641* (originally published London, 1646, reprinted London, 1746), p. 87. 52 John Temple, *The Irish rebellion ... in the year 1641* (originally published London, 1646, reprinted London, 1746), p. 88. 53 John Temple, *The Irish rebellion ... in the year 1641* (originally published London, 1646, reprinted London, 1746), p. 91. 54 *Cal. S. P. Ire., 1647–60*, p. 540.

death, to the war effort. Protestants could not be depended upon to cooperate in the same way and they had a tendency to resist, using force whenever they could. Therefore other methods, such as armed raids, had to be used to secure compliance and, when seizures were made, they had to be processed and secured. For example, in Co. Meath, 'in every barony some were appointed to oversee the threshing out of the Protestant corn' while Mathew Barnewall's house in Bremore in Fingal was specifically designated to store all goods 'as well such as are rebelliously taken ... as other goods ... for their safe keeping'.[55] The observant Luce Spell of Drogheda, who found out about the store-house at Bremore, noted that the friar Malone, who made seizures from a Liverpool barque probably about 5 December 1641, 'distributed a part of the smallest of the said goods' before sending the rest to Bremore for storage. Perhaps these small items were intended as a token fee or reward to his helpers. Luce Spell later saw some of her own goods, including a ruff and an earthen jug, in Dennis Connor's house at Kilmainham (parish of Balrothery). Dennis Connor was an associate of Malone and his wife, Mrs Connor, told Luce that the jug had been given her by the friar. Later, Luce was detained for three weeks as a prisoner in John Passmore's house (an inn) in Balrothery and, while there, she had the opportunity to confirm what she had heard about Bremore and that the goods there really were in safe keeping, when, at her instigation, a messenger was sent to fetch some balsam for Mrs Passmore's sore leg and brought back 'a box of balsam which the deponent saw and knew to be her own'. On the 13 December Friar Malone, when expelling Edward Leech and his family from Lambay, told him 'he did intend the castle of Lambay for a storehouse for the Catholic army'.[56] Kilsallaghan was used by the leaders in Co. Meath as a headquarters for their cavalry horses.[57] Given the size of Co. Meath the choice of the Fingal location was surprising. Kilsallaghan was, however, regarded, even by the enemy, as a particularly secure location.[58] The leaders of the Catholic army in the Pale at a very early stage in the rising realized the need to husband their resources carefully.

Fifty-seven robberies and seizures are known to have taken place in Fingal during the three months from November 1641 to January 1642.[59] While some raids and robberies occurred after that date they were sporadic and may occasionally have been regarded as an intrinsic part of the military campaign. It is sometimes unclear from the evidence whether killings and physical injuries were regarded as acts of war or not. In many cases, of course, the robberies were accompanied by physical violence. The robberies and seizures have been mapped in figure 9.1. This shows two major clusters of raids, one in the coastal area of north-east Fingal stretching from Lambay Island to Balrothery and centred on Holmpatrick, and the other in southern Fingal

55 Examination of Edward Dowdall, 13 March 1642 (TCD, MS 816, f. 47); deposition of Luce Spell, 5 February 1642 (TCD, MS 834, f. 6); 'County Louth depositions, 1641', ed. Thomas Gogarty in *Journal of the County Louth Archaeological Society*, iii, no. 1 (1912), p. 71. 56 Deposition of Edward Leech, 18 March 1644 (TCD, MS 810, f. 244). 57 Examination of Edward Dowdall, 13 March 1642 (TCD, MS 816, f. 47). 58 Ed. Loftus, *Joyfull newes from Ireland, or a true relation of the great overthrow which the English gave the rebels before Drogheda* ... (London, 1642), p. 2 (NLI, Lough Fea pamphlet no. 98); *A relation touching the present state and condition of Ireland* ... (London, 1642), p. 3 (NLI, Thorpe pamphlet no. 323); Simon Harcourt, *A letter from Sr. Simon Harcourt to a worthy member of the house of commons* ... (London, 1642), no page numbers (NLI, Thorpe pamphlet no. 308). 59 'Fingal 1603–60', i, pp 396–8.

Month	*Perpetuated by* rebels	*Perpetuated by* government troops
November	*	+
December	●	○
January	▲	△
Not determined	?	

Fig. 9.1 Robberies and seizures in Fingal November 1641 to January 1642 (incl.)

in the adjoining parishes of Santry and Finglas. Two smaller clusters have been noted in the Clontarf area and around Swords. In certain other areas there were isolated instances of one or, at most, two, attacks and in twenty-two of the forty-one parishes, no raids at all are known to have occurred. One must however enter a *caveat*. The purpose of the depositions was to collect information from survivors about robberies, spoils, murders and massacres committed against the Protestant English.[60] The voices of Catholics were seldom heard by the presiding commissioners except when they were being 'examined' and consequently placed on the defensive. Nevertheless there are occasional clues which provide information which hardly fits in with what these commissioners were expecting to hear as, for example, when Thomas Waller, as well as mentioning losses sustained at the hands of the rebels, complained of the loss of a mare and cart pressed into service by the government reinforcements travelling to Drogheda about the 29 November 1641 and when the clergyman, Randall Dimmock, mentioned that his house was pillaged and he had lost all when 'the town of Clontarf was burned and pillaged by the soldiers of Dublin'.[61] It seems even more likely that in similar circumstances, the property of the Catholic majority was also requisitioned and plundered.

It is not even certain that all the Protestants who lost property filed depositions. Many fled to England at an early stage in the rising. Others, who were in England, were rather reluctant to return. An interesting insight into this problem is given in a letter which Robert Bysse, junior, sent on 16 February 1642 to his brother, John, in England, explaining some of the procedures.[62] The brothers were both experienced lawyers but the process of making a deposition must have been daunting for others who were less familiar with the law. The bias towards the experiences of one side which, inevitably, is found in the depositions can be mitigated somewhat by examining reported burnings in the area over a longer period (1641–7) for which there is a wider variety of source evidence available. (See figure 9.2.) While much can be done to analyze the interplay between perpetrators and victims through the use of computer databases extensive research would be required to examine the background to, and possible explanations for, the various incidents. For this reason, a detailed examination was confined to one of the large clusters, namely, the series of violent incidents centred around Holmpatrick.[63] The area chosen for analysis is particularly interesting in that, for a brief period, the three strands of the rising already mentioned (international/national, gentry-led and popular) were clearly evident there.

Four raids were recorded in the parishes of Garristown (two), Santry and Cloghran (Swords), during November 1641 before the first raid in north-east Fingal took place. There may have been a fifth at Swords but the date of the raid on Christopher Hewetson's property is uncertain. If the date given by Henry Partington for the attack on his home at Killelane (parish of Balrothery) is accurate, the first raid in north-east Fingal took place on 28 November 1641, the very day on which the relief force, which had set out on the previous day from Dublin for Drogheda, marched slowly through the nearby townland of Courtlough on its way from Swords to Balrothery.[64] Henry Partington was not present to witness the raid. Hearing that 'all the English in Fingal were suddenly surprised and stripped of all their goods' he

60 Aidan Clarke, 'The 1641 depositions', in Peter Fox (ed.), *Treasures of the Library: Trinity College Dublin* (Dublin 1986), p. 112. **61** Deposition of Thomas Waller, 29 March 1642 (TCD, MS 810, f. 187); deposition of Randall Dimmock, 1 March 1642 (TCD, MS 809, f. 276). **62** Robert Bysse, junior, to John Bysse, 16 February 1642 (TCD, MS 840, f. 10). **63** 'Fingal 1603–60', i, p. 403; ii, appendix K, tables K.1 to K.3, pp 91–7. **64** Deposition of Henry Partington, 9 June 1642 (TCD, MS 810, f. 171); Richard Bellings, *History of the Irish confederation and the war in Ireland, 1641–3 . . .*, ed. John T. Gilbert (7 vols, Dublin, 1882–91), i, p. 32.

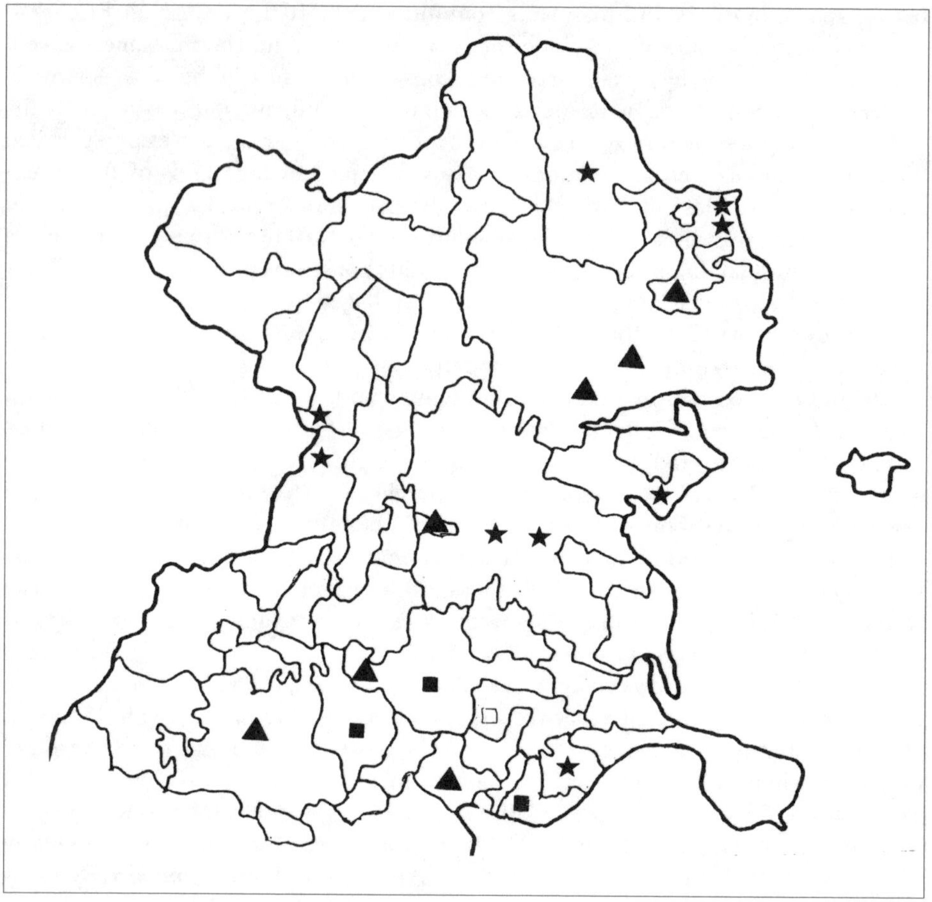

	Perpetuated by	
Year	*rebels/confederates*	*government troops*
1641	□	■
1642		★
1643	▲	

Fig. 9.2 Places in Fingal at which burnings were recorded 1641–7 (incl.)

fled to Dublin with his wife and seven children.[65] Seven of the eight assailants, whose names were passed on to him later by neighbours, lived locally and the surname of the eighth, Edmund Murphy, whose residence was not mentioned, suggests that he, too, was from Balrothery. The assailants, who included one yeoman, one labourer and two innkeepers (the occupations of the other four were not given), divided up his

65 Deposition of Henry Partington, 9 June 1642 (TCD, MS 810, f. 171).

corn, valued at £60, and his household goods, valued at £40, among them. There is no indication of the theft of money. All in all, this was a typical instance of a 'popular' raid. However, four of the participants, Donnogh Connor of Kilmainham, the two innkeepers, the Passmores, father and son, of Balrothery and John Wade of Margaretstown, were to be involved in later raids.

The raid on Killelane took place on the day preceding the battle of Julianstown, in which a government relief force heading for Drogheda was defeated and almost wiped out by the Ulster army under Sir Phelim O'Neill.[66] The next raid, on the home of the widow, Sarah Doughtie in the neighbouring townland of Balcunnin (parish of Lusk), took place 'on or about the last day of November', that is, the day after the battle. It was an armed raid led by 'Cruise the younger of the Naul'. Neither Cruise nor Lieutenant Reilly (Rely), has been identified with certainty. There are several entries for the surname, 'Rely', with addresses at Lusk, Pelletstown and Clontarf, on the list of outlaws but given that the raid took place in the parish of Lusk the most likely candidate appears to have been Connor Reilly, yeoman, of Lusk.[67] His name has not been associated with any other raids in Fingal. As Cruise was the leader of the attackers it should be somewhat easier to identify him. Although only one person with that surname, Peter Cruise, gentleman, of the Naul, was outlawed, five others were accused of being implicated in rebellious activities in Fingal.[68] Apart from Peter, two of these, Christopher, an innkeeper, and Simon, described as a 'captain', had addresses in the Naul.[69] The leader of the military-style attack on Sarah Doughtie's home was probably Simon who was subsequently appointed a captain at the meeting held at Swords from 7 to 10 December 1641.[70] Cruise threatened to kill Sarah and her four children and injured two of her servants.[71] He then turned Sarah and her children out of doors and took money and property (including bills, bonds and other notes for debts) valued at a total of £460. Thomas Doughtie, Sarah's deceased husband, had been rector of Baldongan and perpetual curate of Holmpatrick from 1630 until 1639.[72] The existence of 'notes for debt' may indicate some involvement by one or other of the couple in money-lending. While there is no explanation of why Sarah, in particular, was attacked she mentioned that 'all the Protestants thereabouts' had been robbed.[73] This contrasts with the account of Henry Partington who saw the early raids as attacks on the English (rather than Protestants). Sarah Doughtie, uniquely among those who described or mentioned the murder of Dirrick Huiberts Verveer, accused Cruise of being involved in it.

The following two days saw an intensification of the raids, many of which appear

66 Richard Bellings, *History of the Irish confederation and the war in Ireland, 1641–3* ..., ed. John T. Gilbert (7 vols, Dublin, 1882–91), i, pp 32–4. 67 Deposition of Sarah Doughtie, 20 January 1642 (TCD, MS 809, f. 275); R.C. Simington and John MacLellan, 'Oireachtas Library, List of outlaws, 1641–1647', in *Analecta Hibernica*, no. 23 (1966), p. 343. 68 R.C. Simington and John MacLellan, 'Oireachtas Library, List of outlaws, 1641–1647', in *Analecta Hibernica*, no. 23 (1966), p. 339. 69 Deposition of Thomas Benet, 26 February 1642 (TCD, MS 809, f. 243); deposition of Katherine Magee, 22 April 1642 (TCD, MS 810, f. 174); examination of Robert Walsh, 30 March 1642 (TCD, MS 810, f. 216). 70 Examination of Robert Walsh, 30 March 1642 (TCD, MS 810, f. 216). 71 Deposition of Sarah Doughtie, 20 January 1642 (TCD, MS 809, f. 275). 72 J.B. Leslie, *Clergy of Dublin and Glendalough: biographical succession lists*, ed.W.J.R. Wallace (Belfast and Dublin, 2001), pp 52 and 114. 73 Deposition of Sarah Doughtie, 20 January 1642 (TCD, MS 809, f. 275).

to have been part of a single plan. One which did not quite fit into the general pattern was a raid on the home of John Huxley of Rush, described as a British Protestant, on 1 December.[74] No further information has been discovered about this man who was a tenant of a James Russell. The name of James Russell does not appear either on the list of outlaws or among the rebels mentioned in the local depositions but he may have been a relative of Francis Russell, who was appointed a captain at Swords in December 1641 and who was responsible for capturing Daniel Barwick, captain of the pinnace, *The Swan*, in January 1642.[75] The earl of Ormond was the proprietor of Rush and it is possible that Huxley was an agent or employee of his. Huxley named fifteen of the rebels who attacked his home, all of whom were from the local parish of Lusk, but it is not clear from the text if the 'other Irish rebels to the number of twenty-three' included those fifteen or not. The names of the fifteen men identified do not appear in the accounts of other local attacks although the names of three of them, Thomas Hamilton of Lusk, John Kerrigan of Rathartan and Laughlin Murtagh of Dunganstown, who may have been Murtagh the ploughholder, appear on the list of outlaws.[76] In any event the attack was formidable, if non-violent, but like the attack in Killelane it seems to have been a popular attack by local men taking advantage of the unrest rather than a premeditated raid that was part of a master plan. However, from then on Huxley appears to have been a marked man, as a more serious threat was made to him a few days later.

Another raid which took place on the same day, 1 December, 'in the forenoon' was that on the premises of Darby Lea of Balrothery, described as 'postmaster' though his losses suggest that he was also an innkeeper.[77] Although he was not an exceptionally wealthy man – his total losses amounted to £200 – the fact that as well as being postmaster, he held the lease of the castle of Balrothery, probably made his property a militarily significant target for the rebels. In the course of his deposition Darby Lea mentioned, as hearsay evidence, the murders of 'Dirrick Huiberts of Holmpatrick, gentleman, Mr Pardoe, clerk, the post that came from Dublin, with other English Protestants but to what number he knoweth not'. While Darby Lea gave detailed information about his losses he said little about the raiders except that they were led by Captain Cusack of near Rathaldron in the county of Meath, accompanied with divers other Irish rebels to the number of about forty men. The timing of this raid would indicate that it was the first of a series of raids carried out by Captain Cusack during this period.[78]

While Captain Cusack was a key figure in the attacks in north-east Fingal little is known about him. The Cusack family of Rathaldron was originally from Portraine in Fingal and had links with several prominent Pale families.[79] Rathaldron was situated

74 Deposition of John Huxley, 21 May 1642 (TCD, MS 810, f. 158). 75 Examination of Robert Walsh, 30 March 1642 (TCD, MS 810, f. 216); deposition of Daniel Barwick, 23 May 1642 (TCD, MS 810, f. 114). 76 R.C. Simington and John MacLellan, 'Oireachtas Library, List of outlaws, 1641–1647', in *Analecta Hibernica*, no. 23 (1966), pp 341–3. 77 Deposition of Darby Lea, 25 January 1642 (TCD, MS 809, f. 288). 78 Deposition of Huibart Cromphouts, 2 March 1642 (TCD, MS 809, f. 268); deposition of Darby Lea, 25 January 1642 (TCD, MS 809, f. 288); deposition of Anthony Huiberts, 29 January 1642 (TCD, MS 809, f. 311); deposition of Thomas Clitheroe, 26 May 1642 (TCD, MS 810, f. 126); deposition of Margaret Huiberts, 14 March 1644 (TCD, MS 810, ff 238–9). 79 Hubert Gallwey, 'The Cusack family of Counties Meath and Dublin: part i', in *The Irish Genealogist*, v, no. 3 (November 1976), p. 299

in the parish of Donaghmore, barony of Navan, where Patrick Cusack owned over 500 acres in 1641.[80] This holding was situated at quite a considerable distance from another property, consisting of 120 acres, which he owned at Blackhall in the parish of Balrothery.[81] According to the Civil Survey he had leased this property for six pounds *per annum* to Richard Murphy who, in turn, had leased it to Richard Davis, an English Protestant for twelve pounds *per annum* 'who hath it now in possession'.[82] Richard Davis has not been identified. The buildings on the land consisted of a farm house and two houses of office, as well as a small orchard, which were valued by the jury at fifteen pounds. The buildings valuation seems rather high for the area which suggests that there was probably an inn or business on the site which made sub-letting feasible. The townland of Blackhall immediately adjoined Balrothery on the west and the townland of Ballimad, which was farmed by Anthony Huiberts, son of Dirrick Huiberts Verveer, on the east. According to the genealogist, Hubert Gallwey, Patrick Cusack, who was about sixty-five years old in 1641, took no part in the struggle.[83] He was married twice, first, to Elizabeth Fitzwilliam and, secondly, to Cicely Nangle, daughter of Patrick Nangle, eighteenth baron of Navan.[84] His son, James, had already been active in a raid at Navan on 25 November, and James appears to have been the 'Captain Cusack' who played such a prominent role in the Fingal rising in December.[85]

A characteristic of the events which took place in and around Holmpatrick about this time was the virulence of the attacks on the extended family of the Dutch merchant, Dirrick Huiberts Verveer. The family homes attacked included his own at Holmpatrick as well as those of his son at Ballimad, his sister and nephew at Milverton and his son-in-law, the Revd Henry Birch, possibly at Holmpatrick, though there is some doubt about this and consequently it has been omitted from consideration here. Birch was appointed to Newcastle Lyons in 1641 and was there when he made his deposition on 15 May 1643.[86] In this deposition the date and place of the loss of 'his goods and chattels' were left unspecified. His successor at Holmpatrick was not appointed until 1643. In addition to his involvement in the raid on Darby Lea's house, Captain Cusack was accused of taking part in the raids at Holmpatrick and Milverton as well as being concerned in the murder of Dirrick Huiberts Verveer at Hacketstown and an attack on the home of Thomas Clitheroe, vicar of Balrothery. All of these events were specifically recorded as having taken place on 1 or 2 December, with the exception of the raid on the home of Thomas

and 'The Cusack family of Counties Meath and Dublin: part vi, Cusack of Rathaldron', in *The Irish Genealogist*, vi, no. 3 (November 1982), pp 285–7. 80 *Civil Survey, v, county of Meath, with returns of tithes for the Meath baronies*, p. 225. 81 *Civil Survey, vii, county of Dublin*, pp 11–12. 82 *Civil Survey, vii, county of Dublin*, p. 12. 83 Hubert Gallwey, 'The Cusack family of Counties Meath and Dublin: part vi, Cusack of Rathaldron', in *The Irish Genealogist*, vi, no. 3 (November 1982), pp 288–9. 84 Francis Elrington Ball, *A history of the County Dublin: the people, parishes and antiquities from the earliest times to the close of the eighteenth century: part second* (originally published 1903, reprinted Dublin, 1995), p. 12; Bernard Burke, *A selection of arms authorized by the laws of heraldry: with annotations by Sir Bernard Burke ...* (London, 1863), pp 204–5. 85 Deposition of William Robinson, 7 March 1642 (TCD, MS 816, f. 134); 'The Cusack family of Counties Meath and Dublin: part vi, Cusack of Rathaldron', in *The Irish Genealogist*, vi, no. 3 (November 1982), p. 290. 86 J.B. Leslie, *Clergy of Dublin and Glendalough: biographical succession lists*, ed. W.J.R. Wallace (Belfast and Dublin, 2001), pp 114 and 147.

Clitheroe which took place 'about the beginning of December' after he had fled to Dublin.[87]

Why were Verveer and his family singled out for attack? Undoubtedly, they were wealthy and Protestant. With the exception of his son-in-law, Birch, the male members of his family and his sister, Catherine Cromphouts, were of Dutch origin. The nationalities of Verveer's wife, Margaret, and his son's wife are not known. Although Verveer had lived in Ireland for many years and had been granted 'all the rights and privileges of English subjects' in 1608, he was described 'as a Dutch man' by a neighbour, Sarah Doughtie, in her deposition made on 20 January 1642.[88] He was also described by Sir John Temple as 'a Dutch merchant'.[89] It seems unlikely that anti-English feeling played any part in this series of attacks. The lords justices and council alleged that Dirrick Huiberts Verveer was murdered because he was a Protestant. In a letter to the earl of Leicester, lord lieutenant, on 3 December 1641, the day following the murder, they wrote:

> That the rebels have besieged Drogheda on all sides, a town on the sea coast within twenty miles of this city, and that we cannot relieve the forces there, nor they us, but by sea, we made known to your lordship by our letters of the 30th November, since which time the rebels have, by their multitudes of men and assistance of seamen who readily join with them, seized and manned many boats on the sea coast betwixt this and Drogheda, and have murdered the gentleman that held the island of Lambay, namely Mr Dirrick Huiberts, for no other cause but because he was a Protestant, and now they hinder us from intercourse by sea to be had between us and Drogheda and we fear will presently be able to intercept our passages between this and Chester, so far as multitudes of men and boats can do.[90]

Was Verveer involved in money-lending, a practice in which many merchants were engaged? The Irish Statute Staple Books list only three instances of loans made by him in the period 1613 to 1616, none of which were made to local men.[91] Of course there were other ways of borrowing and lending money besides the staple. All that can be said is that no evidence has been found to connect Verveer with any large-scale involvement in money-lending.

There are two accounts of the raid on the home of Dirrick Huiberts Verveer on 1 December and his murder on the following day. One of these was contained in the deposition of his son, Anthony, who was not an eye-witness but whose account was given to the authorities on 29 January, less than two months after the events took place.[92] The second was deposed by Dirrick's widow, Margaret, who was an eyewit-

87 Deposition of Thomas Clitheroe, 26 May 1642 (TCD, MS 810, f. 126). 88 *Irish patent rolls of James I*, ed. M.C. Griffith (Dublin, 1966), p. 126; deposition of Sarah Doughtie, 20 January 1642 (TCD, MS 809, f. 275). 89 John Temple, *The Irish rebellion ... in the year 1641* (originally published London, 1646, reprinted London, 1746), p. 259. 90 Lords justices and council to the earl of Leicester, lord lieutenant, 3 December 1641, in Historical Manuscripts Commission, *Calendar of the manuscripts of the marquess of Ormonde ...* (new series, 8 vols, London, 1902–20), ii, p. 33. 91 *The Irish statute staple books, 1596–1687*, ed. Jane Ohlmeyer and Éamonn Ó Ciardha (Dublin, 1998), identity numbers 744, 883 and 871, pp 111, 179, 190, 254 and 263. 92 Deposition of Anthony Huiberts, 29 January 1642 (TCD, MS 809, f. 311).

ness but whose deposition (quoted in part in chapter 1) was not made until 14 March 1644, more than two years after his murder.[93] Although the accounts differed and, to a large extent, implicated different people in the robbery and in the murder on the following day, they were not contradictory and, taken together, provide a detailed account of the sequence of events. Both depositions mentioned Captain Cusack and, in addition to the 'neighbours of Fingal' listed by Margaret, Anthony implicated Michael Murphy of Balrothery and Jasper and Thomas Hurlston in both the robbery on 1 December and the subsequent murder.

The Hurlstons of Skerries, sub-tenants of Verveer, bring a additional strand to the complicated network. In his will proved in 1623 Jasper Hurlston, alderman of Drogheda, mentioned his brother, Thomas Hurlston and his sons John and Jasper.[94] Luce Spell of Drogheda accused Jasper Hurlston of Drogheda, merchant (she referred to him later as 'Jasper Hurlston of the Skerries') of being one of those who robbed and imprisoned the passengers of the Liverpool barque at Skerries in early December.[95] She also mentioned that the prisoners were taken first to the house of William Hulson [sic] in Skerries. The names of Thomas Hurlston, gentleman, and William Hurlston, yeoman, both of Skerries, appeared on the Oireachtas list of outlaws for Co. Dublin while that of Jasper Hurlston of Drogheda, merchant, appeared for Co. Louth, although a footnote indicated that his county of residence was listed in the original as 'Dublin'.[96] William may have been a younger son of Thomas Hurlston, perhaps born after his uncle Jasper's death *c.*1623. While little further is known about the family, apart from the fact that they were subsequently involved in the invasion of Lambay and that Jasper Hurlston escaped from jail in Dublin early in 1658, their involvement in so many incidents in the early days of the rising is evidence of co-ordination between the rebels in the port towns of Drogheda and Skerries and what Aidan Clarke has described as the systematic seizure of boats as a result of which the 'Catholic army' was for a time in control of the sea.[97]

Apart from Captain Cusack one of the more interesting visitors to Holmpatrick on 1 December was Bartholomew Russell of Seatown, who held a large estate in the parish of Swords, a small amount of which he possessed in his own right and the remainder of which he leased at a low rent from the archbishop of Dublin.[98] According to the Civil Survey he left his home after the defeat of the Irish at Swords and died about the beginning of the first cessation (which took place on 15 September 1643) with the rebels in the county of Louth.[99] Mr Bellings of Ardla may have been the proprietor of Ardla, Laurence Bellings of Belinstown, who was indicted for rebellion and who held land, much of it in his own right, in all four of the Fingal baronies.[100] On the other hand, it may have been Mark (or Martin) of

93 Deposition of Margaret Huiberts, 14 March 1644 (TCD, MS 810, ff 238–9). 94 Abstract of will of Jasper Hurlston, proved 31 July 1623 (NAI, Betham genealogical abstracts, prerogative wills, series I, vol 31, p. 37). 95 Deposition of Luce Spell, 5 February 1642 (TCD, MS 834, f. 6); 'County Louth depositions, 1641', ed. Thomas Gogarty in *Journal of the County Louth Archaeological Society*, iii, no. 1 (1912), pp 71–2. 96 R.C. Simington and John MacLellan, 'Oireachtas Library, List of outlaws, 1641–1647', in *Analecta Hibernica*, no. 23 (1966), p. 341. 97 *Anc. rec. Dublin*, iv, p. 136; Aidan Clarke, *The Old English in Ireland, 1625–42* (paperback ed., Dublin, 2000), pp 178 and 191. 98 Deposition of Margaret Huiberts, 14 March 1644 (TCD, MS 810, f. 238); *Civil Survey, vii, county of Dublin*, pp 87, 92–3, 102–3. 99 *Civil Survey, vii, county of Dublin*, p. 102. 100 *Civil Survey, vii, county of Dublin*, pp 18, 58, 70, 90,

Ardla, perhaps a son or brother, whose name also appeared on the list of outlaws.[101] The identity of Lieutenant Fleming is uncertain. Several men called Fleming were listed as outlaws for counties Dublin and Meath.[102] Thomas Fitzwilliam and Robert Arthur were represented by their servants. Thomas Fitzwilliam of Baldongan later became marshal of the rebels.[103] The position of the near neighbour, Robert Arthur of Hacketstown, was more ambiguous. It is clear that he sympathized with the rebels and perhaps even collaborated with them, but he has not been identified as an active participant in any violent or military action.[104] Cusack was also accompanied by his tenant at Blackhall, Richard Murphy of Balrothery. Captain Cusack was the only one of the raiders named by both Margaret Huiberts and her son, Anthony.[105] As already mentioned, Anthony also implicated Michael Murphy of Balrothery and Jasper and Thomas Hurlston in the raid.

On arrival at Holmpatrick Captain Cusack first threatened Dirrick Huiberts Verveer with death if he did not hand over his money and then demanded the keys of the trunks which he proceeded to break open and 'took what pleased them'.[106] It is probable that Cusack found documents as well as money and valuables. Margaret Huiberts also deposed that Cusack would have killed Verveer at that point had not Michael Murphy intervened. This, together with the actual murder on the following day in which he was accused of taking part, would suggest that Cusack, in particular, wanted Verveer out of the way. What followed was the strange and significant visit of Katherine Scanlon who 'came to the said Dirrick and called him aside telling him that she was sent to wish him and the rest to depart the house saying that the priest must come there to say Mass (it being an old Abbey)'.[107] There is no indication in the text as to who sent her nor is the identity of the priest known. There were a number of priests in the neighbourhood at the time but the most likely would appear to have been the Friar Malone who came to prominence in Skerries a few days later and who clearly wished to have the Mass restored in the churches.[108] Edward Walsh, a foster-brother of Alderman Robert Arthur, guided Verveer and his wife and sister to Arthur's home at nearby Hacketstown where they spent the night.[109] Anthony Huiberts mentioned their intention of going to Lambay but this was not referred to by Margaret.[110] According to Margaret's account, she, with her husband and sister-in-law, proceeded back towards Holmpatrick on the advice of Edward Walsh and under the guidance of a servant of Alderman Arthur though whether or not this was the same man who had taken part in the raid on the previous day is not clear.[111] What followed was an attack on the small group by ten or twelve men, the robbery and stripping of Margaret and her sister-in-law, Catherine Cromphouts, the particularly

104–5, 119, 155, 168, 236 and 238. **101** R.C. Simington and John MacLellan, 'Oireachtas Library, List of outlaws, 1641–1647', in *Analecta Hibernica*, no. 23 (1966), p. 337. **102** R.C. Simington and John MacLellan, 'Oireachtas Library, List of outlaws, 1641–1647', in *Analecta Hibernica*, no. 23 (1966), pp 340 and 356. **103** Deposition of Daniel Barwick, 23 May 1642 (TCD, MS 810, f. 114). **104** Deposition of Daniel Barwick, 23 May 1642 (TCD, MS 810, f. 114); examination of Anthony Pile, 29 June 1643 (TCD, MS 810, f. 281). **105** Deposition of Anthony Huiberts, 29 January 1642 (TCD, MS 809, f. 311). **106** Deposition of Margaret Huiberts, 14 March 1644 (TCD, MS 810, f. 238). **107** Deposition of Margaret Huiberts, 14 March 1644 (TCD, MS 810, f. 238). **108** Deposition of Edward Leech, 18 March 1644 (TCD, MS 810, f. 245). **109** Deposition of Margaret Huiberts, 14 March 1644 (TCD, MS 810, f. 238). **110** Deposition of Anthony Huiberts, 29 January 1642 (TCD, MS 809, f. 311). **111** Deposition of Margaret Huiberts, 14 March 1644 (TCD, MS 810, f. 238).

brutal murder of Dirrick and the flight of the two women by night to Dublin. Catherine Cromphouts died a few weeks later as a result of her ordeal. The only person recognized by Margaret was Nicholas Russell of Collinstown, but her son mentioned Captain Cusack, Michael Murphy of Balrothery, and the Hurlstons as being among those responsible.[112] Dirrick was refused burial in the church or churchyard until Saturday, 4 December, although the circumstances in which the rebels then relented are not known.

Two other raids took place on the homes of members of the Verveer family on Thursday, 2 December. The first of these was on the Milverton home of Catherine Cromphouts, who had gone to Hacketstown with her brother.[113] Her son, Huibart, who had fled from the scene and hidden himself, named Captain Cusack, Richard Murphy of Balrothery and John Wade of Morganstown (probably the adjoining townland of Margaretstown), as being among those responsible. He also mentioned that he had been informed that William Trevor (Travers) of Ballykea 'had seized upon his haggard of corn valued £100 at least and maketh use of it in this examinant's house'.[114] William Travers was a substantial landholder and, a short time later, a signatory to the letter sent by the Co. Dublin gentry to the lords justices and council.[115] Whether he was making use of the haggard at Milverton for his own use or for the use of the rebel army is unclear. The second raid on 2 December took place at Ballimad (now Hampton Demesne) which adjoined the Cusack-owned Blackhall Farm (figure 9.3) 'about twelve of the clock at midnight'.[116] The lateness of the hour may explain why the only person whose name was mentioned in connection with this raid was the leader of the attackers, Captain Barnewall of Annagor in the parish of Kilsharvan in Co. Meath. The proprietor of Annagor in 1641 was George Stoakes of Mitchelstown, Co. Meath, who was also one of the joint owners of the joint owners of Knocknagin in the parish of Balrothery which was about 5 km from Ballimad.[117] While £500 worth of property was stolen no violence was reported on this occasion. The final raid in the series cannot be dated with certainty. It began with an assault on the Revd Thomas Clitheroe, vicar of Balrothery, by a group of men, whom he named as Michael Murphy of Balrothery, gentleman, Walter St Lawrence of Courtlough, gentleman, George Tankard of Balrothery, labourer, John Passmore of Balrothery, innkeeper, Robert Passmore, 'his son, a popish priest', and Richard Murphy of Balrothery, gentleman.[118] Michael Murphy and Tankard assaulted him and Murphy wounded him in the neck. Thomas Clitheroe fled to Dublin, and after his departure Captain Cusack, John Passmore and Michael Murphy seized his house, pulled it down and carried off his goods.

112 Deposition of Margaret Huiberts, 14 March 1644 (TCD, MS 810, f. 238); deposition of Anthony Huiberts, 29 January 1642 (TCD, MS 809, f. 311). 113 Deposition of Huibart Cromphouts, 2 March 1642 (TCD, MS 809, f. 268); deposition of Margaret Huiberts, 14 March 1644 (TCD, MS 810, f. 238); deposition of Anthony Huiberts, 29 January 1642 (TCD, MS 809, f. 311). 114 Deposition of Huibart Cromphouts, 2 March 1642 (TCD, MS 809, f. 268, original damaged, copy MS 810, f. 38). 115 Gentry of English Pale to lords justices and council in Ireland, 10 December 1641, in John T. Gilbert (ed.), *History of the Irish confederation and the war in Ireland, 1641–3* ... (7 vols, Dublin, 1882–91), i, pp 229–30; *Civil Survey, vii, county of Dublin*, pp 7, 9, 11, 59, 66 and 124. 116 Deposition of Anthony Huiberts, 29 January 1642 (TCD, MS 809, f. 310). 117 *Civil Survey, v, county of Meath, with returns of tithes for the Meath baronies*, p. 36; *Civil Survey, vii, county of Dublin*, p. 3. 118 Deposition of Thomas Clitheroe, 26 May 1642 (TCD, MS 810, f. 126).

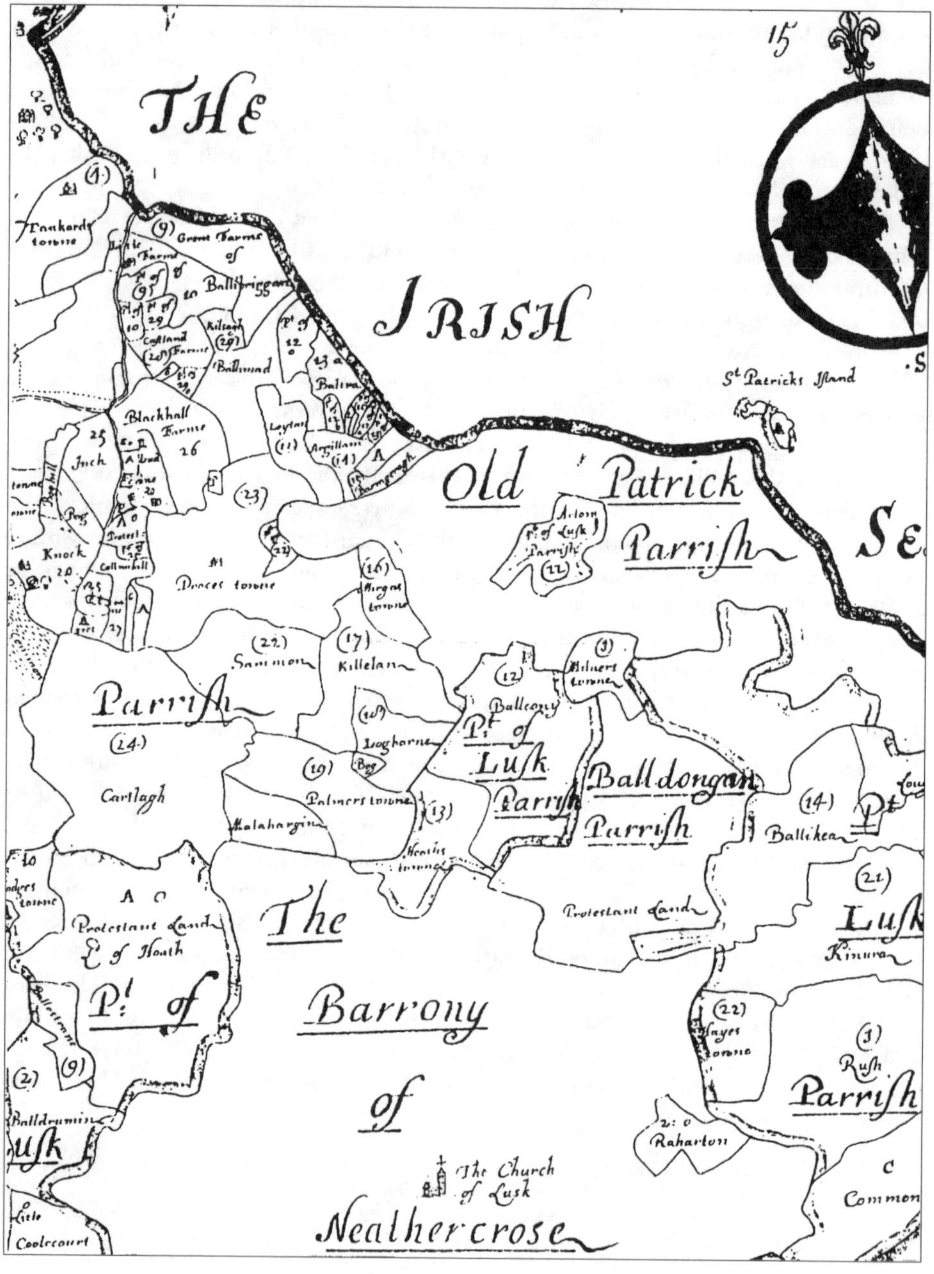

Fig. 9.3 Down Survey barony map, 1657 – barony of Balrothery (detail)

Following this series of assaults there was a lull of a few days, until about Sunday, 5 December 1641, when a number of ships and boats were driven into Skerries by a storm. Since a large number of Protestants had fled from the area many of the incidents which followed were described by outsiders who were caught up in the turmoil. The central figure in this part of the story of the rising in north-east Fingal was John Malone (or O'Malony) generally described as a friar. There was no friary nearer than Drogheda so that the arrival of a friar in a town like Skerries, which had a substantial Protestant population, was bound to arouse keen interest.

Nothing has been established with absolute certainty about John Malone's background. Since, however, he played such a key role in the 1641 rising in Fingal it may be useful to consider the possibilities further. Three instances of this Gaelic-Irish surname occurred in the hearth money roll for Fingal. These were in the parishes of Clontarf, Donabate and Garristown.[119] The name was also found in Dublin and the town of Drogheda and in Co. Meath. The name is, however, fairly common and has been found in many parts of the country. It is virtually certain that Friar John Malone was a Franciscan. In fact, it seems probable that there was more than one friar of the name 'John Malone' in the Franciscan order during the first half of the seventeenth century.[120] A Franciscan preacher with a somewhat similar name, 'Joannes Molanus', who had studied in Paris and who was guardian of the convent in Armagh, died in the year 1610.[121] According to an entry in *Some funeral entries of Ireland* a friar called John Malone, son of Edmond Malone of Co. Westmeath died in the Low Countries, in or before 1638, though in his case the religious order to which he belonged was not stated.[122] In an article published in the *Irish Sword* in 1953, Canice Mooney wrote: 'we know that Bonaventure Fitzgerald and John Molinus (= Mullen, Mallan, Malone?) were preachers in the army in Belgium in the beginning of the seventeenth century'.[123] The document on which this was based was prepared in 1617 and read as follows: '4. *Fr Joannes Molinus, diocesis Casselensis, receptus, 29 Aprilis 1612, nunc est praedicator apud exercitum*'. It would seem, therefore, that the recording of John Malone's (if, indeed, he was the 'Joannes Molinus' mentioned in the entry) association with the army was somewhat later than Canice Mooney's article would, at first glance, suggest. There are three contemporary lists of Franciscans, together with a fourth list, compiled later, of clergy ordained in the Malines archdiocese, which help to trace the career of the Munster man, Joannes Molinus, and to link him with the network of Fingal priests and gentry and to suggest that he was, in fact, the Friar Malone of Skerries. The earliest of these lists, called here the 'Douai list', which was presented to the Archduke Albert and Archduchess Isabella of Austria in 1613, was a list of Douai *alumni* who had entered any branch of the priesthood.[124] Apart from distinguishing between secular and

119 'Hearth money roll for County Dublin, 1664' (second part), *Journal of the County Kildare Archaeological Society*, xi (1930–33), pp 394, 406 and 409. 120 I am most grateful to Fr Ignatius Fennessy, OFM, for drawing my attention to the probability that there was more than one Franciscan called 'John Malone' and for pointing out the connection between John Malone and John Barnewall. 121 'Brussels MS 3947: Donatus Moneyus, de provincia Hiberniae, S. Francisci' presented by Brendan Jennings in *Analecta Hibernica*, no. 6 (November 1934), p. 36. 122 Association for the Preservation of Memorials of the Dead, *Some funeral entries of Ireland* (Dublin, 1907–12), p. 15. 123 Canice Mooney, 'The Irish sword and the Franciscan cowl' in *The Irish Sword*, i (1949–53), p. 85. 124 'A list of the Irish

regular clergy and between the various religious orders and congregations this list supplies no information about the *alumni* other than names. The second list, called here the 'Louvain list', was a list of Franciscans who had been received into the Irish Franciscan College of Louvain between 1607 and 1617, the date at which it was prepared.[125] As can be seen from the Latin entry already quoted, it provided a little more information about the individuals mentioned. The third list, presented to the Archduchess Isabella and printed in 1622 under the title, *Exhibitio consolatoria*, was very similar to the first though, of course, it had been updated to include later *alumni*.[126] The fourth (modern) list, published by Brendan Jennings in the *Irish Ecclesiastical Record* contained the names of those who were ordained in the archdiocese of Malines, in which Louvain was situated from 1602 to 1794.[127] The information derived from the Louvain list and the Malines list about each of three Franciscans, Robert (Father Christopher) Plunket of Dunsoghly, son of Sir Christopher Plunket and brother of Colonel Richard Plunket, John Barnewall, son of Lord Trimleston and associate of Lord Maguire, and 'Joannes Molinus', assumed to be John Malone, has been compared.[128] The names of Robert Plunket and John Malone appeared on the Douai list of 1613 (John Barnewall was not received into the order until 1616) while the names of all three priests appeared in the *Exhibitio consolatoria* of 1622.

All three priests had been educated at Douai and had proceeded from there to the Irish Franciscan College at Louvain. While the fact that Joannes Molinus was from Munster might, at first glance, suggest that it was unlikely that this priest was the 'Friar Malone of Skerries', the Franciscan connection, his army career and the dates are compatible with the experience of a man who, as he himself, as well as Colonel Plunket, claimed, had spent many years planning for a rising in Ireland.[129] Roger Holland's deposition was particularly interesting. He stated:

> that he being in company with Colonel Plunket at Newry and Carlingford, the said colonel told him, this deponent, and many others, that this said plot was for these seventeen years past a plotting: and that the said Friar Malone and himself and one of the lord of Trimleston's sons (which is a friar), with many others of the nobility of the Pale and in the north, knew it of a long time. But that others of the nobles knew not of it but of late. But as for the rest, they had known of it the space of years aforesaid ...[130]

priests and Jesuits that have been students in Doway, written in a complimentary letter to the Princes Albert and Isabella, archduke and archduchess of Austria & c. in 1613' in *Calendar of the Carew manuscripts preserved in the archiepiscopal library at Lambeth* (6 vols, London, 1867–73), vi, pp 285–6; *Louvain papers 1606–1827*, ed. Brendan Jennings (Dublin, 1968), p. 38 (footnote 1). **125** Historical Manuscripts Commission, *Fourth report*, appendix (London, 1874), pp 602–3; *Louvain papers 1606–1827*, ed. Brendan Jennings (Dublin, 1968), pp 54–8. **126** 'The Irish colleges in the Low Countries: (a) *Exhibitio consolatoria*', ed. John Brady in *Archivium Hibernicum*, xiv (1949), pp 66–83; *Louvain papers 1606–1827*, ed. Brendan Jennings (Dublin, 1968), p. 72 (footnote 1). **127** Brendan Jennings, 'Irish names in the Malines ordination registers, 1602–1794' in *The Irish Ecclesiastical Record*, lxxv-lxxvii (1951–2). **128** 'Fingal 1603–60', i, p. 417. **129** Deposition of Edward Leech, 18 March 1644 (TCD, MS 810, f. 244); deposition of Roger Holland, 4 March 1642 (TCD, MS 834, f. 63); deposition of John Kerdiff, 28 February 1642 (TCD, MS 839, ff 3 and 4). **130** Deposition of Roger Holland, 4 March 1642 (TCD, MS 834, f. 63).

Little further is known of the career of John Malone. In 1618 a Franciscan residence was erected at Cashel '*instituo superiore P. Joanne Molina, theologo et predicatore zelosissimo*'.[131] A priest called 'Johannes Molon' (indexed as 'Malone') was appointed a confessor at a Franciscan provincial chapter held in Limerick in 1629.[132] A Franciscan, 'Joannes O Malloon', is found among the names of priests in the diocese of Ardfert and Aghadoe in 1636.[133] At a middle chapter held in Kildare in 1639 a 'Johannes Mollouny' was continued as guardian of convent of Irialagh (Muckross, Co. Kerry).[134] While one cannot be certain if any of these references were to Friar Malone of Skerries, the dates are not incompatible with an ordination to the priesthood in 1615 though they would imply that Malone's initial army career in the Low Countries was short though the gaps in the information which is available would certainly have allowed for a possible return to the continent. In his conversation with Edward Leech he claimed that 'some colonels in Dublin had had money of him, for to raise men for Spain and that he had kept them aboard for some time within the harbour of Dublin ...', which may indicate an association with the attempts to transport the disbanded army to Spain in 1641.[135] Disappointingly however, despite his local importance, Friar John Malone remains a shadowy figure in the history of the period.

The first formal examination in the Co. Dublin depositions which recorded Fingal's involvement in the war, as opposed to the sporadic raiding discussed above, was that of Christopher Hampton. This examination was carried out less than a week after the events which he described as follows:

> The said Hampton being sworn by the Clerk of the Council saith that he and divers others running ashore on the fifth of this present at the Skerries within ten miles of this city, one called Father Malone, with many accompanying of him laid hands upon this examinant and the rest and stripped them of all they had and likewise entered into the ship and there rifled and took away what was there, which being done, the said Malone sent this examinant and the other passengers by a warrant under his hand from constable unto constable to Roger Moore, colonel in the army. According unto the warrant of the said Malone the examinant being brought before Mr Roger Moore who after some while let the examinant and the rest free and at large. The examinant further saith that, at the same place and since, there was present at the Church of Duleek in consultation sundry of the lords of the Pale, namely, the lord of Gormanstown, the Lord Nettervill, the lord of Slane, the Lord Louth, the Lord Iveagh, the rest were unknown to the examinant.[136]

131 'Brevis synopsis provinciae Hiberniae FF. Minorum', presented by Brendan Jennings in *Analecta Hibernica*, no. 6 (November 1934), p. 147. 132 *Liber Lovaniensis: a collection of Irish Franciscan documents 1629–1717* ed. Cathaldus Giblin (Dublin, 1956), pp 7 and 405. 133 Brendan Jennings, 'Miscellaneous documents, II, 1625–1640' in *Archivium Hibernicum*, xiv (1949), p. 10. 134 *Liber Lovaniensis: a collection of Irish Franciscan documents 1629–1717* ed. Cathaldus Giblin (Dublin, 1956), pp 356–7. 135 Deposition of Edward Leech, 18 March 1644 (TCD, MS 810, ff 244–5). 136 Examination of Christopher Hampton, 11 December 1641 (TCD, MS 809, f. 212).

It was clear from this examination that Malone had access to the leaders of the rising. This information was transmitted to London on 14 December by which time events had overtaken the lords justices and council.[137] A much more detailed account of the affair is found in the deposition of Luce Spell, a Drogheda widow, which was made in the following February.[138] She had the advantage of knowing many of those involved. She explained that the vessel had been driven into Skerries by contrary winds and that John Malone had been accompanied to the ship by John Wotton of Tankardstown as well as by Jasper Hurlston. When she and the other prisoners arrived at the house of William Hurlston in Skerries she saw the friar in the company of four Drogheda merchants and gentlemen, namely, Barnaby Bellings, Alderman Francis St Lawrence, Christopher Malone and Robert Plunket as well as Michael Murphy of Balrothery. It is not clear why these prisoners were brought to Duleek but after the meeting held there they were brought back to Balrothery and lodged in John Passmore's inn, where she again saw Michael Murphy together with four Drogheda merchants, namely, Garrett Nugent, John Griffin, Patrick Griffin and Roger Bellings and heard them in their conference say:

> We will shortly have the prince of England here in Ireland and make him viceroy; and we will tutor him and bring him up in the Catholic religion and the king himself shall live in Scotland, and before Easter day next we shall have an army out of Spain, and then we will go all into England and with the help of the Catholics there (all whose names the said friar said that he had) we will put all the puritans to the sword.

Once again the primary purpose of the Fingal and Drogheda rebels appears to have been the restoration of Catholicism.

Others mentioned as being in the company of the friar were Walter St Lawrence of Courtlough (who had been involved in the attack on Thomas Clitheroe), Mark Bellings of Ardla (probably the 'Mr Bellings' who had been concerned in the robbery at Holmpatrick on 1 December) and Dennis Connor of Kilmainham, who was a close associate of the Friar Malone and who had taken part in the raid on the home of Henry Partington on 28 November.[139] Luce Spell also provided a useful cross-check on the stories told by examinants when she described the visit of George Devenish and his family and servants to Balrothery.[140] She also reported a brief conversation which George had with his wife who said to him: 'What have these English brought us unto, the curse of God upon them.' To which he replied: 'Be contented, wife, for

137 Lords justices and council to the earl of Leicester, lord lieutenant, 14 December 1641, in Historical Manuscripts Commission, *Calendar of the manuscripts of the marquess of Ormonde* ... (new series, 8 vols, London, 1902–20), ii, p. 37. 138 Deposition of Luce Spell, 5 February 1642 (TCD, MS 834, f. 6); 'County Louth depositions, 1641', ed. Thomas Gogarty in *Journal of the County Louth Archaeological Society*, iii, no. 1 (1912), pp 71–2. 139 Deposition of Thomas Clitheroe, 26 May 1642 (TCD, MS 810, f. 126); deposition of Margaret Huiberts, 14 March 1644 (TCD, MS 810, f. 238); deposition of Henry Partington, 9 June 1642 (TCD, MS 810, f. 171). 140 Deposition of Luce Spell, 5 February 1642 (TCD, MS 834, f. 6); 'County Louth depositions, 1641', ed. Thomas Gogarty in *Journal of the County Louth Archaeological Society*, iii, no. 1 (1912), p. 72; examination of George Devenish, 24 March 1642 (TCD, MS 816, f. 31).

within this two or three days Dublin will be taken and then we shall be paid double for what we have lost.'[141] Once again there is evidence that, for some people at least, the English, rather than Protestants, were the principal enemy.

Others who found themselves cast ashore in Skerries at that time were John Kerdiff of Co. Tyrone and Roger Holland of Glaslough in Co. Monaghan.[142] Both of these commentators mentioned the kindly treatment they had received from the friar but both also recorded the fact that he had burned bibles which he found in the boats. Of particular interest was a private conversation with the friar recorded by Roger Holland which gives some further insight into the motives of the rebels. Holland deposed as follows:

> And this deponent, sitting by him alone, demanded of him what might be the reason of their going out in such manner as in killing and robbing the English, and persuading him to make peace, he replied unless all men that had estates lost by the king's giving them to great men, that were little worth in former times, unless they had their estates given them again under the king's broad seal, that they would not yield. And withal that if they had not the duke of York for their governor and ruler in this kingdom and to be a papist, they would not yield as aforesaid. And further said that they would have the whole kingdom to themselves and that they have been about this plot for this seventeen years past but never had so fitting opportunity as now they had.[143]

John Kerdiff also reported that 'at Mr Connor's house, where the friar was, they had Hanmer's *Chronicle*, out of which they animated the rebels with the stories of the Danes discomfiture by the Irish (though for the most part unarmed) and paralleled the history with these times.'[144]

When the private conversations of the Friar Malone with Roger Holland and Edward Leech (see p. 224 above) and the discussions based on Hanmer's *Chronicle* at Mr Connor's house are considered together with the conversations overheard by Luce Spell at the Passmore's inn in Balrothery they show that the rebels had given serious thought to the wider implications of their military actions.

A different side of John Malone's character was recorded by John Huxley of Rush:

> And this deponent further saith: that one Malone (who, as he heard, is a friar) and called himself the chaplain major to the Irish host, about the 6th of December last 1641 said that he was the beginner of this rebellion, and that it cost him to bring it to pass three and twenty thousand pounds, the said Malone did say that this deponent and his wife should be both hanged by him,

141 Deposition of Luce Spell, 5 February 1642 (TCD, MS 834, f. 6); 'County Louth depositions, 1641', ed. Thomas Gogarty in *Journal of the County Louth Archaeological Society*, iii, no. 1 (1912), p. 72. 142 Deposition of John Kerdiff, 28 February 1642 (TCD, MS 839, f. 4); Mary Hickson, *Ireland in the seventeenth century* ... (2 vols, London, 1884), i, pp 192–5; deposition of Roger Holland, 4 March 1642 (TCD, MS 834, f. 63); Thomas Fitzpatrick, *The bloody bridge and other papers relating to the insurrection of 1641 (Sir Phelim O'Neill's rebellion)* (first published Dublin, 1903, reissued New York and London, 1970), p. 170. 143 Deposition of Roger Holland, 4 March 1642 (TCD, MS 834, f. 63). 144 Deposition of John Kerdiff, 28 February 1642 (TCD, MS 839, f. 4).

> that there might be none of their breed left, but with much entreaty of a gentlewoman, Mr James Russell's wife (falling upon her knees unto him to spare their lives) he was contented, but gave present order to take away all their corn and goods and to send it to the army called the Irish host.[145]

The last known movements of Malone were those which followed the successful invasion and capture of Lambay Island with the help of a court clerk, Dennis Connor (probably the Dennis or Donnogh Connor who owned the house at Kilmainham where the rebels had so assiduously studied Hanmer's *Chronicle*), and Thomas and Jasper Hurlston of Skerries, together with many of the inhabitants of Rush.[146] This was the most daring and successful enterprise of the rising in the area, and it was accomplished without bloodshed as the servants and tenants of the island 'being Papists' deserted Edward Leech, who had charge of the castle. With Dirrick Huiberts Verveer dead the task of the invaders was made somewhat easier. The lords justices and council summarized the events described by Leech in a letter to the lord lieutenant as follows:

> One of the rebels, styling himself chaplain major and overseer of the coasts and harbours, lately sent a summons in a proud and vaunting manner to one Edward Leech, that was entrusted to keep the island of Lambay, requiring the delivering up of that island to the rebels, which being done, he gave Leech a pass, wherein he styles the rebels 'the Catholic army', copies of which summons and pass we send your lordship here enclosed, and Leech told us that the mighty chaplain declared openly to him that he was the plotter of this rebellion, that he had spent in travels and prosecution of that design beyond seas four thousand pounds, and that all the kings in Christendom, excepting the king of England and the king of Denmark, have hands in this business.[147]

By taking over Skerries and capturing Lambay, Malone cut off the sea route from Dublin to Drogheda and in the overall scheme of things bought time for Sir Phelim O'Neill and the Ulster army then besieging Drogheda. O'Neill was unable to avail of this opportunity. Malone disappeared from the history of Fingal at that point. He was later outlawed as 'John Malone, Skerries, clerk'.[148]

The government forces exacted a terrible revenge. Captain Thomas Stutevile set out with relief for Drogheda on Sunday night, 9 January 1642, in *The Swan*, a pinnace, together with two frigates, one gabbard and two long boats.[149] According to Stutevile 'the captain sent out of *The Swan* some musketeers to the Skerries, where he found the enemy fled, but had left behind them much goods, which being all taken aboard by them, they set the town on fire; and with it got above 500*l.* worth of corn.

145 Deposition of John Huxley, 21 May 1642 (TCD, MS 810, f. 158). **146** Deposition of Edward Leech, 18 March 1644 (TCD, MS 810, f. 244). **147** Lords justices and council to the earl of Leicester, lord lieutenant, 14 December 1641, in Historical Manuscripts Commission, *Calendar of the manuscripts of the marquess of Ormonde* ... (new series, 8 vols, London, 1902–20), ii, p. 38. **148** R.C. Simington and John MacLellan, 'Oireachtas Library, List of outlaws, 1641–1647', in *Analecta Hibernica*, no. 23 (1966), p. 342. **149** Thomas Stutevile, *A true relation of every remarkable circumstance in relieving of Tredagh ...* (place of publication not stated, 1642), p. 3 (NLI, Lough Fea pamphlet no. 42).